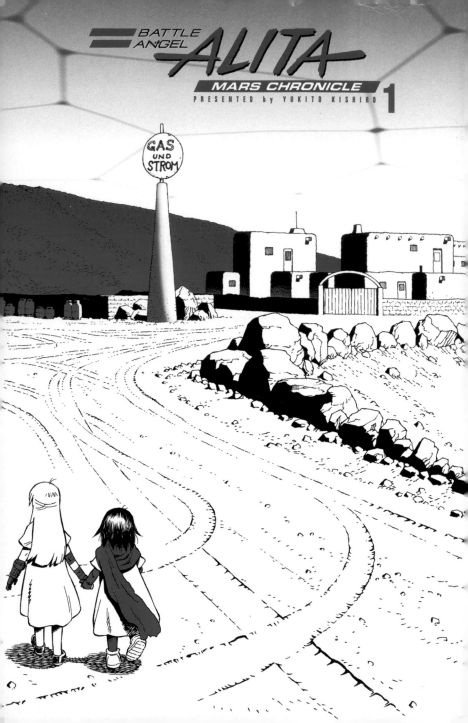

BATTLE ANGEL ALITA MARS CHRONICLE
PRESENTED by YUKITO KISHIRO

CONTENTS

Additional Staff: Tsutomu Kishiro / Emiya Kinari

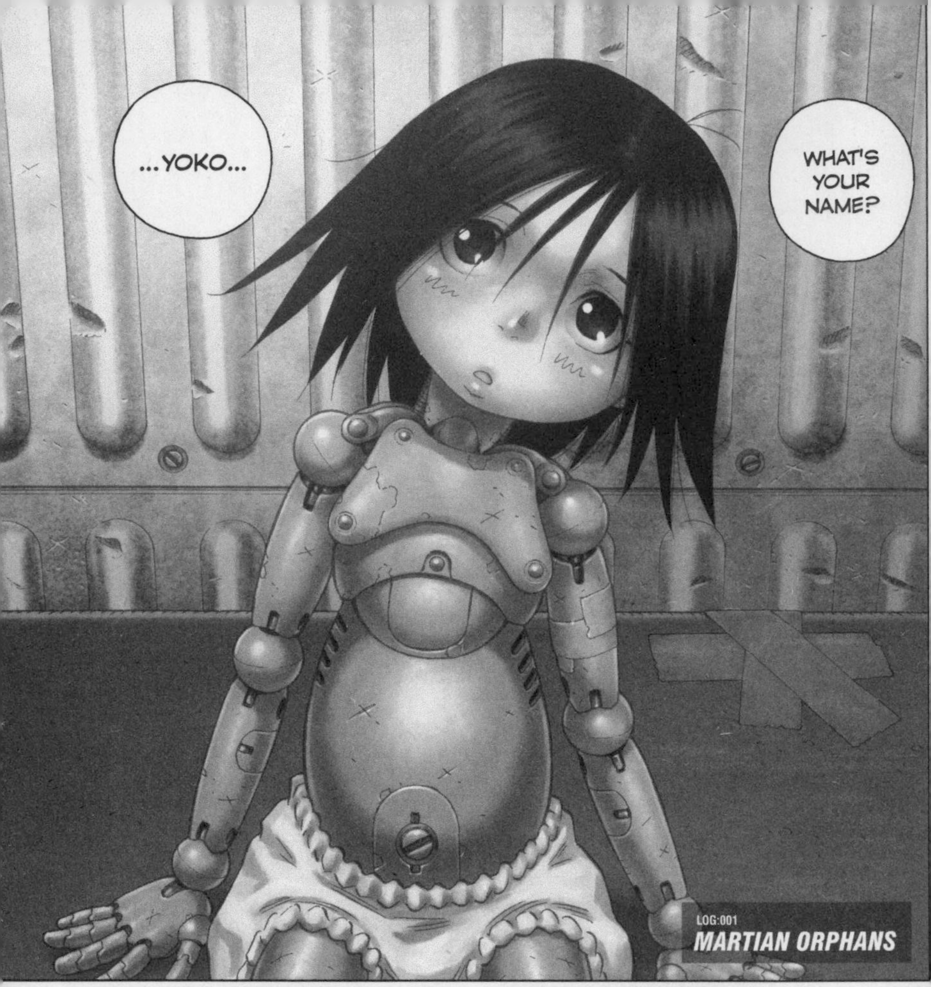
WHAT'S YOUR NAME?
...YOKO...
LOG:001
MARTIAN ORPHANS

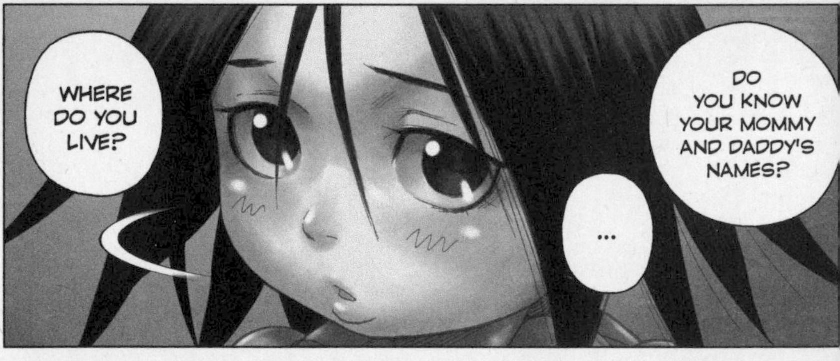
DO YOU KNOW YOUR MOMMY AND DADDY'S NAMES?
...
WHERE DO YOU LIVE?

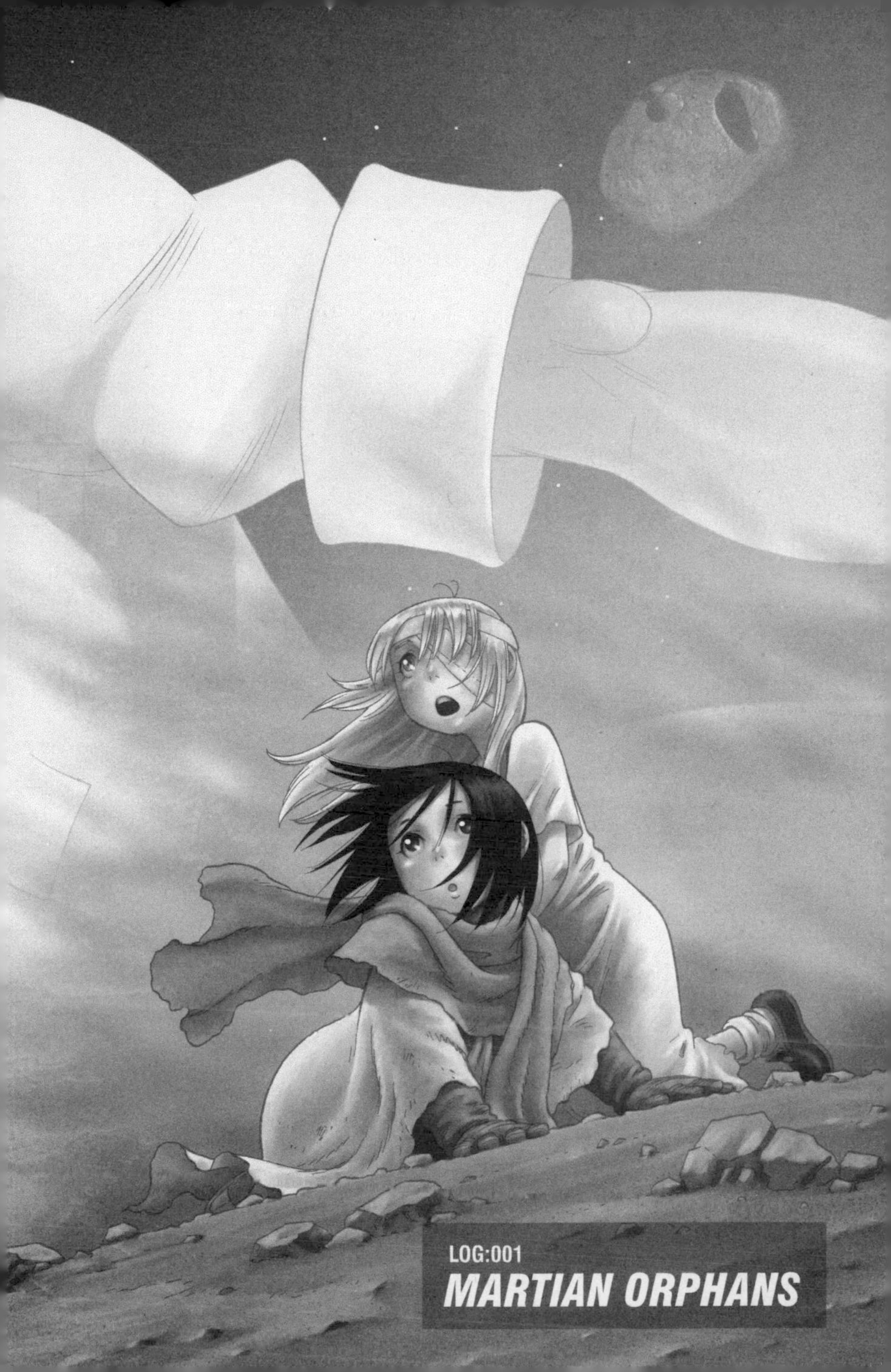
LOG:001
MARTIAN ORPHANS

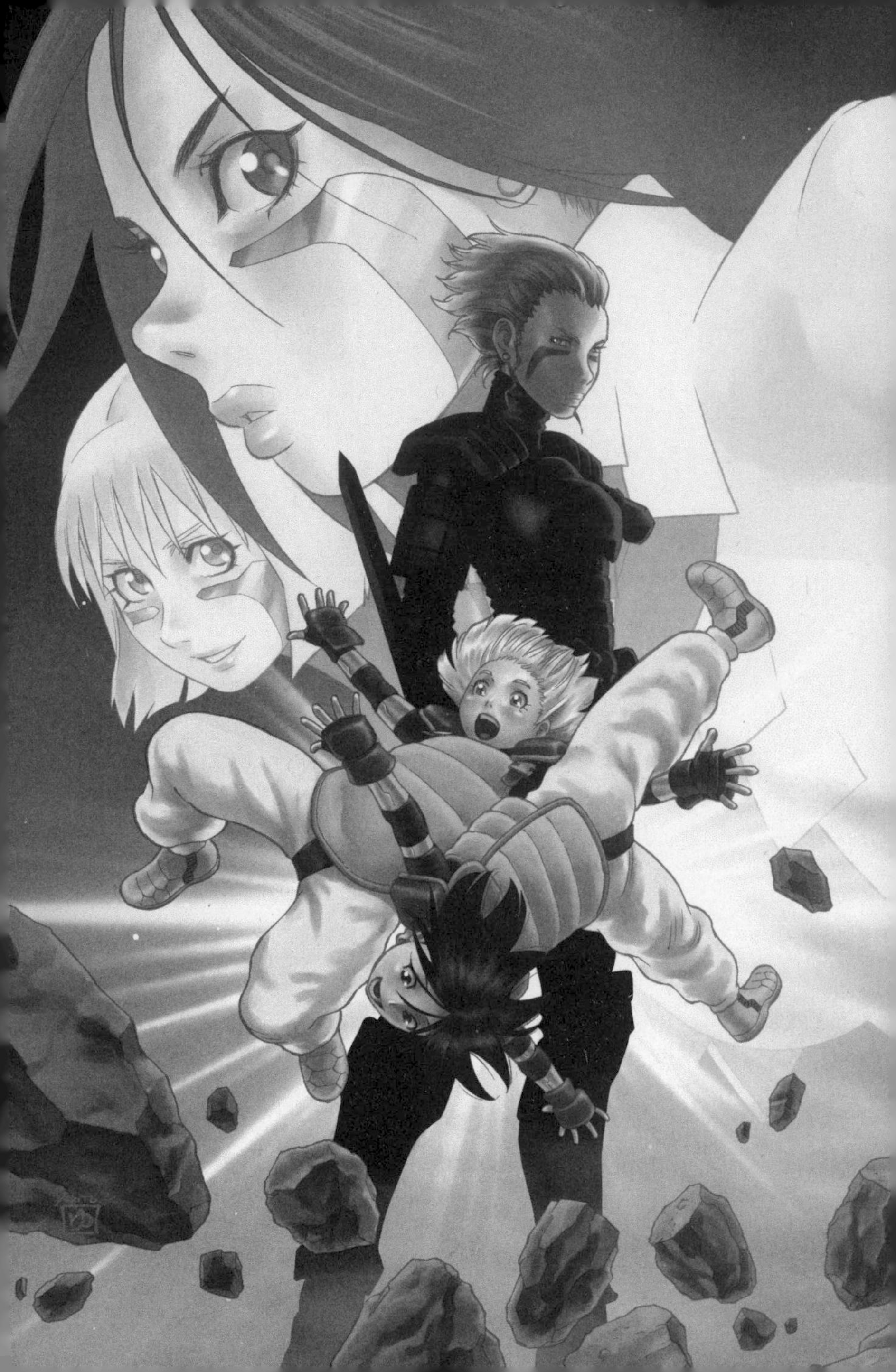

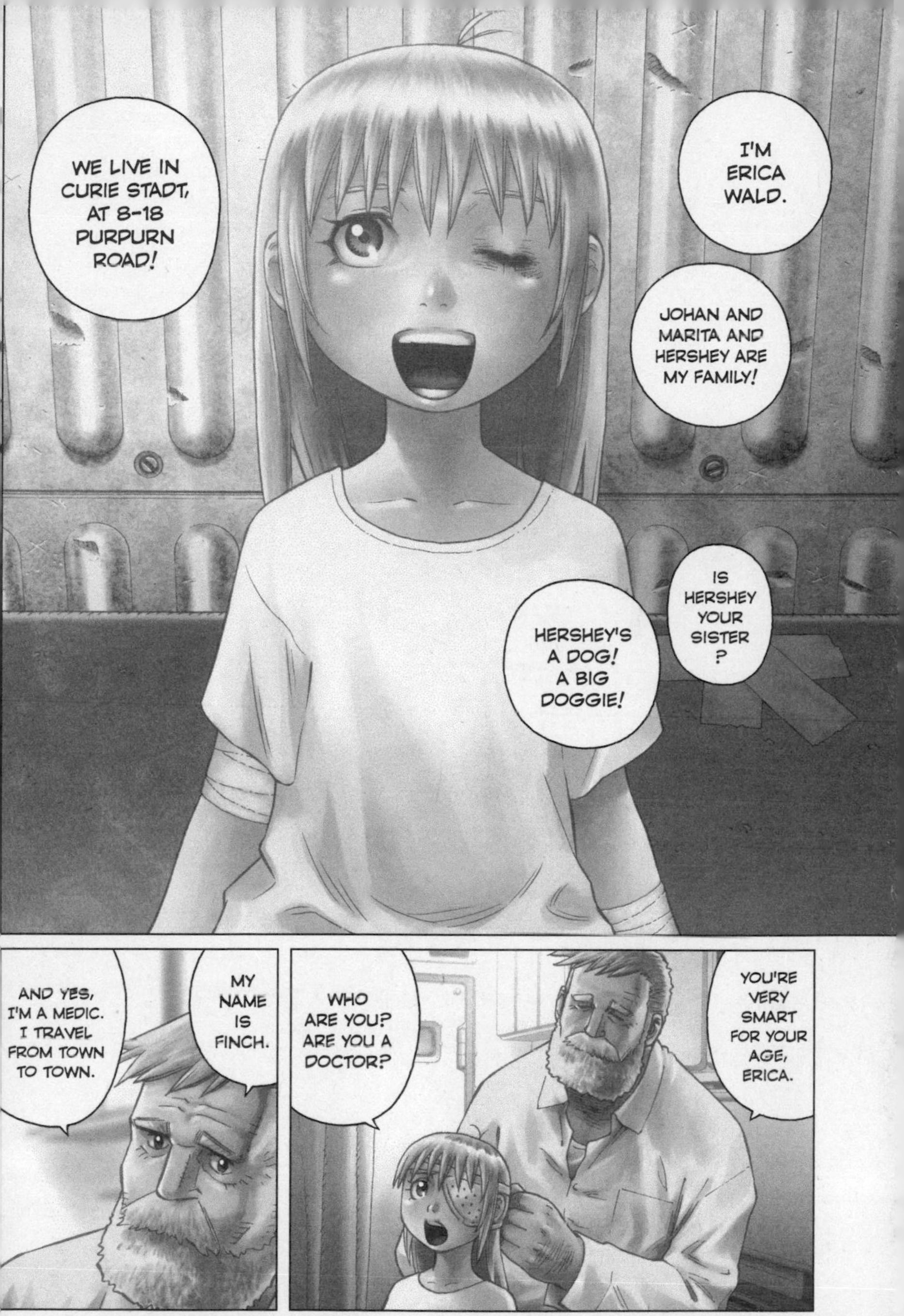
I'M ERICA WALD.
WE LIVE IN CURIE STADT, AT 8-18 PURPURN ROAD!
JOHAN AND MARITA AND HERSHEY ARE MY FAMILY!
IS HERSHEY YOUR SISTER?
HERSHEY'S A DOG! A BIG DOGGIE!
YOU'RE VERY SMART FOR YOUR AGE, ERICA.
WHO ARE YOU? ARE YOU A DOCTOR?
MY NAME IS FINCH.
AND YES, I'M A MEDIC. I TRAVEL FROM TOWN TO TOWN.

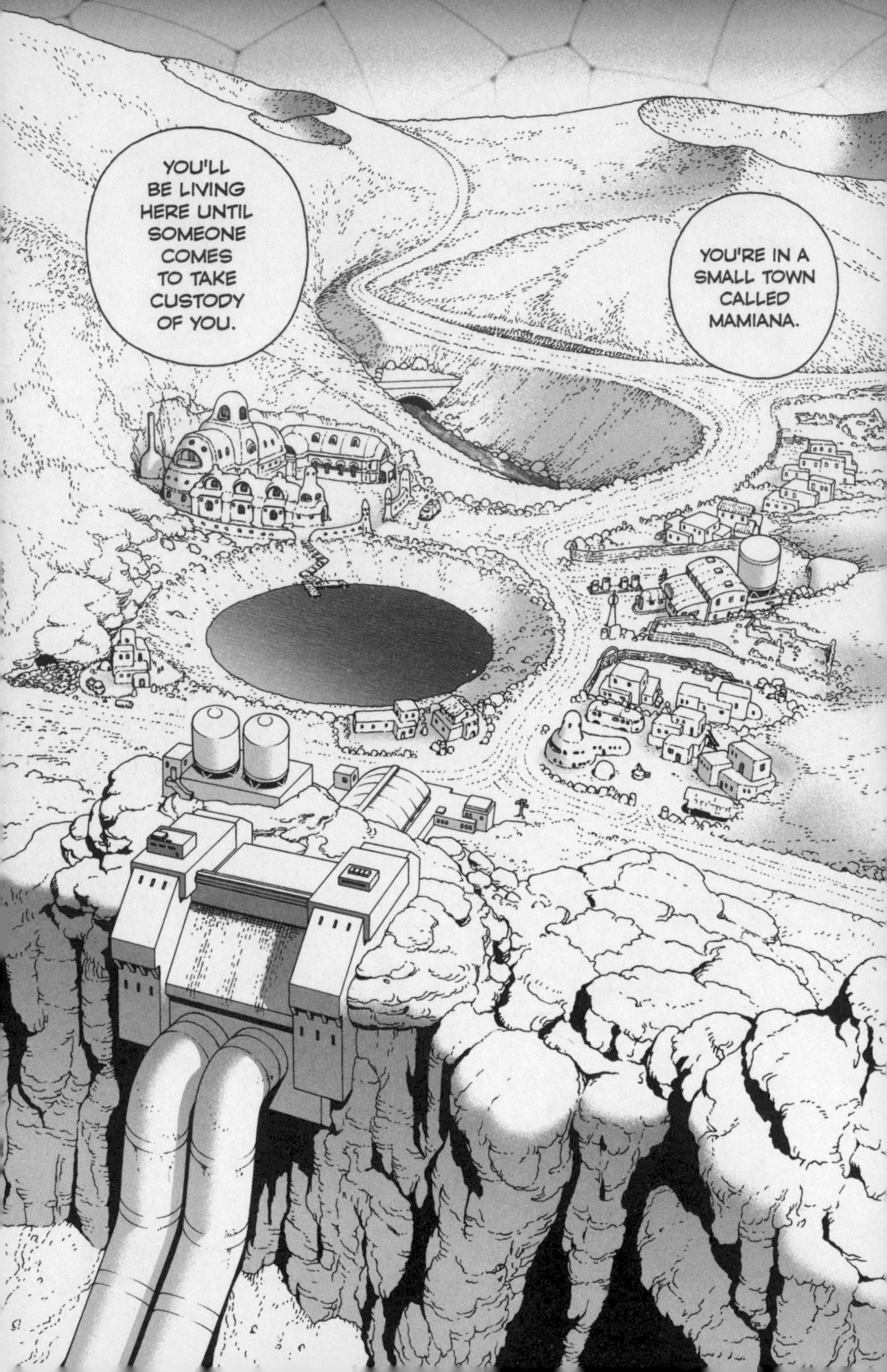
YOU'RE IN A SMALL TOWN CALLED MAMIANA.
YOU'LL BE LIVING HERE UNTIL SOMEONE COMES TO TAKE CUSTODY OF YOU.

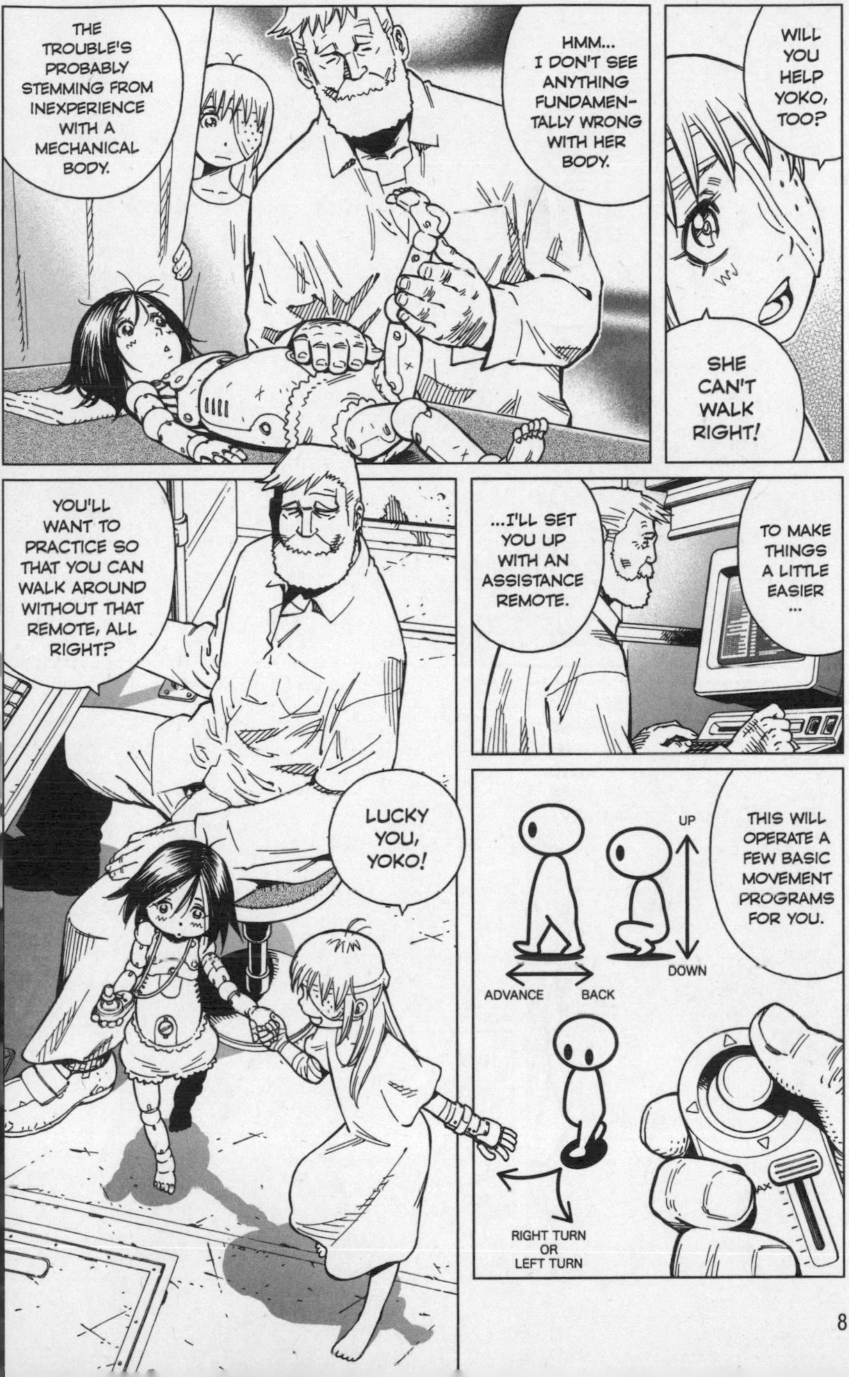
WILL YOU HELP YOKO, TOO?
SHE CAN'T WALK RIGHT!
HMM... I DON'T SEE ANYTHING FUNDAMENTALLY WRONG WITH HER BODY.
THE TROUBLE'S PROBABLY STEMMING FROM INEXPERIENCE WITH A MECHANICAL BODY.
TO MAKE THINGS A LITTLE EASIER ...
...I'LL SET YOU UP WITH AN ASSISTANCE REMOTE.
THIS WILL OPERATE A FEW BASIC MOVEMENT PROGRAMS FOR YOU.
UP
DOWN
ADVANCE
BACK
RIGHT TURN OR LEFT TURN
YOU'LL WANT TO PRACTICE SO THAT YOU CAN WALK AROUND WITHOUT THAT REMOTE, ALL RIGHT?
LUCKY YOU, YOKO!

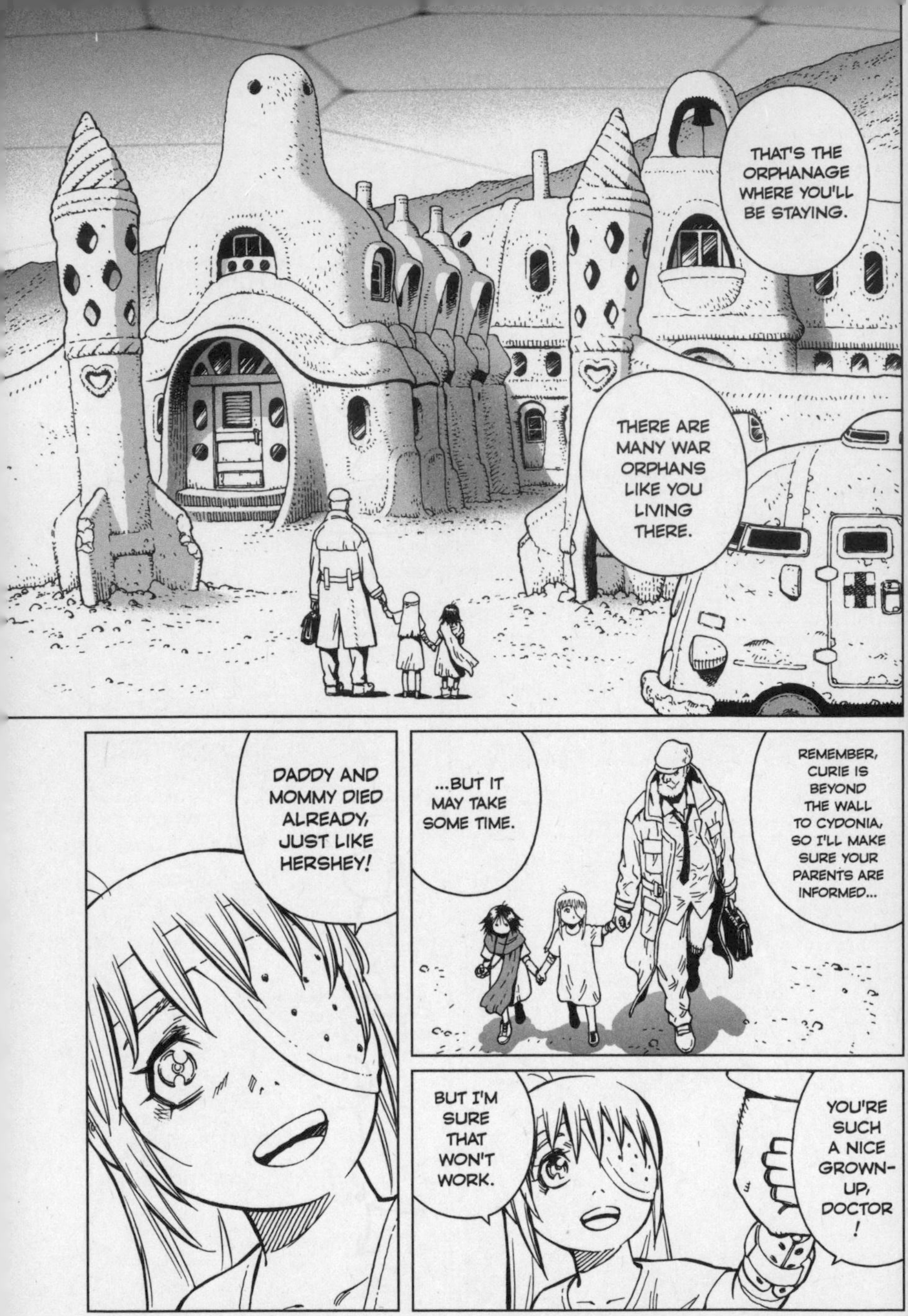
THAT'S THE ORPHANAGE WHERE YOU'LL BE STAYING.
THERE ARE MANY WAR ORPHANS LIKE YOU LIVING THERE.
REMEMBER, CURIE IS BEYOND THE WALL TO CYDONIA, SO I'LL MAKE SURE YOUR PARENTS ARE INFORMED...
...BUT IT MAY TAKE SOME TIME.
YOU'RE SUCH A NICE GROWN-UP, DOCTOR!
BUT I'M SURE THAT WON'T WORK.
DADDY AND MOMMY DIED ALREADY, JUST LIKE HERSHEY!

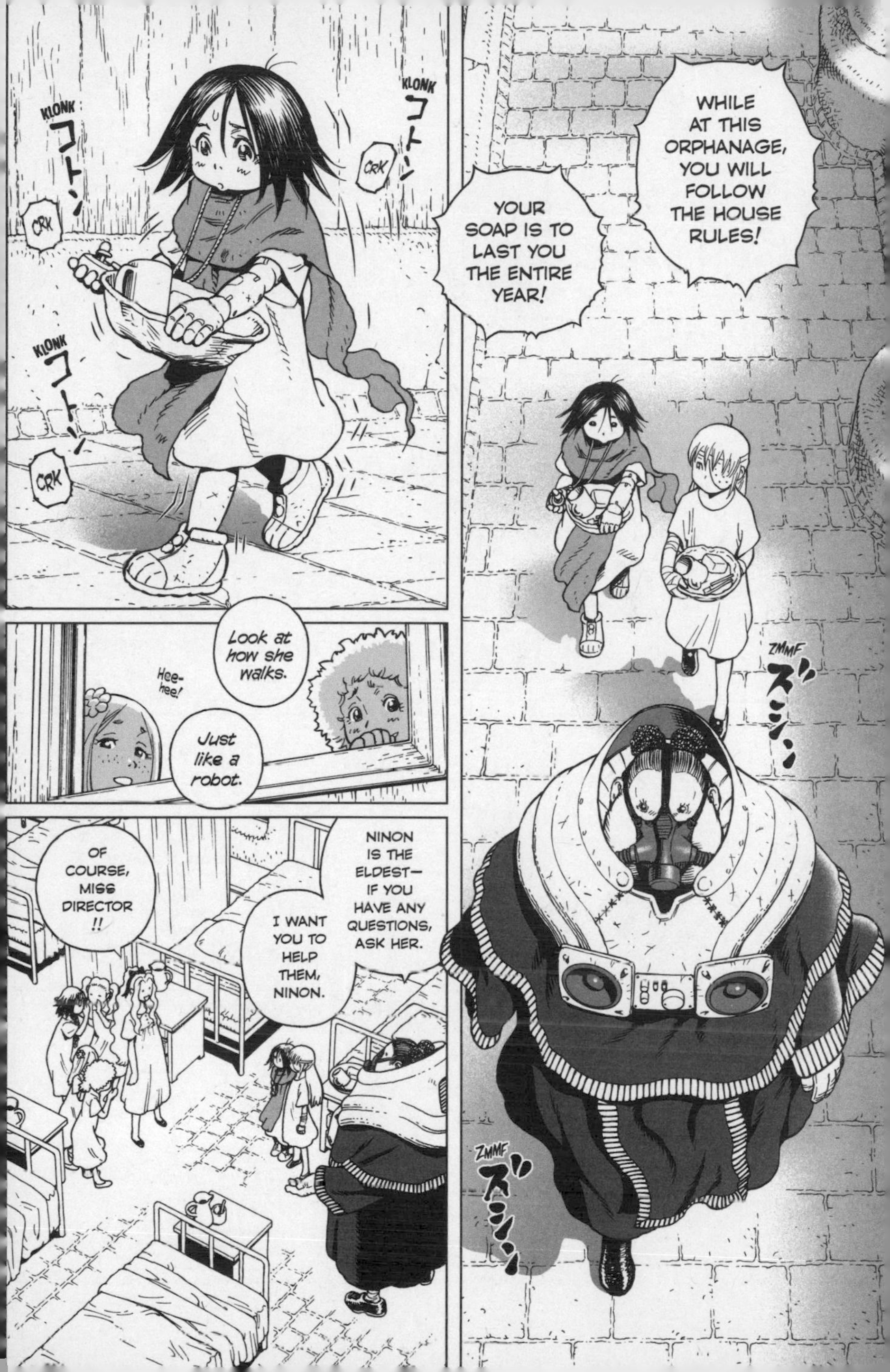
WHILE AT THIS ORPHANAGE, YOU WILL FOLLOW THE HOUSE RULES!
YOUR SOAP IS TO LAST YOU THE ENTIRE YEAR!
ZMMF
ズシン
ZMMF
ズシン
KLONK
コトン
CRK
KLONK
コトン
CRK
KLONK
コトン
CRK
Look at how she walks.
Hee-hee!
Just like a robot.
NINON IS THE ELDEST— IF YOU HAVE ANY QUESTIONS, ASK HER.
I WANT YOU TO HELP THEM, NINON.
OF COURSE, MISS DIRECTOR !!

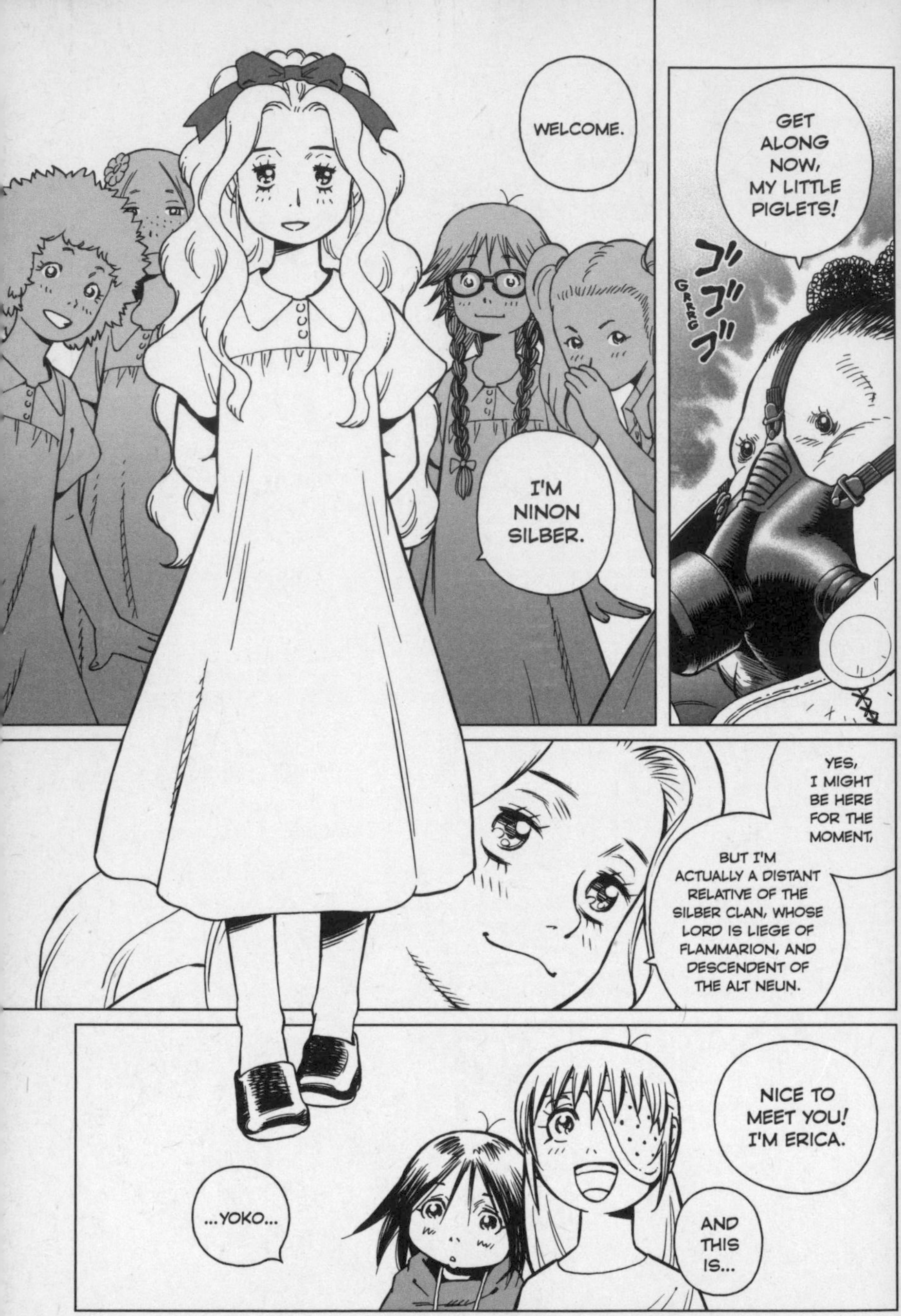
GET ALONG NOW, MY LITTLE PIGLETS!
ゴゴゴ
GRRRG
WELCOME.
I'M NINON SILBER.
YES, I MIGHT BE HERE FOR THE MOMENT,
BUT I'M ACTUALLY A DISTANT RELATIVE OF THE SILBER CLAN, WHOSE LORD IS LIEGE OF FLAMMARION, AND DESCENDENT OF THE ALT NEUN.
NICE TO MEET YOU! I'M ERICA.
AND THIS IS...
...YOKO...

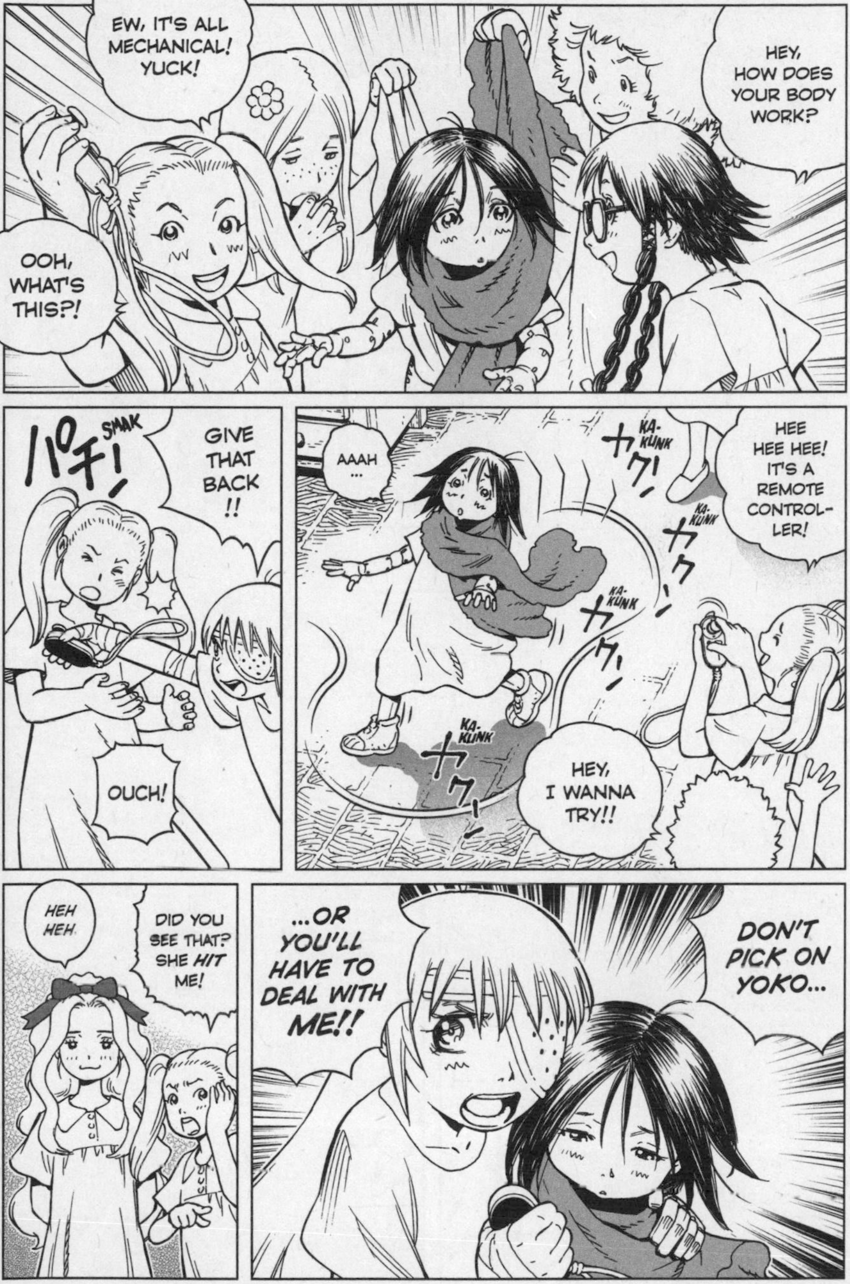
HEY, HOW DOES YOUR BODY WORK?
EW, IT'S ALL MECHANICAL! YUCK!
OOH, WHAT'S THIS?!
HEE HEE HEE! IT'S A REMOTE CONTROLLER!
カクン KA-KUNK
カクン KA-KUNK
AAAH ...
カクン KA-KUNK
カクン KA-KUNK
HEY, I WANNA TRY!!
GIVE THAT BACK!!
パチ! SMAK
OUCH!
DON'T PICK ON YOKO...
...OR YOU'LL HAVE TO DEAL WITH ME!!
DID YOU SEE THAT? SHE HIT ME!
HEH HEH.

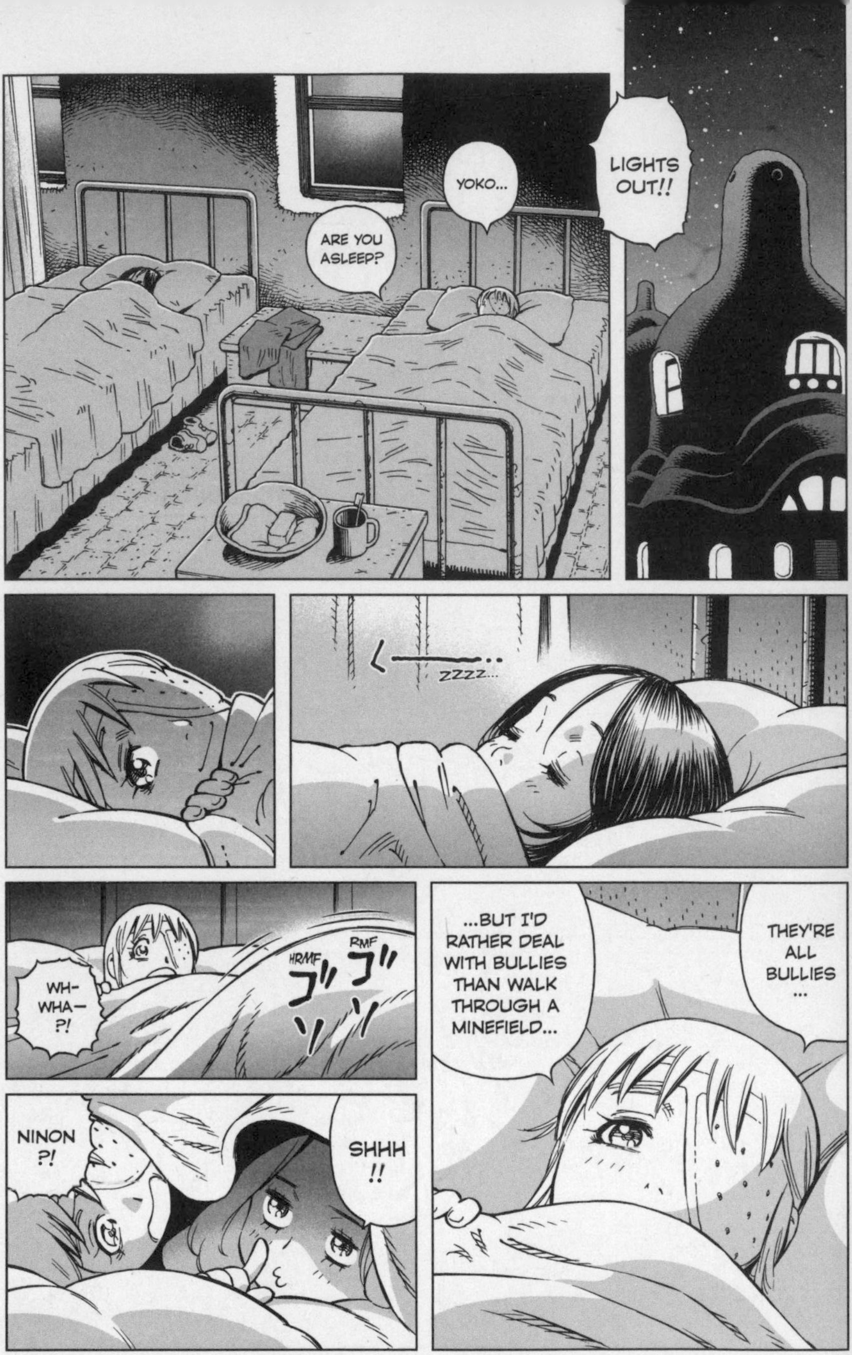
LIGHTS OUT!!
YOKO...
ARE YOU ASLEEP?
ZZZZ...
THEY'RE ALL BULLIES ...
...BUT I'D RATHER DEAL WITH BULLIES THAN WALK THROUGH A MINEFIELD...
RMF
ゴソ
HRMF
ゴソ
WH-WHA- ?!
SHHH !!
NINON ?!

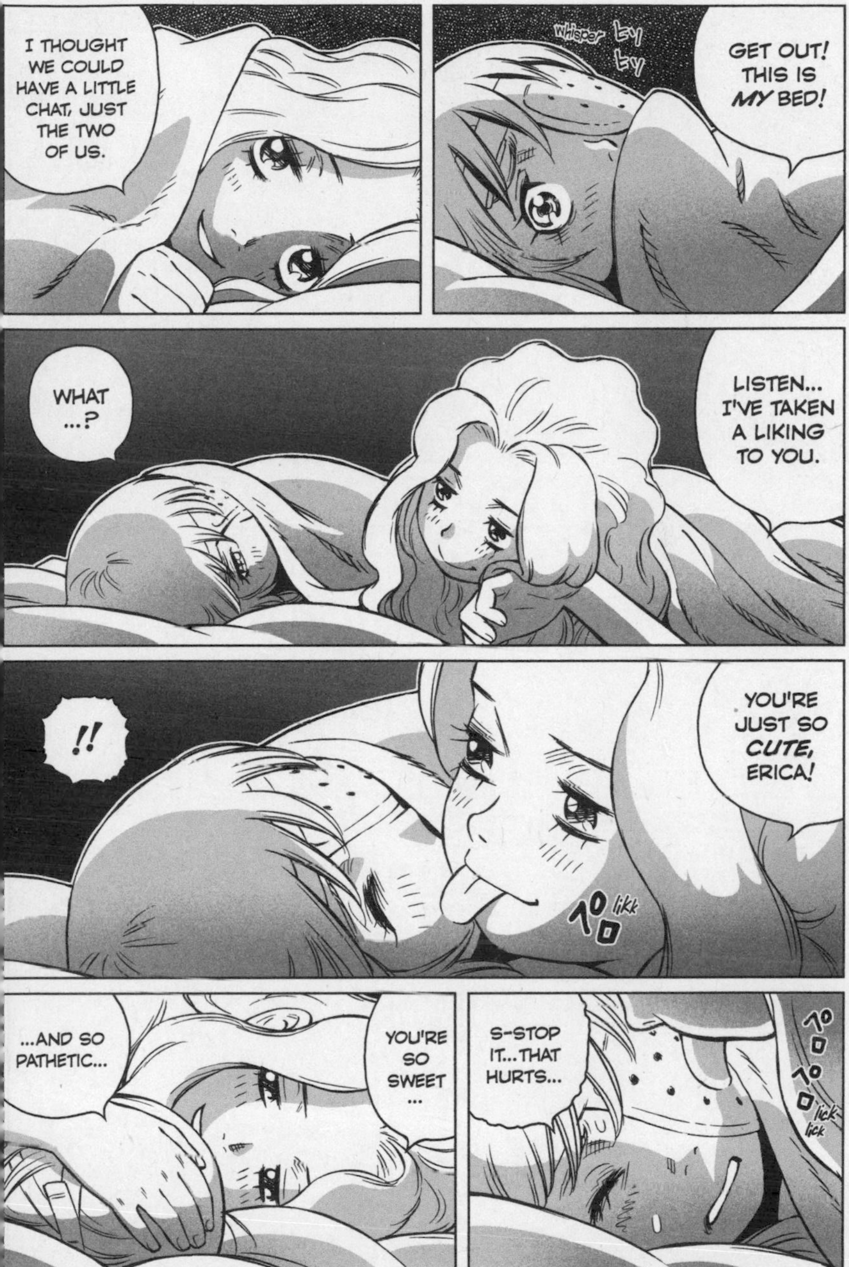
whisper
GET OUT! THIS IS MY BED!
I THOUGHT WE COULD HAVE A LITTLE CHAT, JUST THE TWO OF US.
LISTEN... I'VE TAKEN A LIKING TO YOU.
WHAT ...?
YOU'RE JUST SO CUTE, ERICA!
likk
!!
lick lick
S-STOP IT...THAT HURTS...
YOU'RE SO SWEET ...
...AND SO PATHETIC...

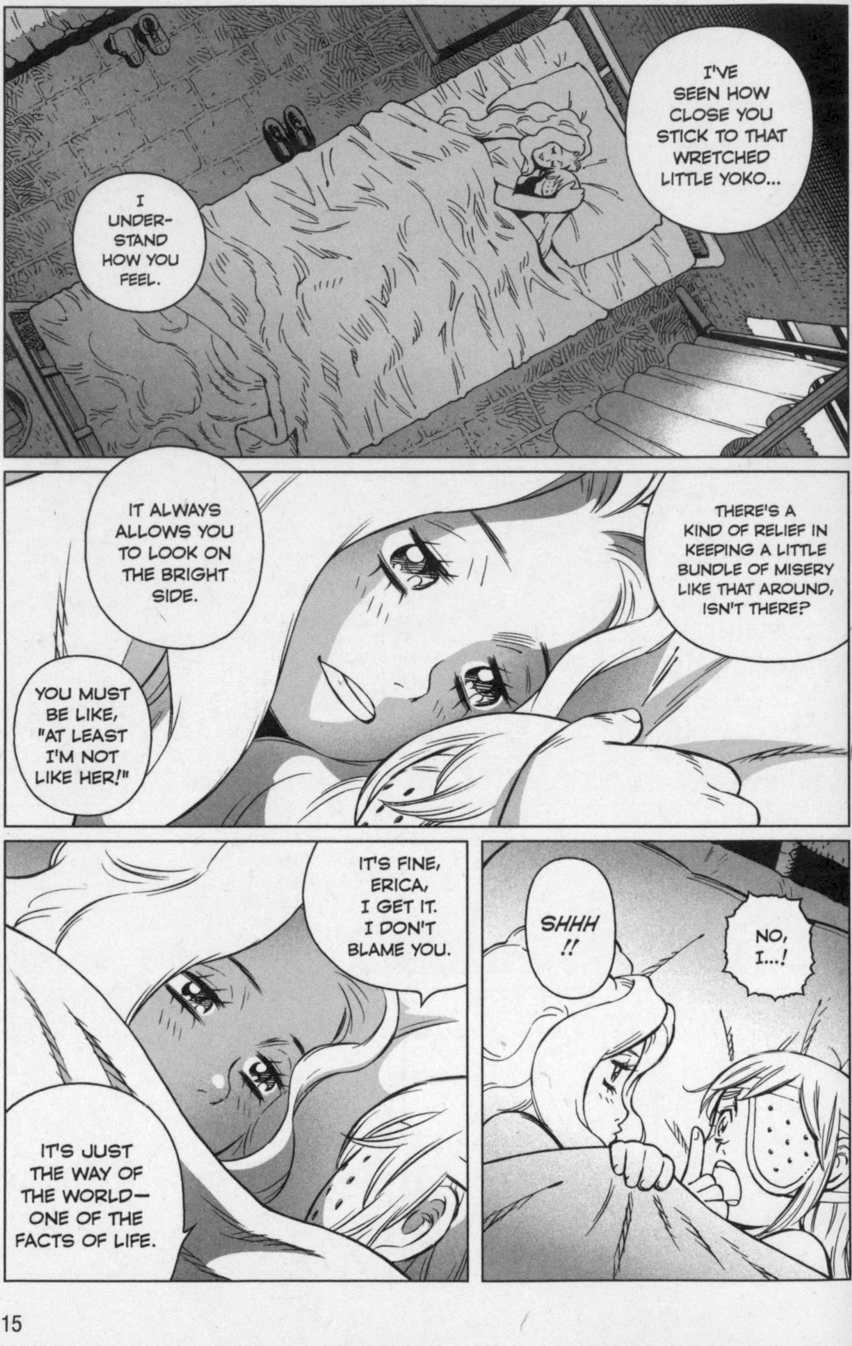
I'VE SEEN HOW CLOSE YOU STICK TO THAT WRETCHED LITTLE YOKO...
I UNDER-STAND HOW YOU FEEL.
THERE'S A KIND OF RELIEF IN KEEPING A LITTLE BUNDLE OF MISERY LIKE THAT AROUND, ISN'T THERE?
IT ALWAYS ALLOWS YOU TO LOOK ON THE BRIGHT SIDE.
YOU MUST BE LIKE, "AT LEAST I'M NOT LIKE HER!"
NO, I...!
SHHH !!
IT'S FINE, ERICA, I GET IT. I DON'T BLAME YOU.
IT'S JUST THE WAY OF THE WORLD— ONE OF THE FACTS OF LIFE.

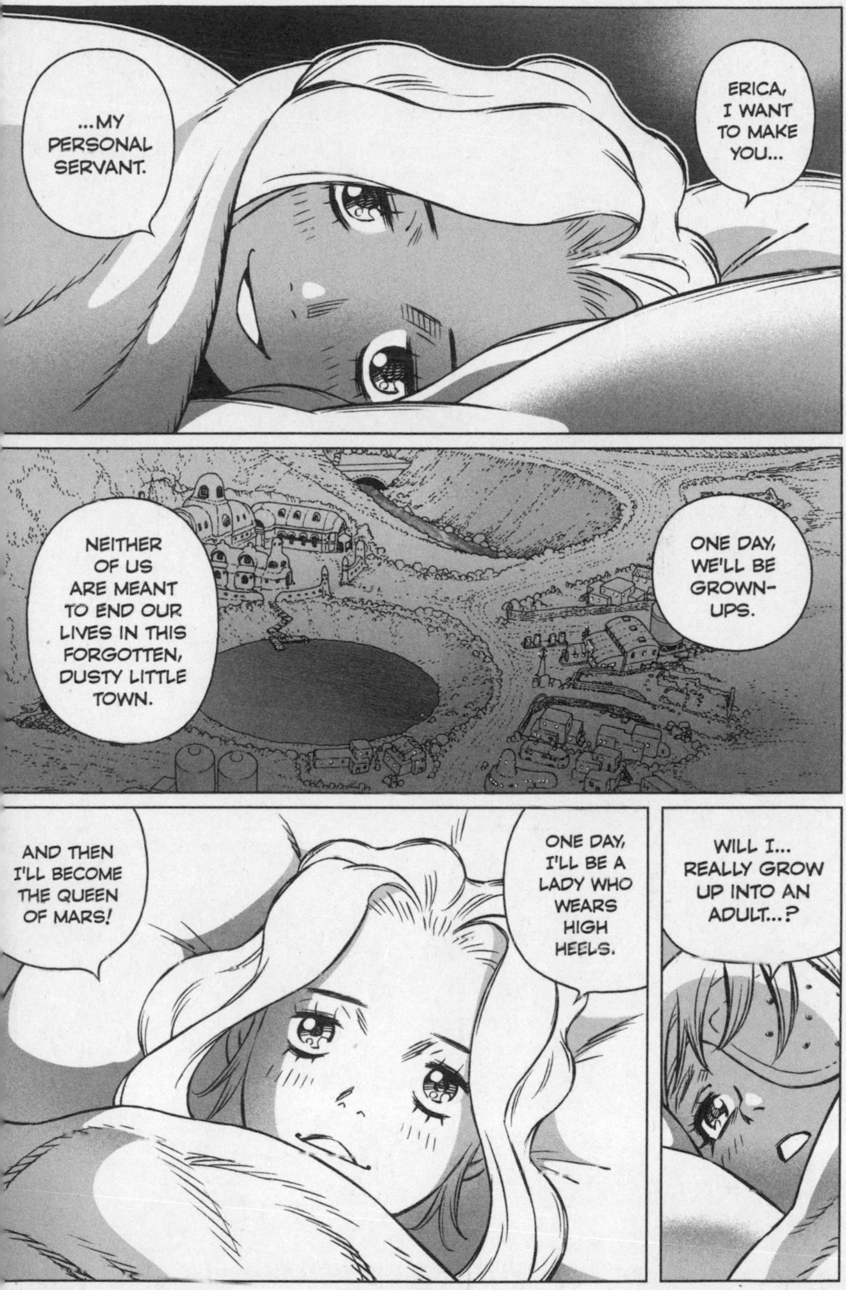
ERICA, I WANT TO MAKE YOU...
...MY PERSONAL SERVANT.
ONE DAY, WE'LL BE GROWN-UPS.
NEITHER OF US ARE MEANT TO END OUR LIVES IN THIS FORGOTTEN, DUSTY LITTLE TOWN.
WILL I... REALLY GROW UP INTO AN ADULT...?
ONE DAY, I'LL BE A LADY WHO WEARS HIGH HEELS.
AND THEN I'LL BECOME THE QUEEN OF MARS!

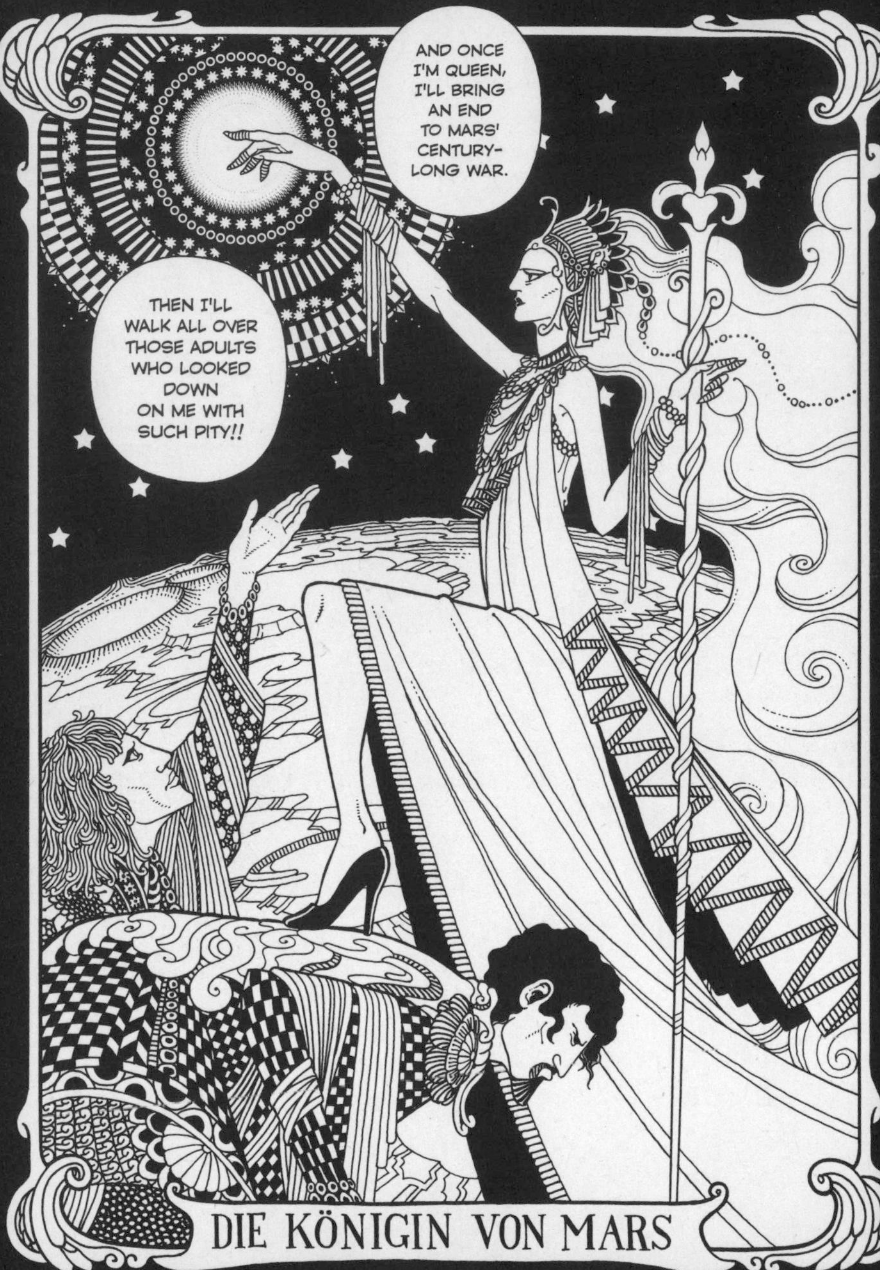
AND ONCE I'M QUEEN, I'LL BRING AN END TO MARS' CENTURY-LONG WAR.
THEN I'LL WALK ALL OVER THOSE ADULTS WHO LOOKED DOWN ON ME WITH SUCH PITY!!
DIE KÖNIGIN VON MARS

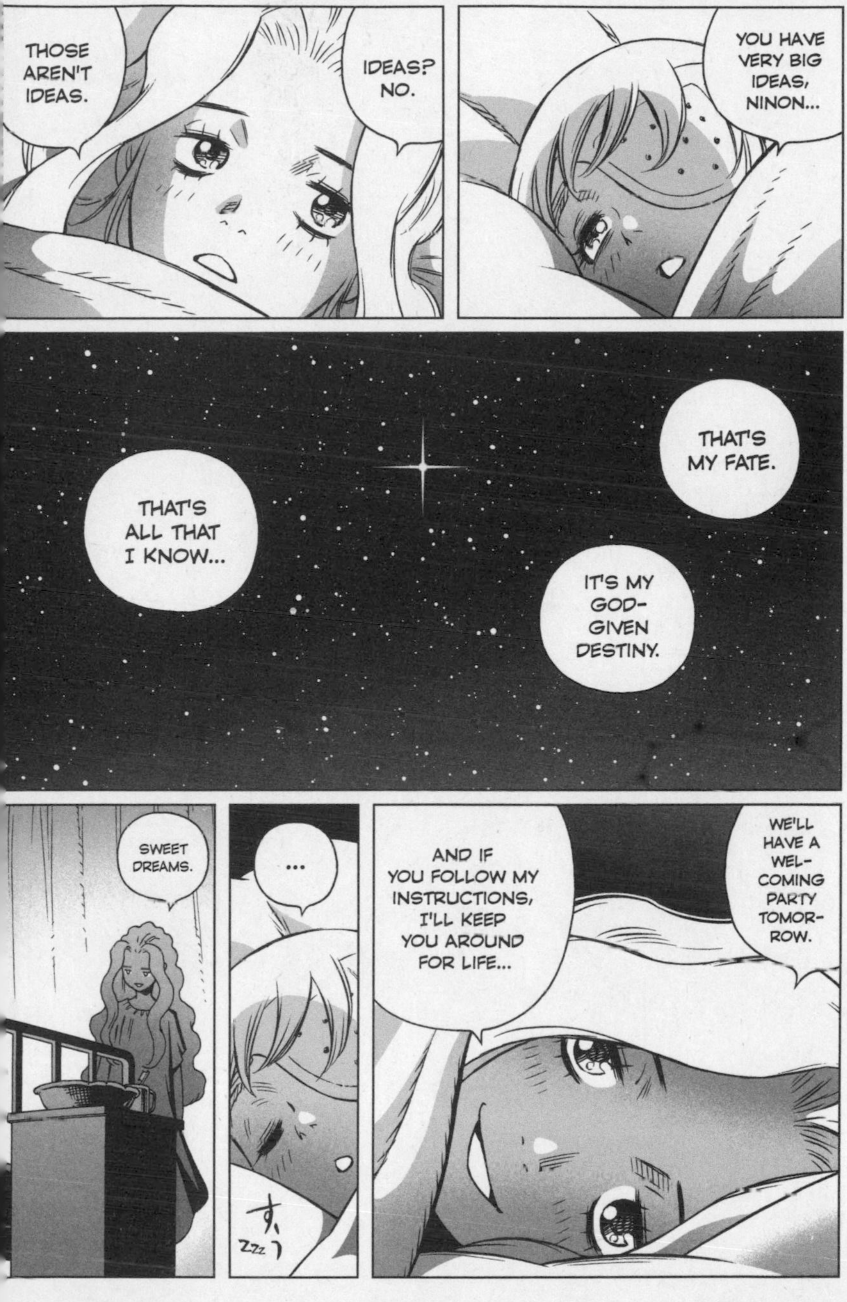
YOU HAVE VERY BIG IDEAS, NINON...
IDEAS? NO.
THOSE AREN'T IDEAS.
THAT'S MY FATE.
IT'S MY GOD-GIVEN DESTINY.
THAT'S ALL THAT I KNOW...
WE'LL HAVE A WEL-COMING PARTY TOMOR-ROW.
AND IF YOU FOLLOW MY INSTRUCTIONS, I'LL KEEP YOU AROUND FOR LIFE...
...
す
ZZZ
SWEET DREAMS.

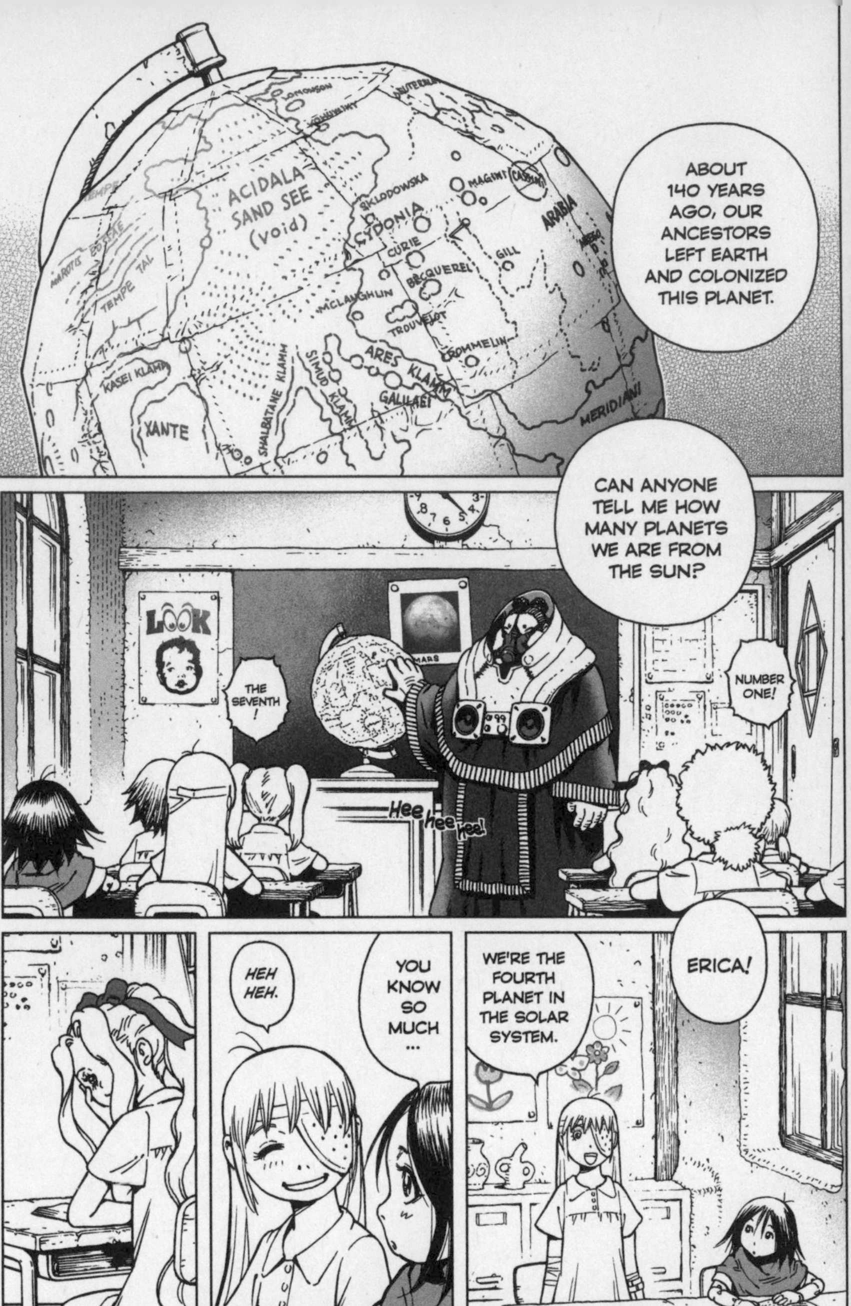
ABOUT 140 YEARS AGO, OUR ANCESTORS LEFT EARTH AND COLONIZED THIS PLANET.
ACIDALA SAND SEE (void)
CYDONIA
ARABIA
SKLODOWSKA
MAGINI
CASSINI
CURIE
GILL
BECQUEREL
MCLANGHLIN
TROUVELOT
ARES KLAMM
GALILAEI
MERIDIANI
SIMUD KLAMM
SHALBATANE KLAMM
KASEI KLAMM
XANTE
TEMPE TAL
CAN ANYONE TELL ME HOW MANY PLANETS WE ARE FROM THE SUN?
NUMBER ONE!
MARS
THE SEVENTH!
LOOK
Hee hee hee!
ERICA!
WE'RE THE FOURTH PLANET IN THE SOLAR SYSTEM.
YOU KNOW SO MUCH...
HEH HEH.

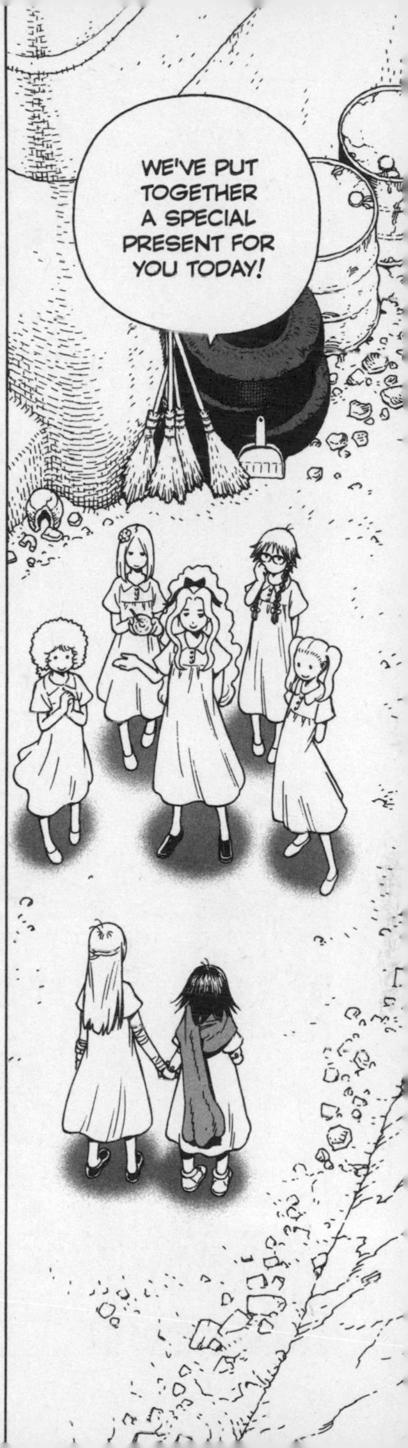
WE'VE PUT TOGETHER A SPECIAL PRESENT FOR YOU TODAY!

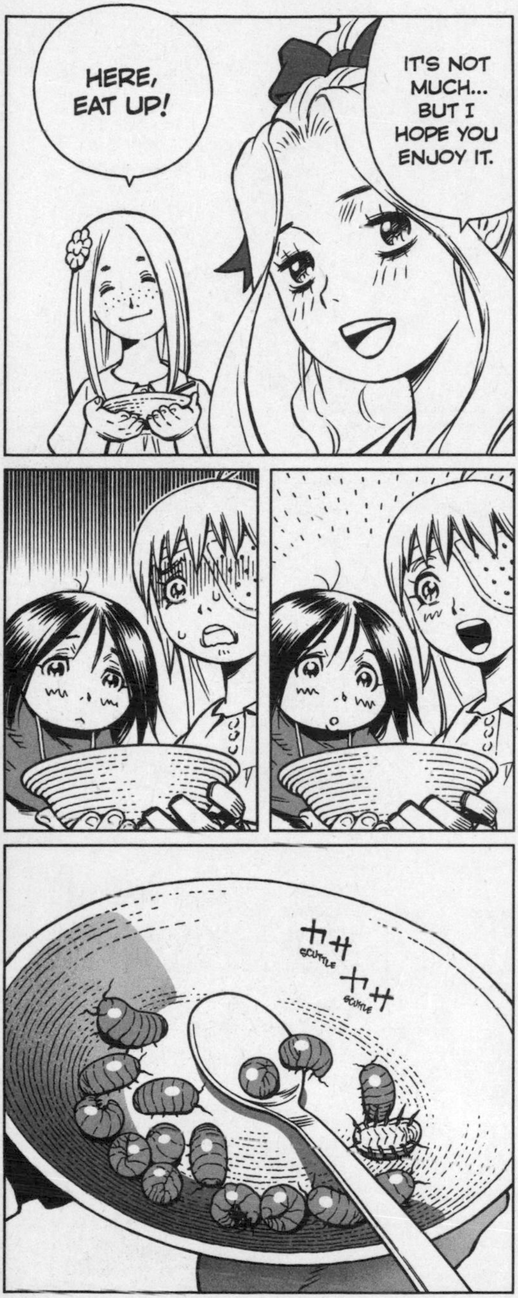
IT'S NOT MUCH... BUT I HOPE YOU ENJOY IT.
HERE, EAT UP!
カサ SCUTTLE
カサ SCUTTLE

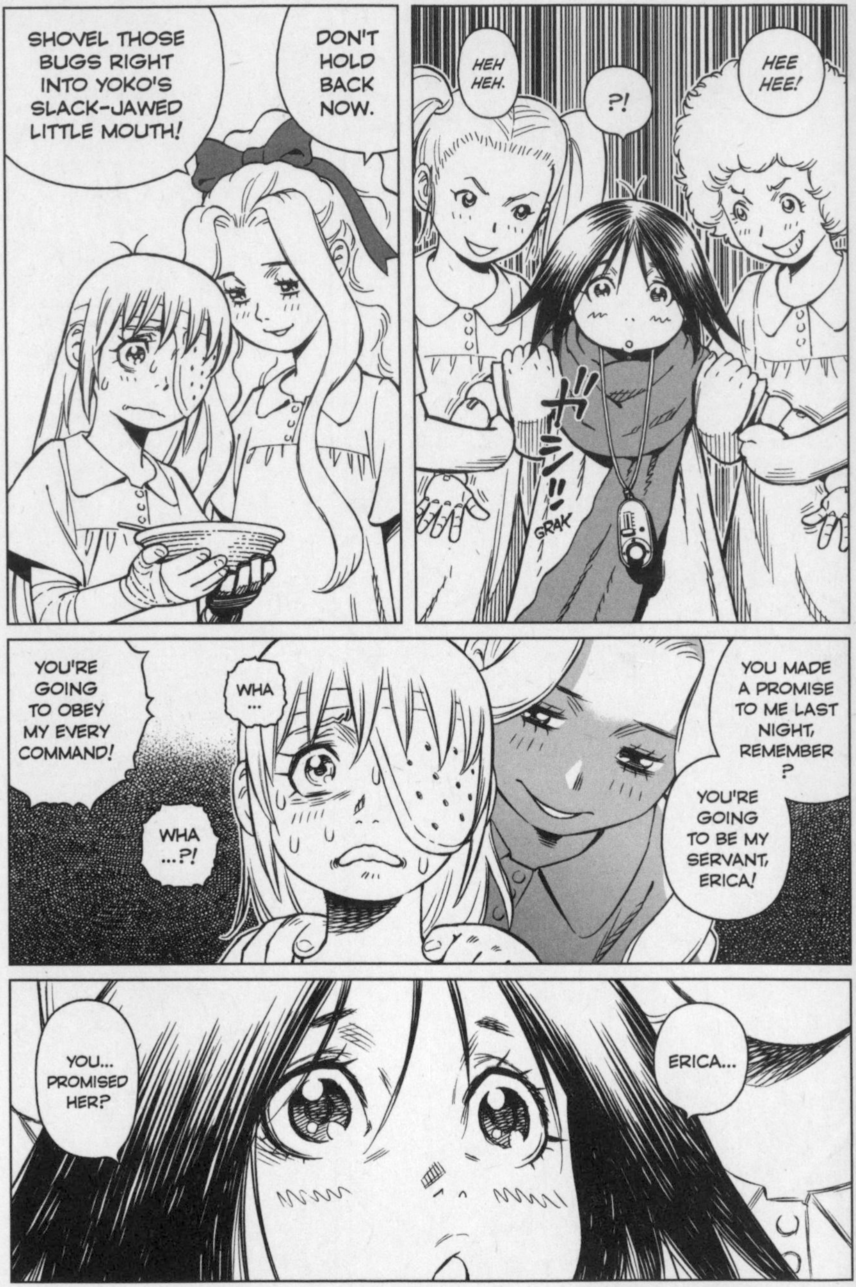
HEE HEE!
?!
HEH HEH.
GRAK
DON'T HOLD BACK NOW.
SHOVEL THOSE BUGS RIGHT INTO YOKO'S SLACK-JAWED LITTLE MOUTH!
YOU MADE A PROMISE TO ME LAST NIGHT, REMEMBER ?
YOU'RE GOING TO BE MY SERVANT, ERICA!
WHA ...
YOU'RE GOING TO OBEY MY EVERY COMMAND!
WHA ...?!
ERICA...
YOU... PROMISED HER?

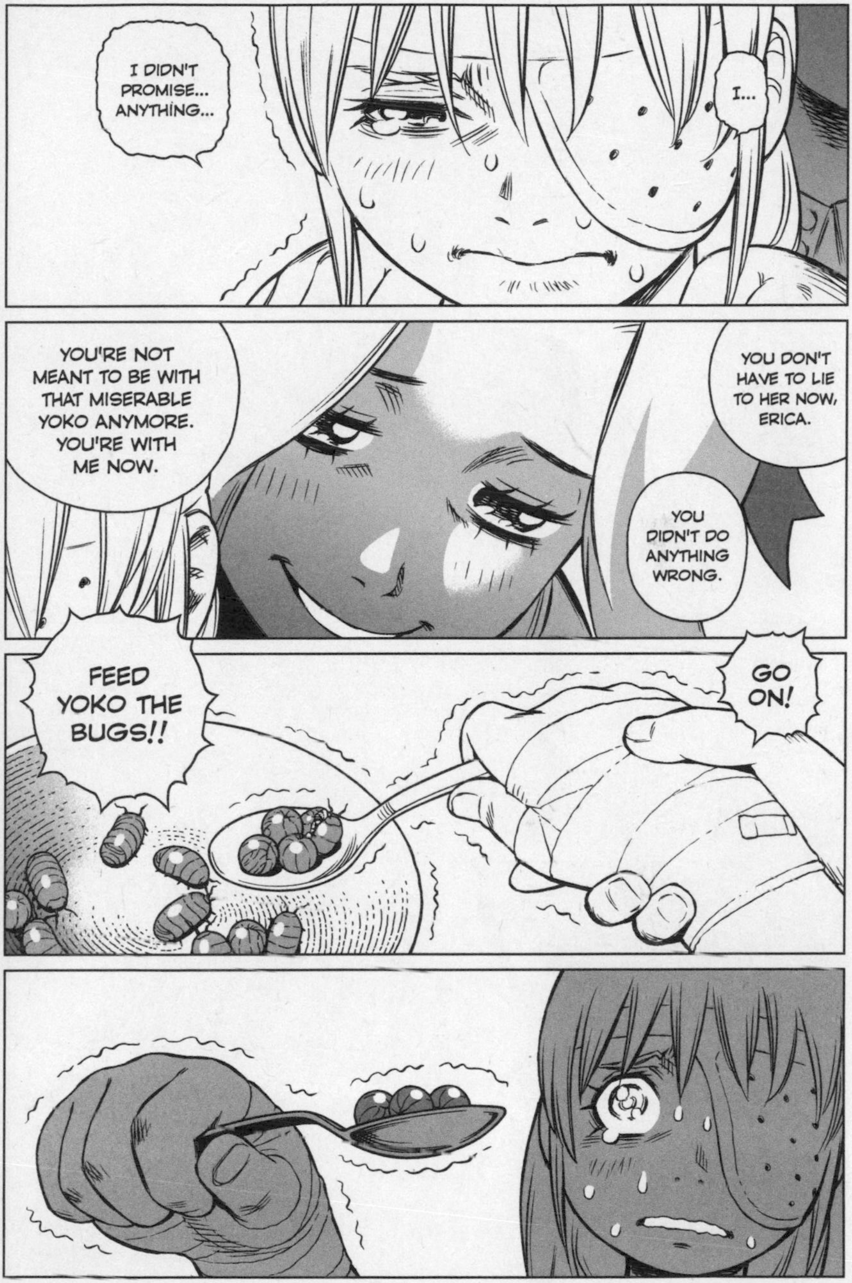
I...
I DIDN'T PROMISE... ANYTHING...
YOU DON'T HAVE TO LIE TO HER NOW, ERICA.
YOU DIDN'T DO ANYTHING WRONG.
YOU'RE NOT MEANT TO BE WITH THAT MISERABLE YOKO ANYMORE. YOU'RE WITH ME NOW.
GO ON!
FEED YOKO THE BUGS!!

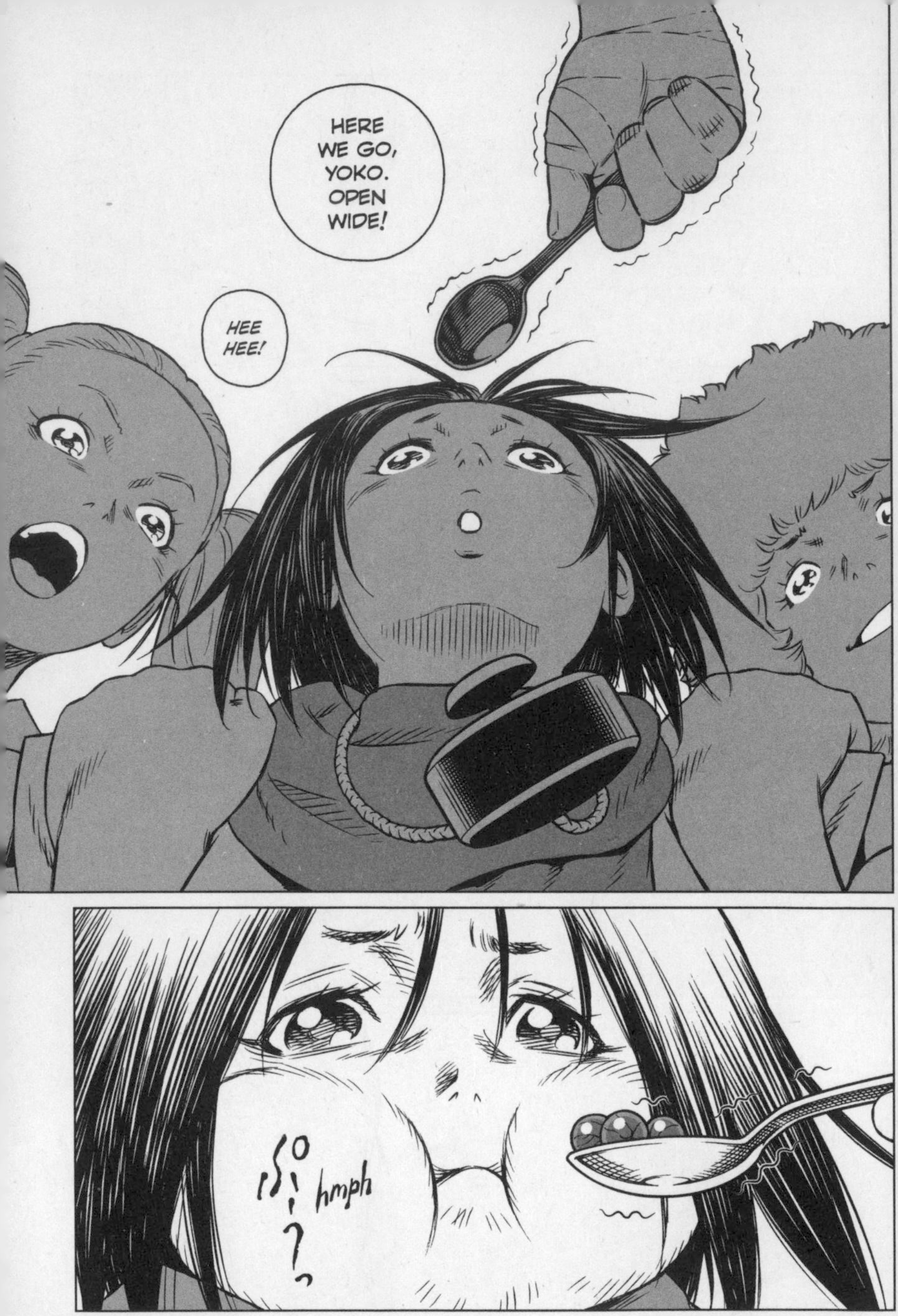
HERE WE GO, YOKO. OPEN WIDE!
HEE HEE!
hmph
!?

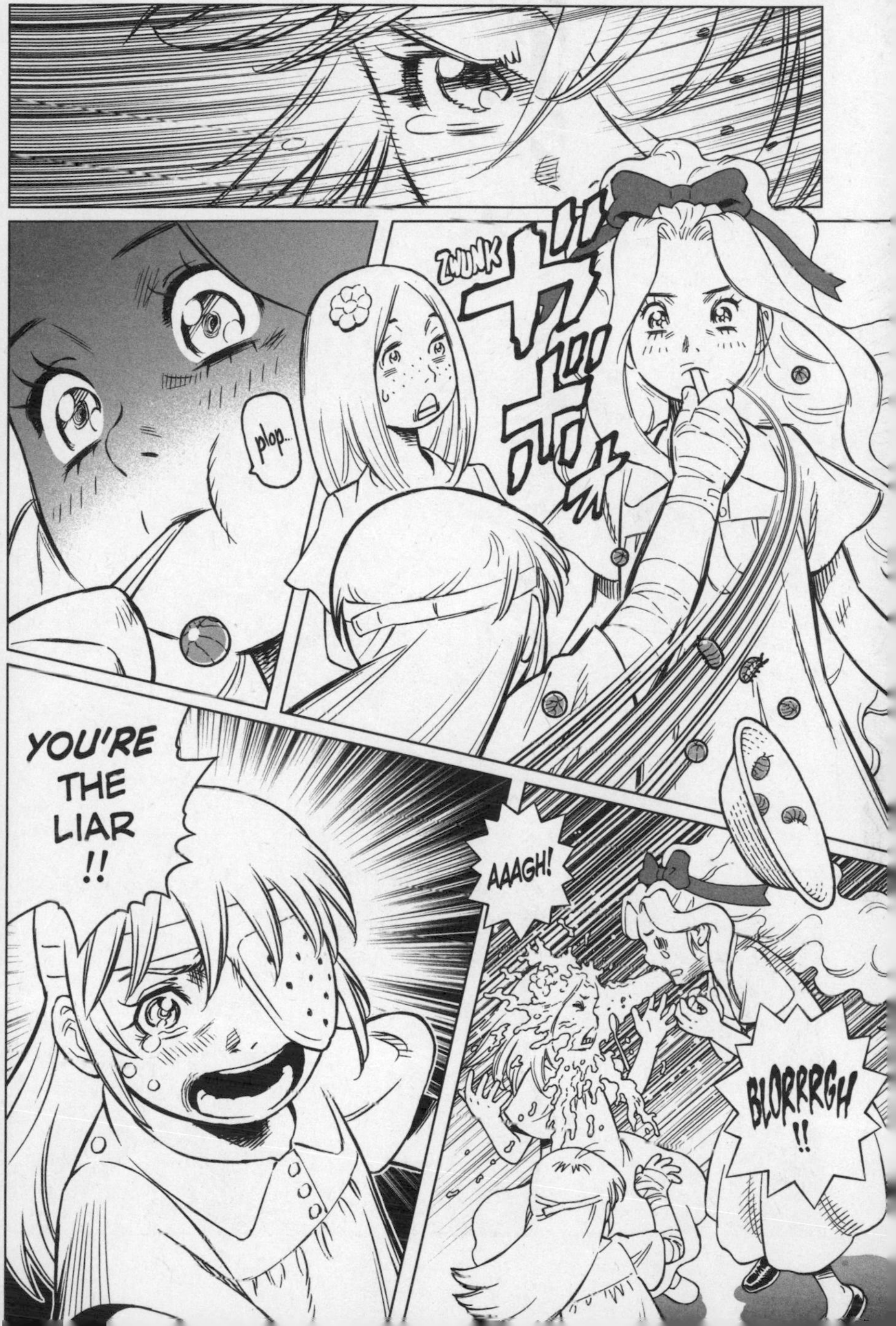
ZWUNK
plop...
AAAGH!
BLORRRGH !!
YOU'RE THE LIAR !!

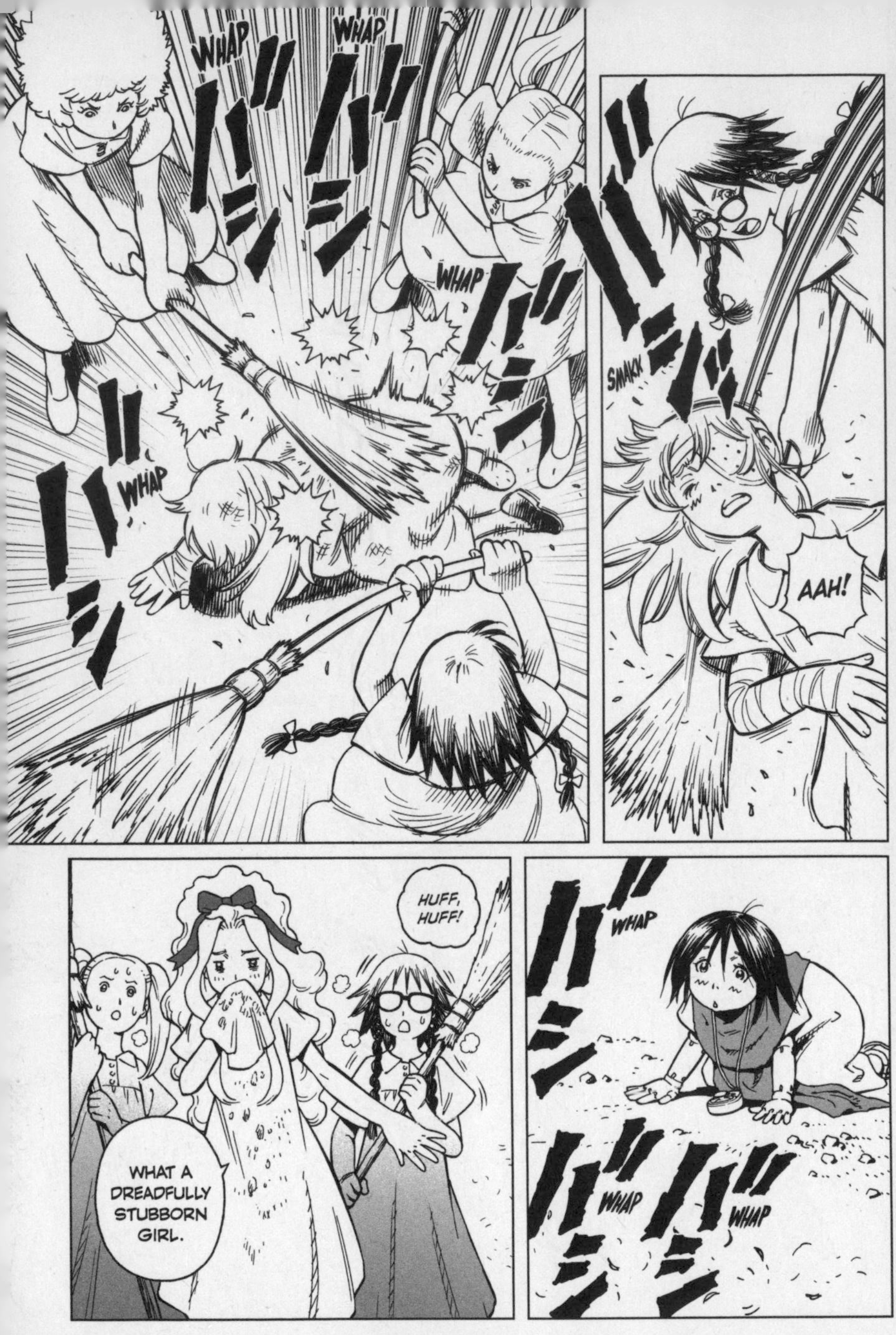
SMAKK
AAH!
WHAP
WHAP
WHAP
WHAP
WHAP
WHAP
WHAP
HUFF, HUFF!
WHAT A DREADFULLY STUBBORN GIRL.

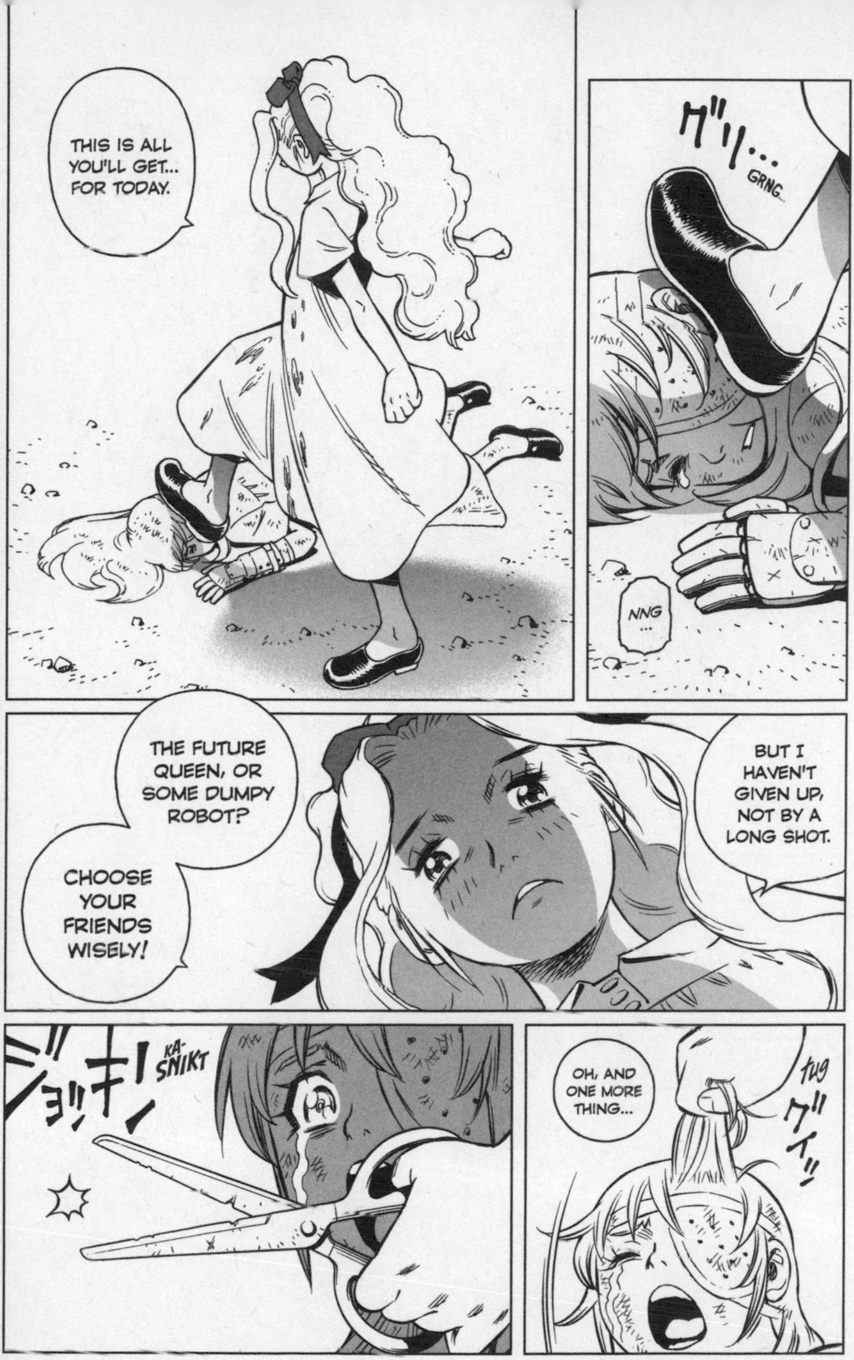
グリ…
GRNG...
NNG ...
THIS IS ALL YOU'LL GET... FOR TODAY.
BUT I HAVEN'T GIVEN UP, NOT BY A LONG SHOT.
THE FUTURE QUEEN, OR SOME DUMPY ROBOT?
CHOOSE YOUR FRIENDS WISELY!
OH, AND ONE MORE THING...
TUG
グイッ
ジョッキ!
KA-SNIKT

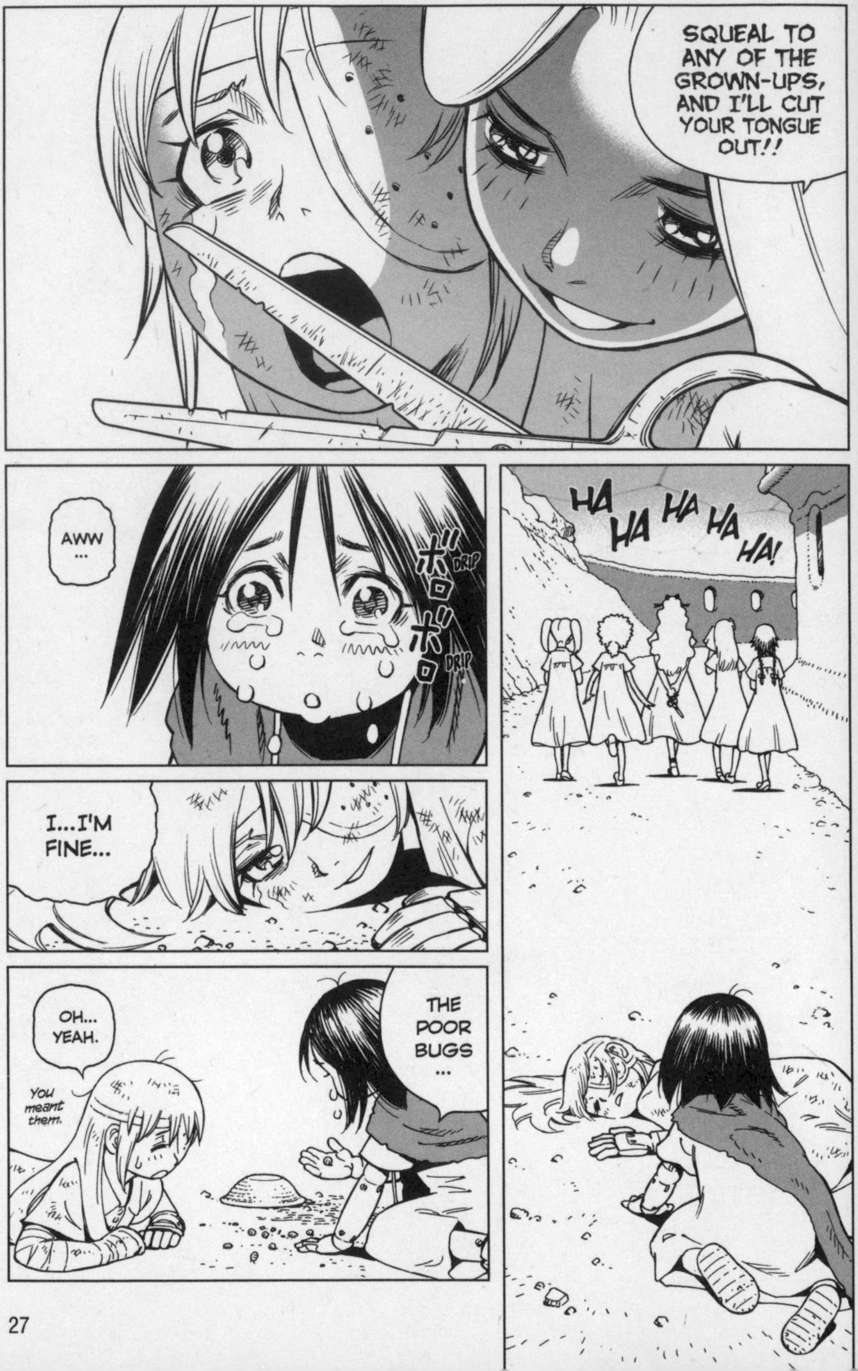
SQUEAL TO ANY OF THE GROWN-UPS, AND I'LL CUT YOUR TONGUE OUT!!
HA HA HA HA HA HA!
AWW ...
ボロボロ
DRIP
DRIP
I...I'M FINE...
THE POOR BUGS ...
OH... YEAH.
You meant them.

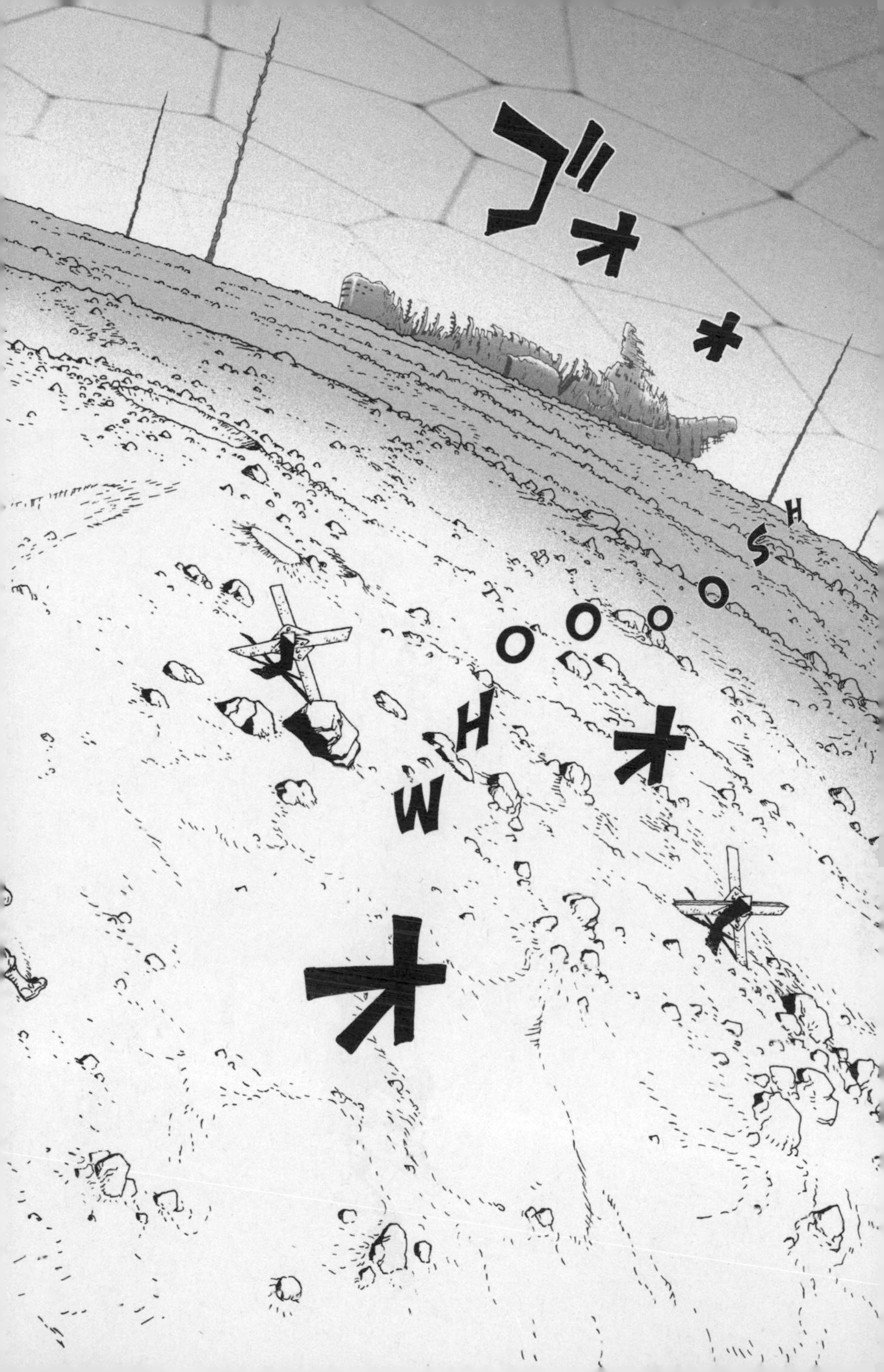
ゴォォオオ
WHOOOOSH

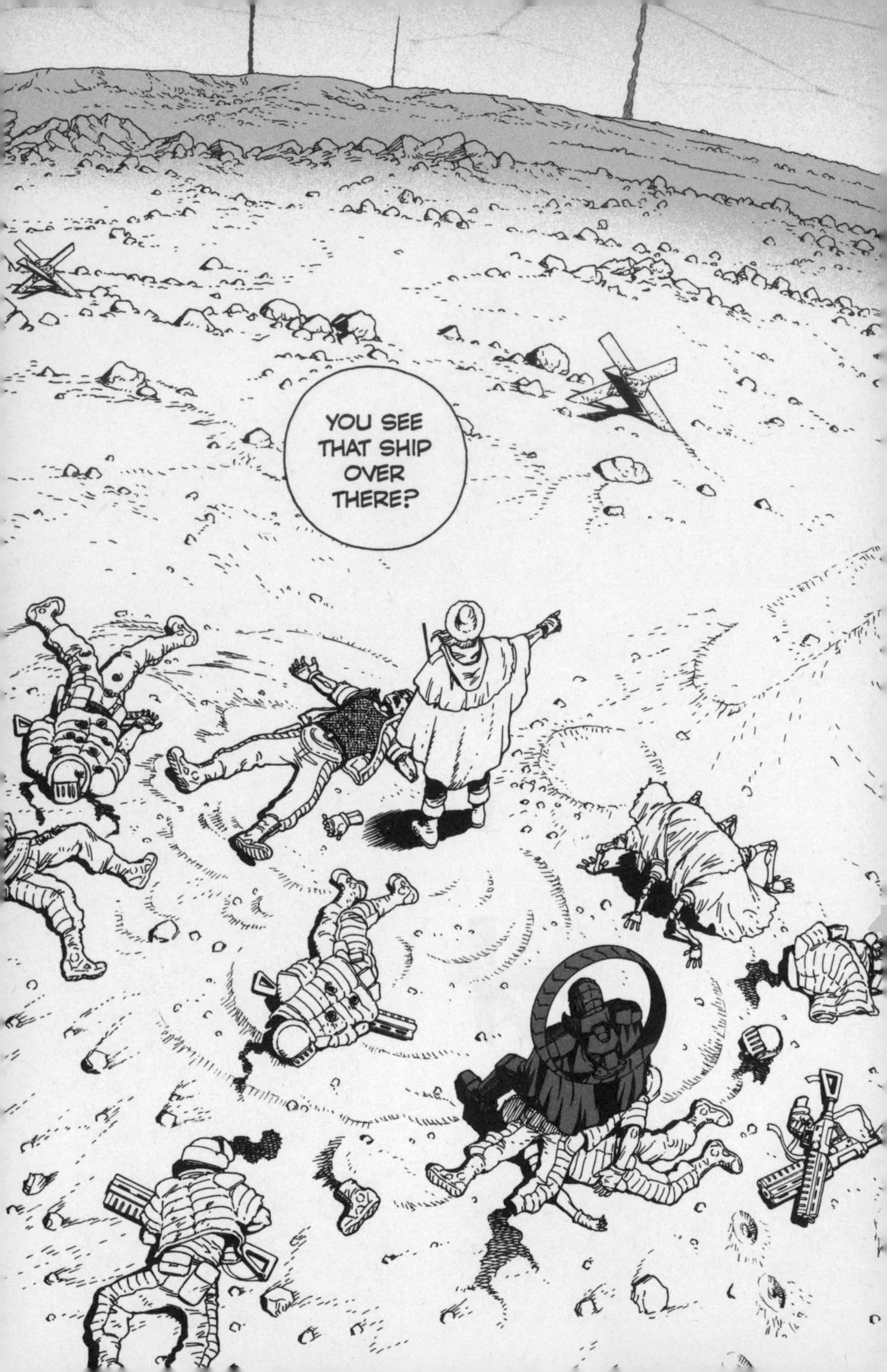
YOU SEE THAT SHIP OVER THERE?

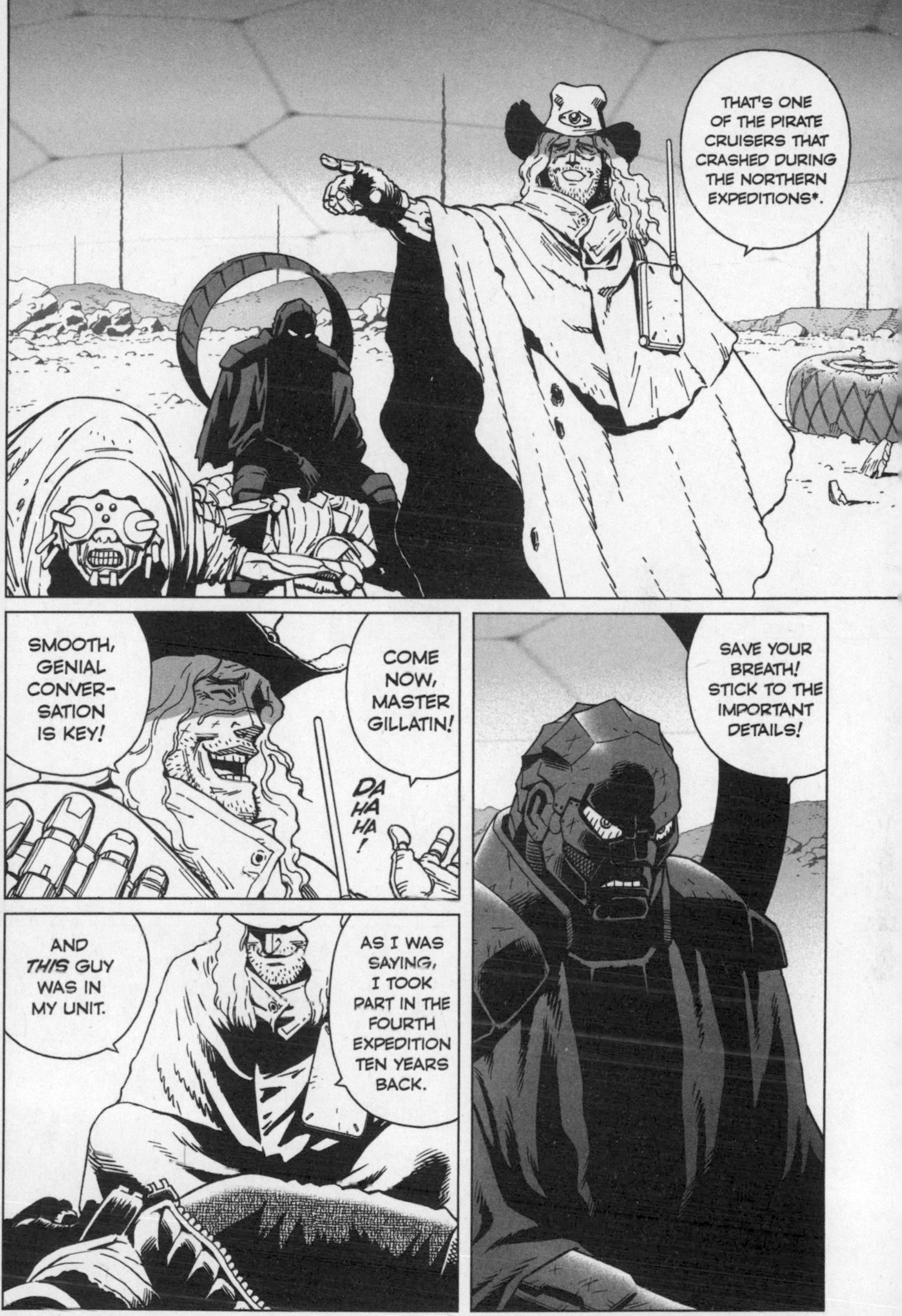
THAT'S ONE OF THE PIRATE CRUISERS THAT CRASHED DURING THE NORTHERN EXPEDITIONS*.
SAVE YOUR BREATH! STICK TO THE IMPORTANT DETAILS!
COME NOW, MASTER GILLATIN!
SMOOTH, GENIAL CONVER-SATION IS KEY!
DA HA HA!
AS I WAS SAYING, I TOOK PART IN THE FOURTH EXPEDITION TEN YEARS BACK.
AND *THIS* GUY WAS IN MY UNIT.

***Northern Expeditions:** Officially, the Martian North Pole Conflict. A war that broke out between Martian forces and space pirates when the pirates attempted to build a base on the north pole of Mars. Conflicts arose four times during ES 361-363, each time with a decisive Martian victory.

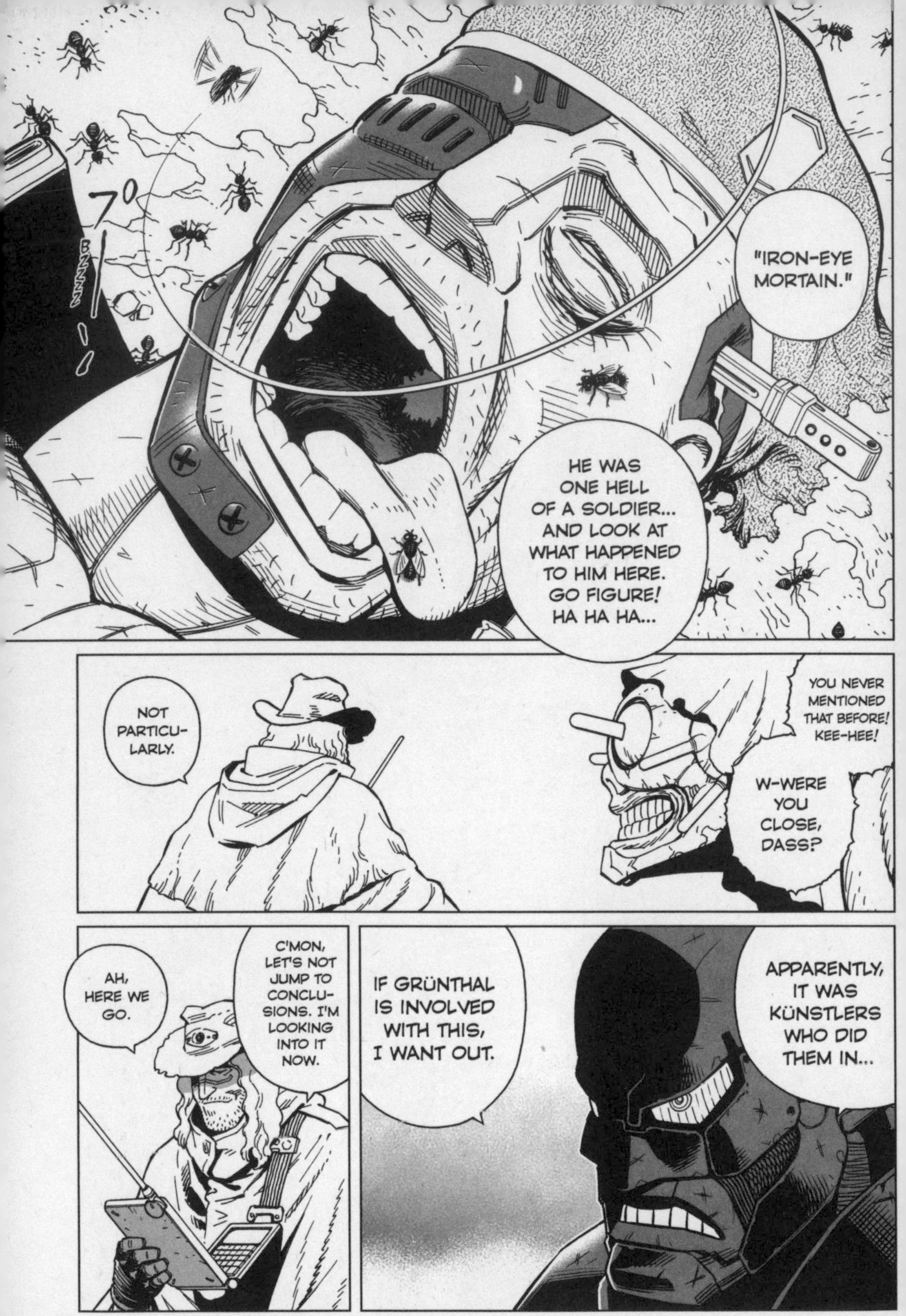
"IRON-EYE MORTAIN."
HE WAS ONE HELL OF A SOLDIER... AND LOOK AT WHAT HAPPENED TO HIM HERE. GO FIGURE! HA HA HA...
YOU NEVER MENTIONED THAT BEFORE! KEE-HEE!
W-WERE YOU CLOSE, DASS?
NOT PARTICU-LARLY.
APPARENTLY, IT WAS KÜNSTLERS WHO DID THEM IN...
IF GRÜNTHAL IS INVOLVED WITH THIS, I WANT OUT.
C'MON, LET'S NOT JUMP TO CONCLU-SIONS. I'M LOOKING INTO IT NOW.
AH, HERE WE GO.

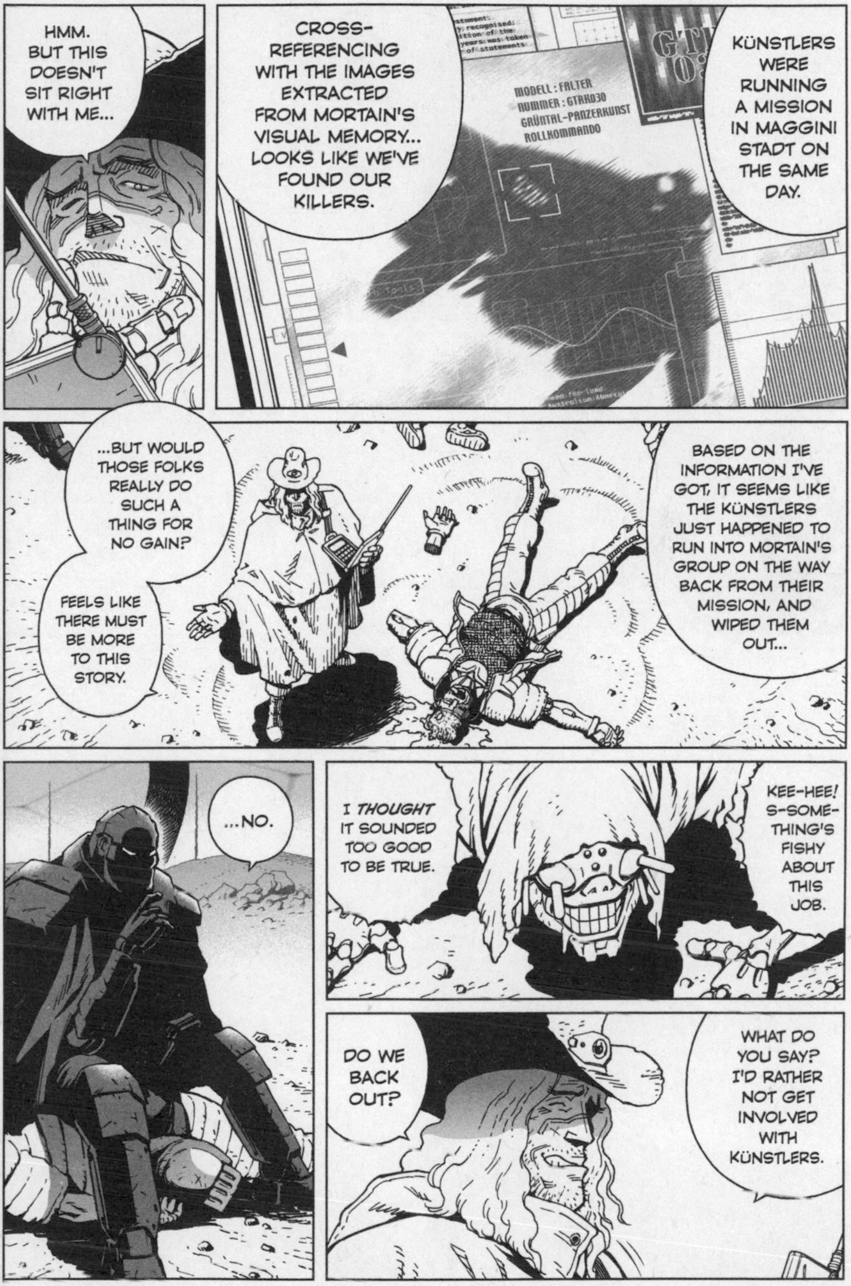
KÜNSTLERS WERE RUNNING A MISSION IN MAGGINI STADT ON THE SAME DAY.
CROSS-REFERENCING WITH THE IMAGES EXTRACTED FROM MORTAIN'S VISUAL MEMORY... LOOKS LIKE WE'VE FOUND OUR KILLERS.
MODELL : FALTER
NUMMER : GTRK030
GRÜNTAL-PANZERKUNST
ROLLKOMMANDO
HMM. BUT THIS DOESN'T SIT RIGHT WITH ME...
BASED ON THE INFORMATION I'VE GOT, IT SEEMS LIKE THE KÜNSTLERS JUST HAPPENED TO RUN INTO MORTAIN'S GROUP ON THE WAY BACK FROM THEIR MISSION, AND WIPED THEM OUT...
...BUT WOULD THOSE FOLKS REALLY DO SUCH A THING FOR NO GAIN?
FEELS LIKE THERE MUST BE MORE TO THIS STORY.
KEE-HEE! S-SOME-THING'S FISHY ABOUT THIS JOB.
I *THOUGHT* IT SOUNDED TOO GOOD TO BE TRUE.
WHAT DO YOU SAY? I'D RATHER NOT GET INVOLVED WITH KÜNSTLERS.
DO WE BACK OUT?
...NO.

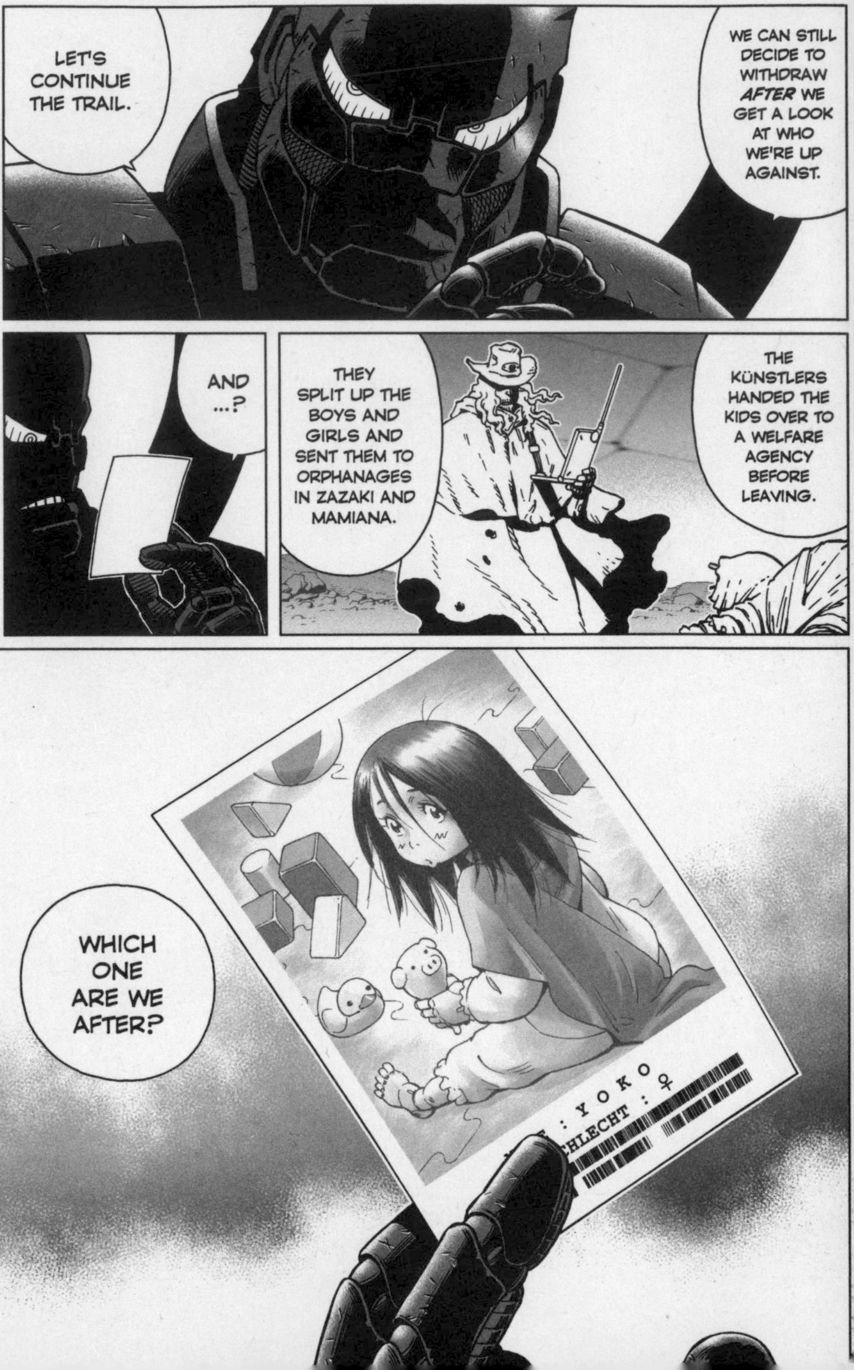
WE CAN STILL DECIDE TO WITHDRAW *AFTER* WE GET A LOOK AT WHO WE'RE UP AGAINST.
LET'S CONTINUE THE TRAIL.
THE KÜNSTLERS HANDED THE KIDS OVER TO A WELFARE AGENCY BEFORE LEAVING.
THEY SPLIT UP THE BOYS AND GIRLS AND SENT THEM TO ORPHANAGES IN ZAZAKI AND MAMIANA.
AND ...?
WHICH ONE ARE WE AFTER?
YOKO

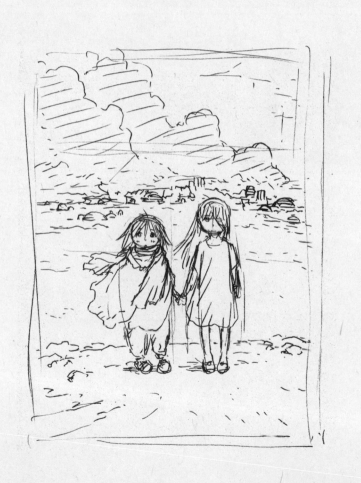

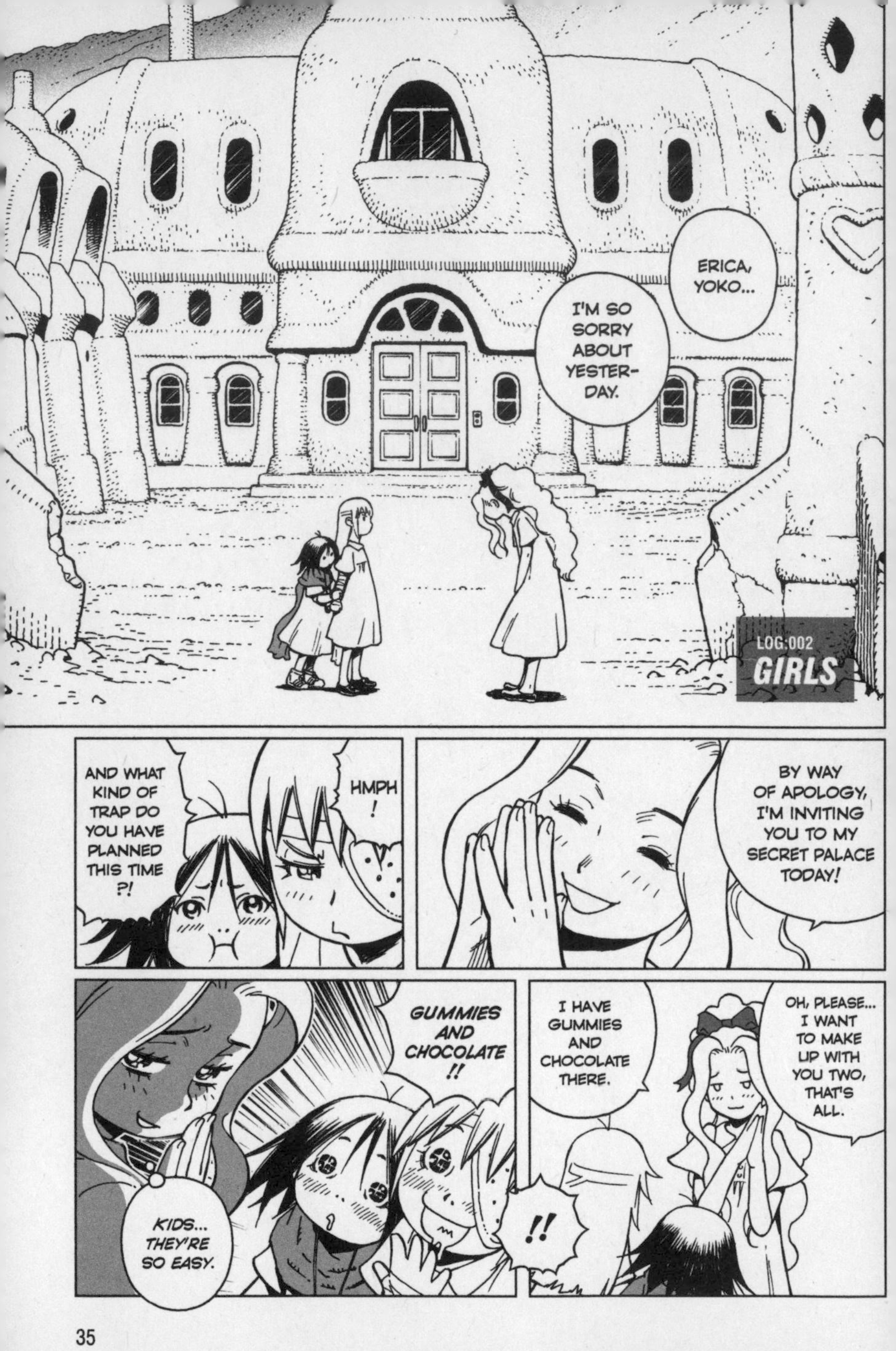
ERICA, YOKO...
I'M SO SORRY ABOUT YESTER-DAY.
LOG:002
GIRLS
BY WAY OF APOLOGY, I'M INVITING YOU TO MY SECRET PALACE TODAY!
HMPH!
AND WHAT KIND OF TRAP DO YOU HAVE PLANNED THIS TIME?!
OH, PLEASE... I WANT TO MAKE UP WITH YOU TWO, THAT'S ALL.
I HAVE GUMMIES AND CHOCOLATE THERE.
!!
GUMMIES AND CHOCOLATE!!
KIDS... THEY'RE SO EASY.

LOG:002

GIRLS

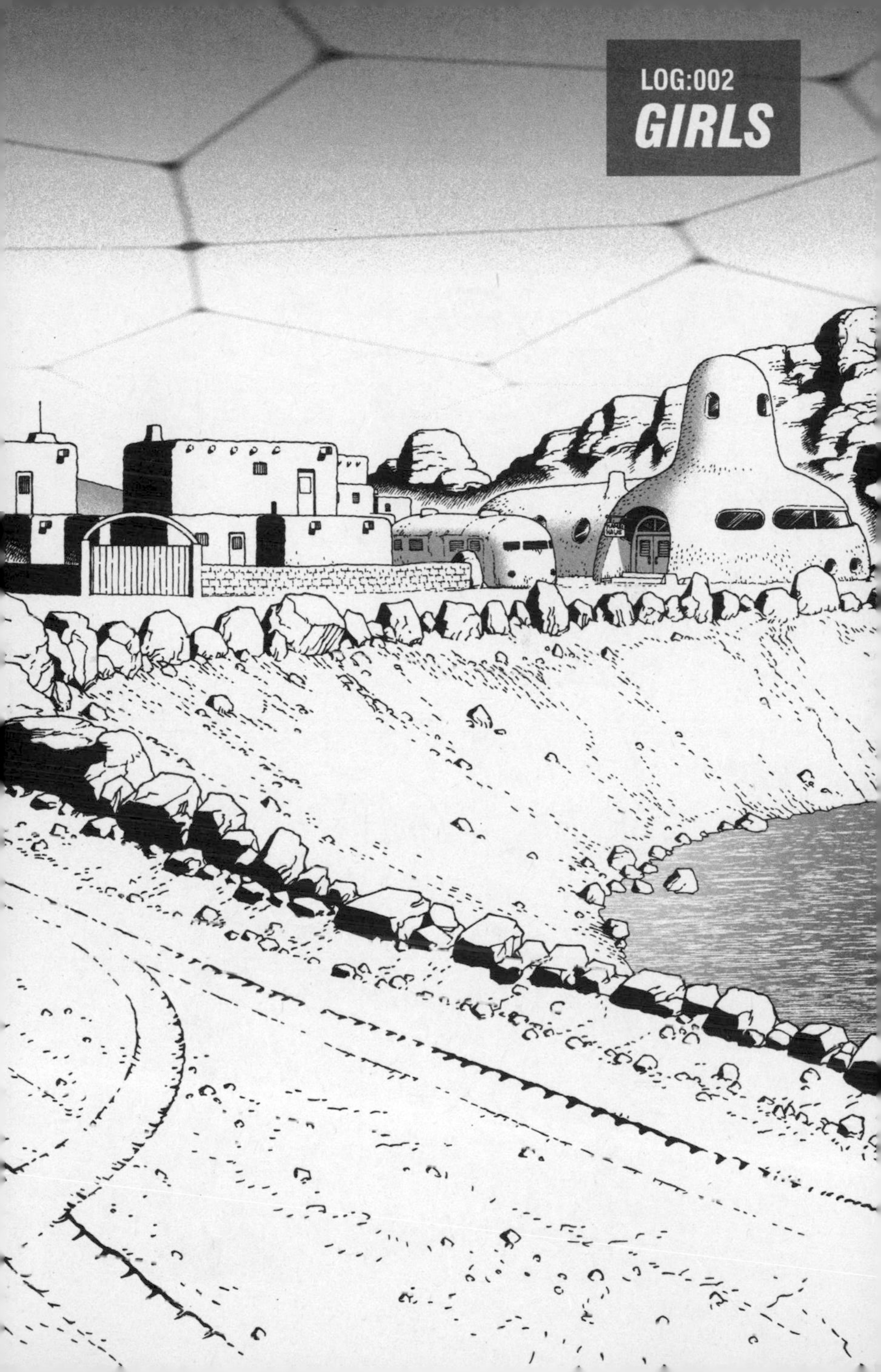

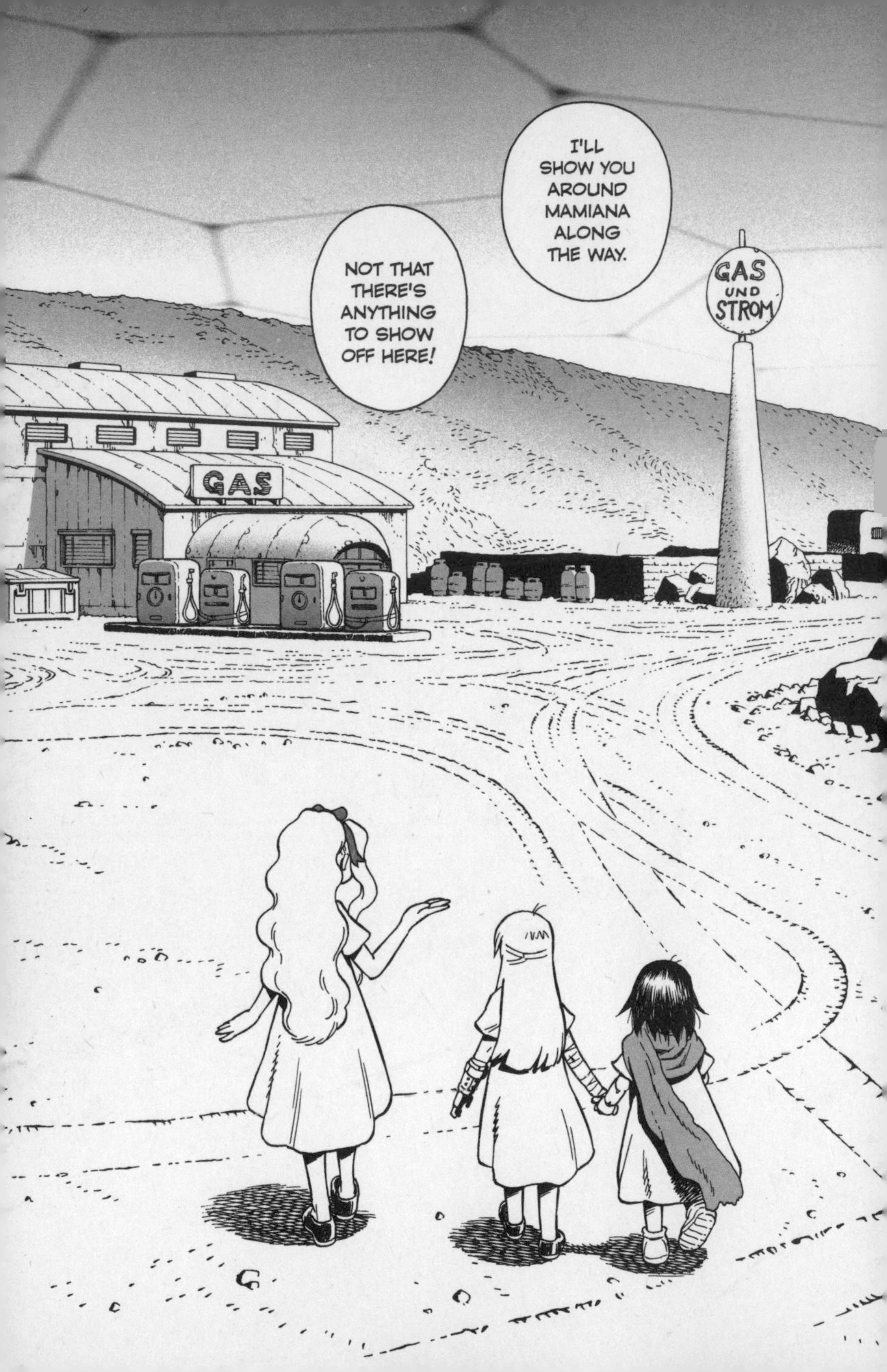
I'LL SHOW YOU AROUND MAMIANA ALONG THE WAY.
NOT THAT THERE'S ANYTHING TO SHOW OFF HERE!
GAS UND STROM
GAS

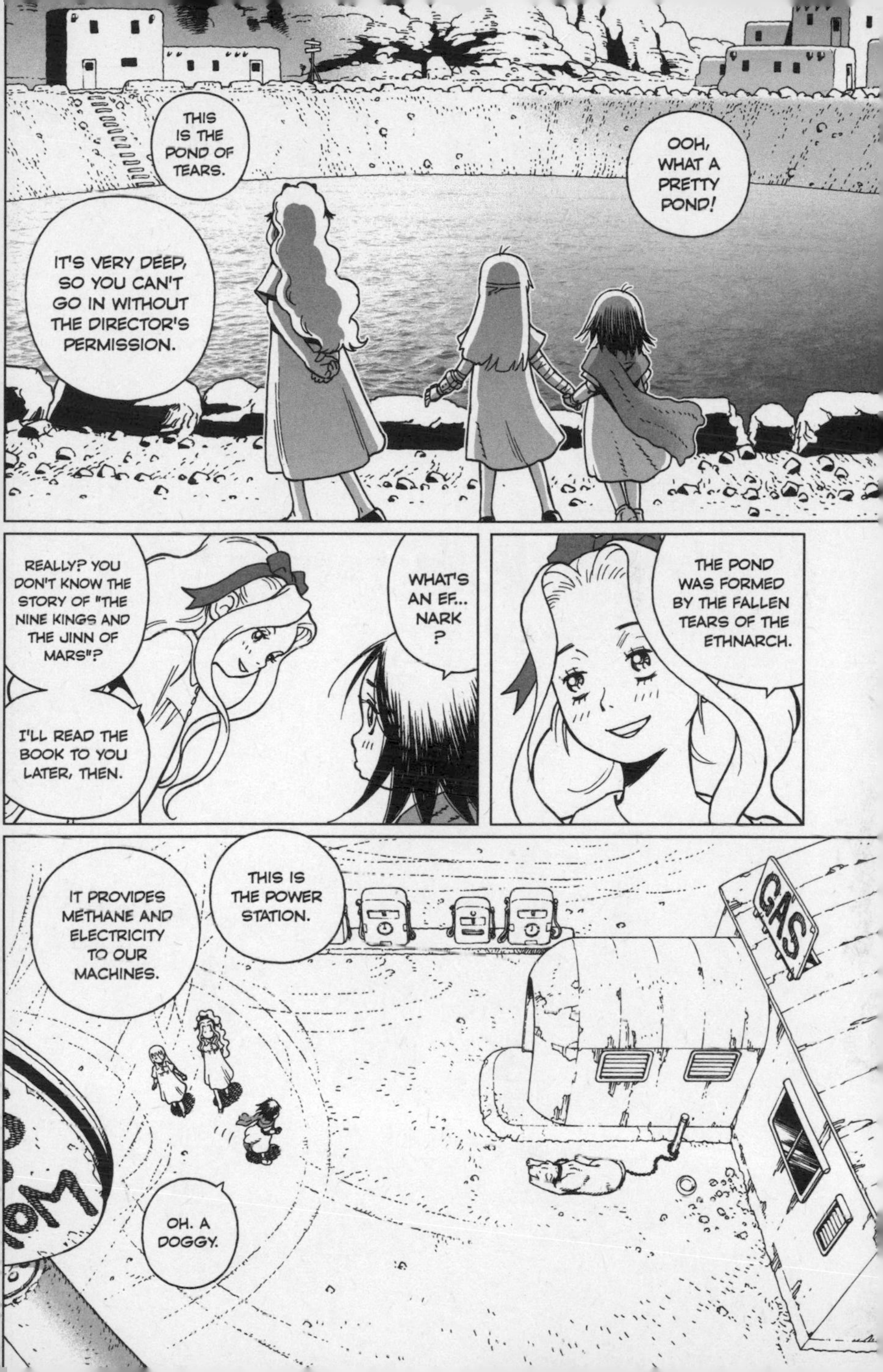
OOH, WHAT A PRETTY POND!
THIS IS THE POND OF TEARS.
IT'S VERY DEEP, SO YOU CAN'T GO IN WITHOUT THE DIRECTOR'S PERMISSION.
THE POND WAS FORMED BY THE FALLEN TEARS OF THE ETHNARCH.
WHAT'S AN EF... NARK ?
REALLY? YOU DON'T KNOW THE STORY OF "THE NINE KINGS AND THE JINN OF MARS"?
I'LL READ THE BOOK TO YOU LATER, THEN.
GAS
THIS IS THE POWER STATION.
IT PROVIDES METHANE AND ELECTRICITY TO OUR MACHINES.
OH. A DOGGY.

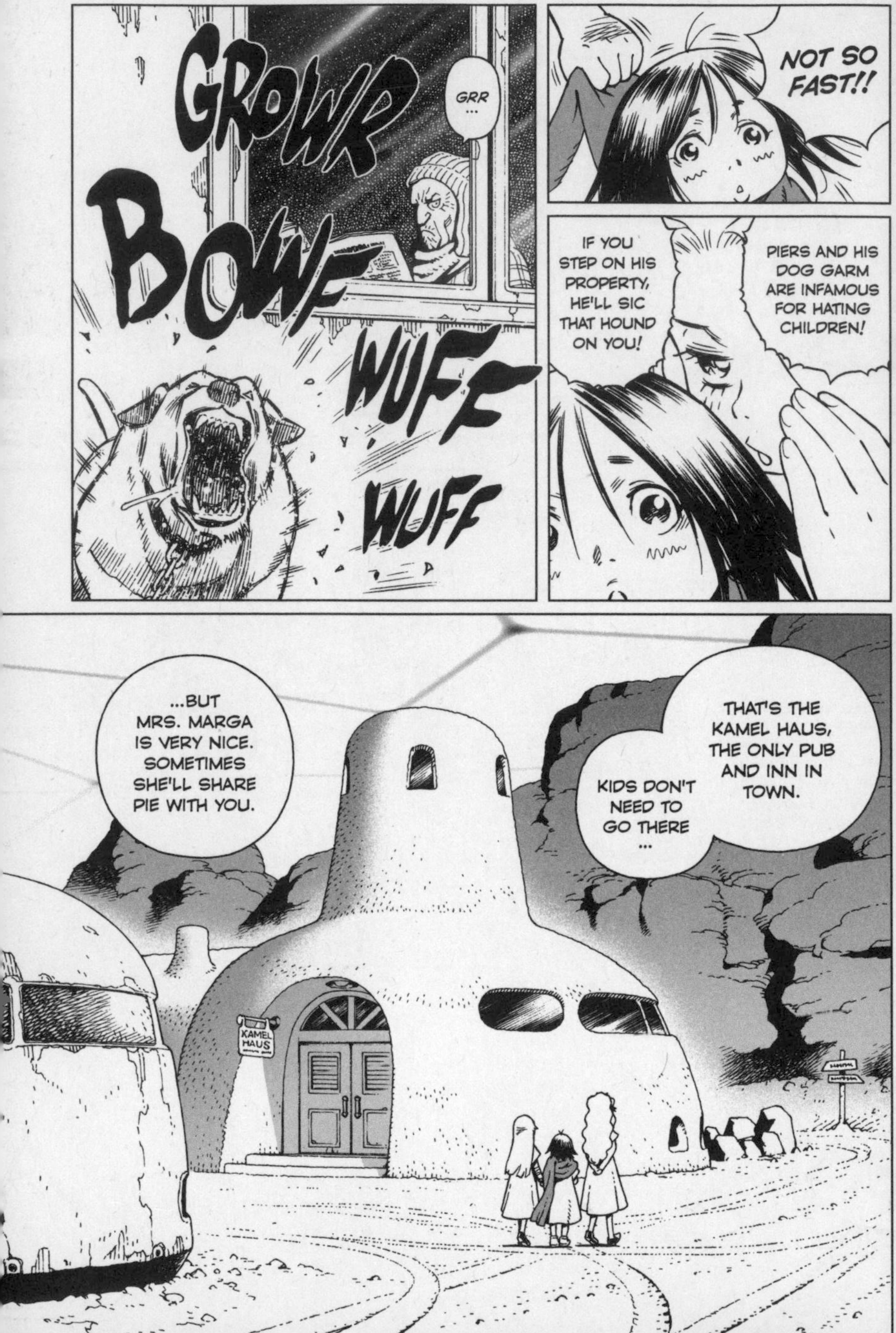
NOT SO FAST!!
PIERS AND HIS DOG GARM ARE INFAMOUS FOR HATING CHILDREN!
IF YOU STEP ON HIS PROPERTY, HE'LL SIC THAT HOUND ON YOU!
GRR ...
GROWR
BOWF
WUFF
WUFF
THAT'S THE KAMEL HAUS, THE ONLY PUB AND INN IN TOWN.
KIDS DON'T NEED TO GO THERE ...
...BUT MRS. MARGA IS VERY NICE. SOMETIMES SHE'LL SHARE PIE WITH YOU.
KAMEL HAUS

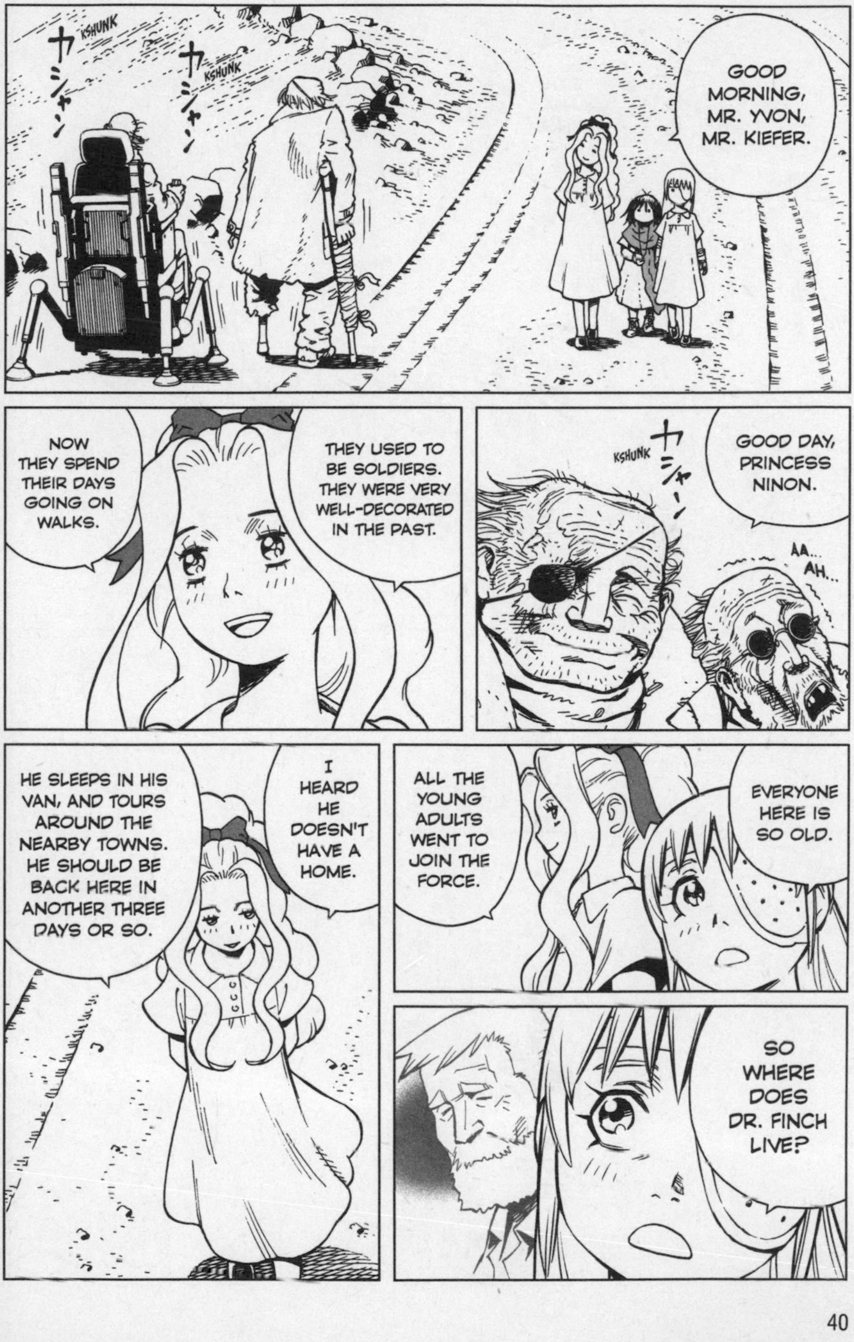
GOOD MORNING, MR. YVON, MR. KIEFER.
カシャン KSHUNK
カシャン KSHUNK
GOOD DAY, PRINCESS NINON.
カシャーン KSHUNK
AA... AH...
THEY USED TO BE SOLDIERS. THEY WERE VERY WELL-DECORATED IN THE PAST.
NOW THEY SPEND THEIR DAYS GOING ON WALKS.
EVERYONE HERE IS SO OLD.
ALL THE YOUNG ADULTS WENT TO JOIN THE FORCE.
SO WHERE DOES DR. FINCH LIVE?
I HEARD HE DOESN'T HAVE A HOME.
HE SLEEPS IN HIS VAN, AND TOURS AROUND THE NEARBY TOWNS. HE SHOULD BE BACK HERE IN ANOTHER THREE DAYS OR SO.

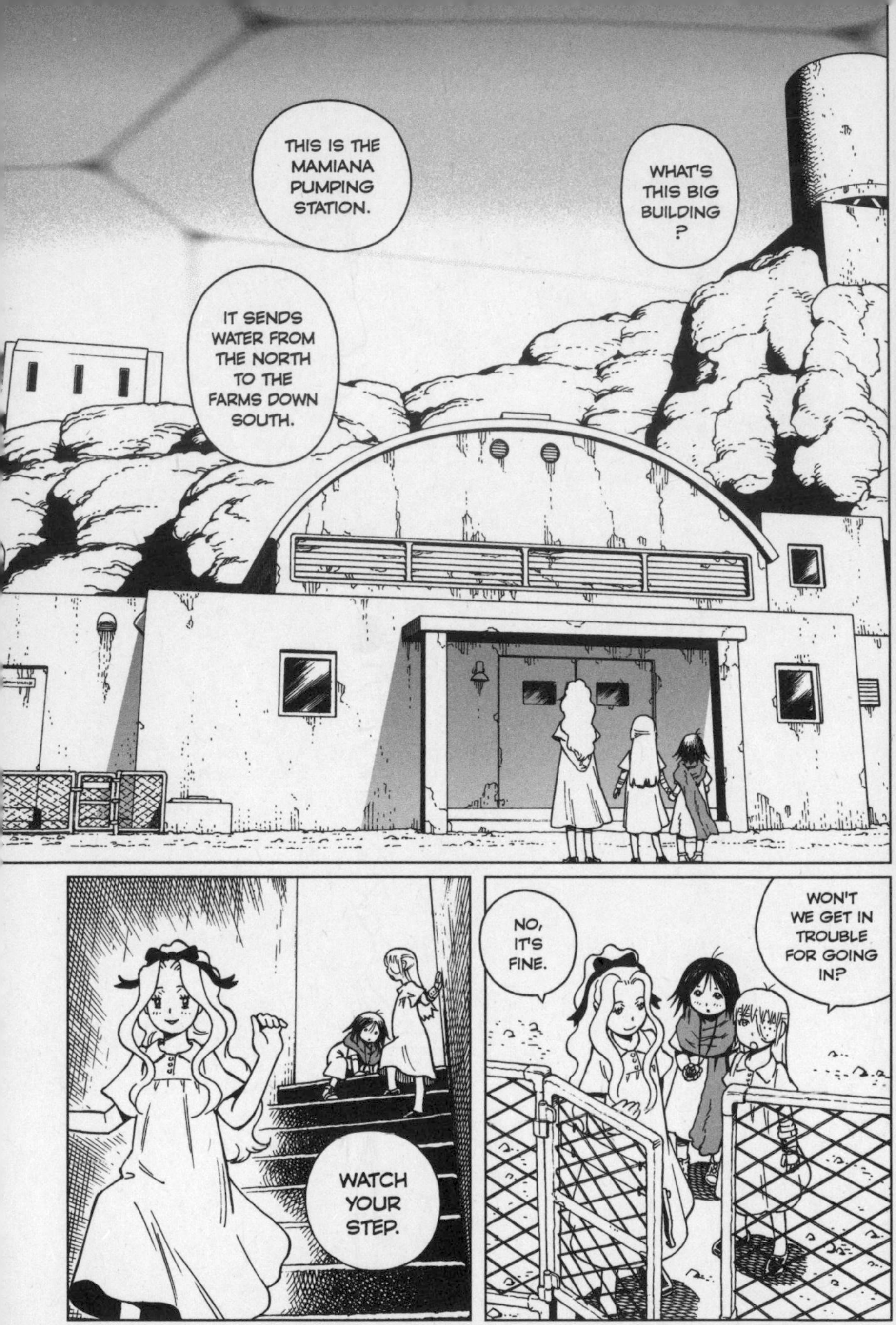
WHAT'S THIS BIG BUILDING?
THIS IS THE MAMIANA PUMPING STATION.
IT SENDS WATER FROM THE NORTH TO THE FARMS DOWN SOUTH.
WON'T WE GET IN TROUBLE FOR GOING IN?
NO, IT'S FINE.
WATCH YOUR STEP.

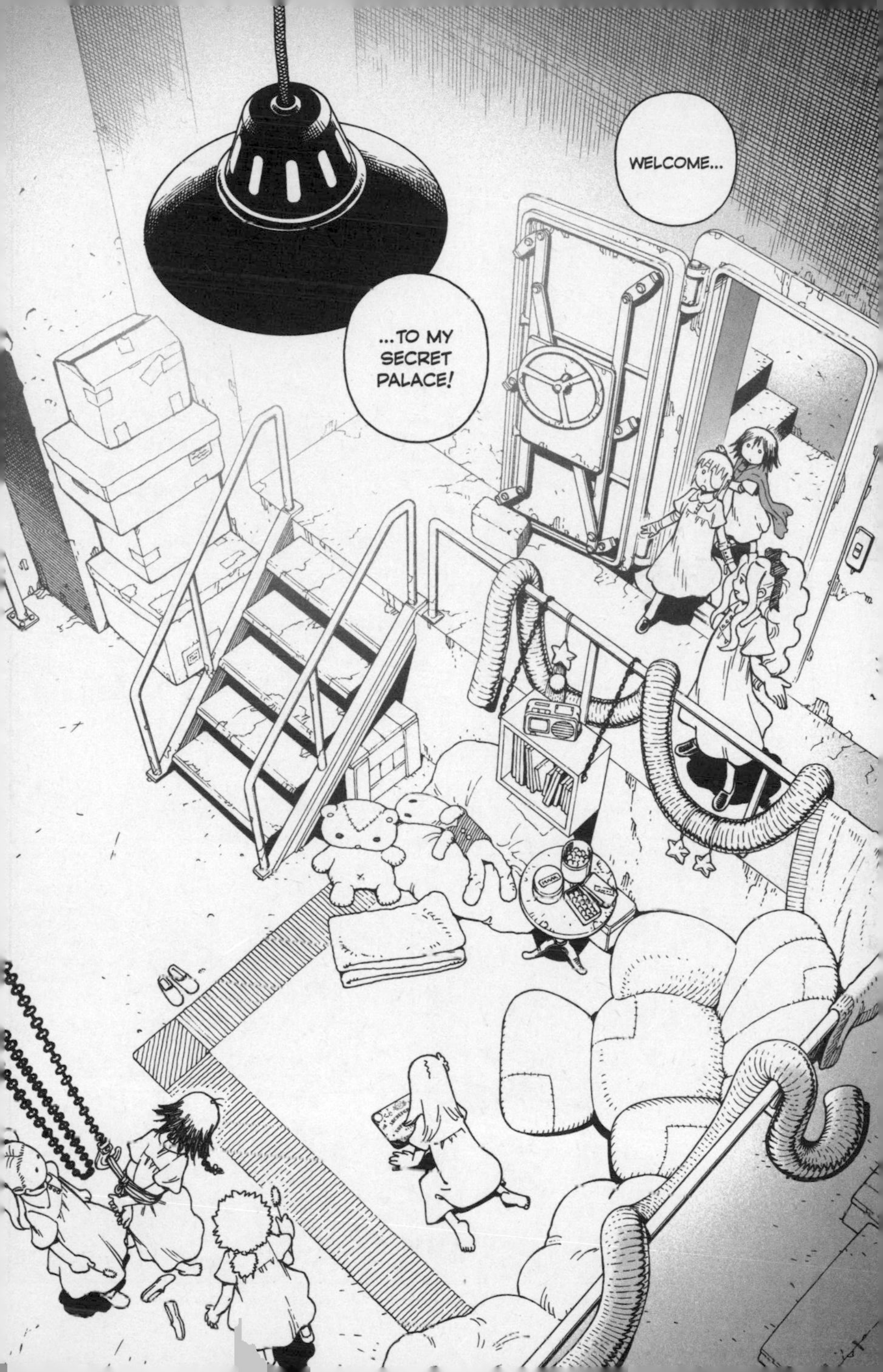
WELCOME...
...TO MY SECRET PALACE!

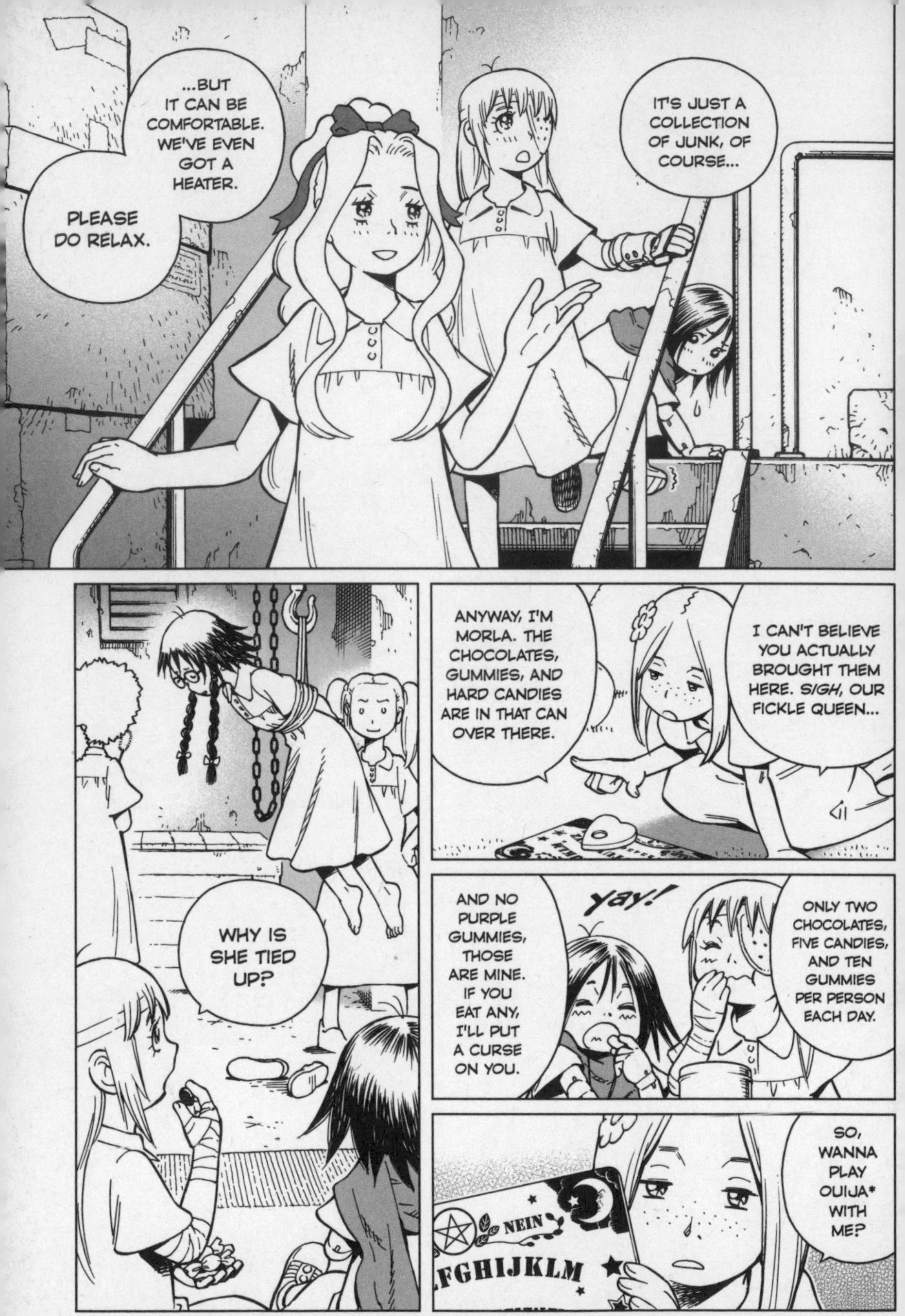
IT'S JUST A COLLECTION OF JUNK, OF COURSE...
...BUT IT CAN BE COMFORTABLE. WE'VE EVEN GOT A HEATER.
PLEASE DO RELAX.
I CAN'T BELIEVE YOU ACTUALLY BROUGHT THEM HERE. *SIGH*, OUR FICKLE QUEEN...
ANYWAY, I'M MORLA. THE CHOCOLATES, GUMMIES, AND HARD CANDIES ARE IN THAT CAN OVER THERE.
ONLY TWO CHOCOLATES, FIVE CANDIES, AND TEN GUMMIES PER PERSON EACH DAY.
yay!
AND NO PURPLE GUMMIES, THOSE ARE MINE. IF YOU EAT ANY, I'LL PUT A CURSE ON YOU.
SO, WANNA PLAY OUIJA* WITH ME?
NEIN
FGHIJKLM
WHY IS SHE TIED UP?

***Ouija board:** A letter board for communing with spirits, first developed in America in 1892. It's a Western version of an old game called *Kokkuri-san* in Japan.

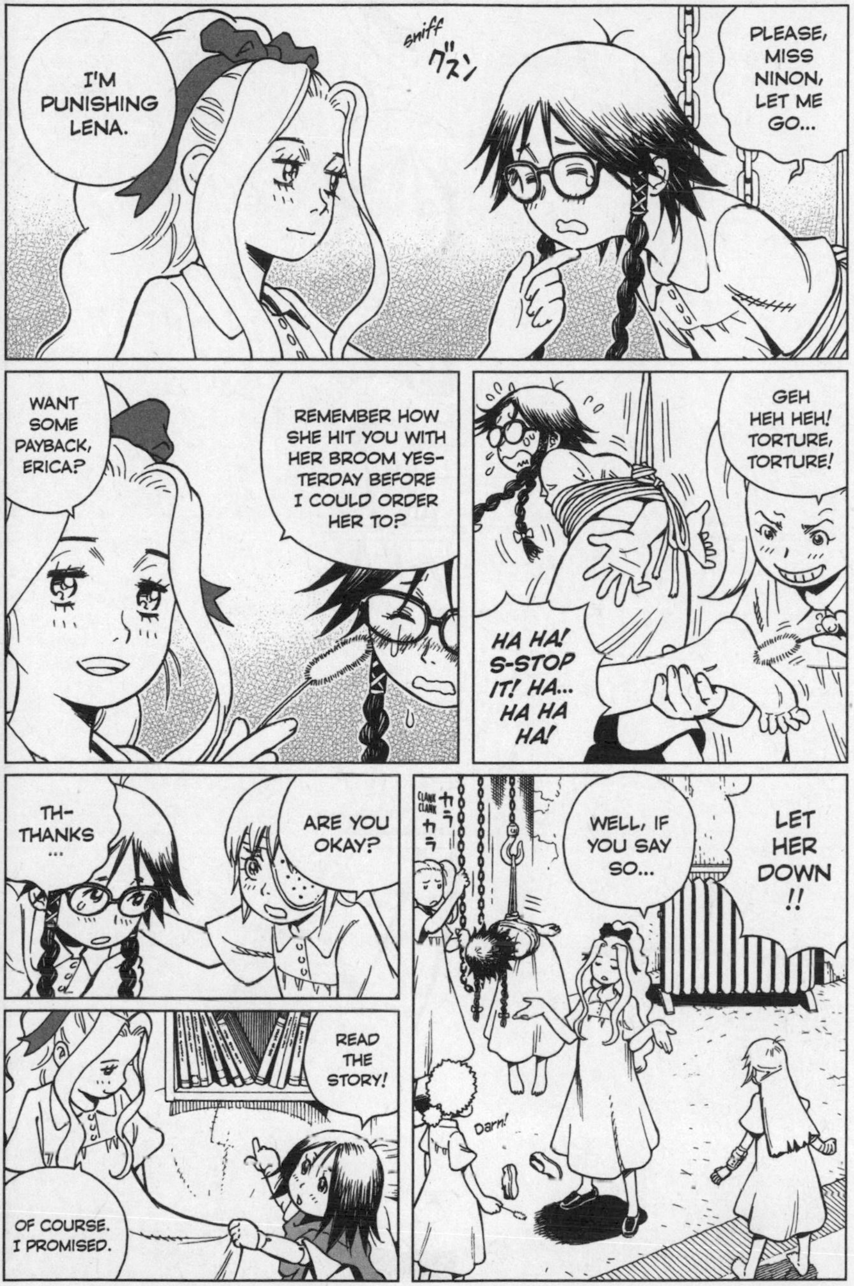
PLEASE, MISS NINON, LET ME GO...
sniff
グスン
I'M PUNISHING LENA.
GEH HEH HEH! TORTURE, TORTURE!
HA HA! S-STOP IT! HA... HA HA HA!
REMEMBER HOW SHE HIT YOU WITH HER BROOM YES-TERDAY BEFORE I COULD ORDER HER TO?
WANT SOME PAYBACK, ERICA?
LET HER DOWN!!
WELL, IF YOU SAY SO...
CLANK CLANK
カラ カラ
Darn!
ARE YOU OKAY?
TH-THANKS...
READ THE STORY!
OF COURSE. I PROMISED.

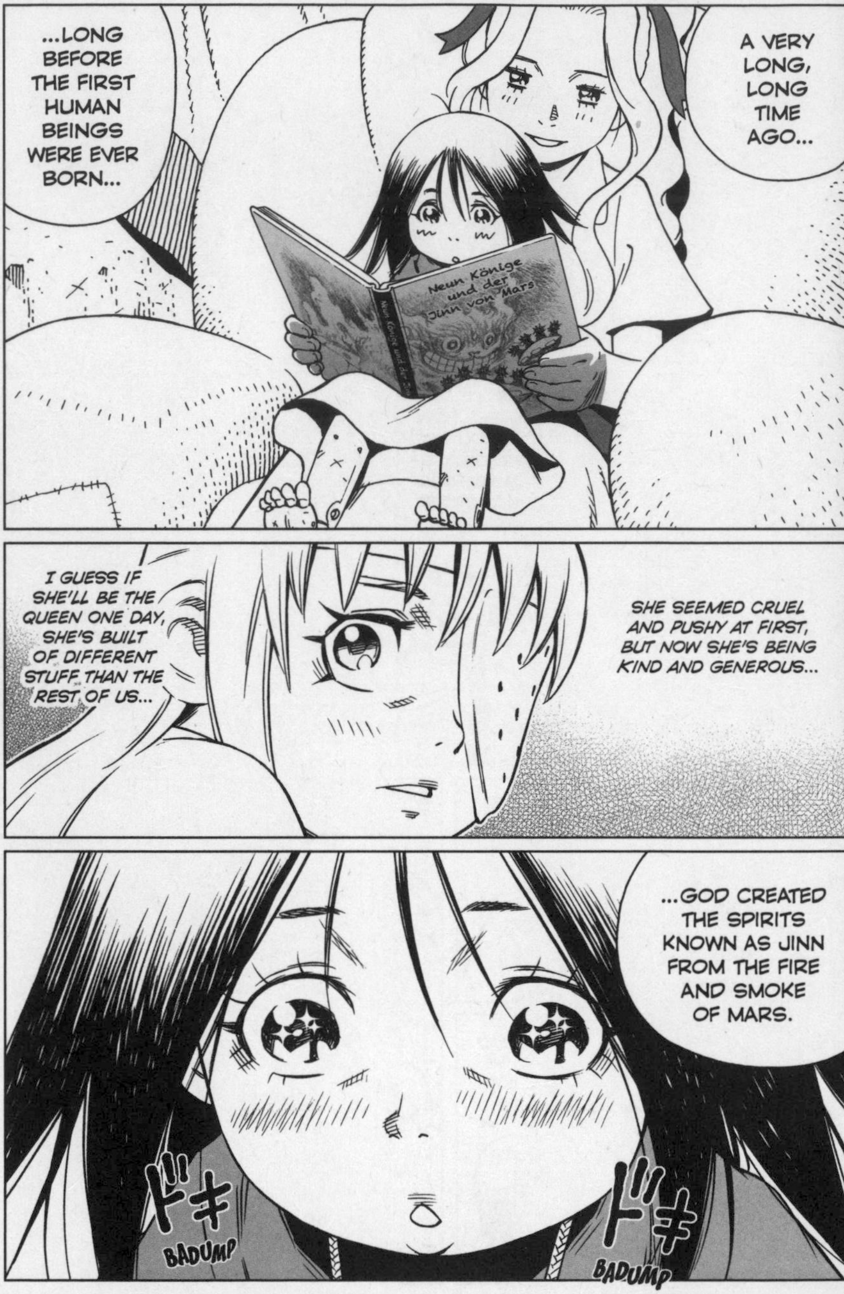
A VERY LONG, LONG TIME AGO...
...LONG BEFORE THE FIRST HUMAN BEINGS WERE EVER BORN...
Neun Könige und der Jinn von Mars
SHE SEEMED CRUEL AND PUSHY AT FIRST, BUT NOW SHE'S BEING KIND AND GENEROUS...
I GUESS IF SHE'LL BE THE QUEEN ONE DAY, SHE'S BUILT OF DIFFERENT STUFF THAN THE REST OF US...
...GOD CREATED THE SPIRITS KNOWN AS JINN FROM THE FIRE AND SMOKE OF MARS.
ドキ
BADUMP
ドキ
BADUMP

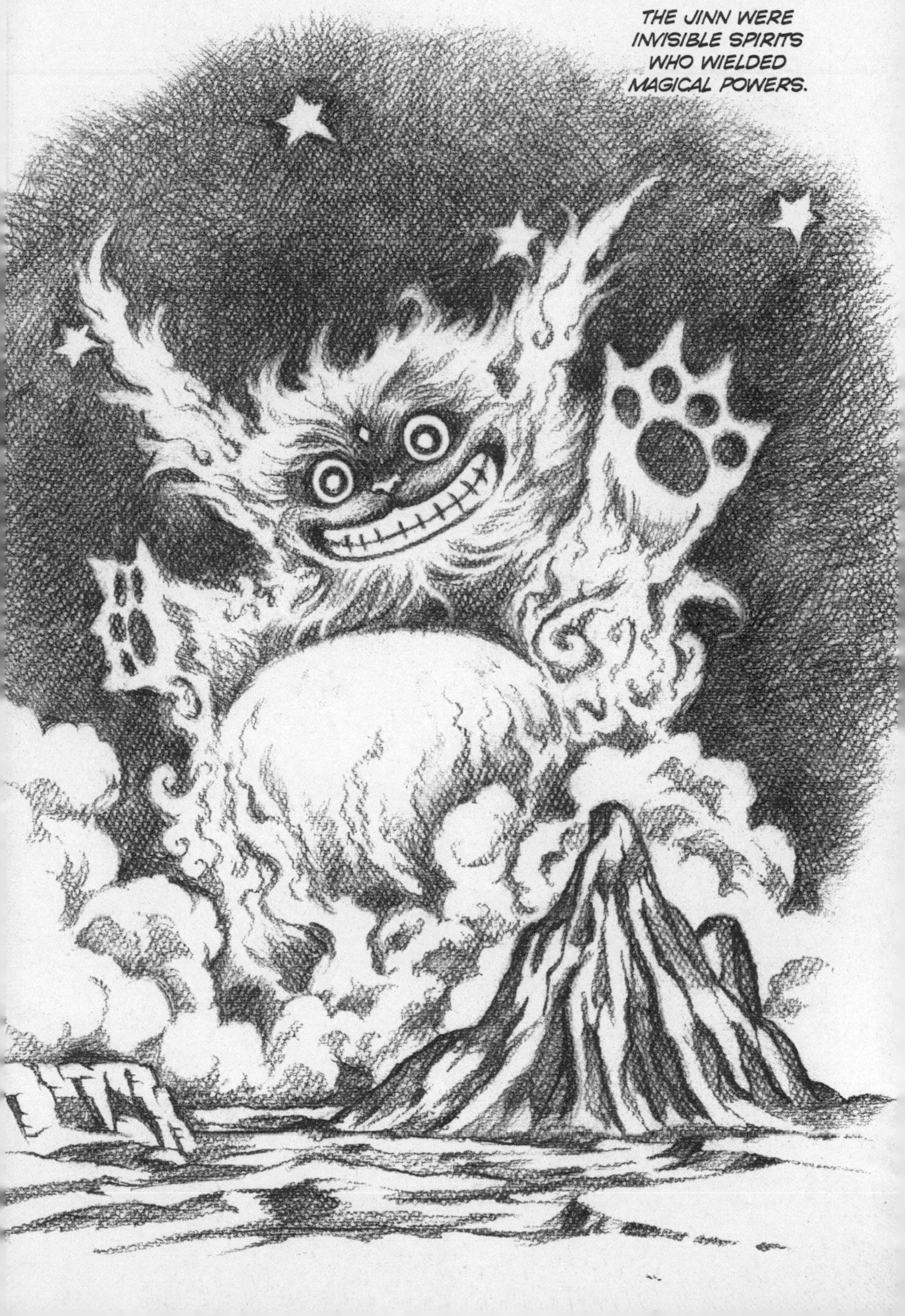
THE JINN WERE INVISIBLE SPIRITS WHO WIELDED MAGICAL POWERS.

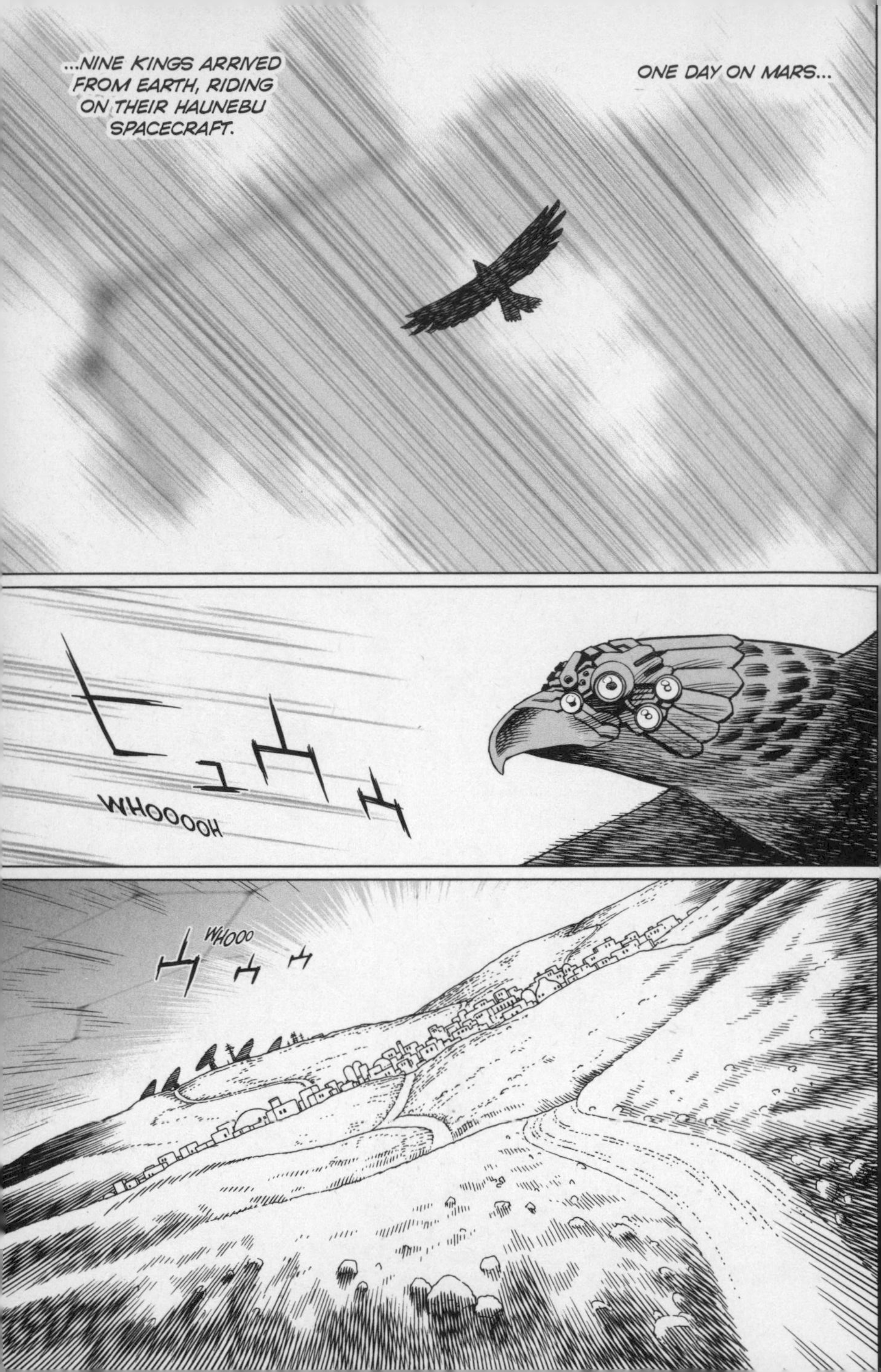
ONE DAY ON MARS...
...NINE KINGS ARRIVED FROM EARTH, RIDING ON THEIR HAUNEBU SPACECRAFT.
WHOOOOH
WHOOO

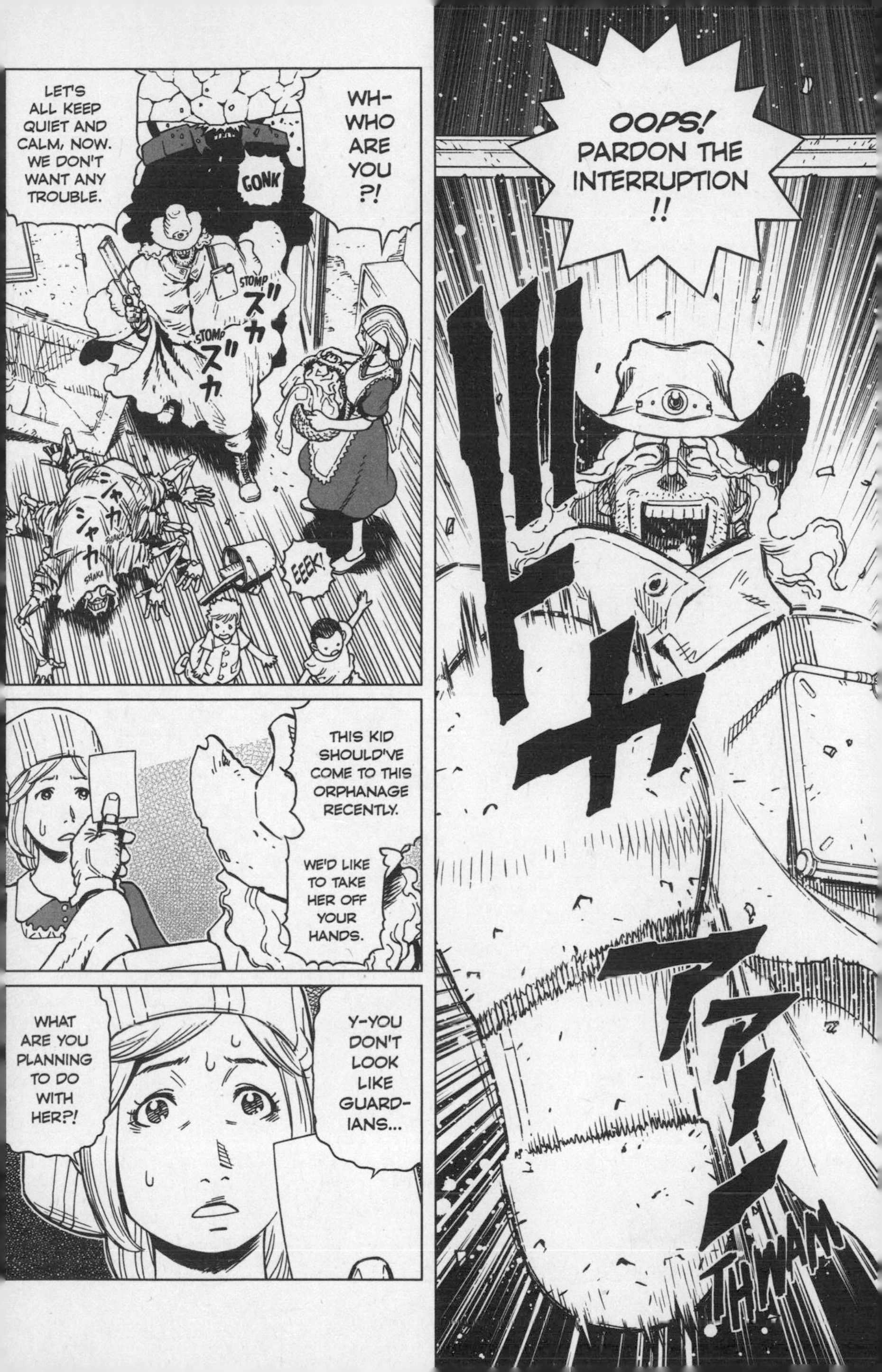
OOPS! PARDON THE INTERRUPTION !!
THWAM
WH-WHO ARE YOU ?!
LET'S ALL KEEP QUIET AND CALM, NOW. WE DON'T WANT ANY TROUBLE.
GONK
STOMP
STOMP
EEEK!
SHAKA
SHAKA
THIS KID SHOULD'VE COME TO THIS ORPHANAGE RECENTLY.
WE'D LIKE TO TAKE HER OFF YOUR HANDS.
Y-YOU DON'T LOOK LIKE GUARD-IANS...
WHAT ARE YOU PLANNING TO DO WITH HER?!

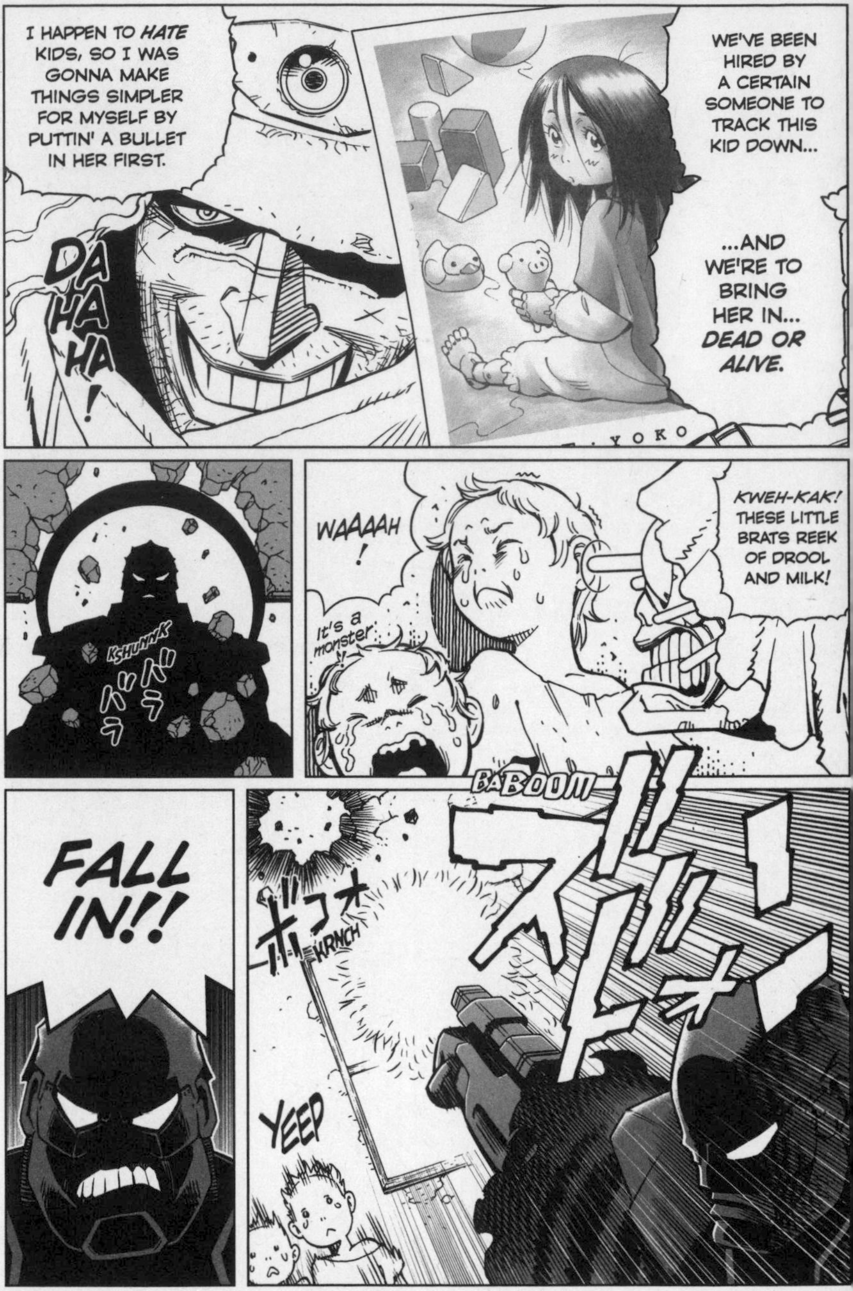

WE'VE BEEN HIRED BY A CERTAIN SOMEONE TO TRACK THIS KID DOWN...
...AND WE'RE TO BRING HER IN... DEAD OR ALIVE.
I HAPPEN TO HATE KIDS, SO I WAS GONNA MAKE THINGS SIMPLER FOR MYSELF BY PUTTIN' A BULLET IN HER FIRST.
DAHAHAHA!
YOKO
KWEH-KAK! THESE LITTLE BRATS REEK OF DROOL AND MILK!
WAAAAH!
It's a monster!
KSHUNNNK
バラバラ
BABOOM
ボコォ
KRNCH
YEEP
FALL IN!!

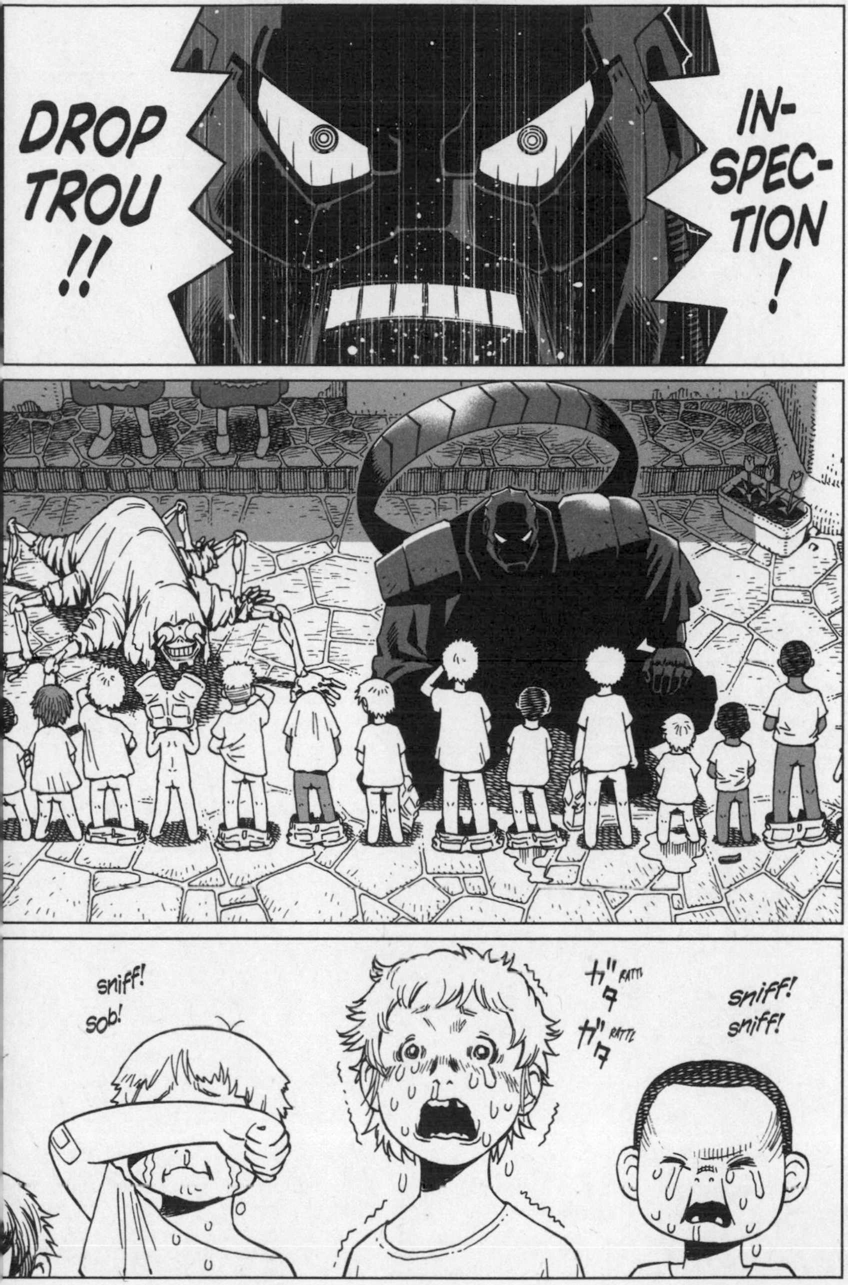
IN-SPECTION!
DROP TROU!!
sniff! sniff!
ガタ RATTL
ガタ RATTL
sniff! sob!

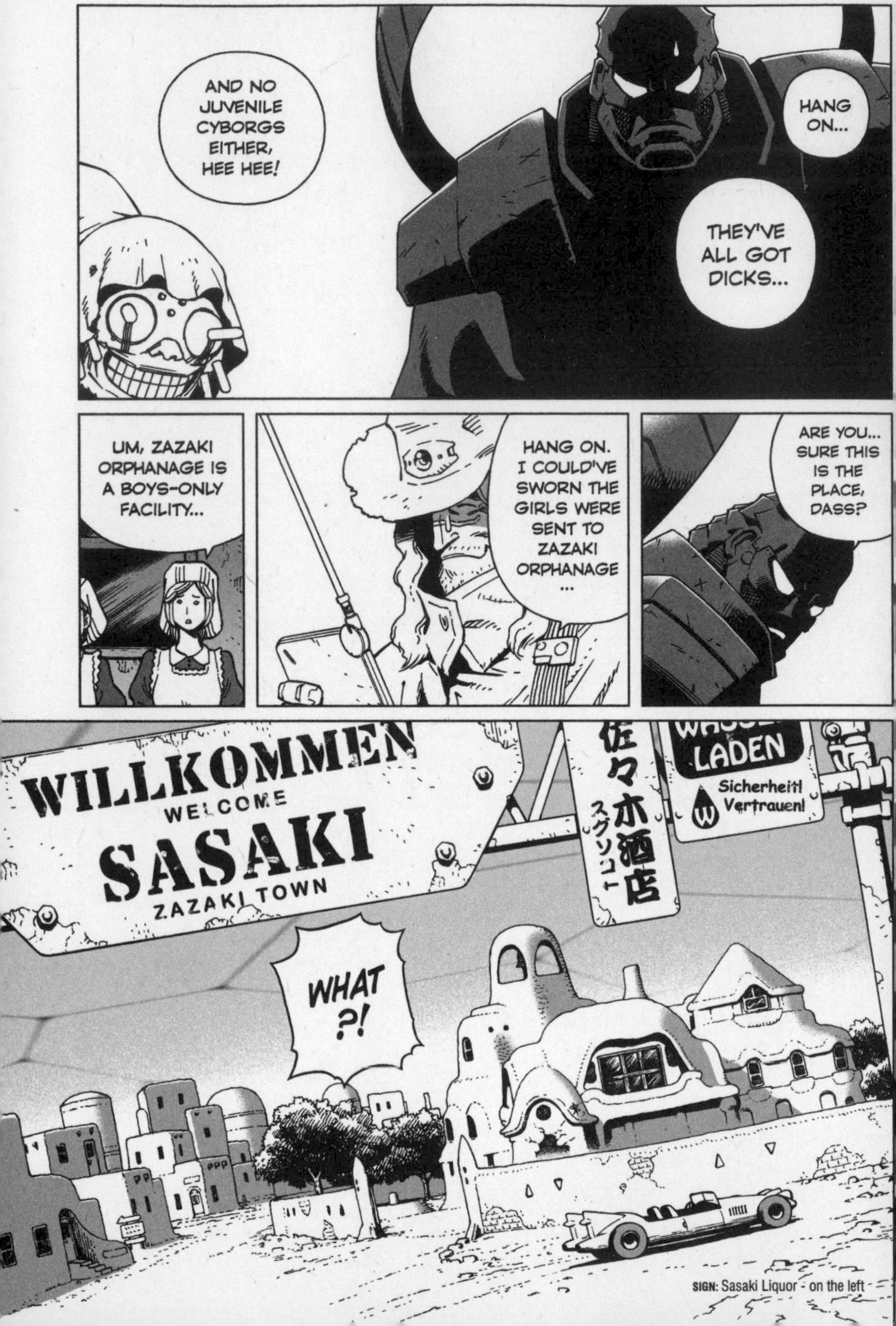
AND NO JUVENILE CYBORGS EITHER, HEE HEE!
HANG ON...
THEY'VE ALL GOT DICKS...
ARE YOU... SURE THIS IS THE PLACE, DASS?
HANG ON. I COULD'VE SWORN THE GIRLS WERE SENT TO ZAZAKI ORPHANAGE ...
UM, ZAZAKI ORPHANAGE IS A BOYS-ONLY FACILITY...
LADEN
Sicherheit! Vertrauen!
佐々木酒店
スグソコ→
WILLKOMMEN
WELCOME
SASAKI
ZAZAKI TOWN
WHAT ?!

SIGN: Sasaki Liquor - on the left

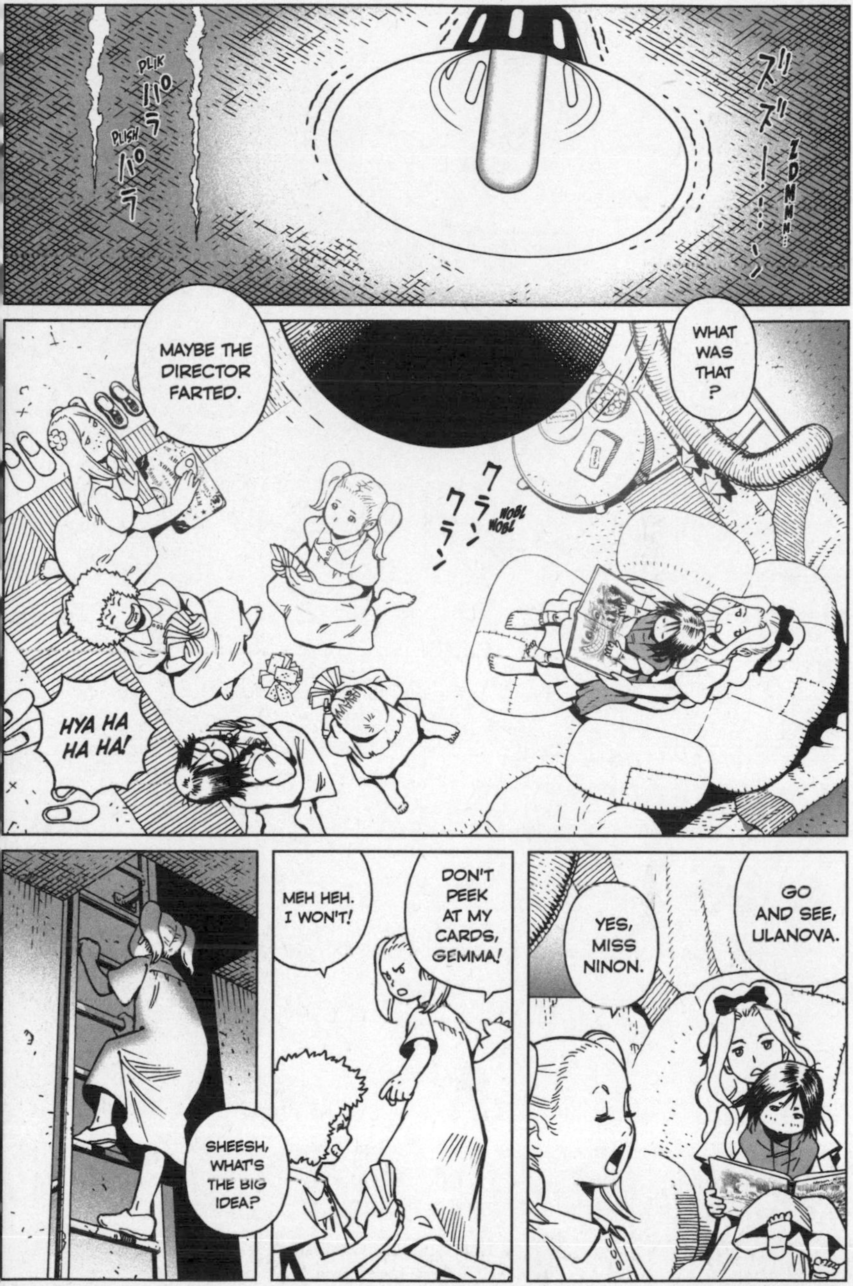
ズズー…ン
ZDMMM...
パラ
PLIK
パラ
PLISH
WHAT WAS THAT?
クランクラン
WOBL WOBL
MAYBE THE DIRECTOR FARTED.
HYA HA HA HA!
GO AND SEE, ULANOVA.
YES, MISS NINON.
DON'T PEEK AT MY CARDS, GEMMA!
MEH HEH. I WON'T!
SHEESH, WHAT'S THE BIG IDEA?

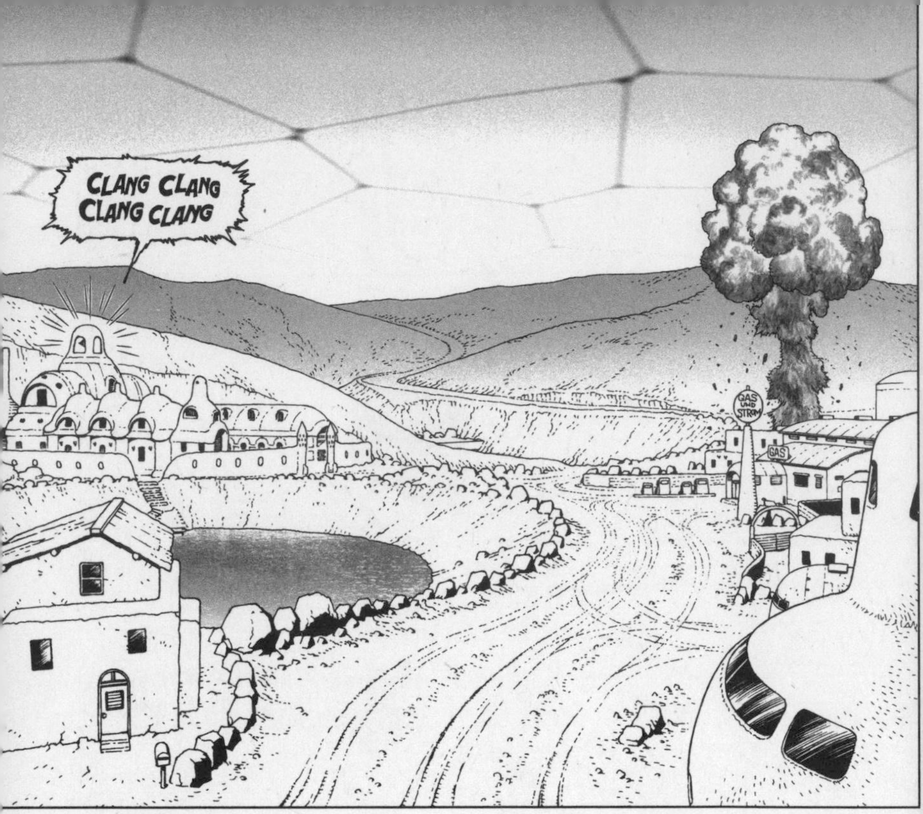
GAS UND STROM
GAS
CLANG CLANG
CLANG CLANG

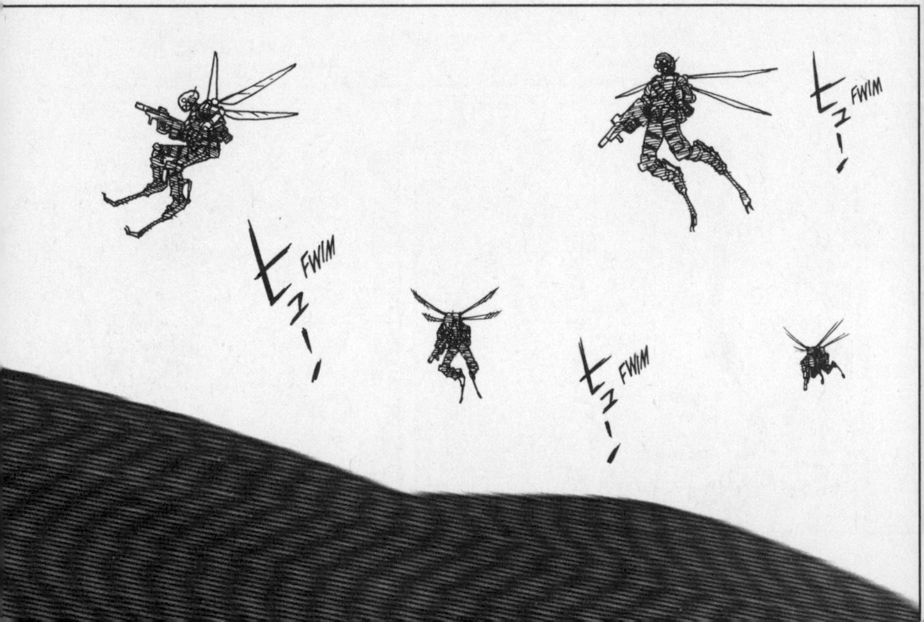
FWIM
FWIM
FWIM

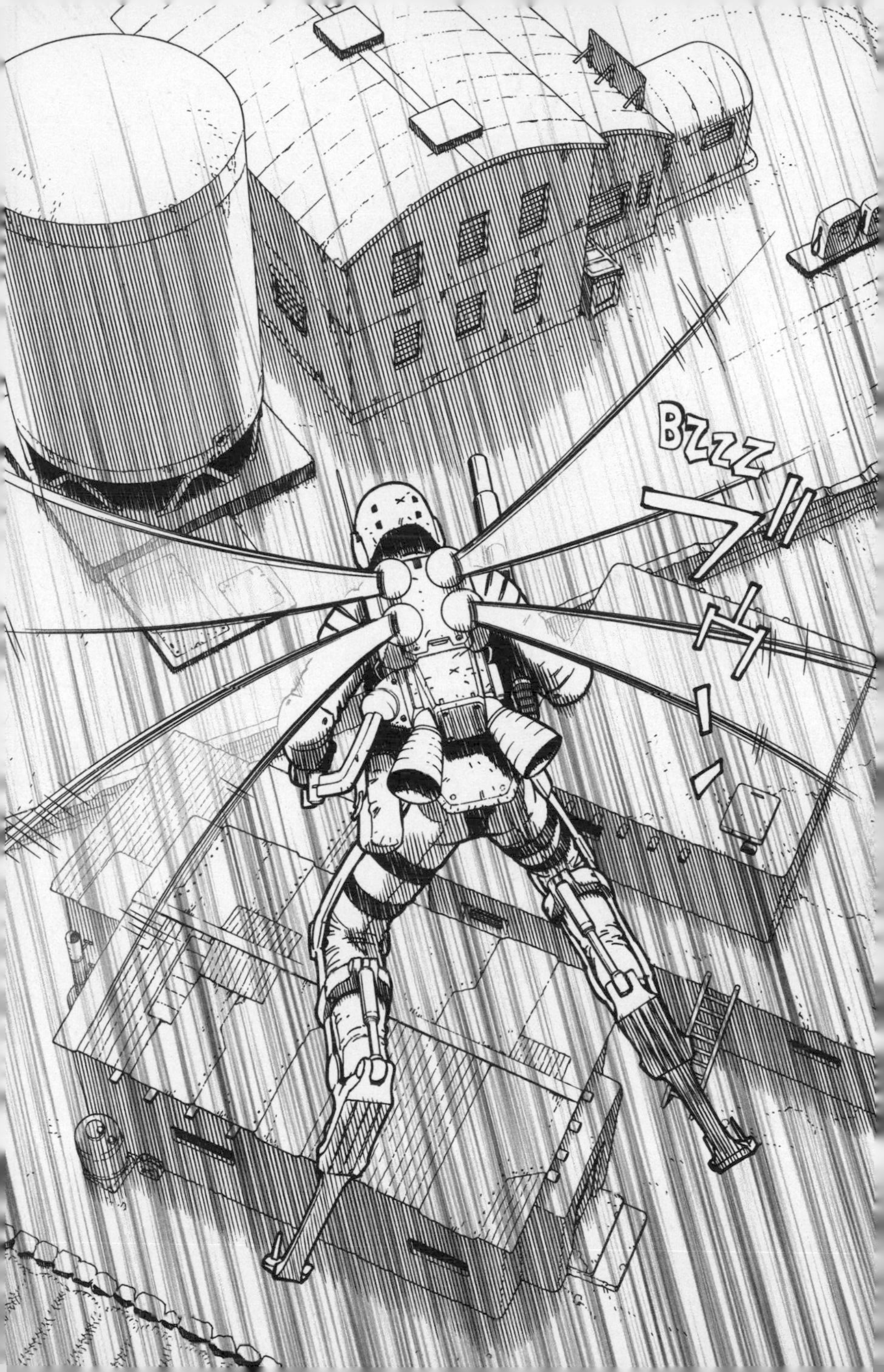
Bzzz

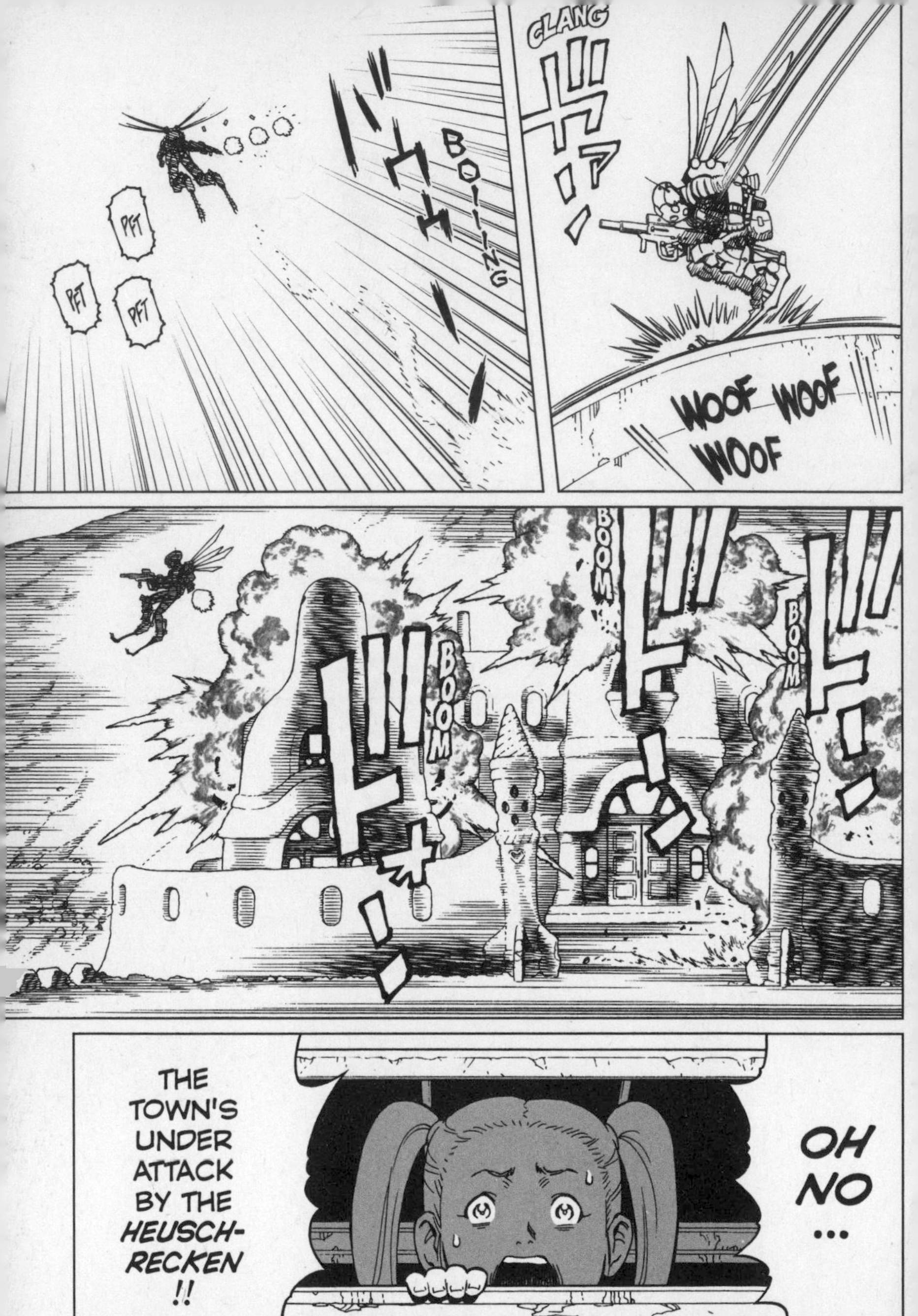
CLANG
WOOF WOOF WOOF
BOIIING
PFT
PFT
PFT
BOOM
BOOM
BOOM
OH NO ...
THE TOWN'S UNDER ATTACK BY THE HEUSCHRECKEN!!

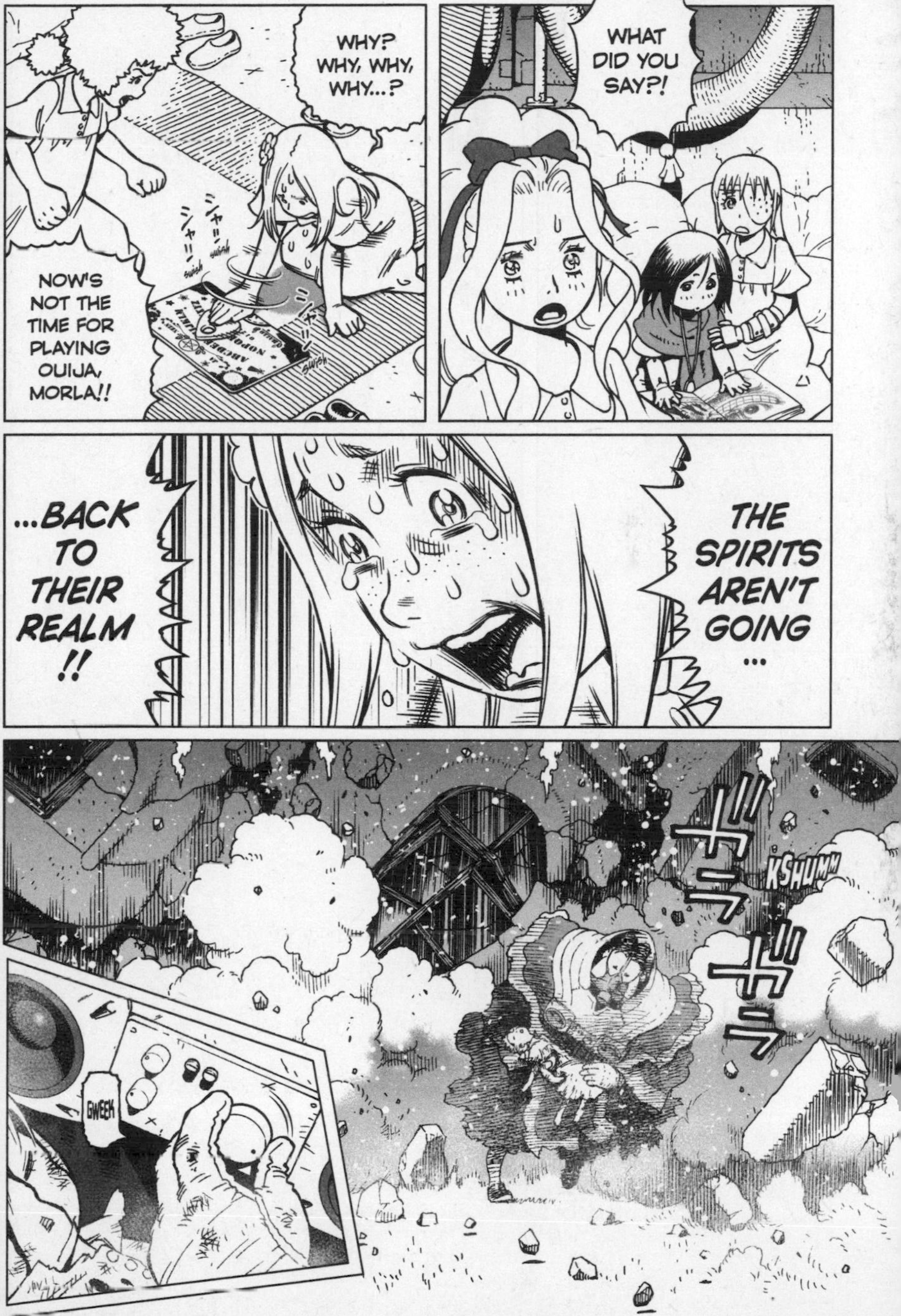
WHAT DID YOU SAY?!
WHY? WHY, WHY, WHY...?
swish
NOW'S NOT THE TIME FOR PLAYING OUIJA, MORLA!!
THE SPIRITS AREN'T GOING ...
...BACK TO THEIR REALM!!
KSHUMM
GWEEK

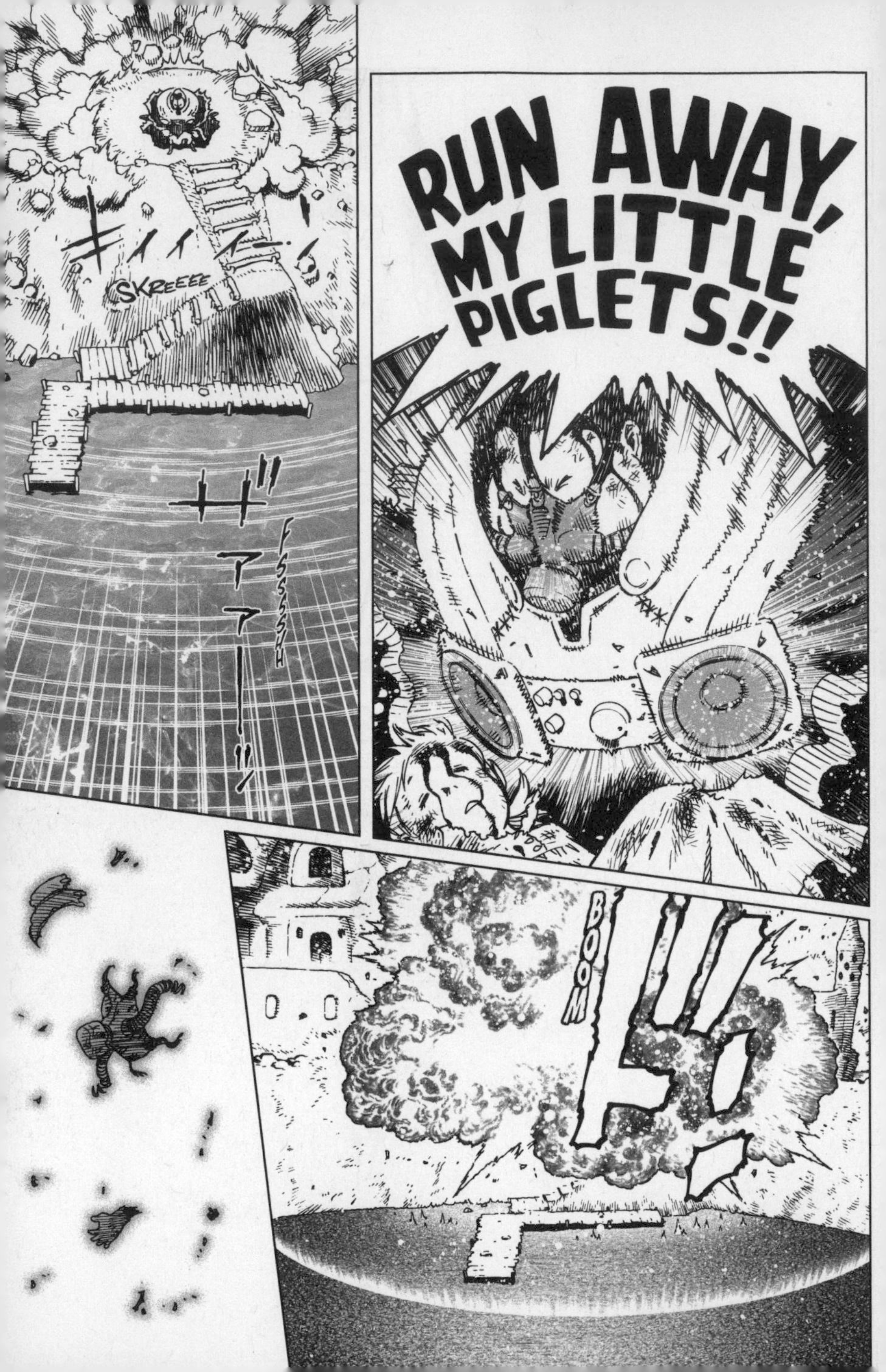
RUN AWAY, MY LITTLE PIGLETS!!
SKREEEE
FSSSSSH
BOOM

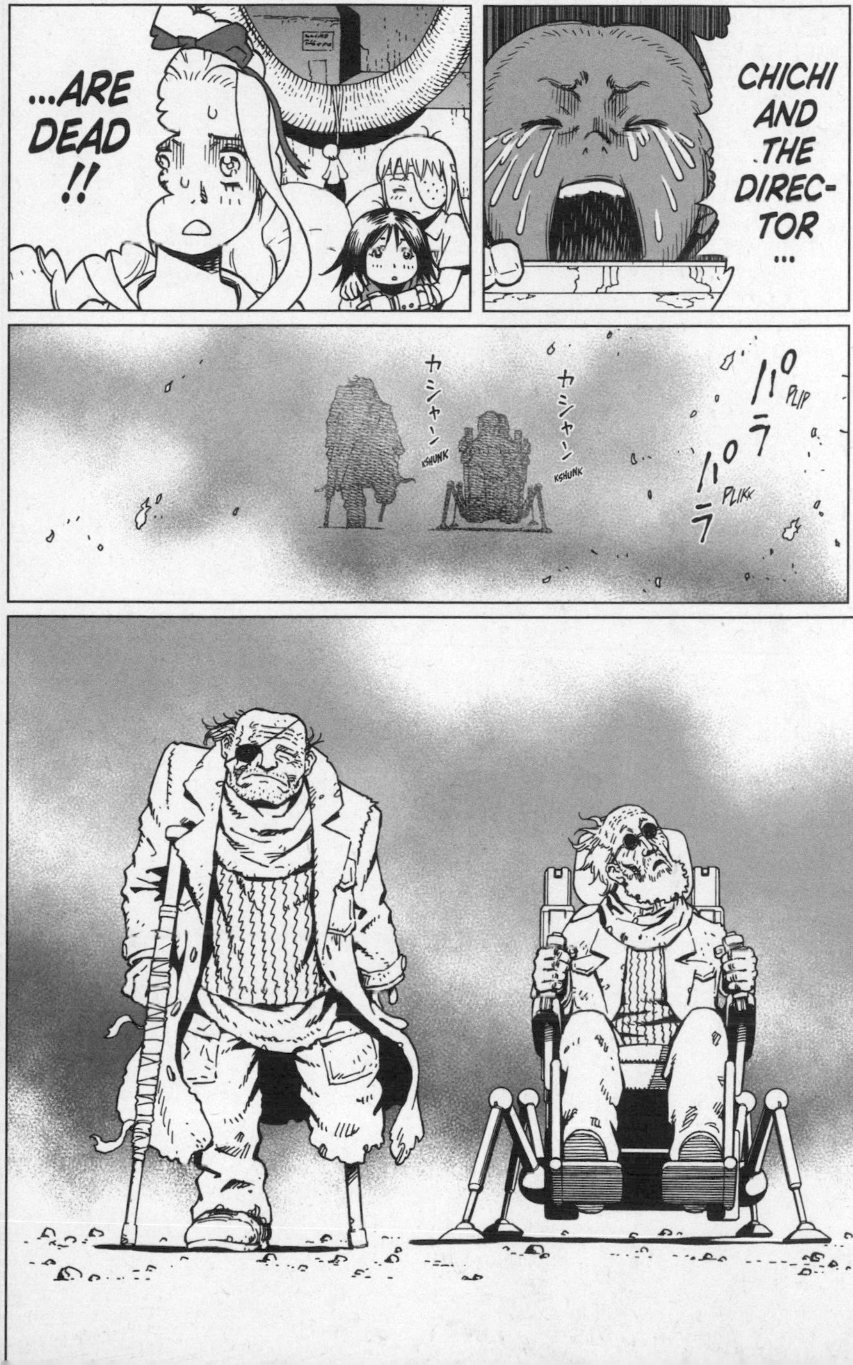
CHICHI AND THE DIRECTOR ...
...ARE DEAD !!
パラ
PLIP
パラ
PLIKK
カシャン
KSHUNK
カシャン
KSHUNK

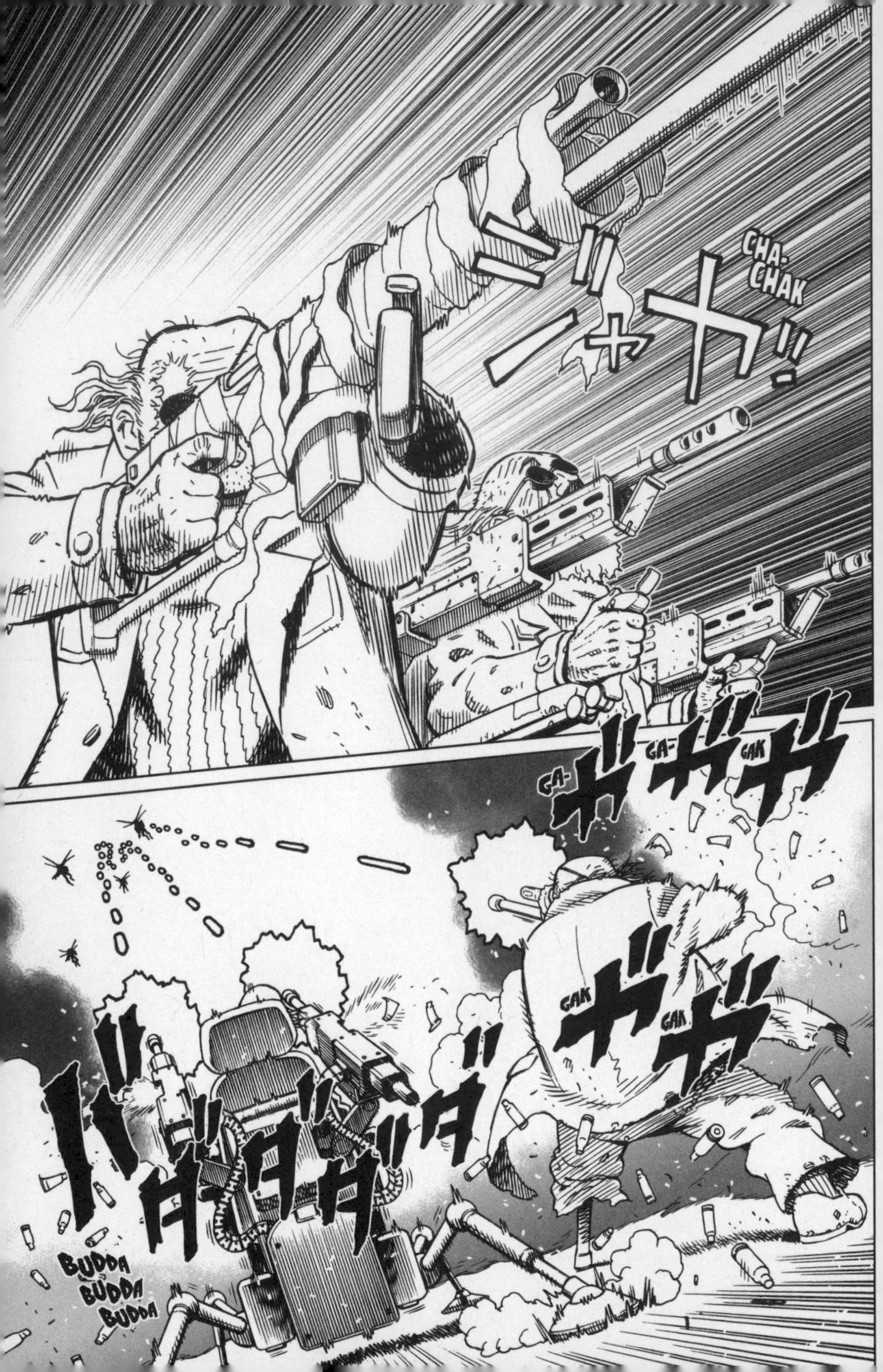
ジャカ!!
CHA-CHAK
GA-
GA-GAK
GAK
GAK
BUDDA
BUDDA
BUDDA

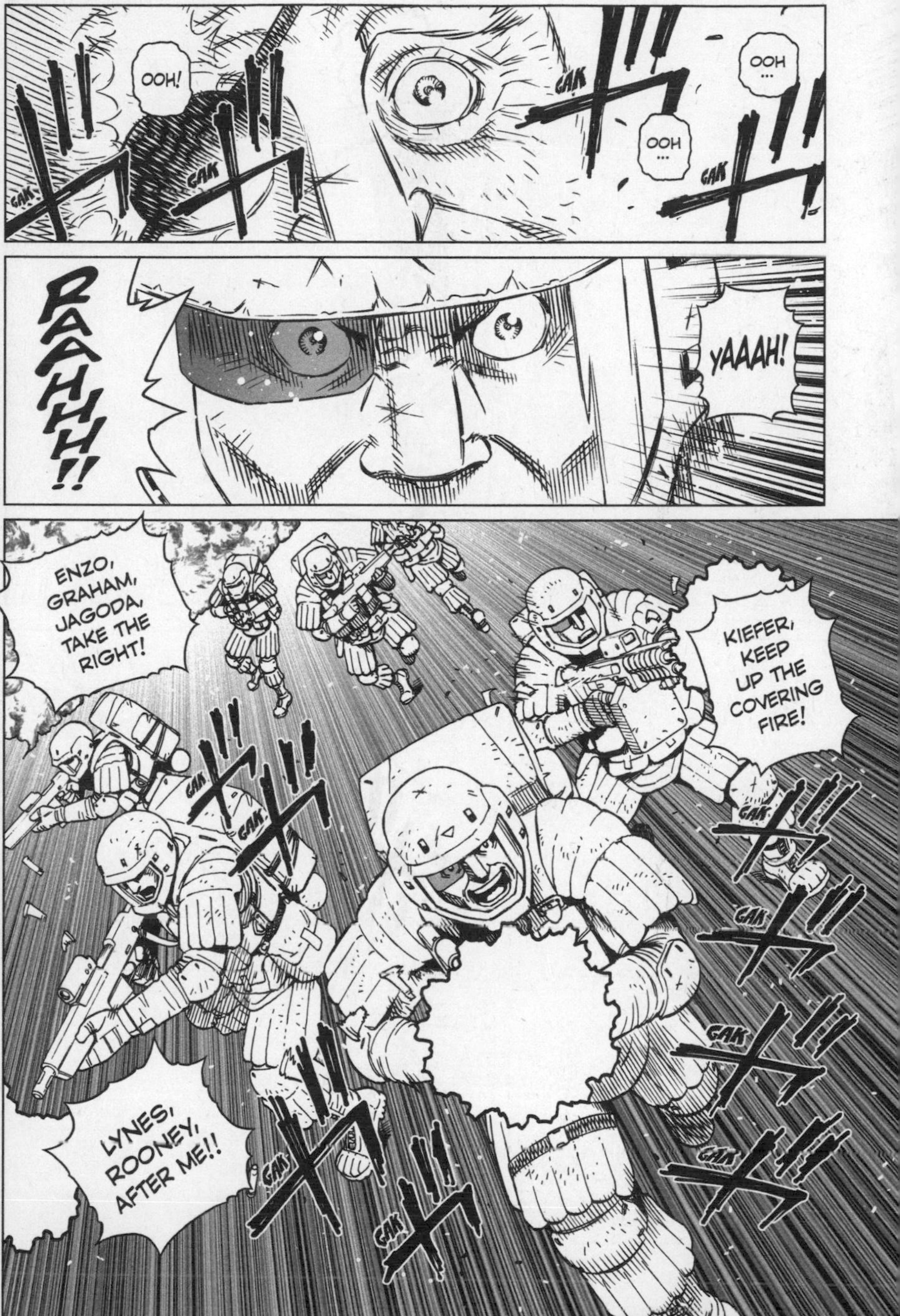
OOH ...
GAK
OOH ...
GAK
OOH!
GAK
GAK
YAAAH!
RAAHHH!!
KIEFER, KEEP UP THE COVERING FIRE!
ENZO, GRAHAM, JAGODA, TAKE THE RIGHT!
GAK
GAK
GAK
GAK
GAK
GAK
GAK
LYNES, ROONEY, AFTER ME!!

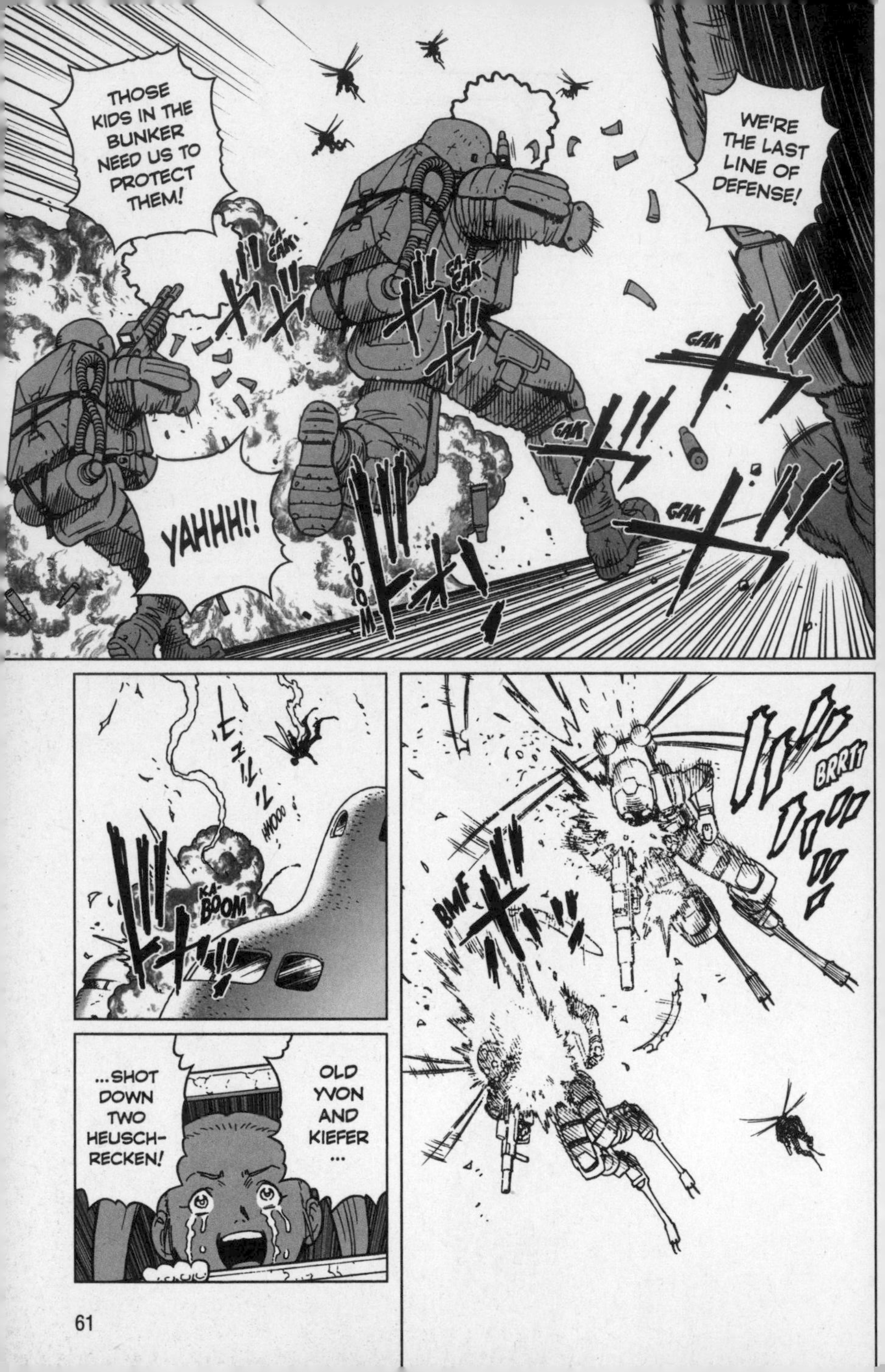
WE'RE THE LAST LINE OF DEFENSE!
THOSE KIDS IN THE BUNKER NEED US TO PROTECT THEM!
GA-GAK
GA-GAK
GAK
GAK
GAK
YAHHH!!
BOOM
BRRTT
BMF
HWOOO
KA-BOOM
OLD YVON AND KIEFER ...
...SHOT DOWN TWO HEUSCH-RECKEN!

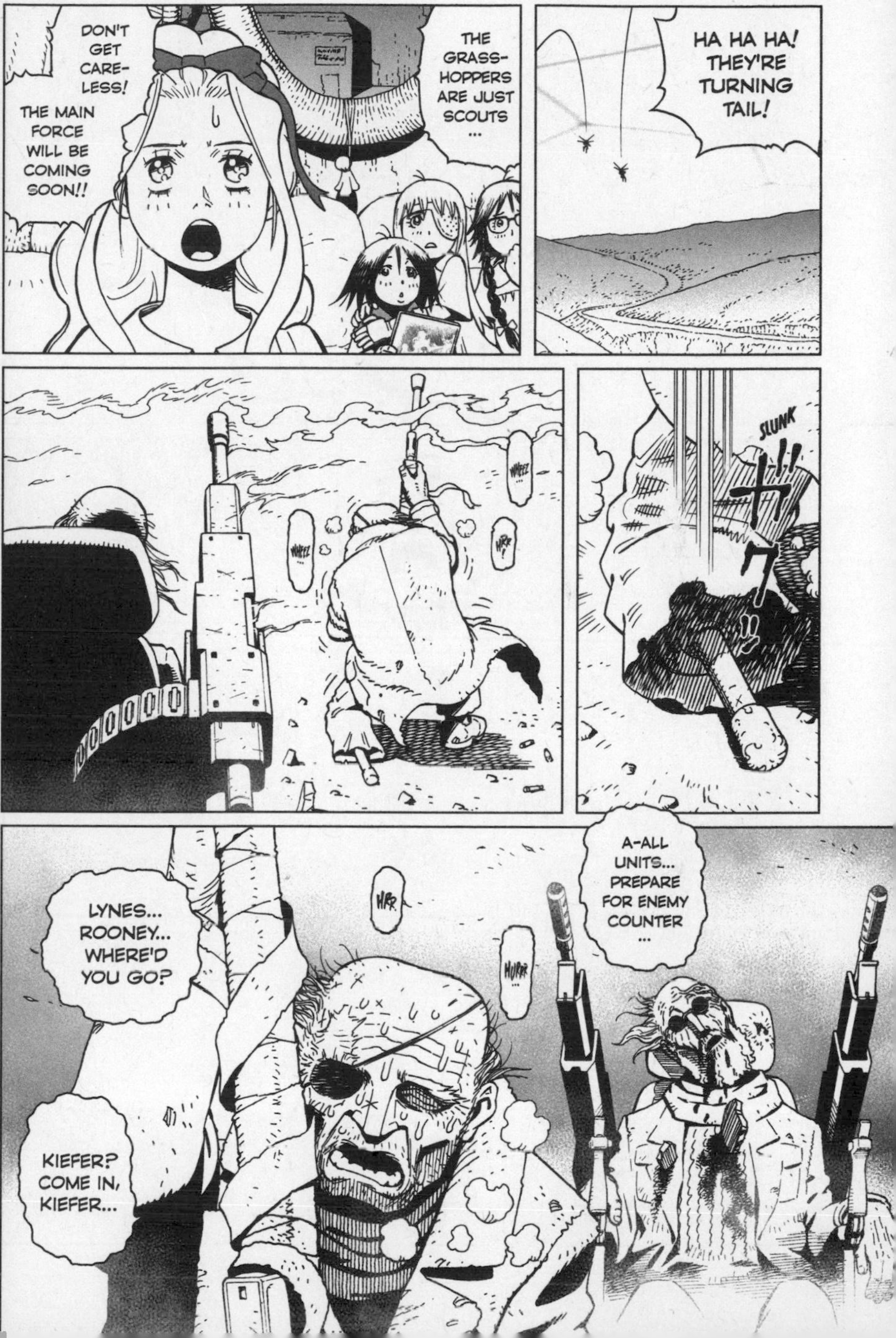
HA HA HA! THEY'RE TURNING TAIL!
THE GRASS-HOPPERS ARE JUST SCOUTS ...
DON'T GET CARE-LESS!
THE MAIN FORCE WILL BE COMING SOON!!
SLUNK
A-ALL UNITS... PREPARE FOR ENEMY COUNTER ...
LYNES... ROONEY... WHERE'D YOU GO?
KIEFER? COME IN, KIEFER...

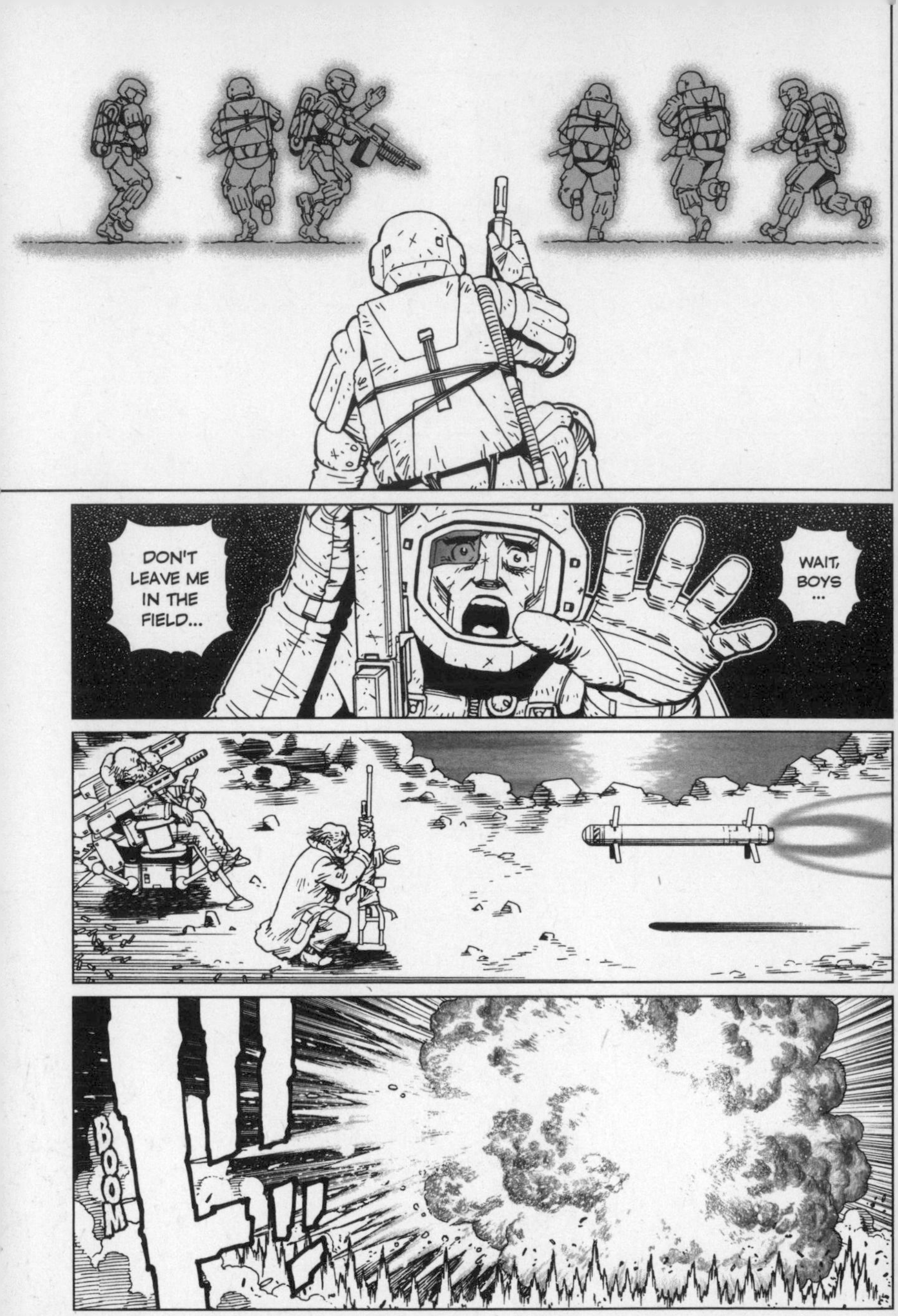

WAIT, BOYS ...
DON'T LEAVE ME IN THE FIELD...
BOOM

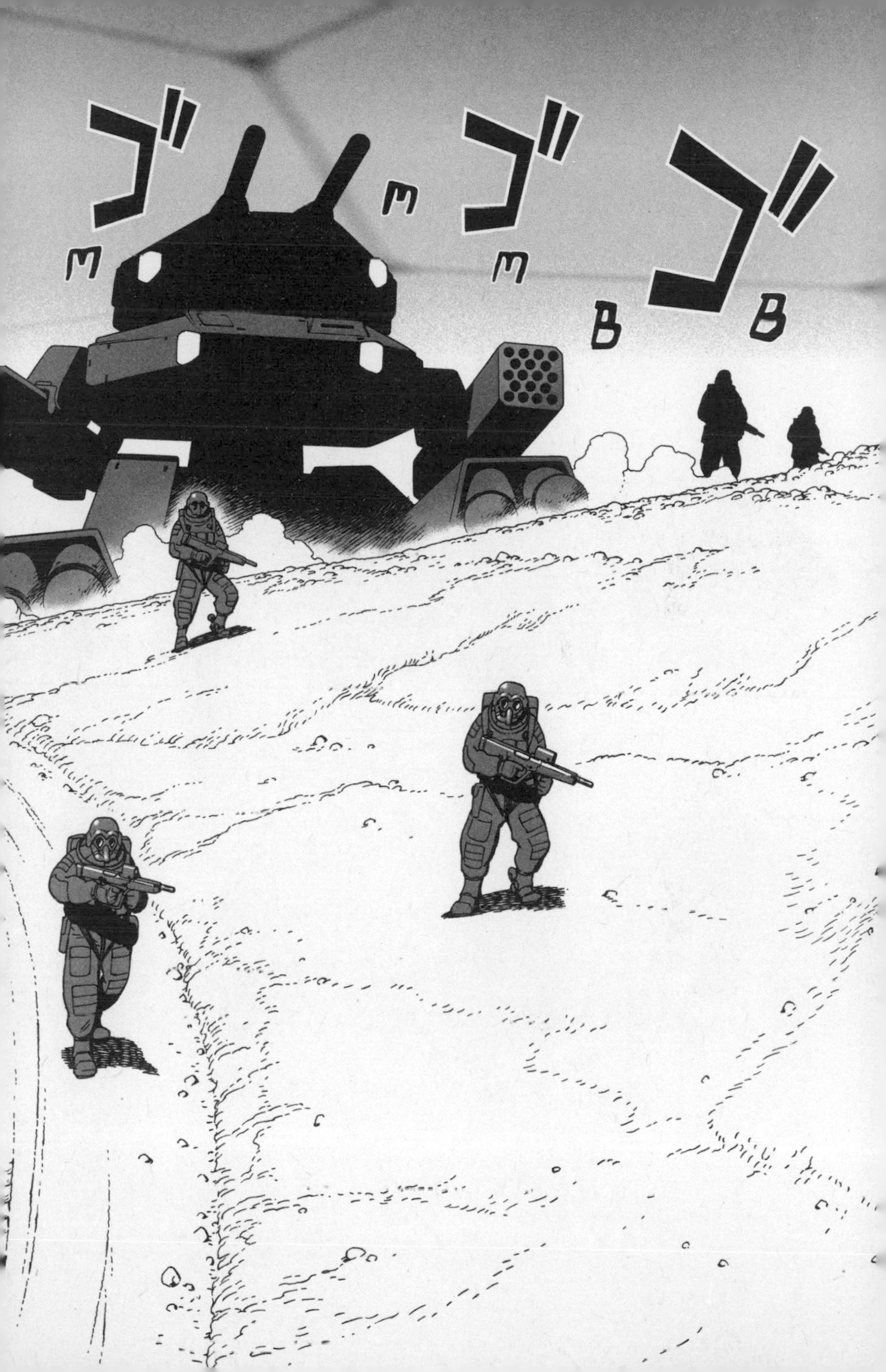
ゴ B B
ゴ m m
ゴ m m

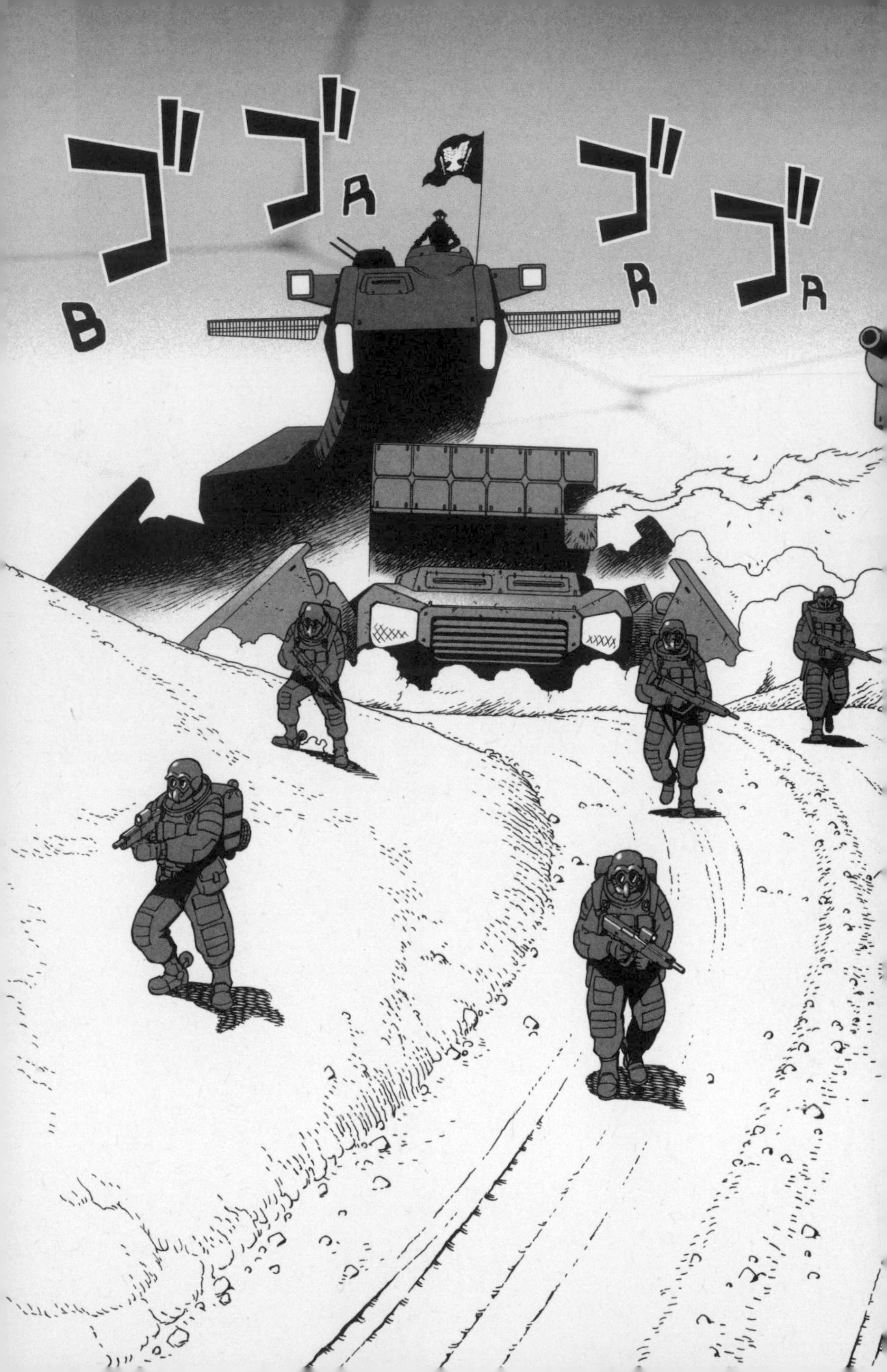
ゴゴゴゴ
BRRR

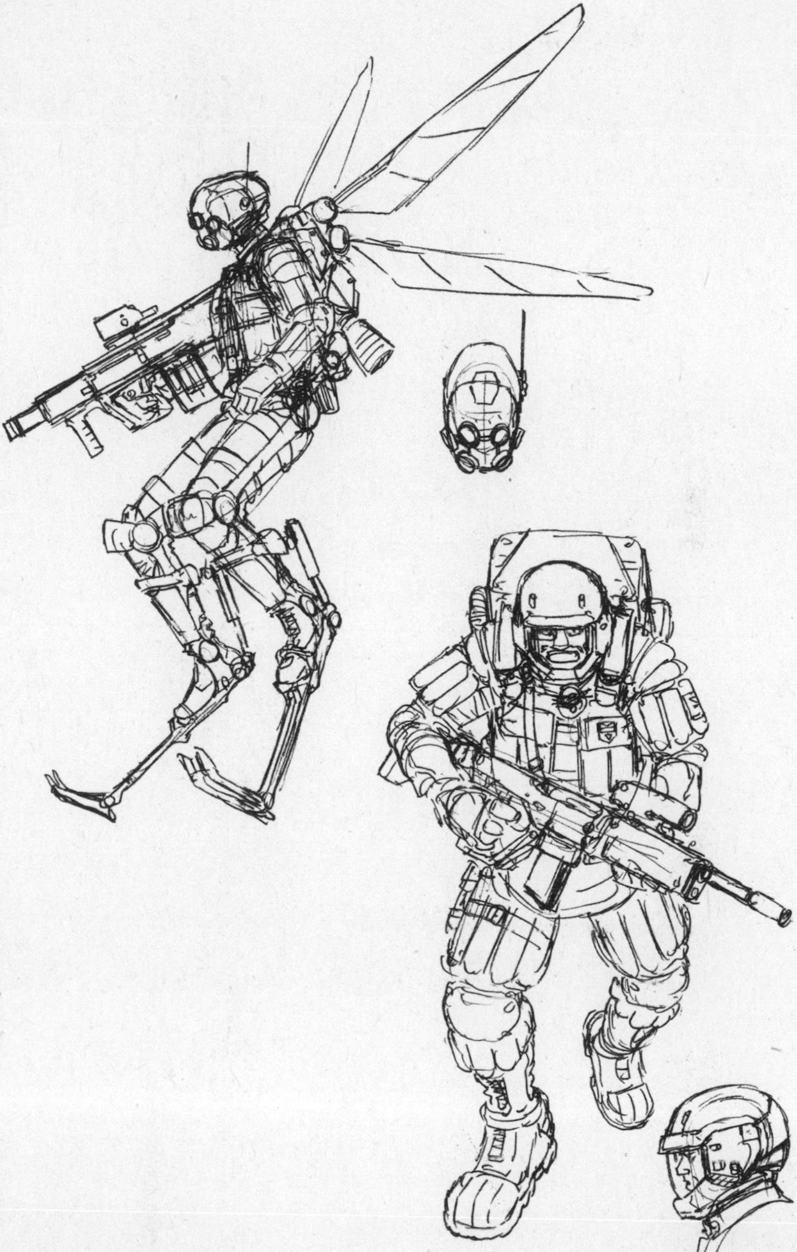

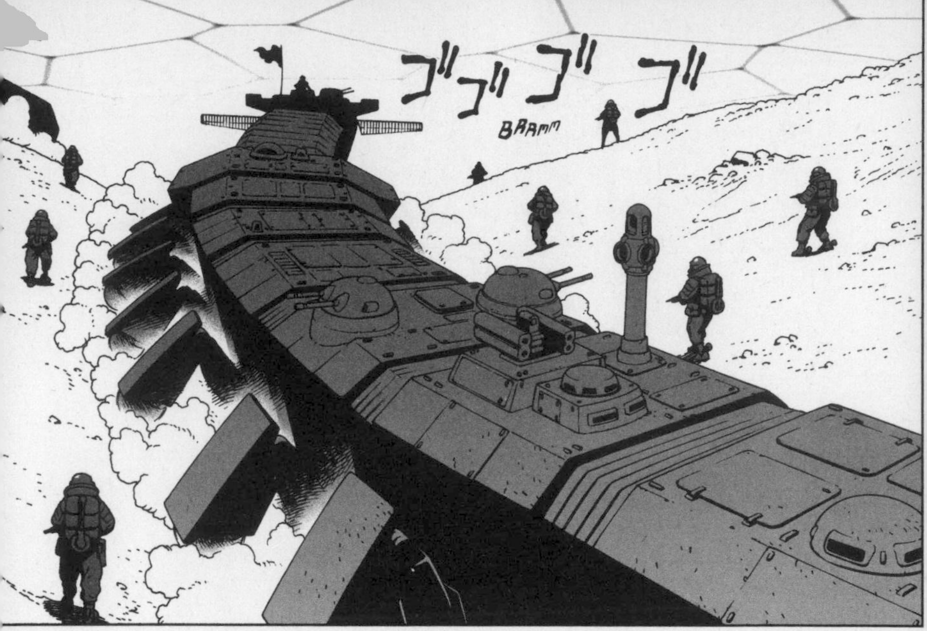
ゴゴゴゴ
BRAMM

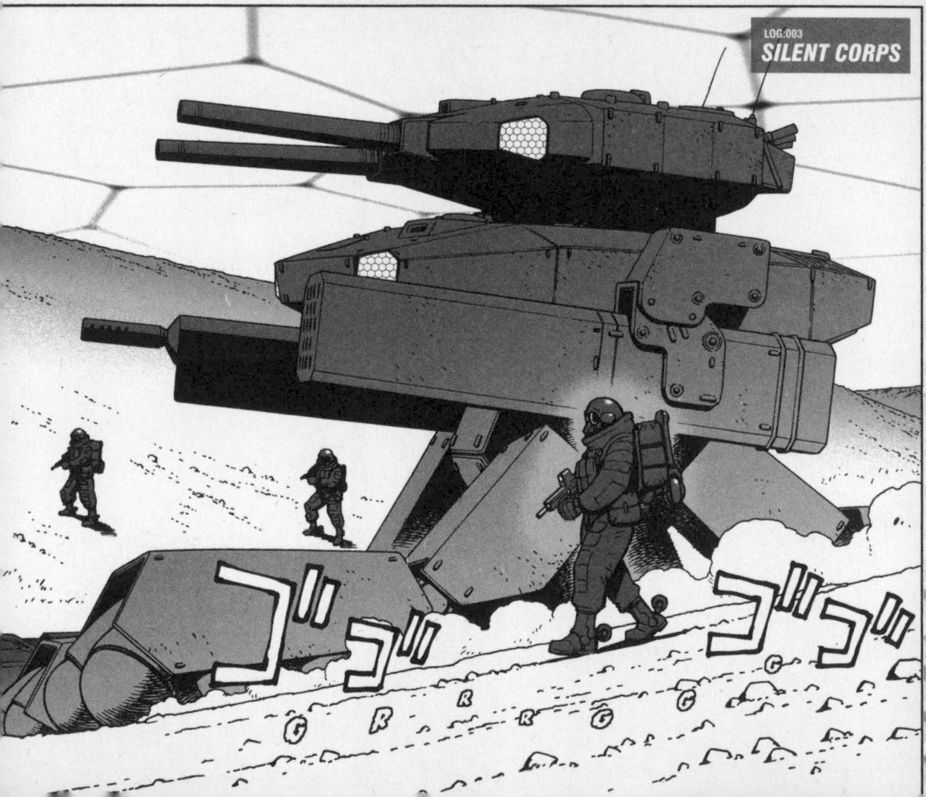
LOG:003
SILENT CORPS
ゴゴ
ゴゴゴ
G R R R G G G

LOG:003
SILENT CORPS

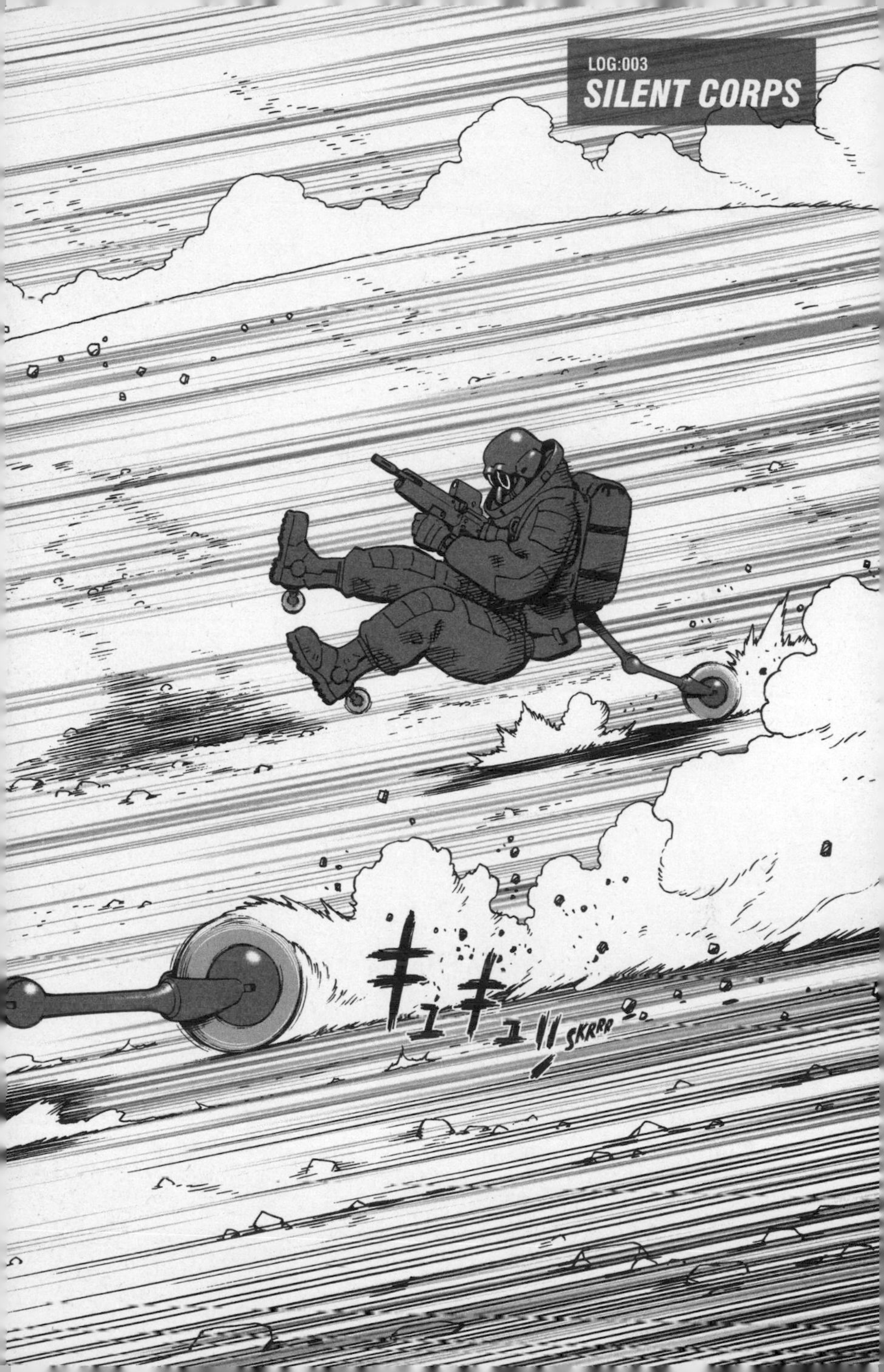
キュキュ!!
SKRRR

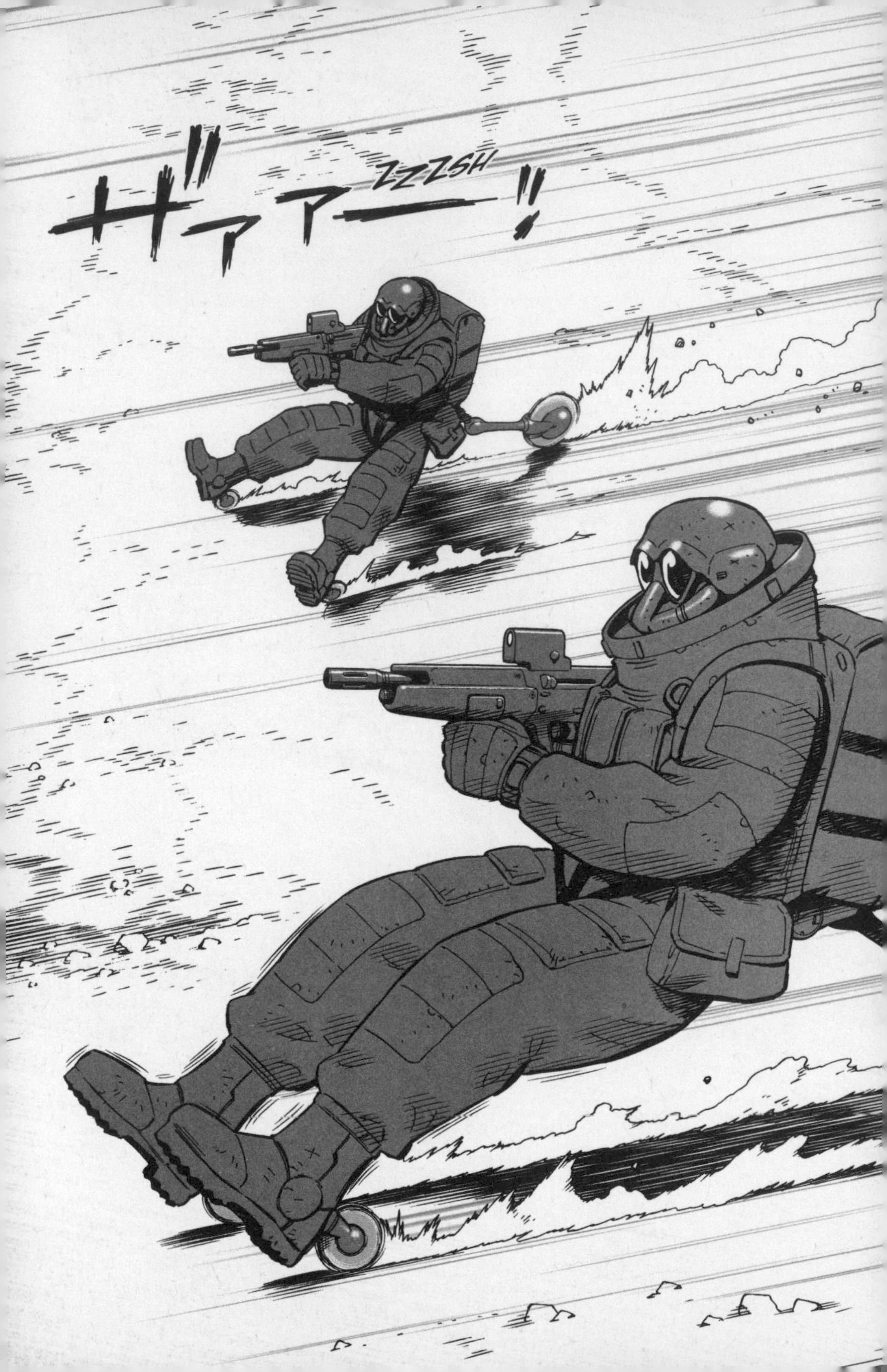
ザァアー‼
ZZZSH
ZZZSH

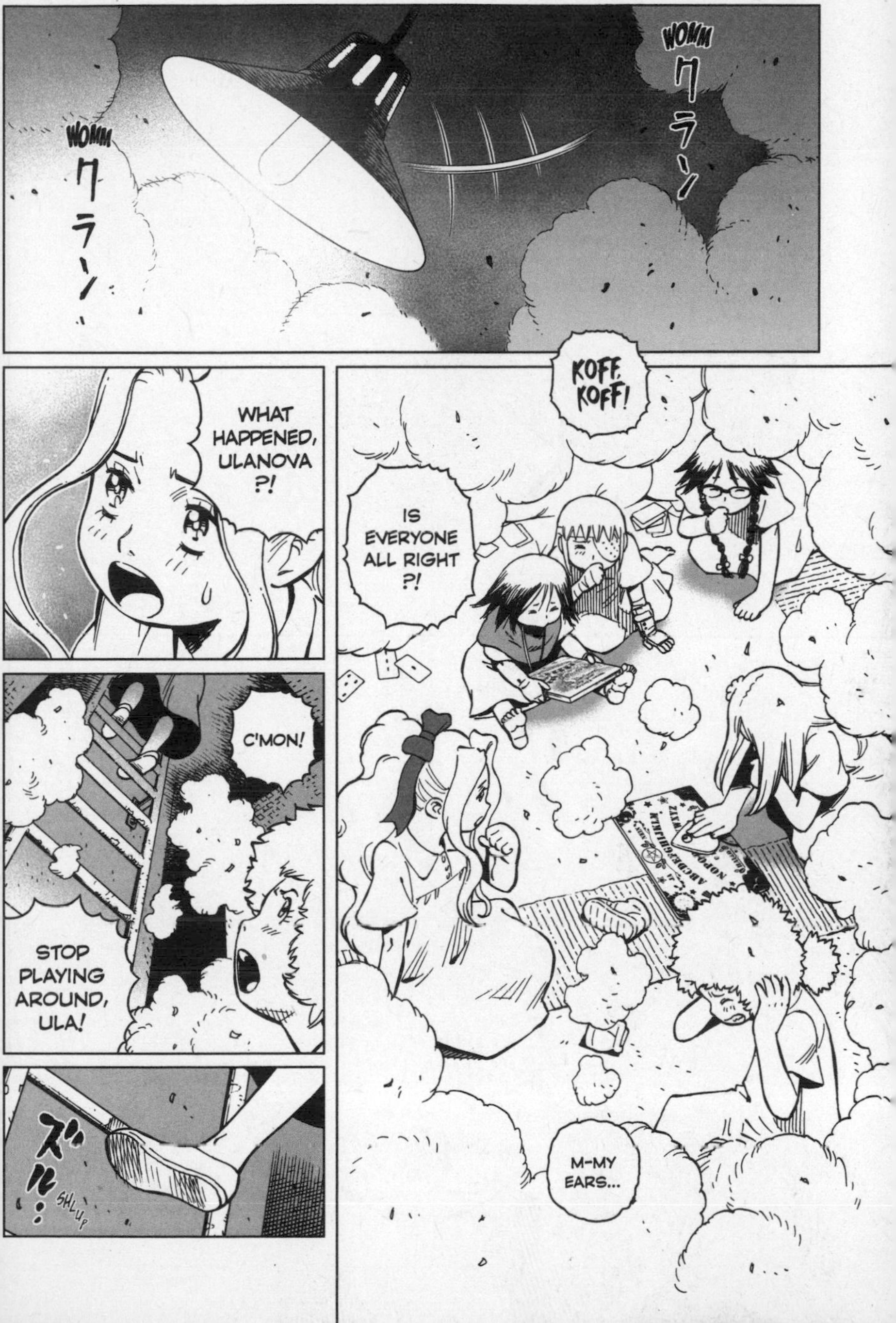
WOMM
クラン
WOMM
クラン
KOFF, KOFF!
IS EVERYONE ALL RIGHT?!
M-MY EARS...
WHAT HAPPENED, ULANOVA?!
C'MON!
STOP PLAYING AROUND, ULA!
ズル
SHLUP

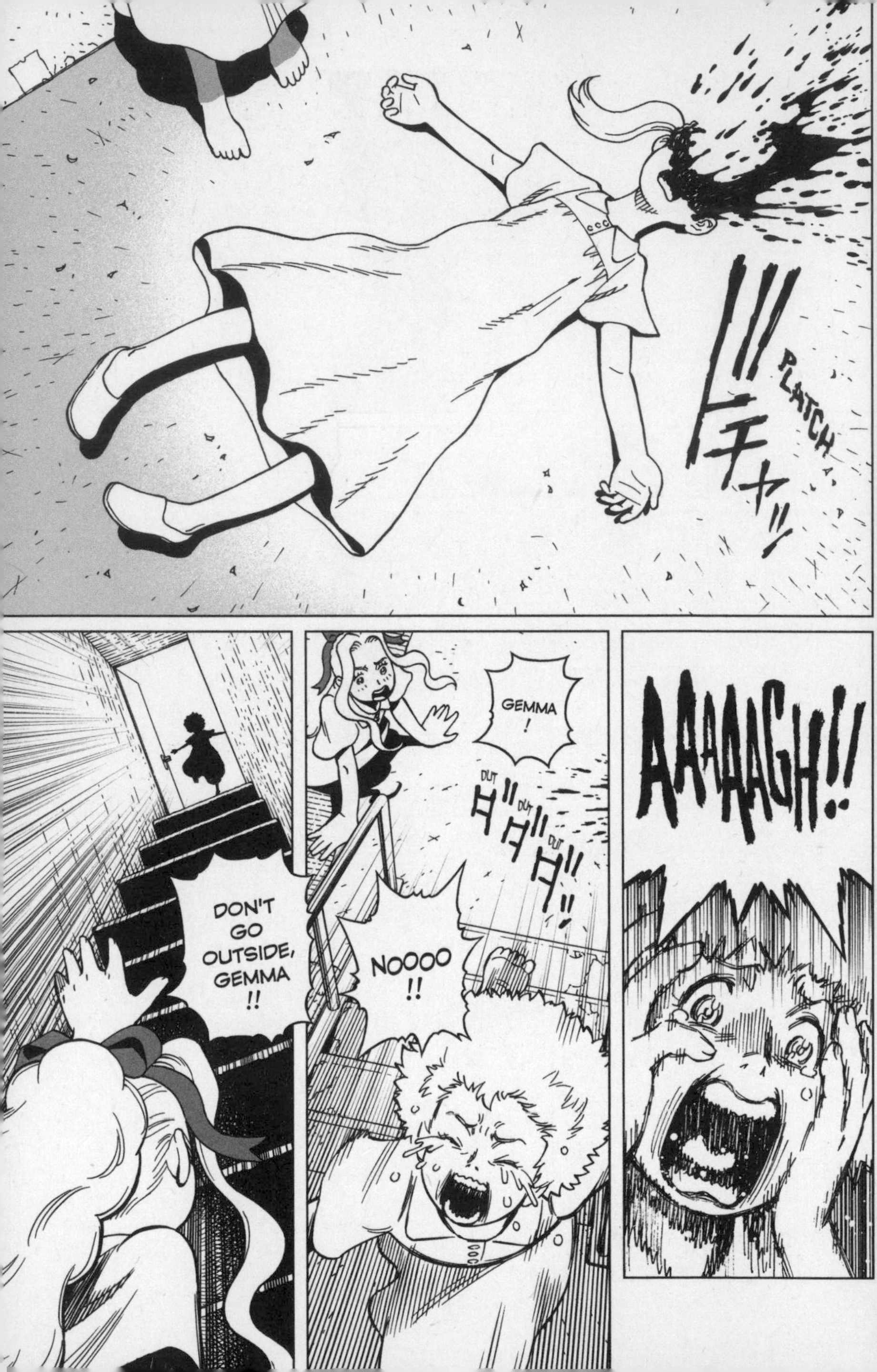
PLATCH
AAAAGH!!
GEMMA!
DUT DUT DUT
NOOOO!!
DON'T GO OUTSIDE, GEMMA!!

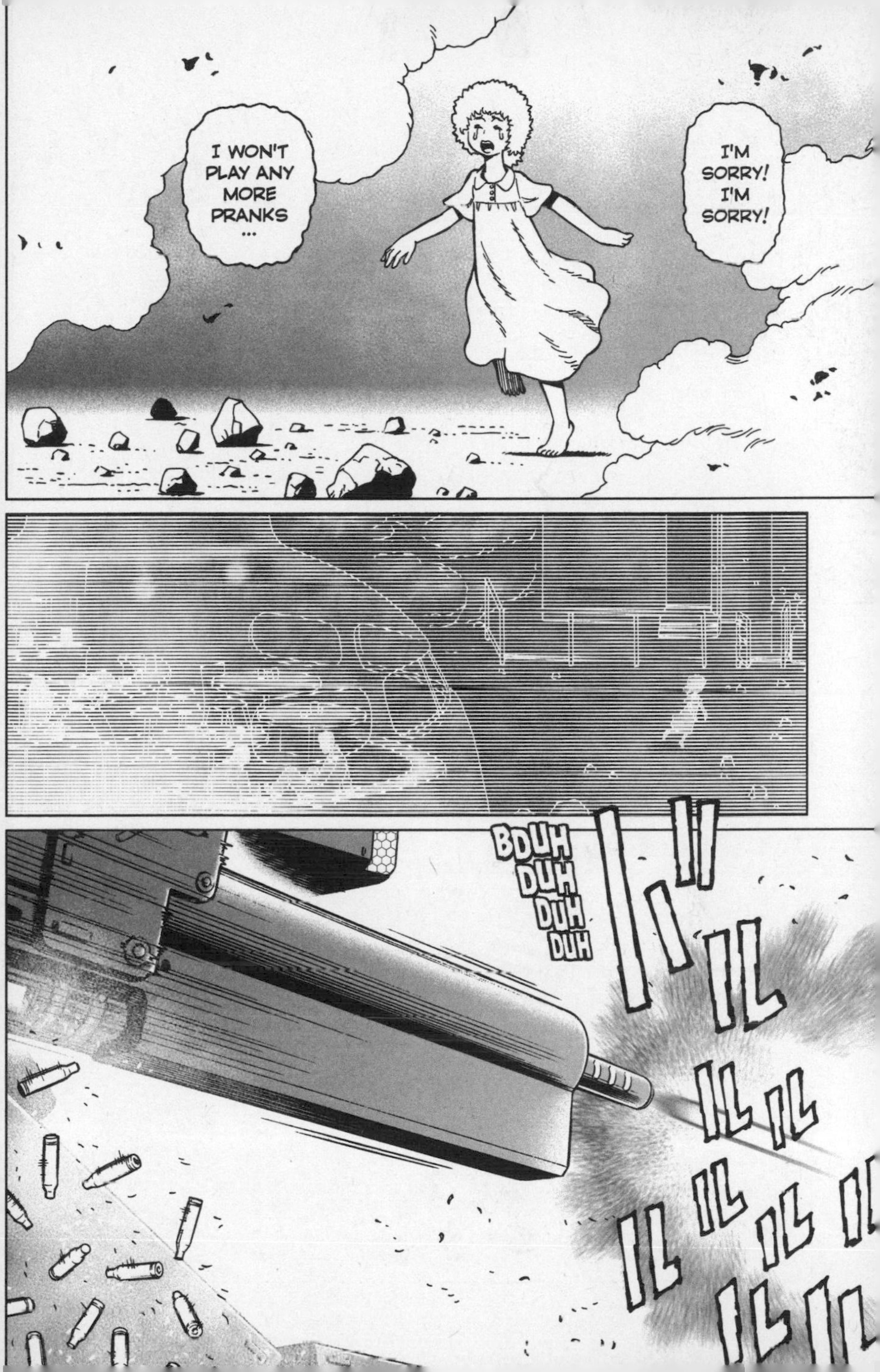
I'M SORRY! I'M SORRY!
I WON'T PLAY ANY MORE PRANKS ...
BDUH DUH DUH DUH

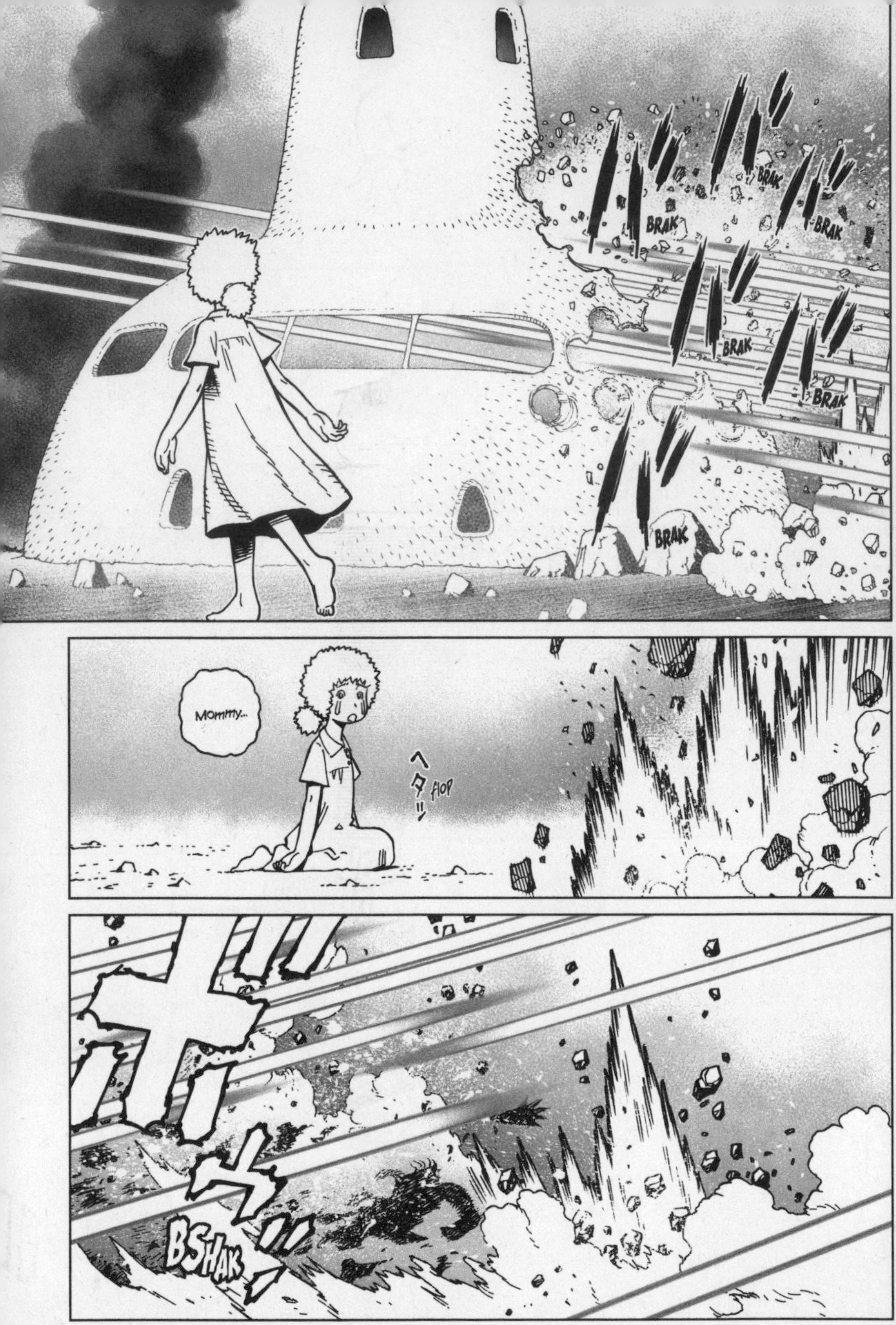
BRAK
BRAK
BRAK
BRAK
BRAK
BRAK
Mommy...
ヘタッ
flop
BSHAK

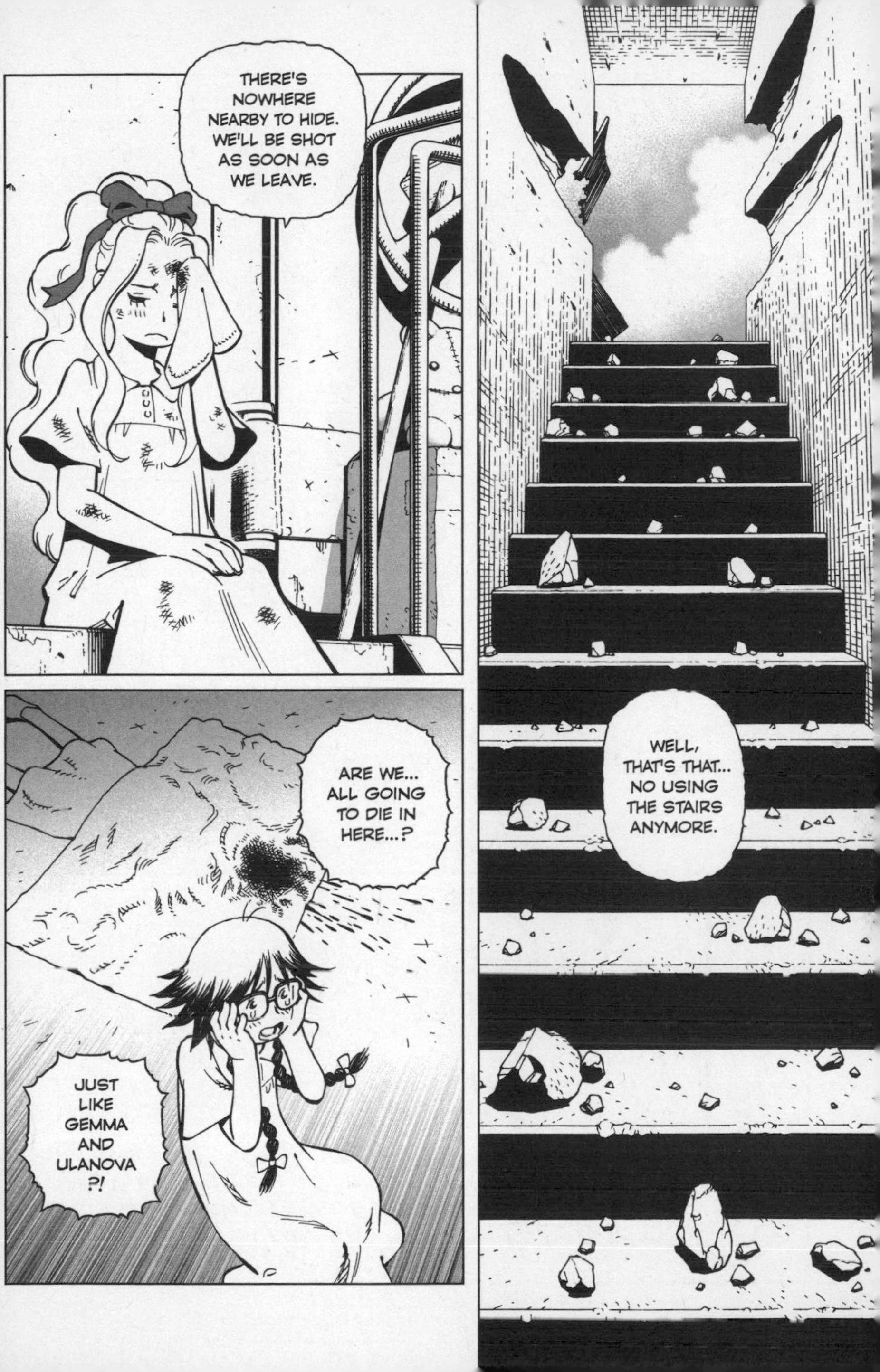
WELL, THAT'S THAT... NO USING THE STAIRS ANYMORE.
THERE'S NOWHERE NEARBY TO HIDE. WE'LL BE SHOT AS SOON AS WE LEAVE.
ARE WE... ALL GOING TO DIE IN HERE...?
JUST LIKE GEMMA AND ULANOVA ?!

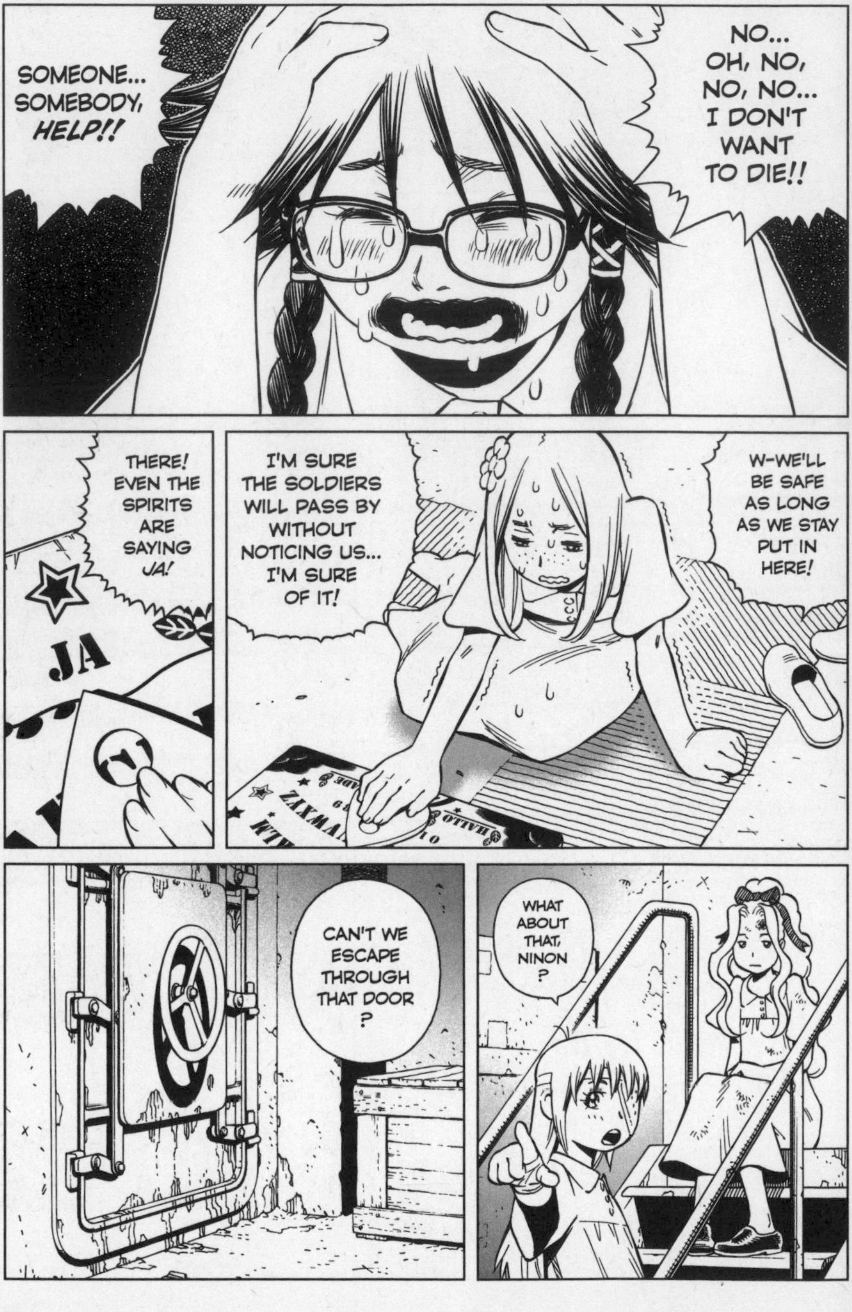
NO... OH, NO, NO, NO... I DON'T WANT TO DIE!!
SOMEONE... SOMEBODY, HELP!!
W-WE'LL BE SAFE AS LONG AS WE STAY PUT IN HERE!
I'M SURE THE SOLDIERS WILL PASS BY WITHOUT NOTICING US... I'M SURE OF IT!
THERE! EVEN THE SPIRITS ARE SAYING JA!
JA
WHAT ABOUT THAT, NINON?
CAN'T WE ESCAPE THROUGH THAT DOOR?

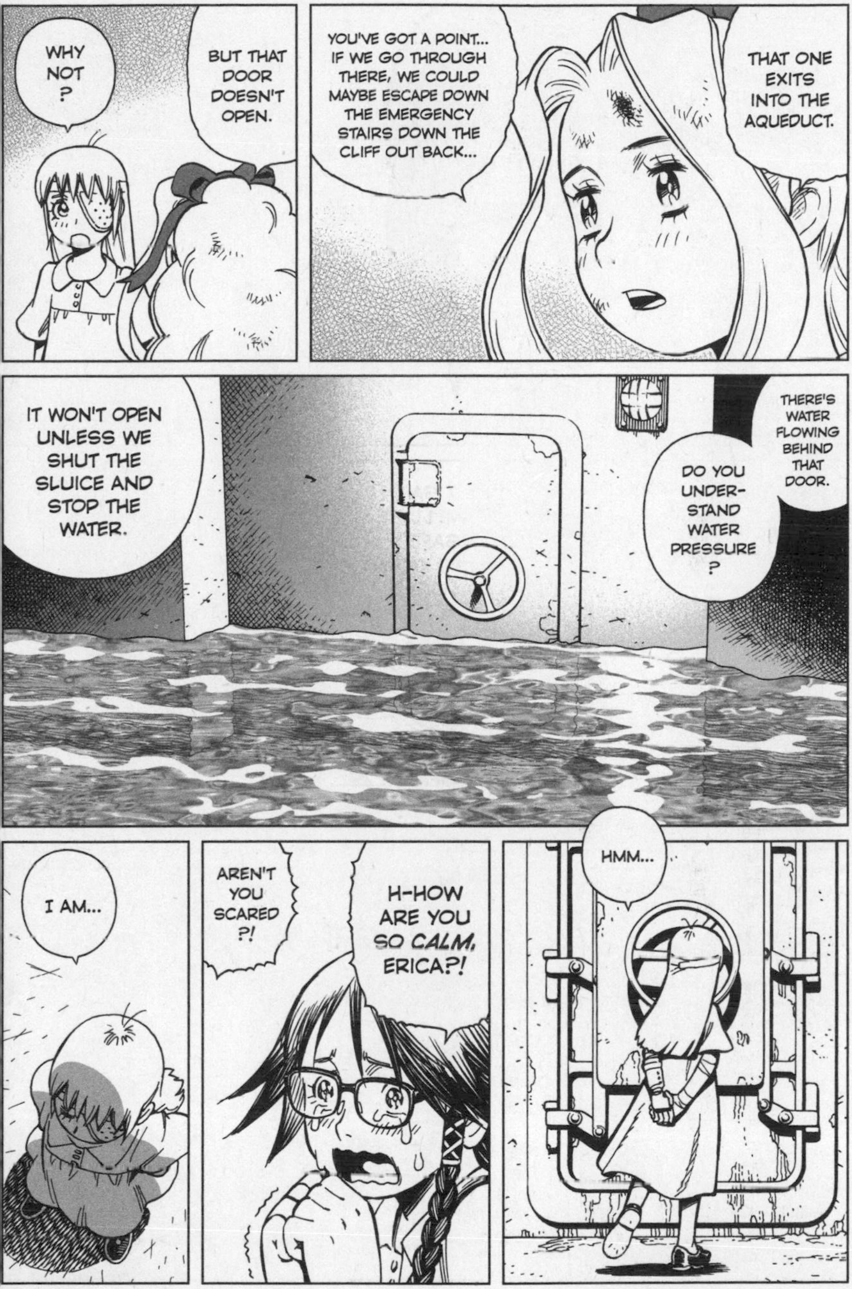
THAT ONE EXITS INTO THE AQUEDUCT.
YOU'VE GOT A POINT... IF WE GO THROUGH THERE, WE COULD MAYBE ESCAPE DOWN THE EMERGENCY STAIRS DOWN THE CLIFF OUT BACK...
BUT THAT DOOR DOESN'T OPEN.
WHY NOT ?
THERE'S WATER FLOWING BEHIND THAT DOOR.
DO YOU UNDER-STAND WATER PRESSURE ?
IT WON'T OPEN UNLESS WE SHUT THE SLUICE AND STOP THE WATER.
HMM...
H-HOW ARE YOU SO *CALM,* ERICA?!
AREN'T YOU SCARED ?!
I AM...

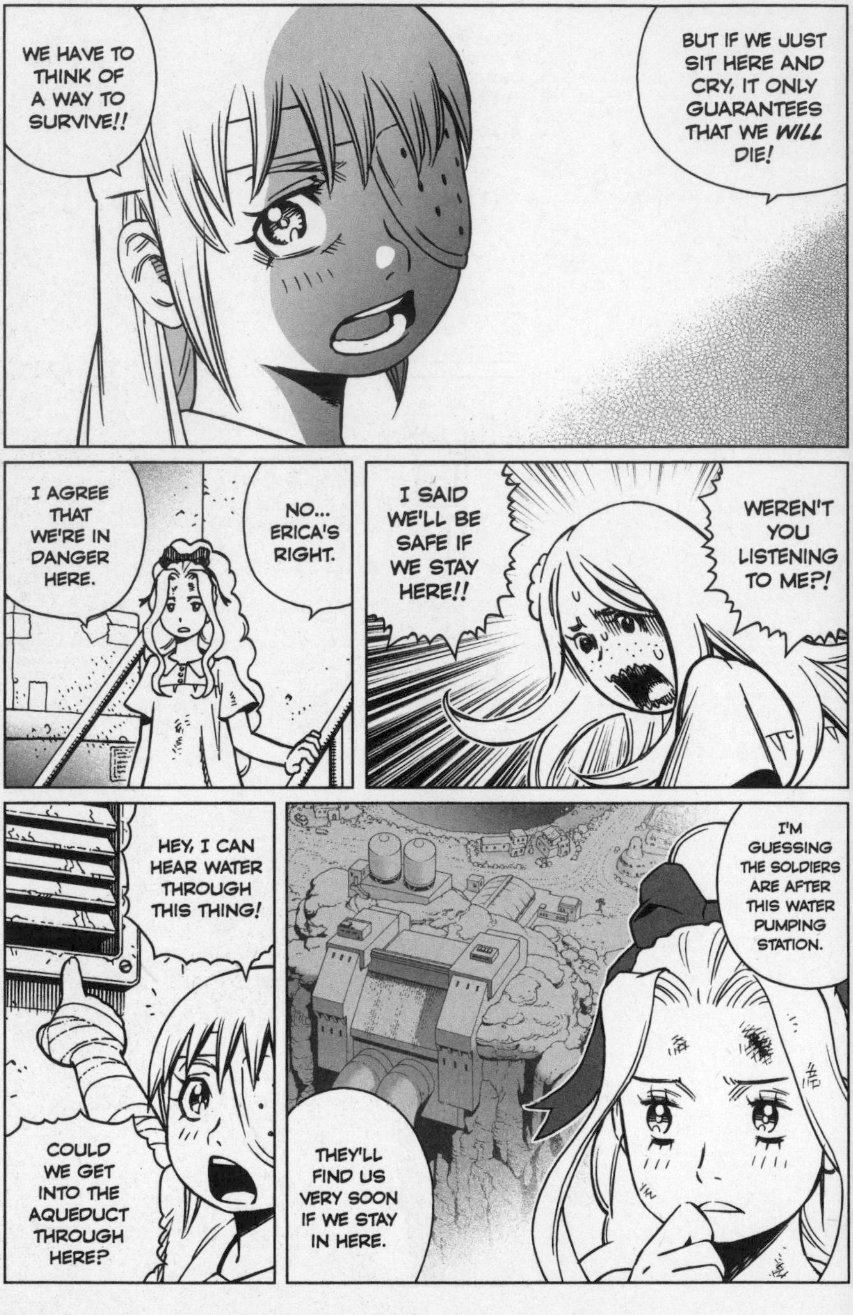
BUT IF WE JUST SIT HERE AND CRY, IT ONLY GUARANTEES THAT WE *WILL* DIE!
WE HAVE TO THINK OF A WAY TO SURVIVE!!
WEREN'T YOU LISTENING TO ME?!
I SAID WE'LL BE SAFE IF WE STAY HERE!!
NO... ERICA'S RIGHT.
I AGREE THAT WE'RE IN DANGER HERE.
I'M GUESSING THE SOLDIERS ARE AFTER THIS WATER PUMPING STATION.
THEY'LL FIND US VERY SOON IF WE STAY IN HERE.
HEY, I CAN HEAR WATER THROUGH THIS THING!
COULD WE GET INTO THE AQUEDUCT THROUGH HERE?

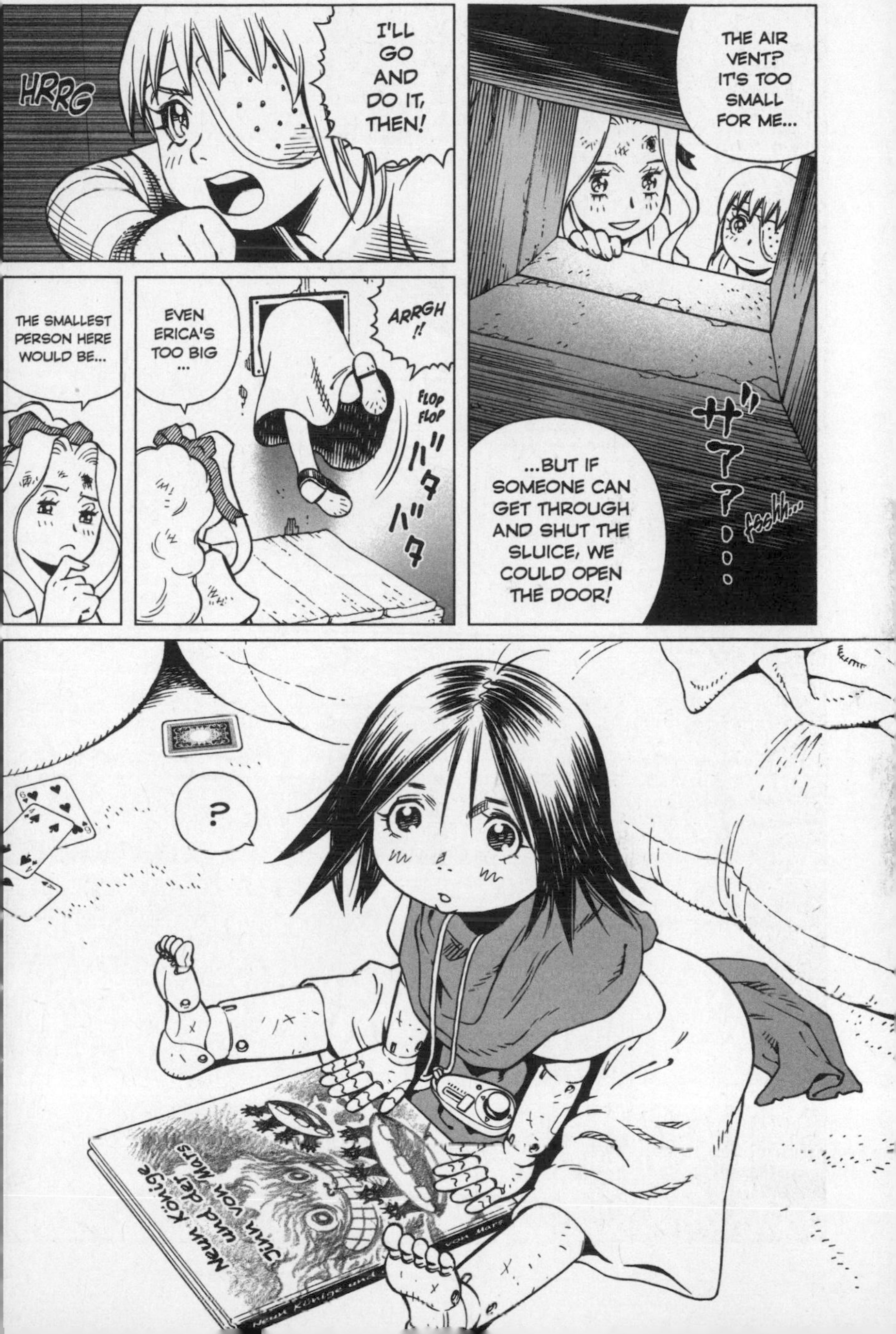
THE AIR VENT? IT'S TOO SMALL FOR ME...
...BUT IF SOMEONE CAN GET THROUGH AND SHUT THE SLUICE, WE COULD OPEN THE DOOR!
ザァァ...
fsshh...
I'LL GO AND DO IT, THEN!
HRRG
ARRGH !!
FLOP FLOP
バタバタ
EVEN ERICA'S TOO BIG ...
THE SMALLEST PERSON HERE WOULD BE...
?

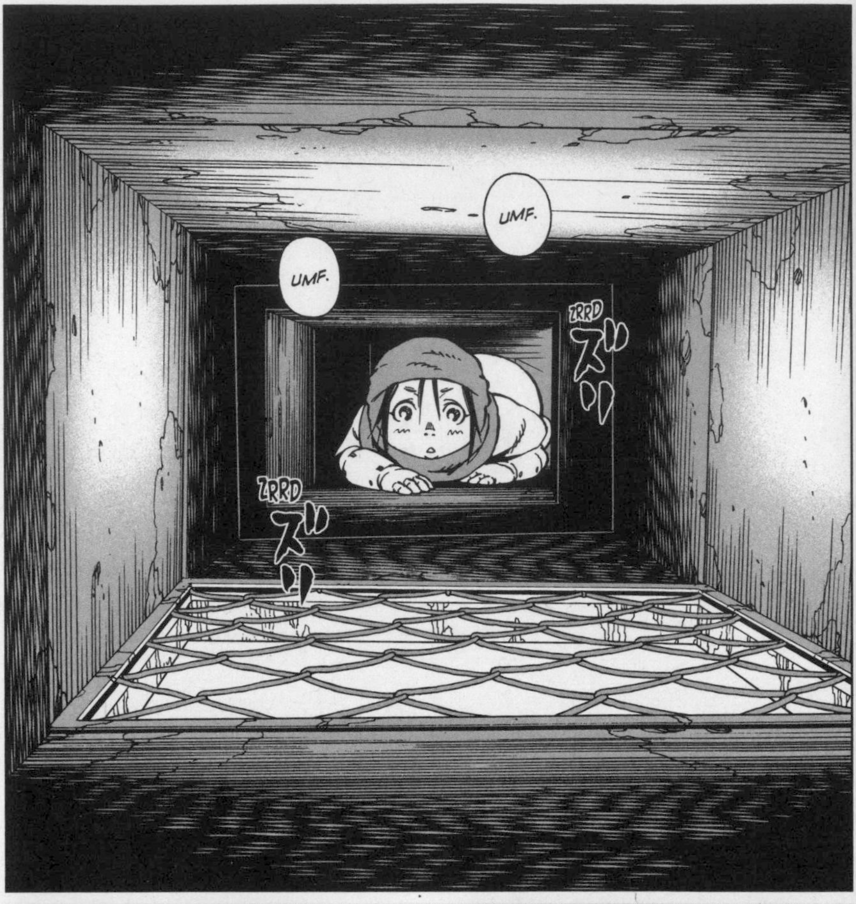
UMF.
UMF.
ZRRD ズリ
ZRRD ズリ

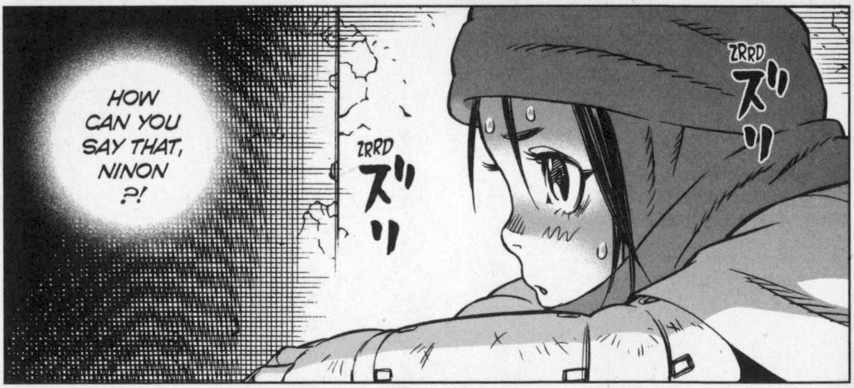
ZRRD ズリ
ZRRD ズリ
HOW CAN YOU SAY THAT, NINON ?!

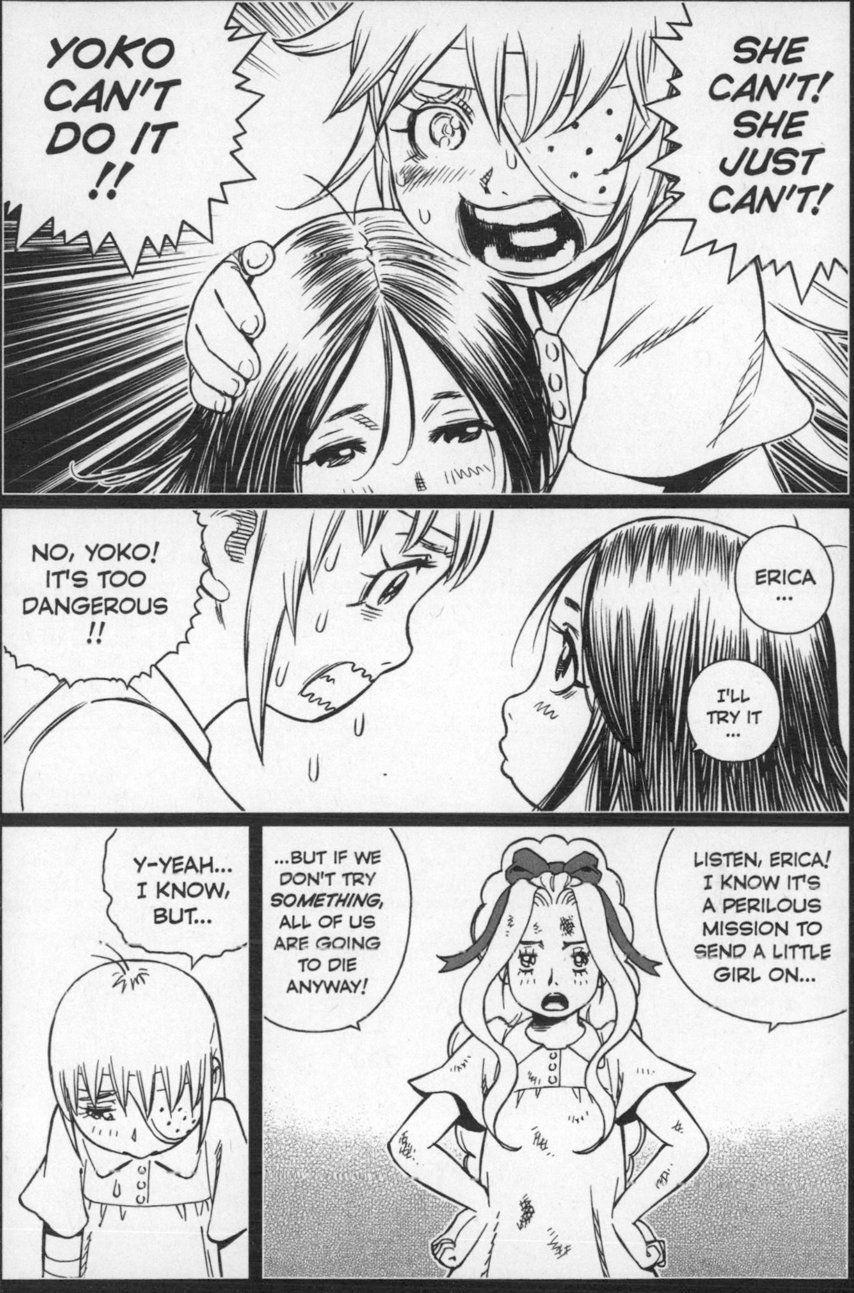
SHE CAN'T! SHE JUST CAN'T!
YOKO CAN'T DO IT!!
ERICA...
I'LL TRY IT...
NO, YOKO! IT'S TOO DANGEROUS!!
LISTEN, ERICA! I KNOW IT'S A PERILOUS MISSION TO SEND A LITTLE GIRL ON...
...BUT IF WE DON'T TRY *SOMETHING*, ALL OF US ARE GOING TO DIE ANYWAY!
Y-YEAH... I KNOW, BUT...

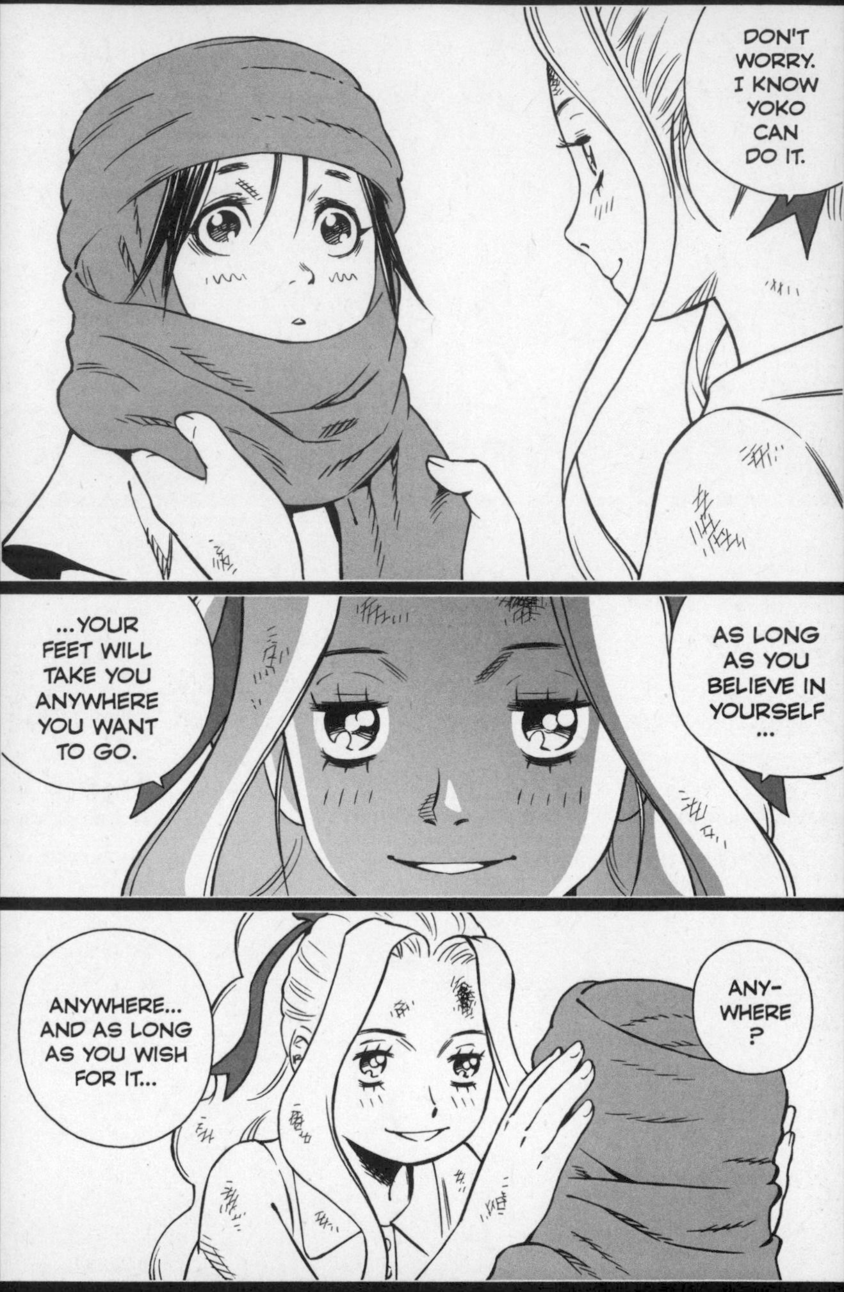
DON'T WORRY. I KNOW YOKO CAN DO IT.
AS LONG AS YOU BELIEVE IN YOURSELF...
...YOUR FEET WILL TAKE YOU ANYWHERE YOU WANT TO GO.
ANY-WHERE?
ANYWHERE... AND AS LONG AS YOU WISH FOR IT...

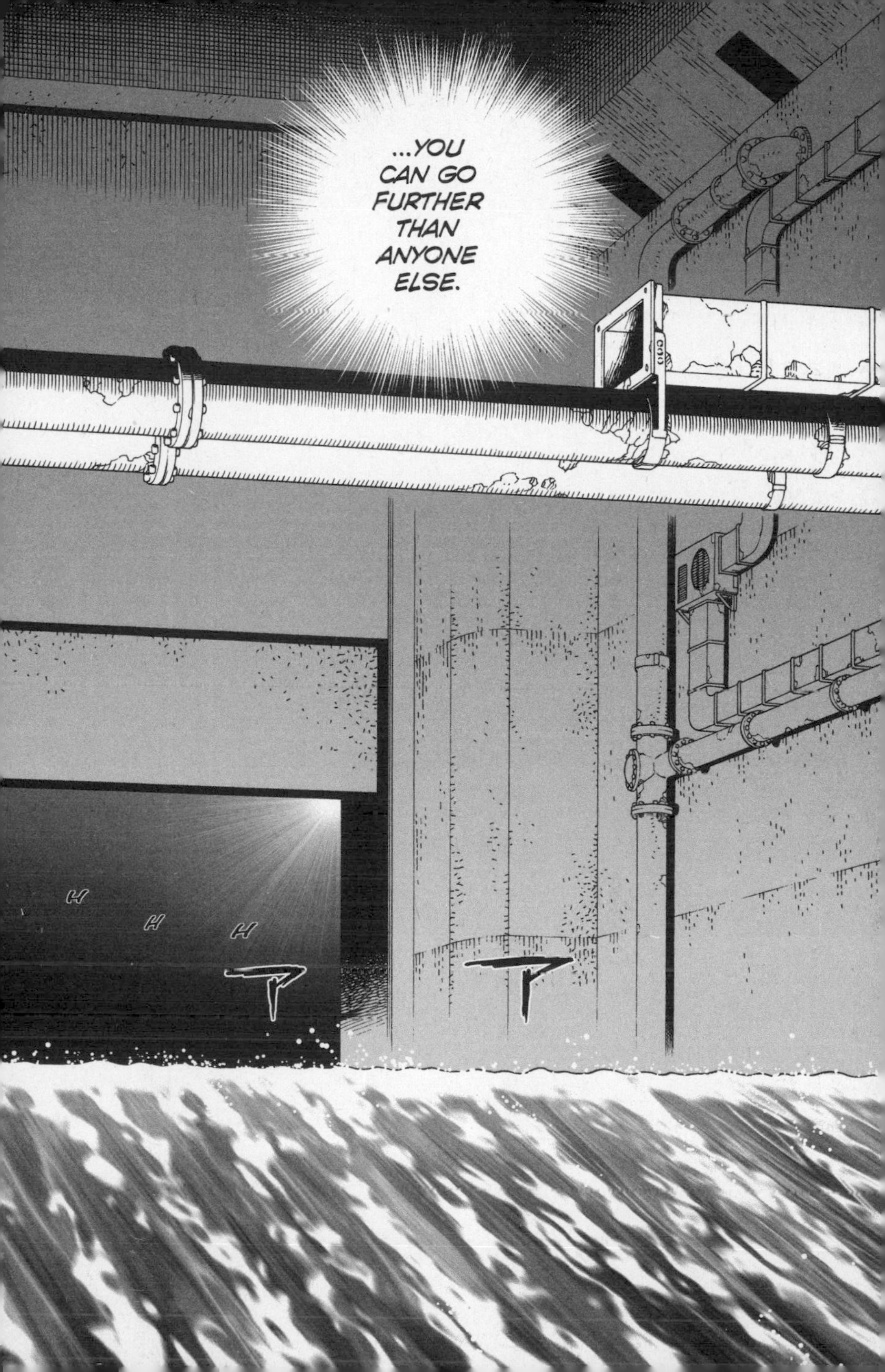
...YOU CAN GO FURTHER THAN ANYONE ELSE.
H
H
H

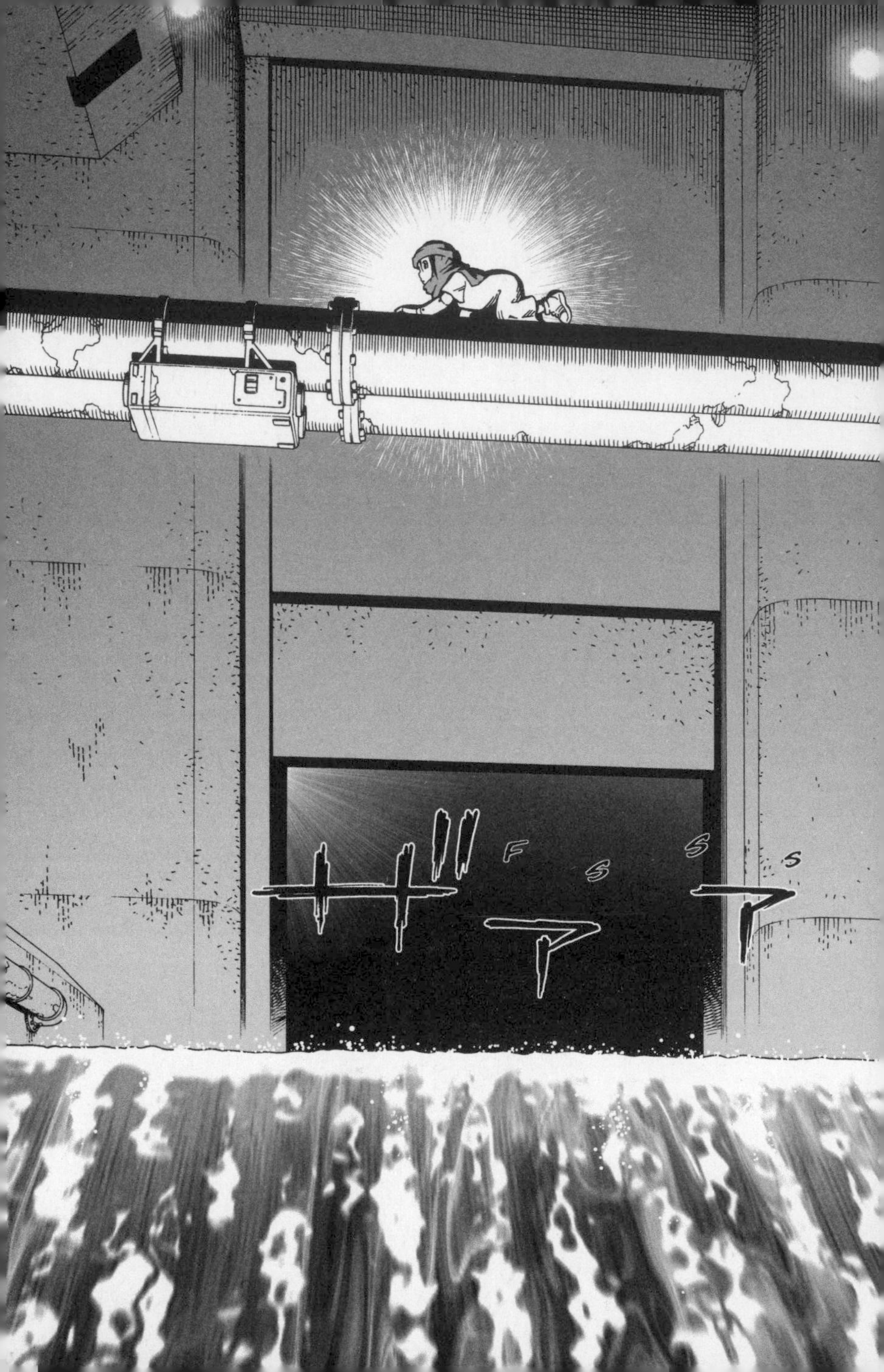
サザァァ
FSSS

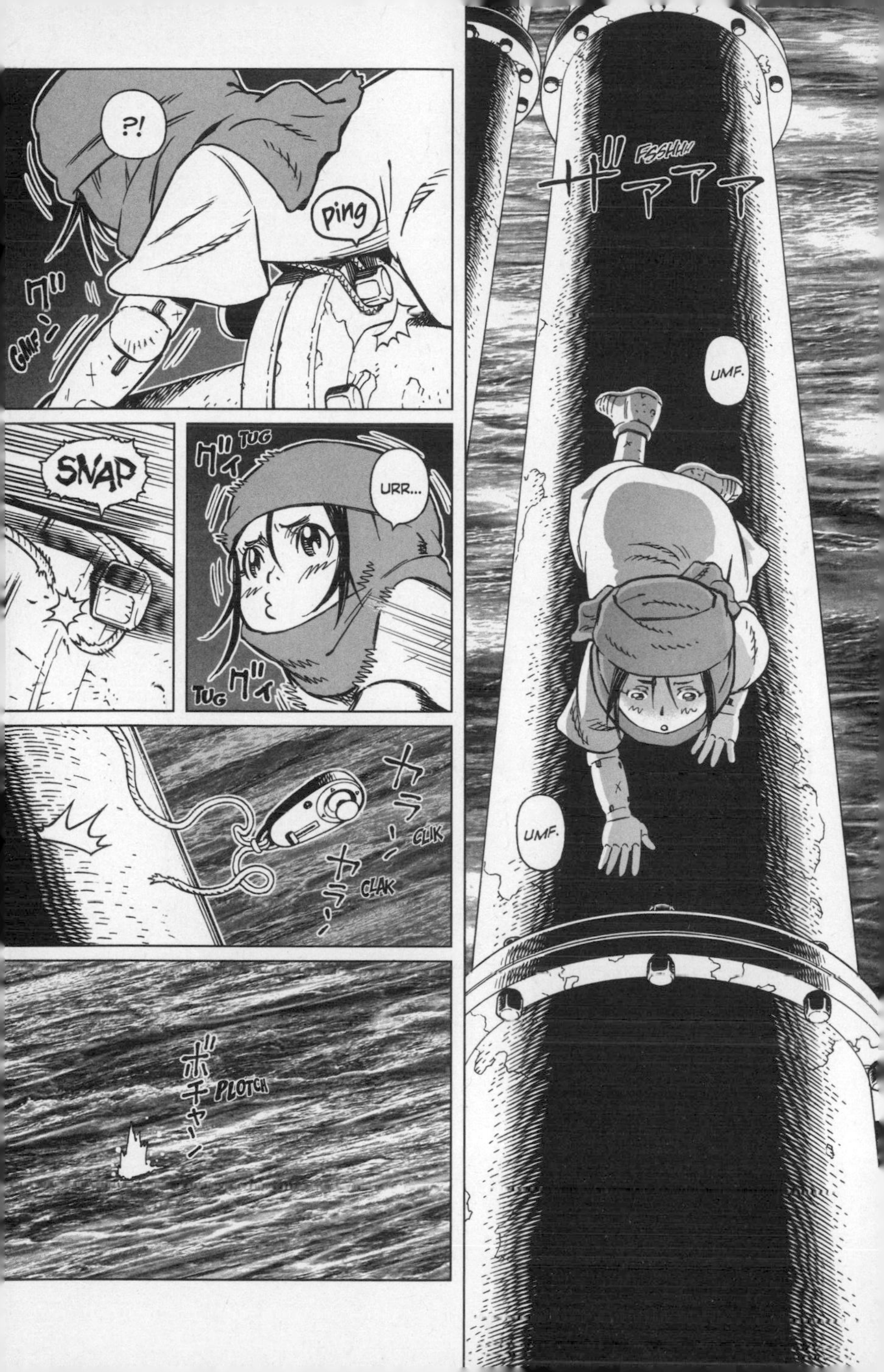
ザアアア
FSSHHH
UMF.
UMF.
?!
ping
グン
GMF
グイ
TUG
URR...
TUG
グイ
SNAP
カラーン
GLIK
カラーン
CLAK
ボチャーン
PLOTCH

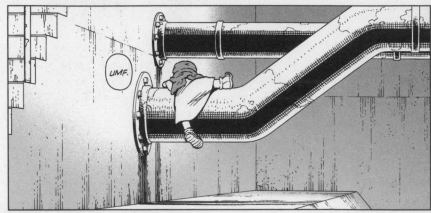

UMF.

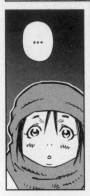

...

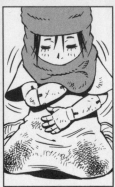

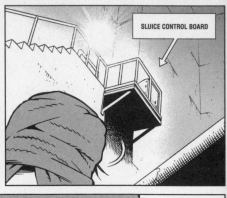

SLUICE CONTROL BOARD

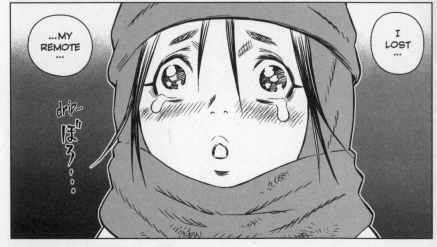

...MY
REMOTE
...

I
LOST
...

drip...
ぼ
ろ...

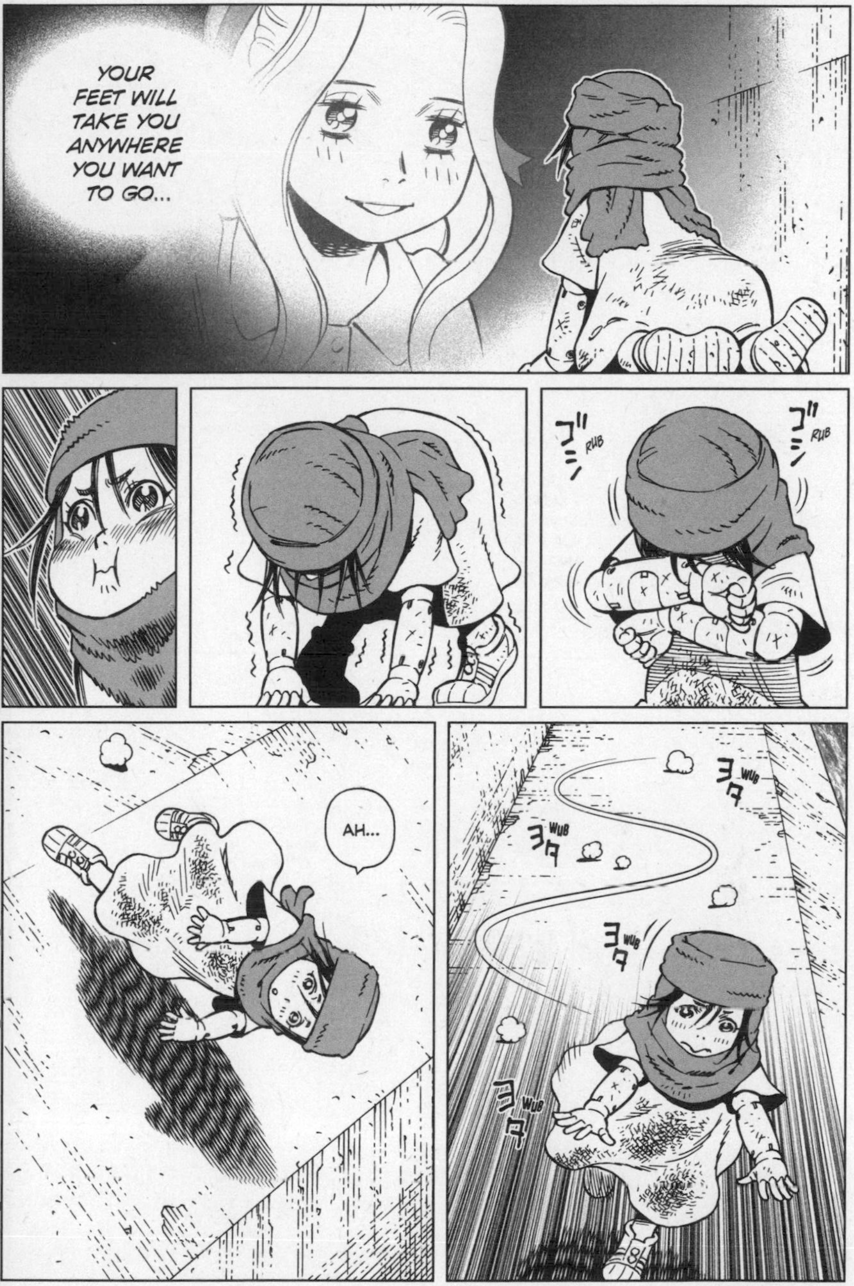
YOUR FEET WILL TAKE YOU ANYWHERE YOU WANT TO GO...
ゴシ RUB
ゴシ RUB
ヨタ WUB
ヨタ WUB
ヨタ WUB
ヨタ WUB
AH...

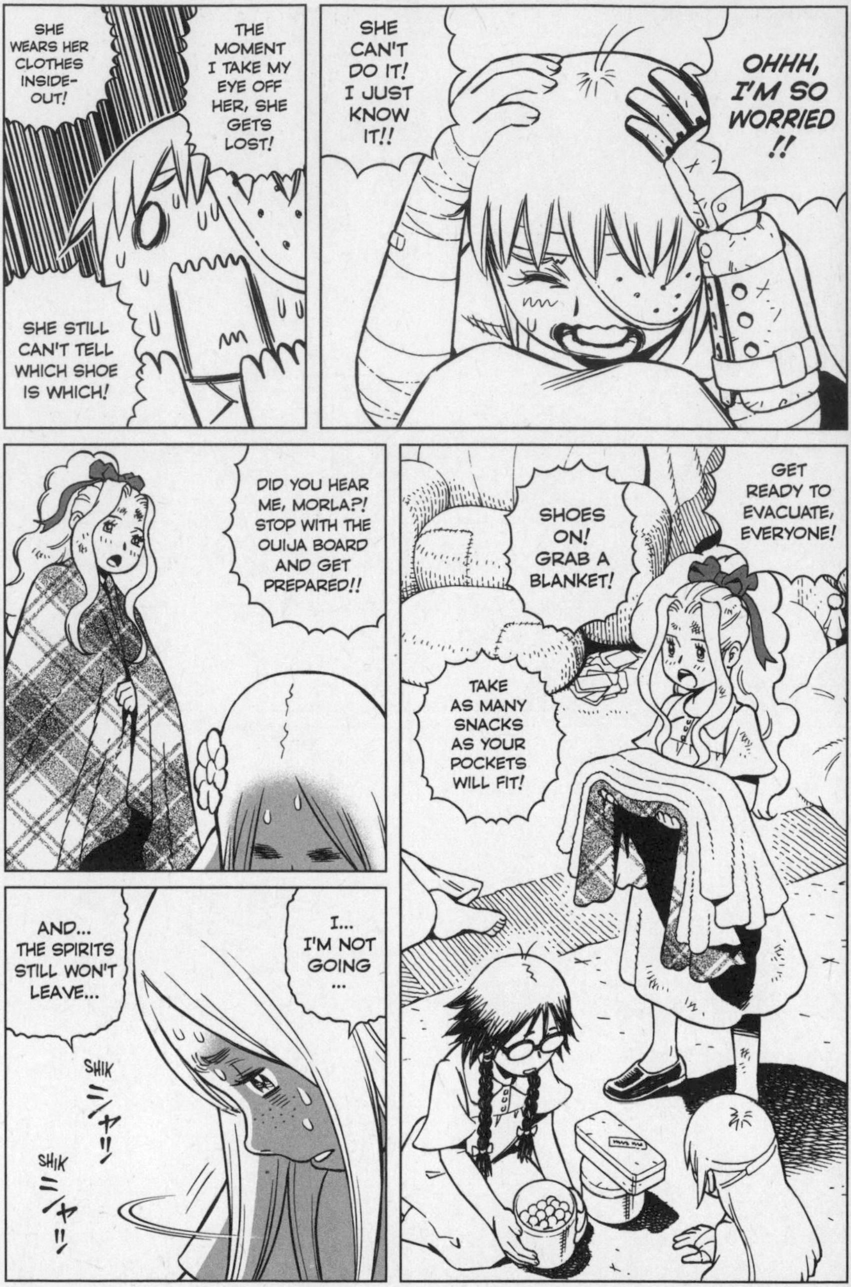
OHHH, I'M SO WORRIED!!
SHE CAN'T DO IT! I JUST KNOW IT!!
THE MOMENT I TAKE MY EYE OFF HER, SHE GETS LOST!
SHE WEARS HER CLOTHES INSIDE-OUT!
SHE STILL CAN'T TELL WHICH SHOE IS WHICH!
GET READY TO EVACUATE, EVERYONE!
SHOES ON! GRAB A BLANKET!
TAKE AS MANY SNACKS AS YOUR POCKETS WILL FIT!
DID YOU HEAR ME, MORLA?! STOP WITH THE OUIJA BOARD AND GET PREPARED!!
I... I'M NOT GOING...
AND... THE SPIRITS STILL WON'T LEAVE...
SHIK
シャ!!
SHIK
シャ!!

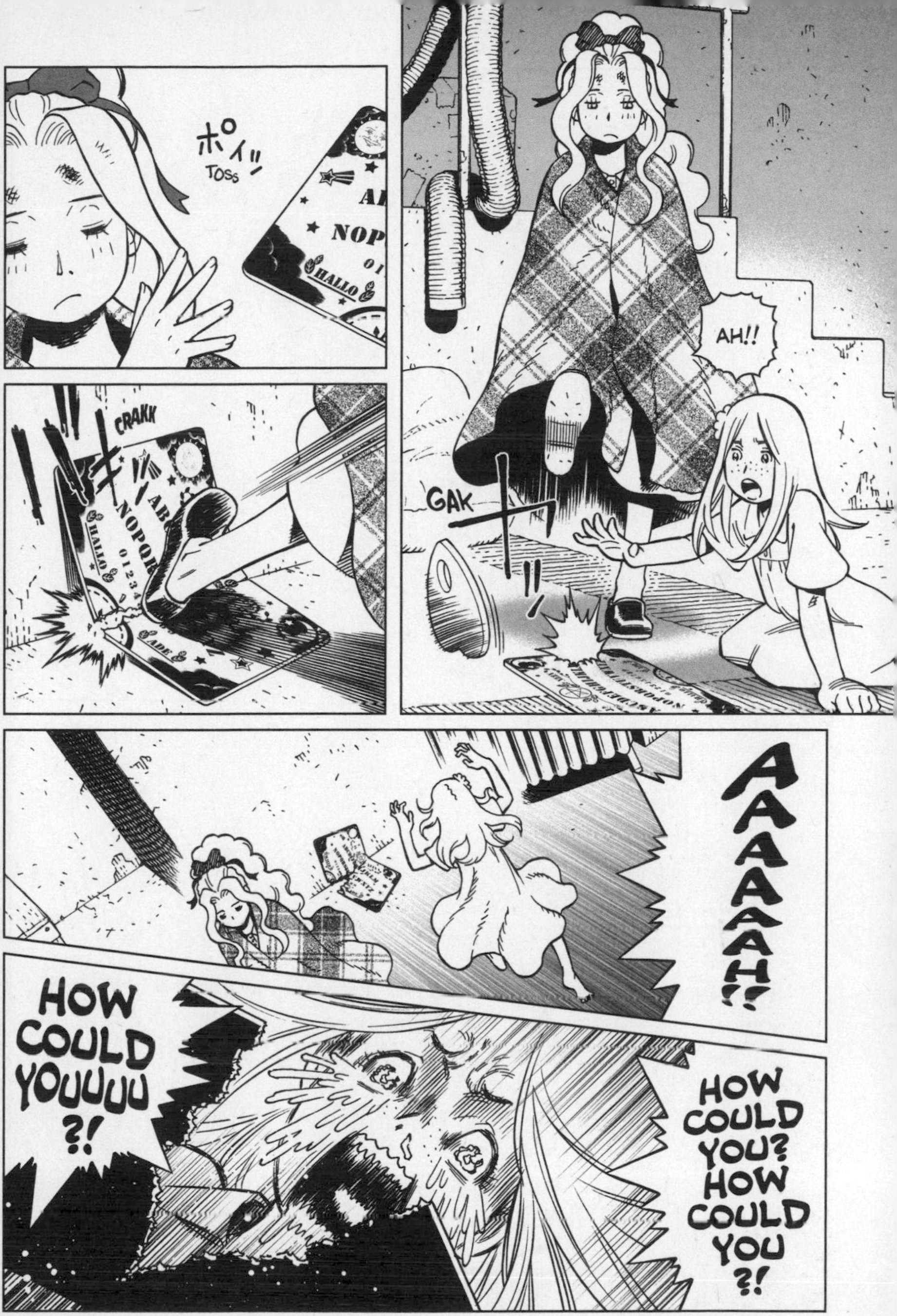
AH!!
GAK
ポイッ
TOSS
CRAKK
AAAAAAH!!
HOW COULD YOU? HOW COULD YOU?!
HOW COULD YOUUUU?!

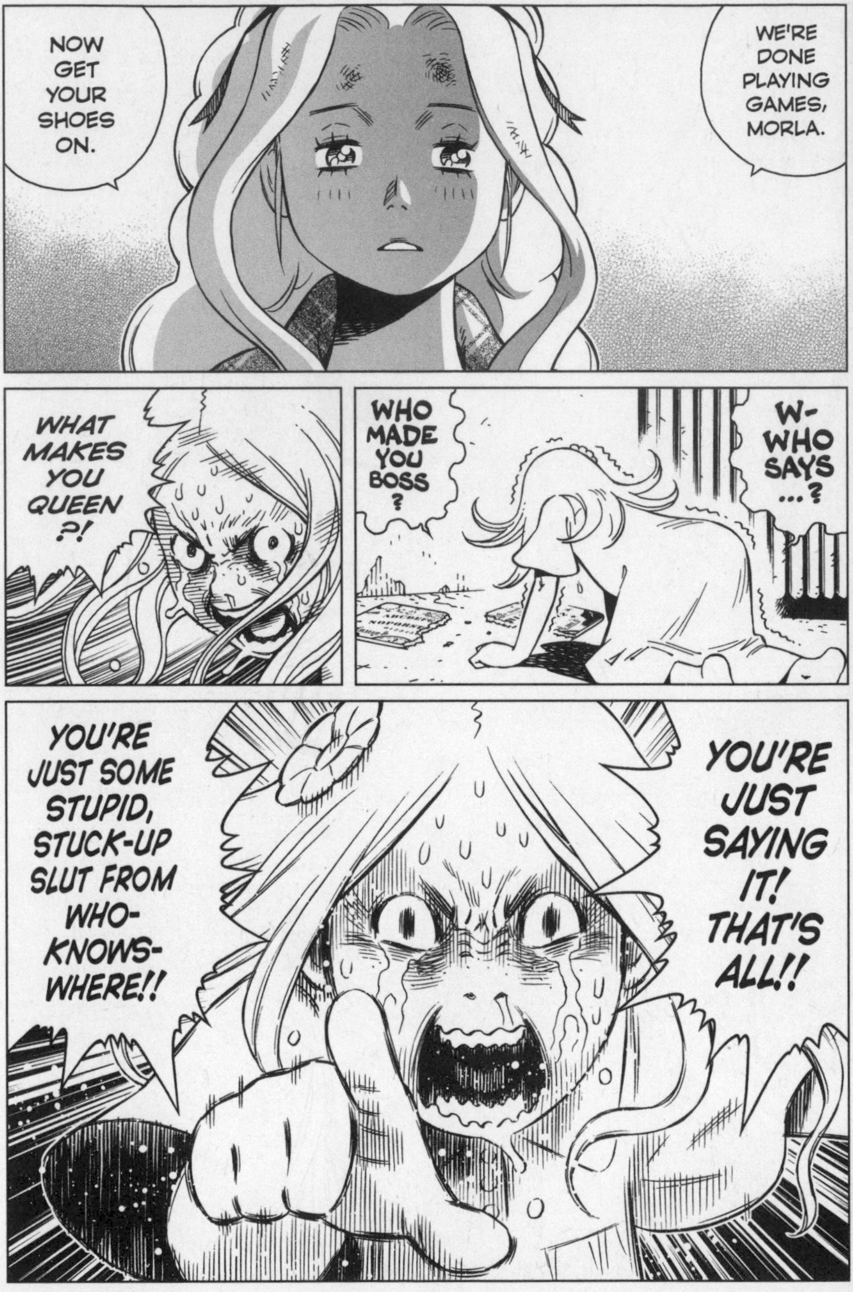
WE'RE DONE PLAYING GAMES, MORLA.
NOW GET YOUR SHOES ON.
W-WHO SAYS...?
WHO MADE YOU BOSS?
WHAT MAKES YOU QUEEN?!
YOU'RE JUST SAYING IT! THAT'S ALL!!
YOU'RE JUST SOME STUPID, STUCK-UP SLUT FROM WHO-KNOWS-WHERE!!

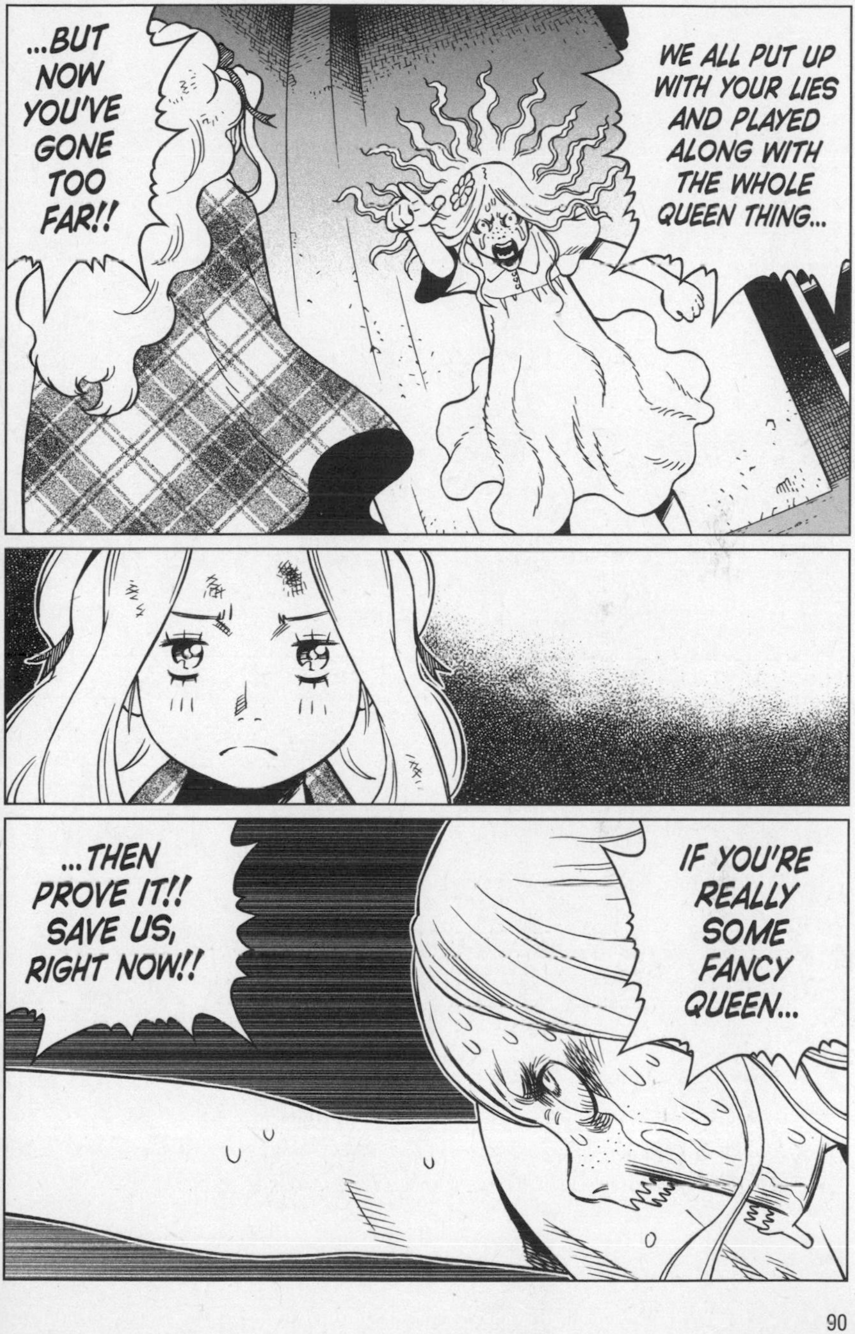
WE ALL PUT UP WITH YOUR LIES AND PLAYED ALONG WITH THE WHOLE QUEEN THING...
...BUT NOW YOU'VE GONE TOO FAR!!
IF YOU'RE REALLY SOME FANCY QUEEN...
...THEN PROVE IT!! SAVE US, RIGHT NOW!!

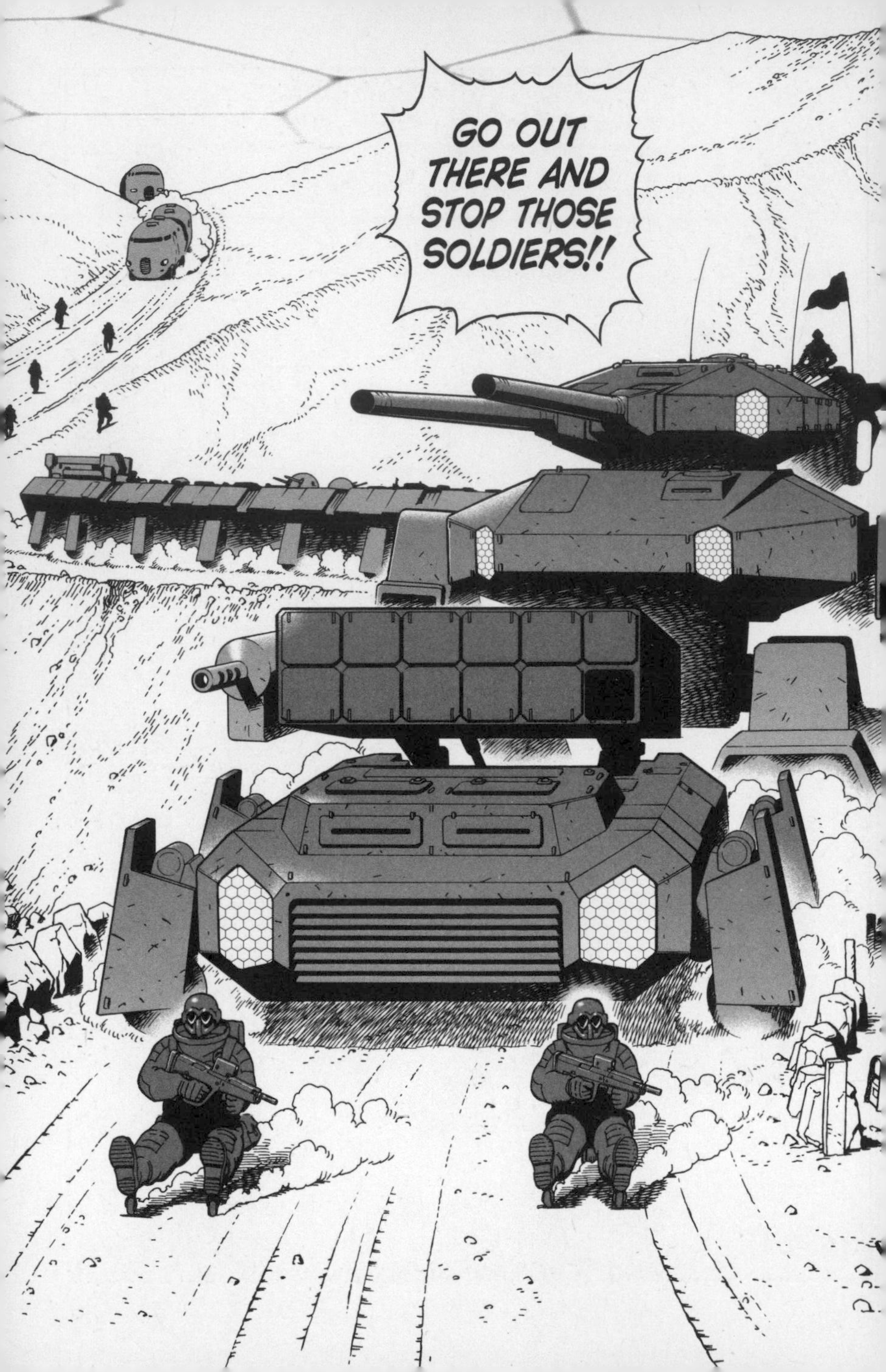
GO OUT THERE AND STOP THOSE SOLDIERS!!

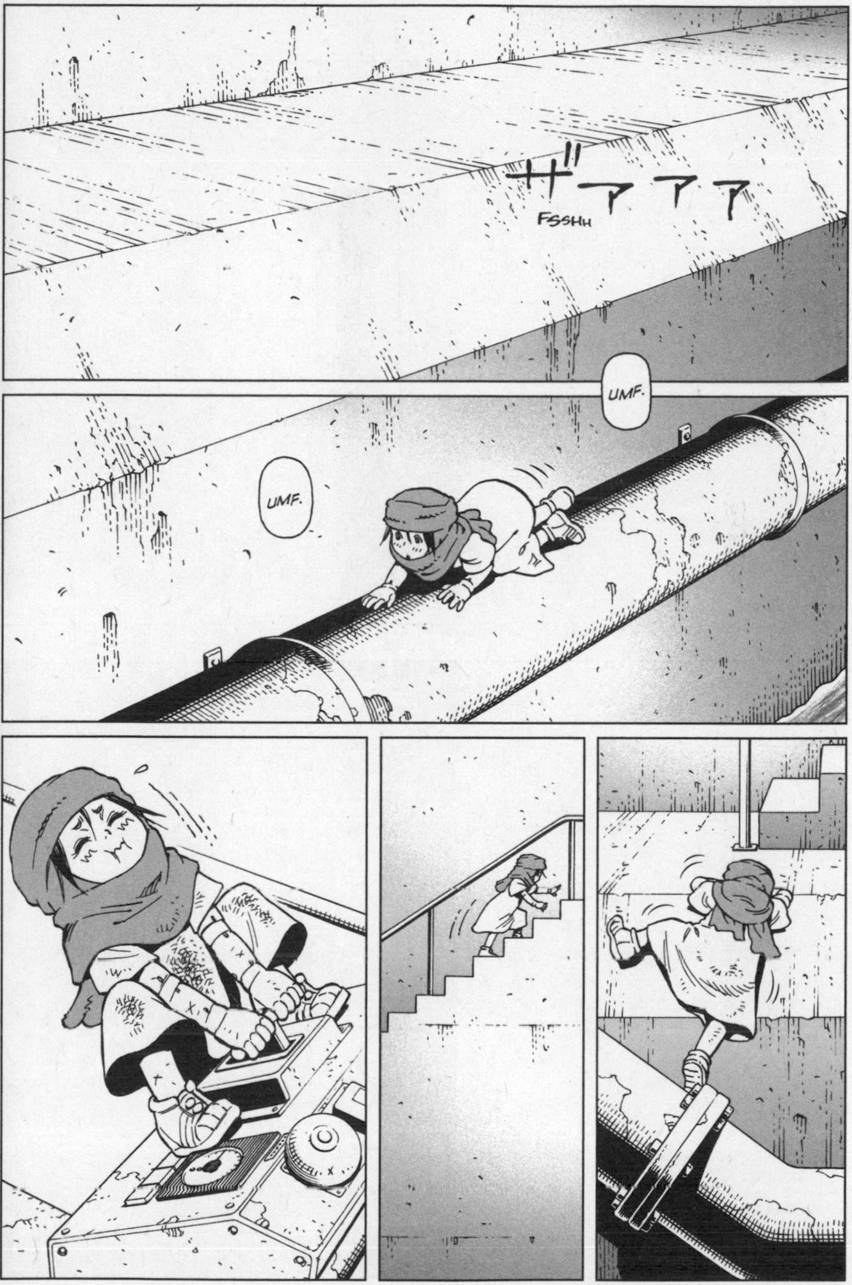
ザアアア
FSSHH
UMF.
UMF.

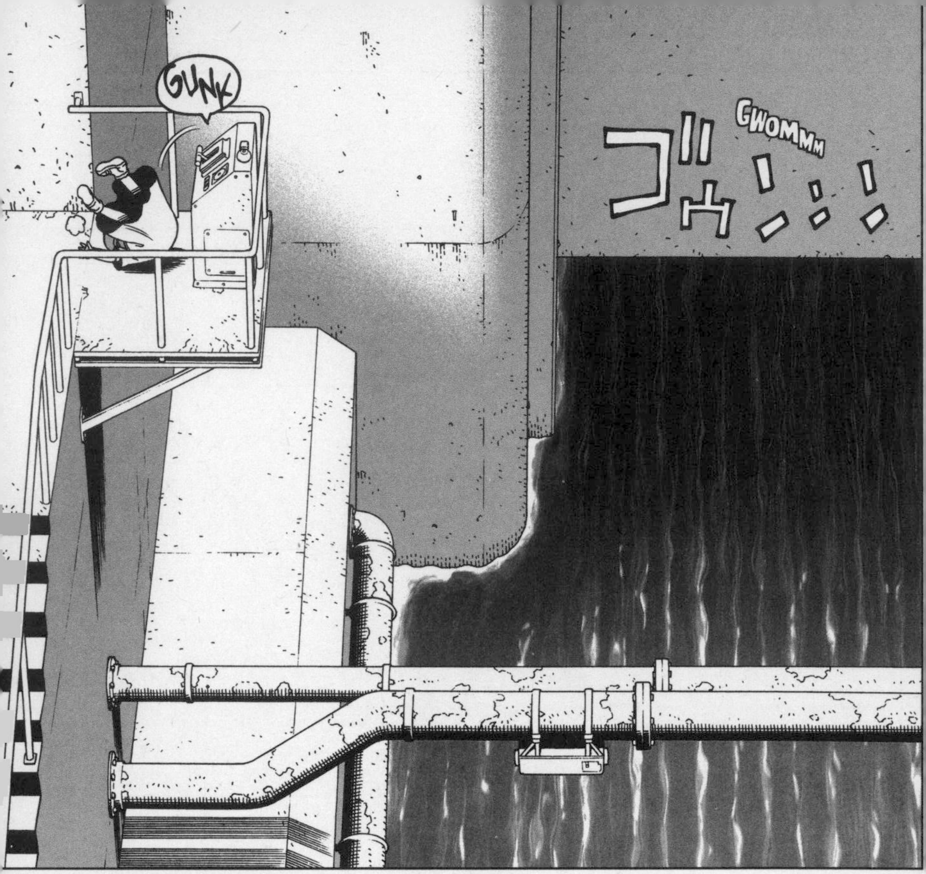
GWOMMM
GUNK

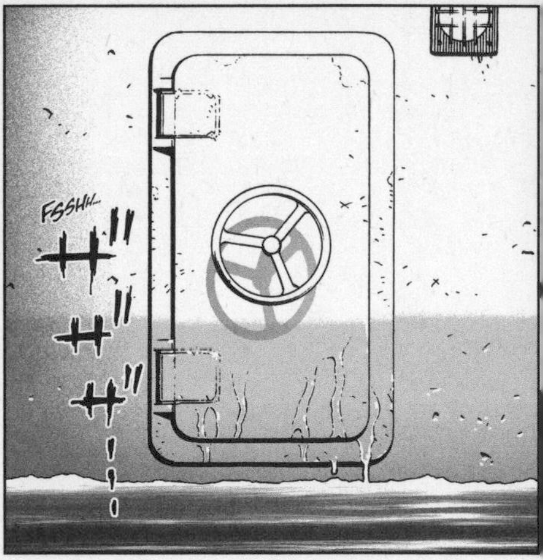
FSSHH

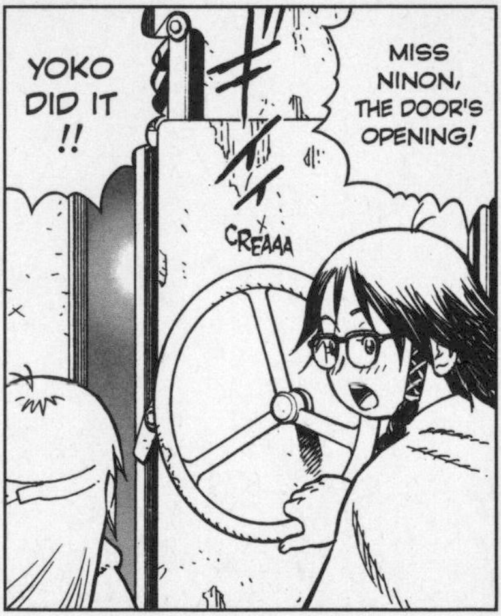
MISS NINON, THE DOOR'S OPENING!
CREAAA
YOKO DID IT !!

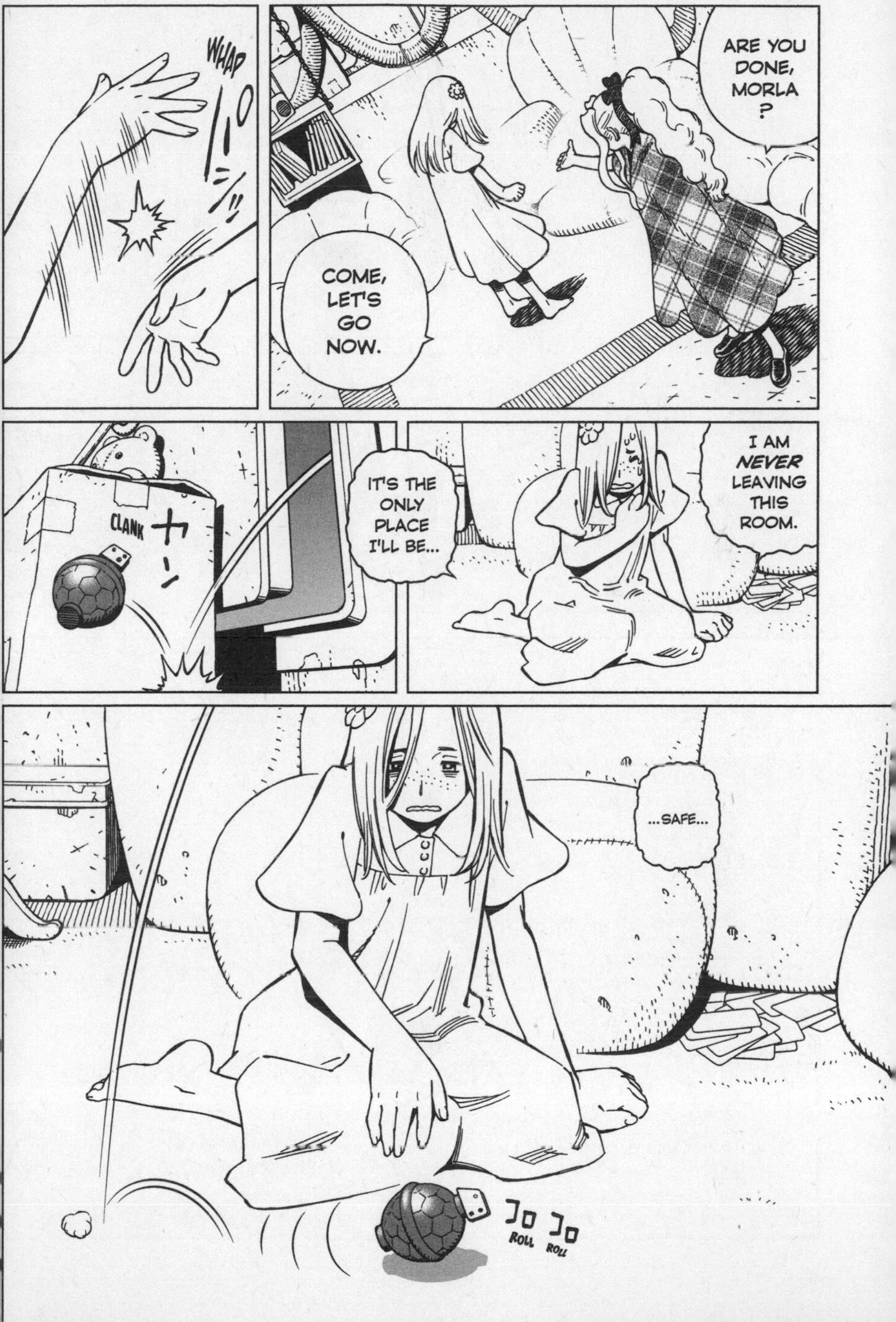
ARE YOU DONE, MORLA?
COME, LET'S GO NOW.
WHAP
I AM *NEVER* LEAVING THIS ROOM.
IT'S THE ONLY PLACE I'LL BE...
CLANK
...SAFE...
コロ コロ
ROLL ROLL

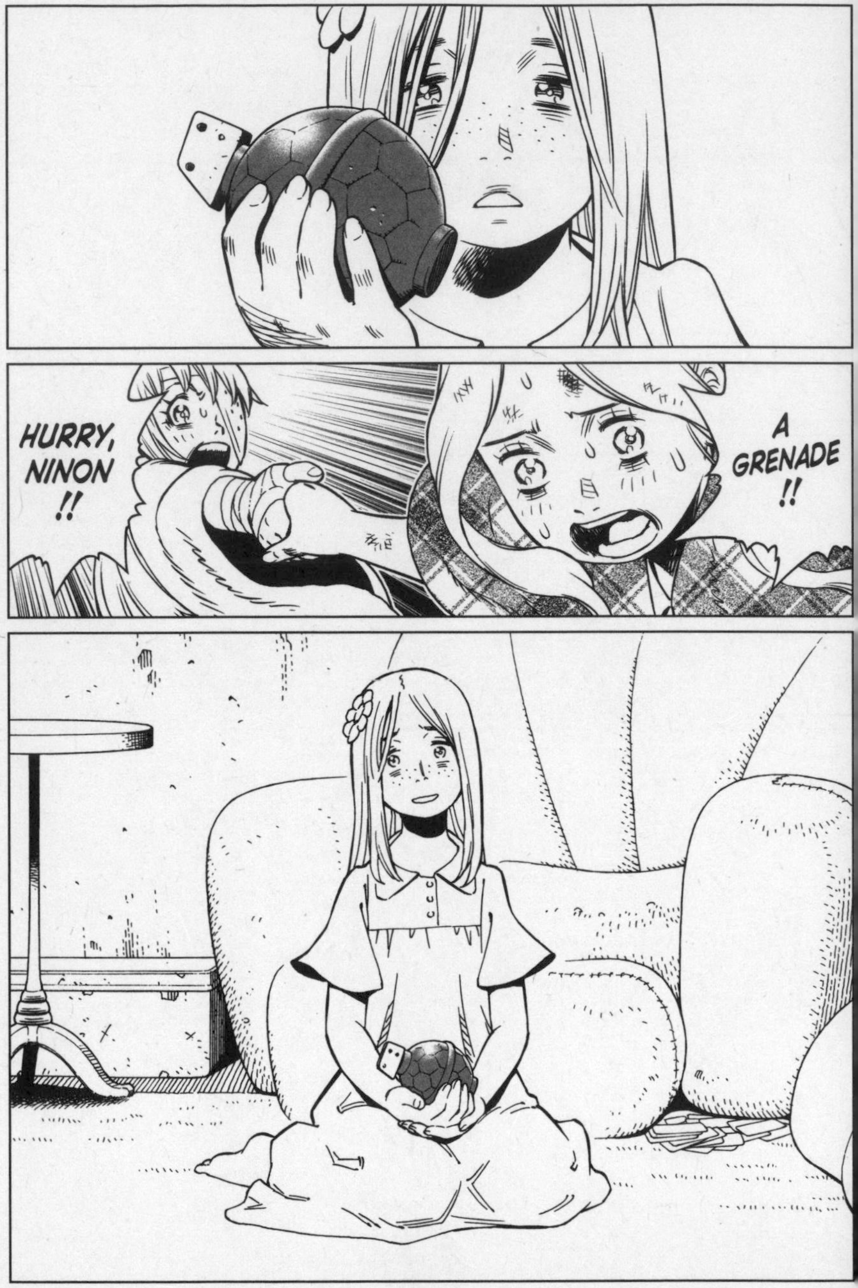
A GRENADE !!
HURRY, NINON !!

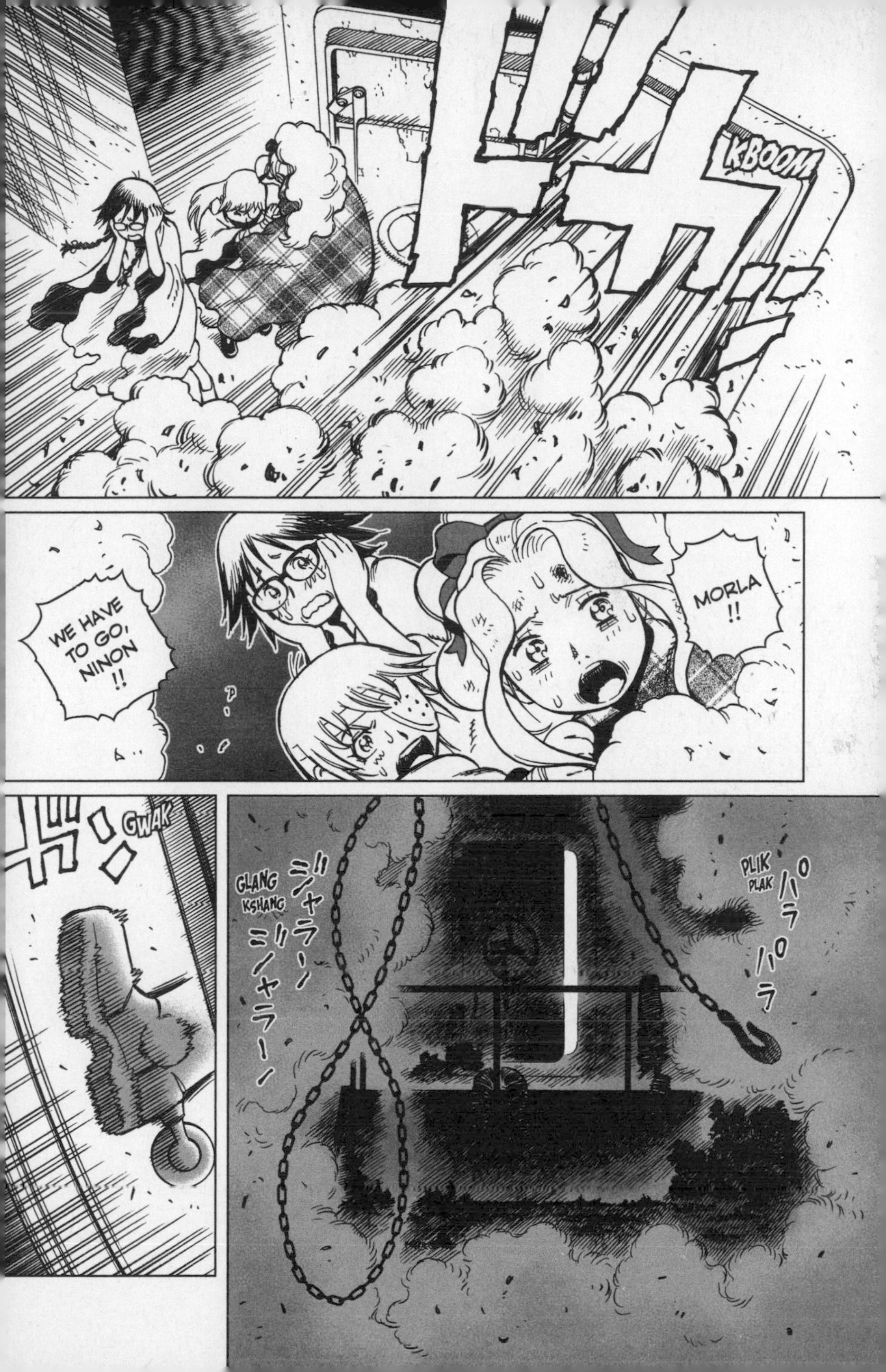
KBOOM
MORLA !!
WE HAVE TO GO, NINON !!
PLIK PLAK
パラパラ
GLANG KSHANG
ジャラーン
ジャラーン
GWAK

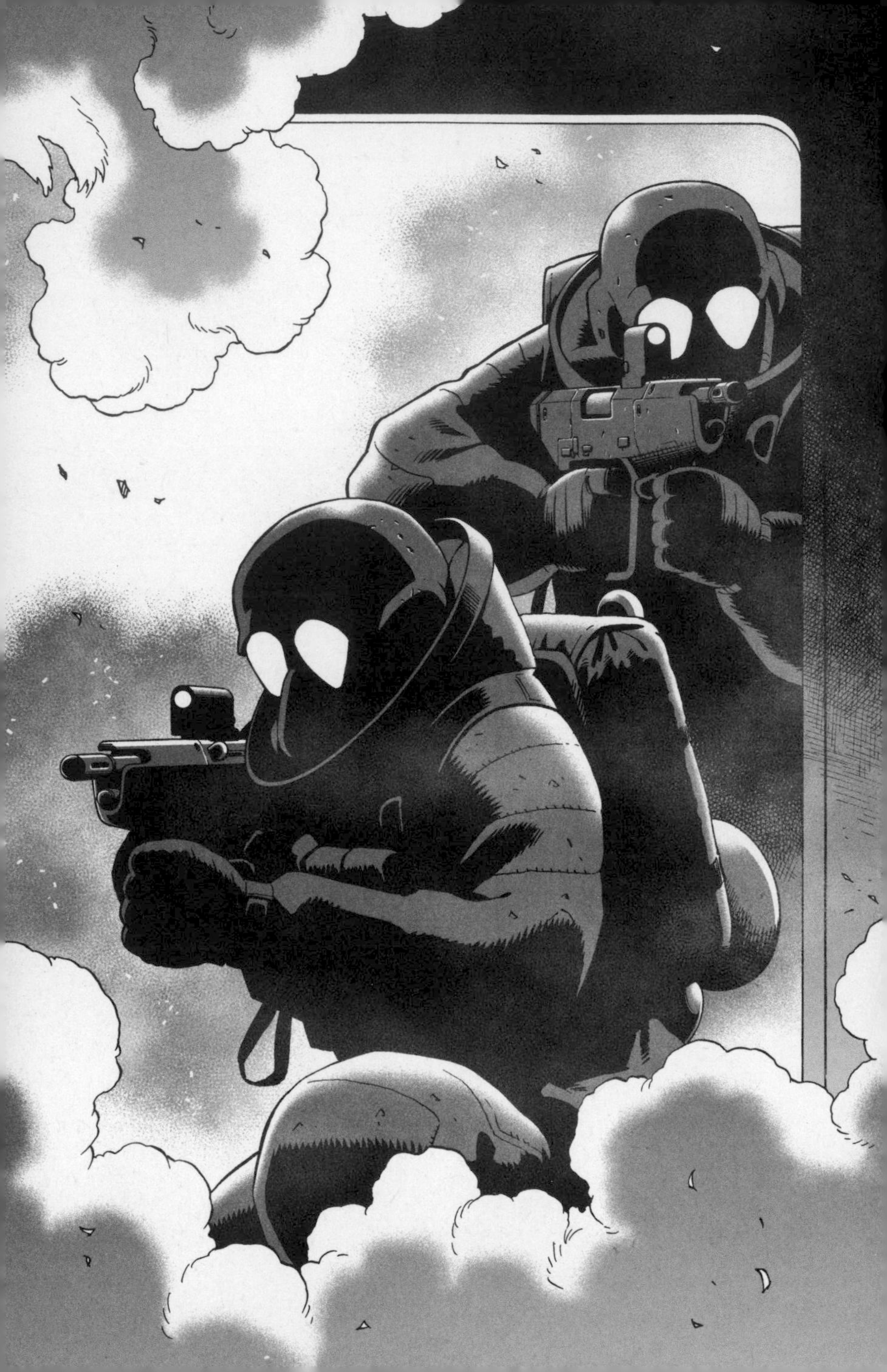

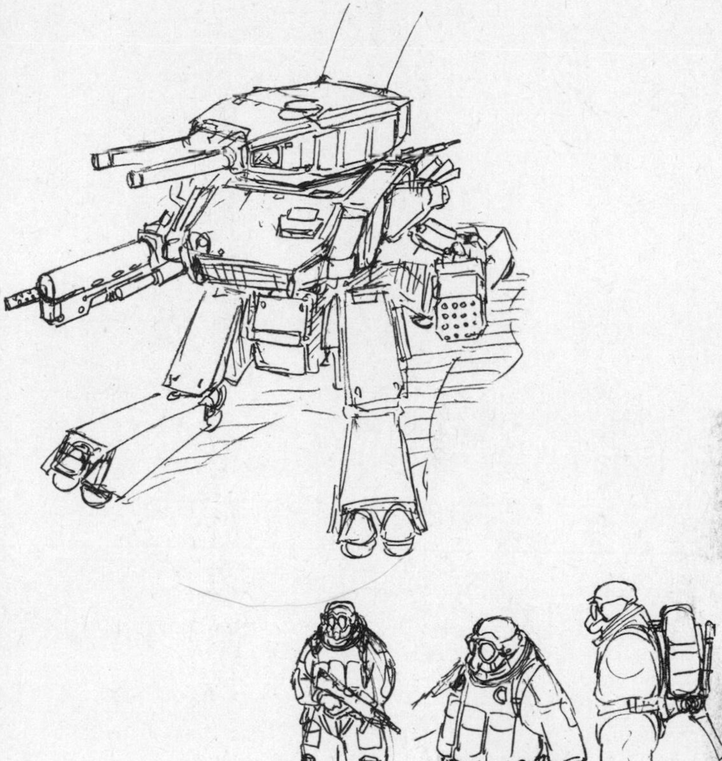

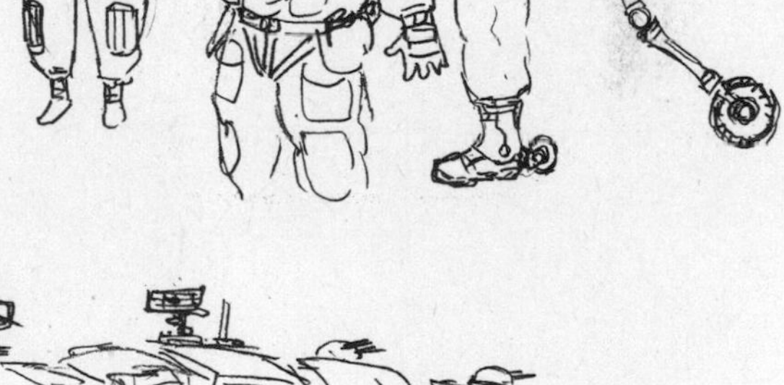

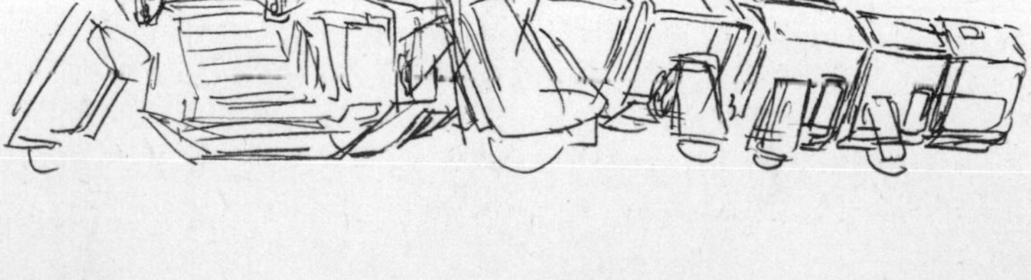

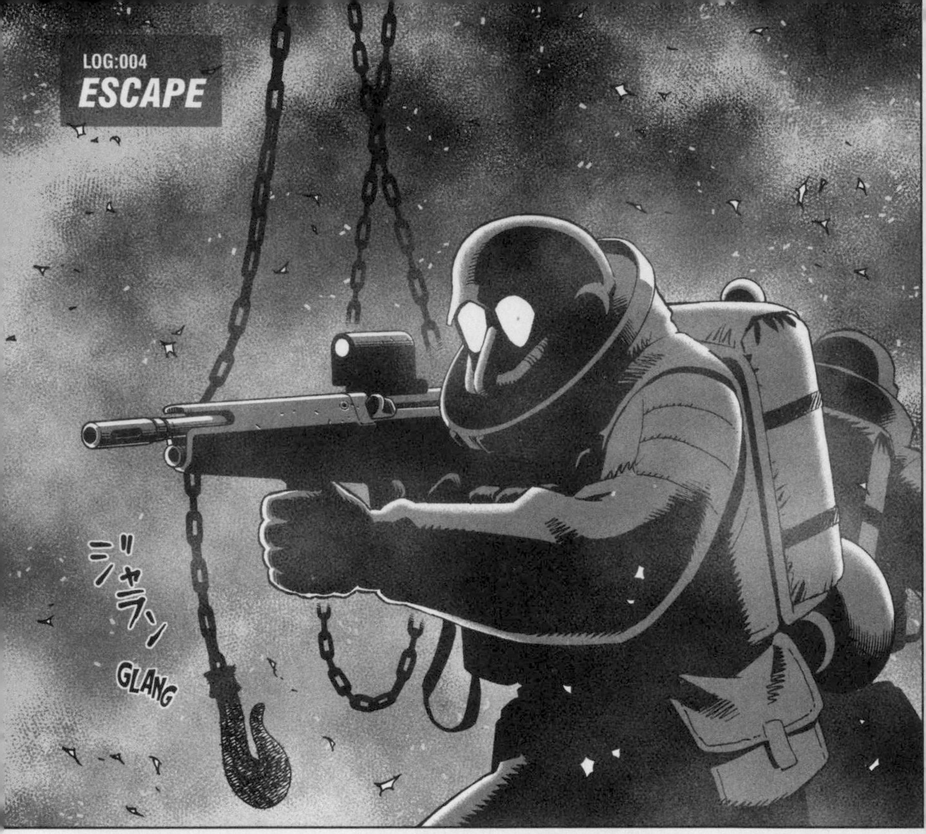
LOG:004
ESCAPE
ジャラン
GLANG

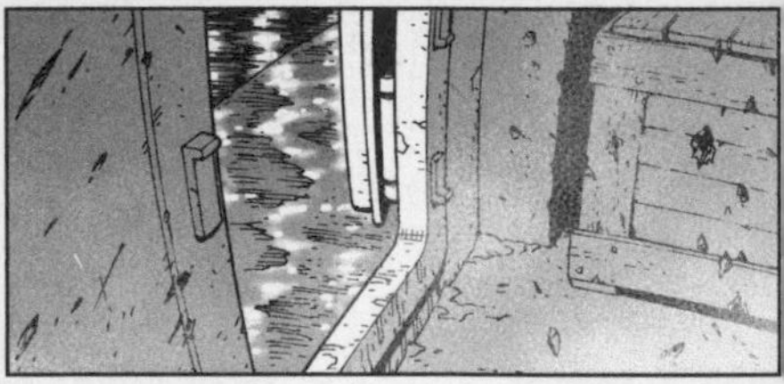

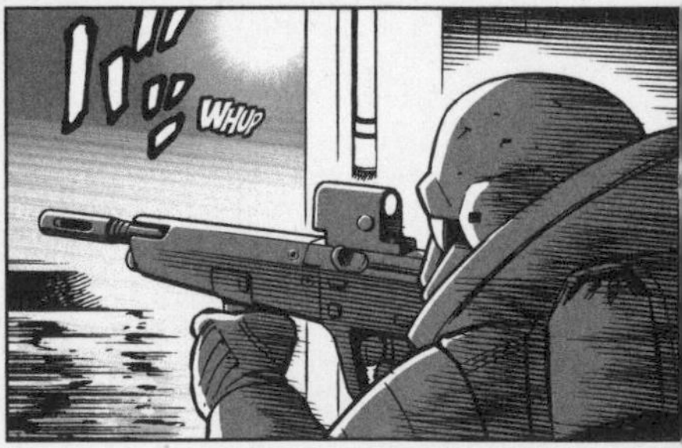
WHUP

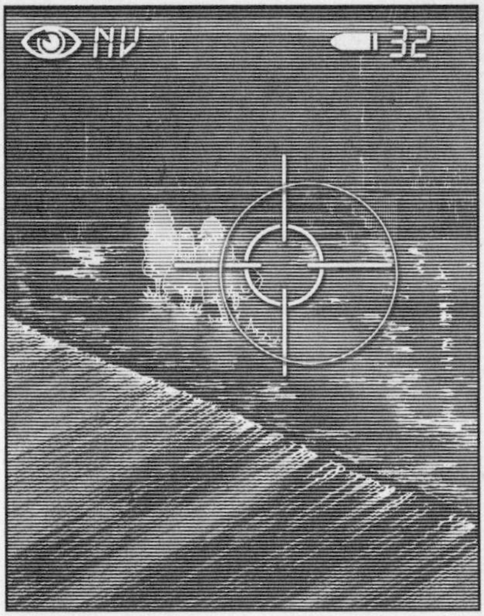
NV
32

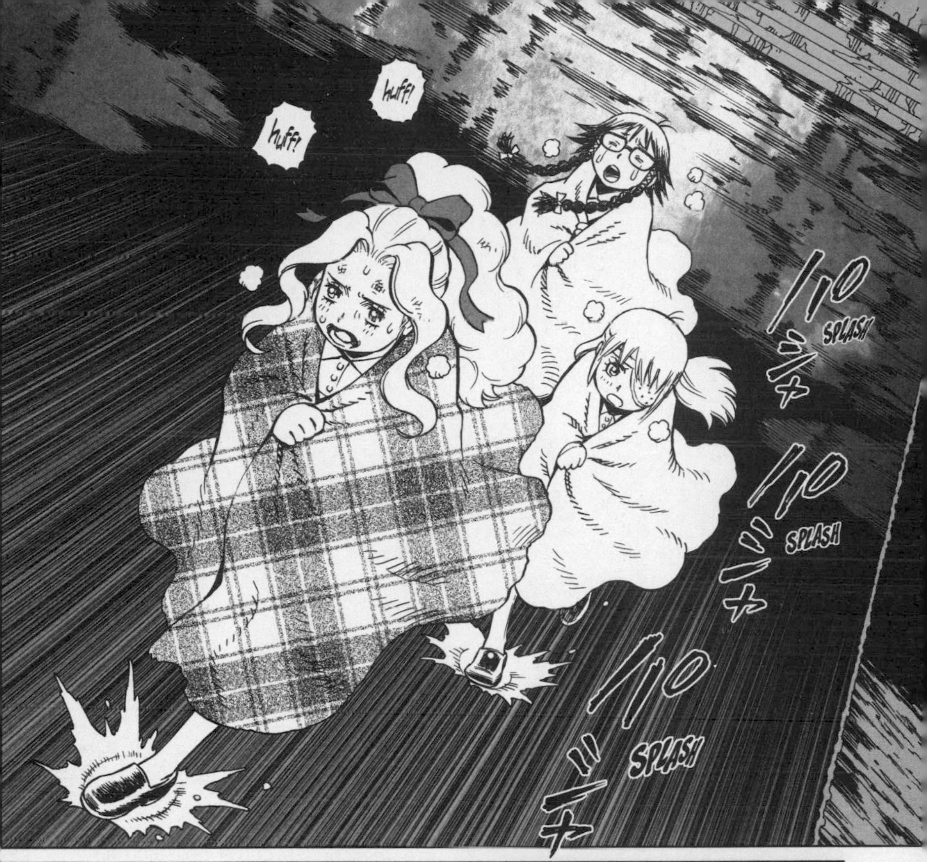
パシャ
SPLASH
パシャ
SPLASH
パシャ
SPLASH
huff!
huff!

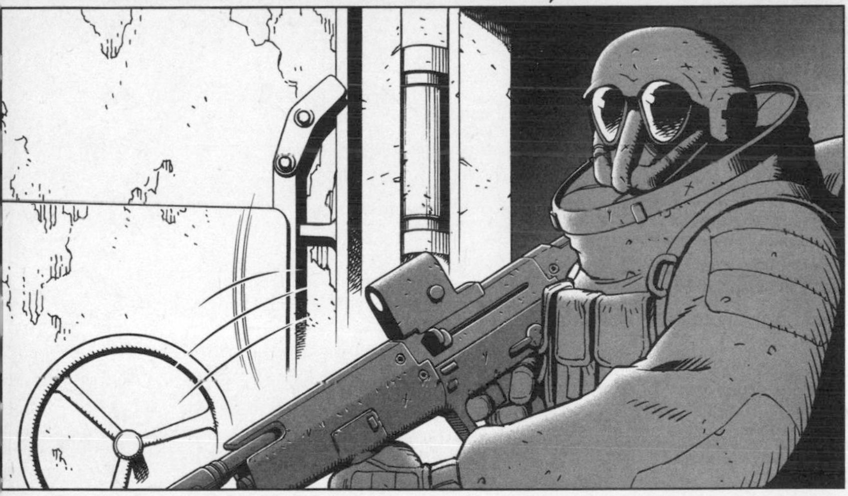

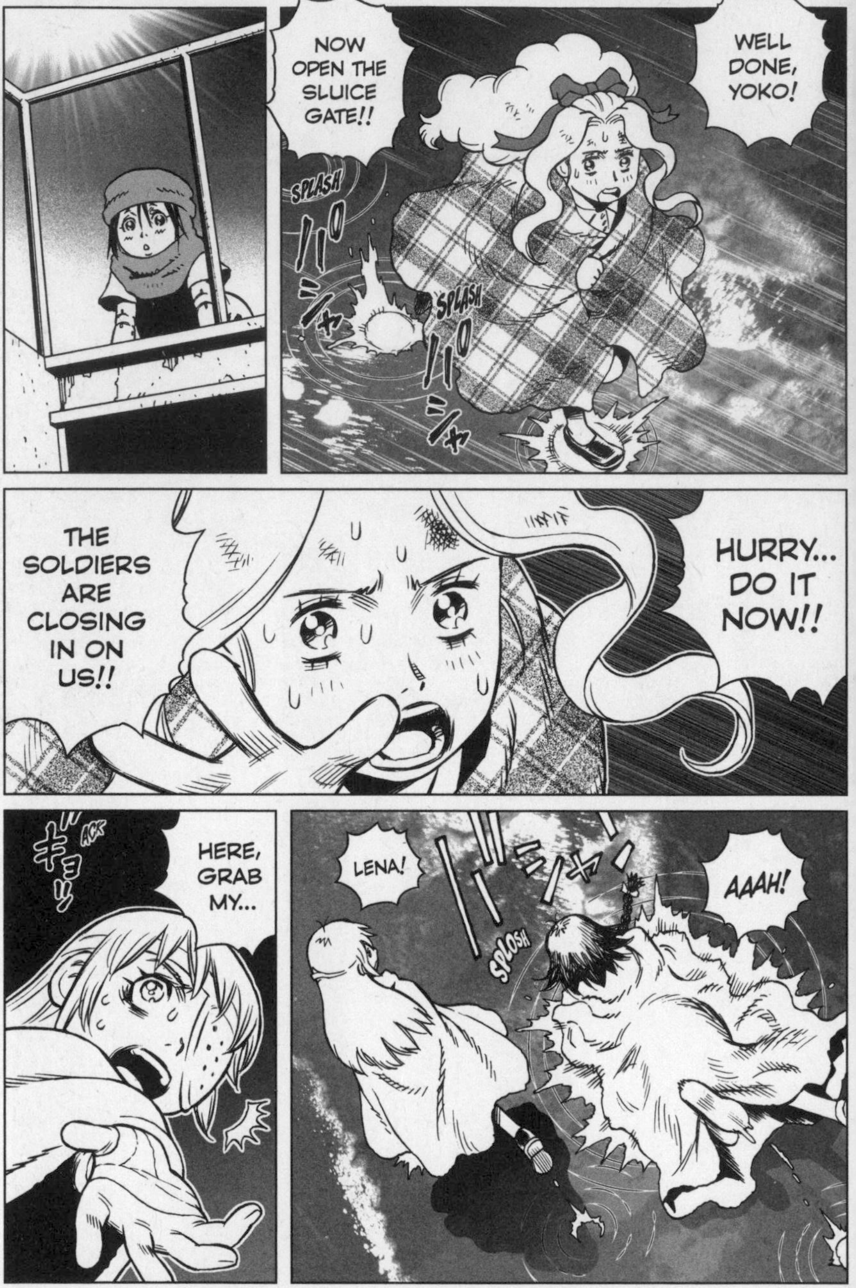
WELL DONE, YOKO!
NOW OPEN THE SLUICE GATE!!
SPLASH
SPLASH
HURRY... DO IT NOW!!
THE SOLDIERS ARE CLOSING IN ON US!!
AAAH!
LENA!
SPLOSH
HERE, GRAB MY...
ACK

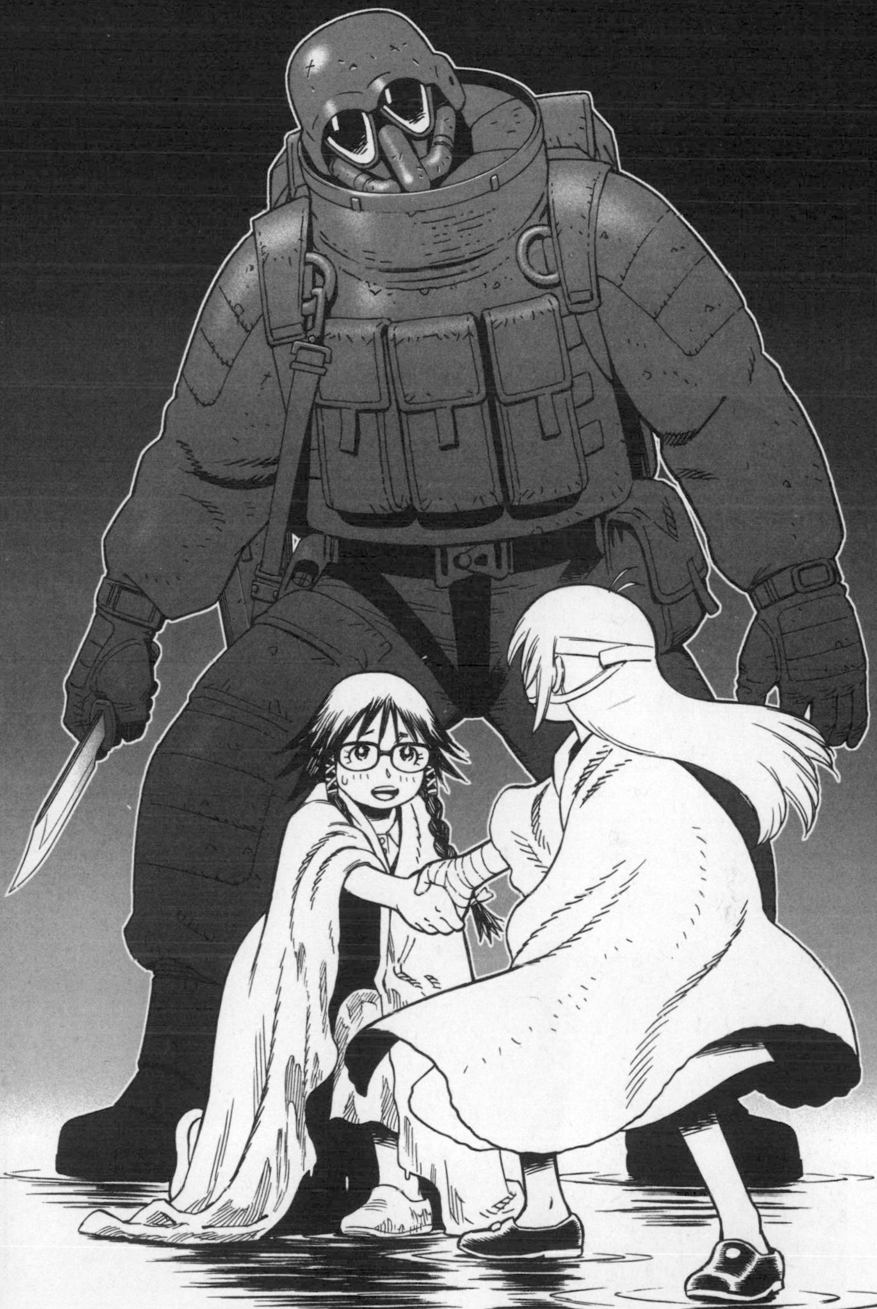

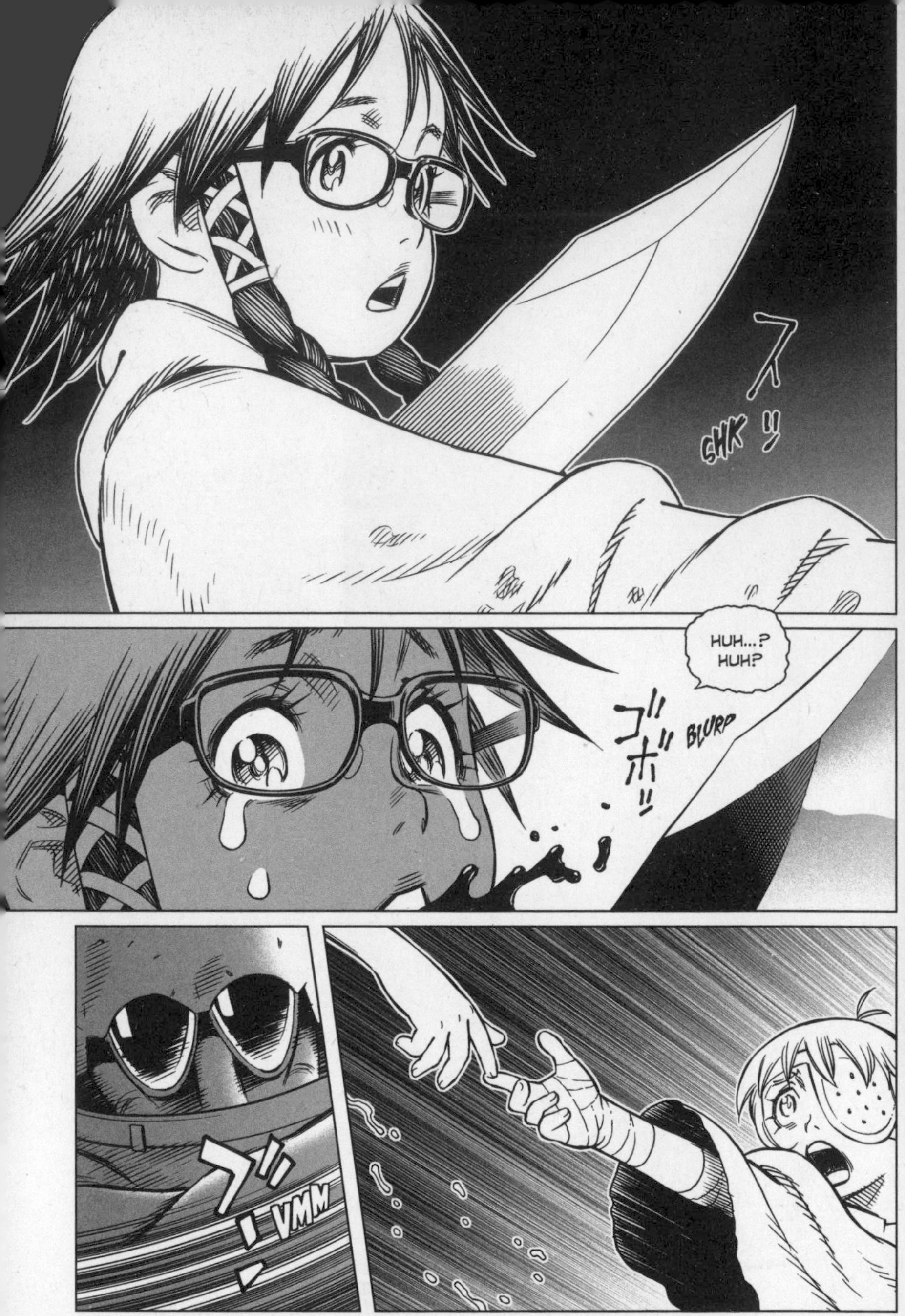
ス
SHK!!
HUH...? HUH?
ゴボ!!
BLURP
ブ!!
VMM

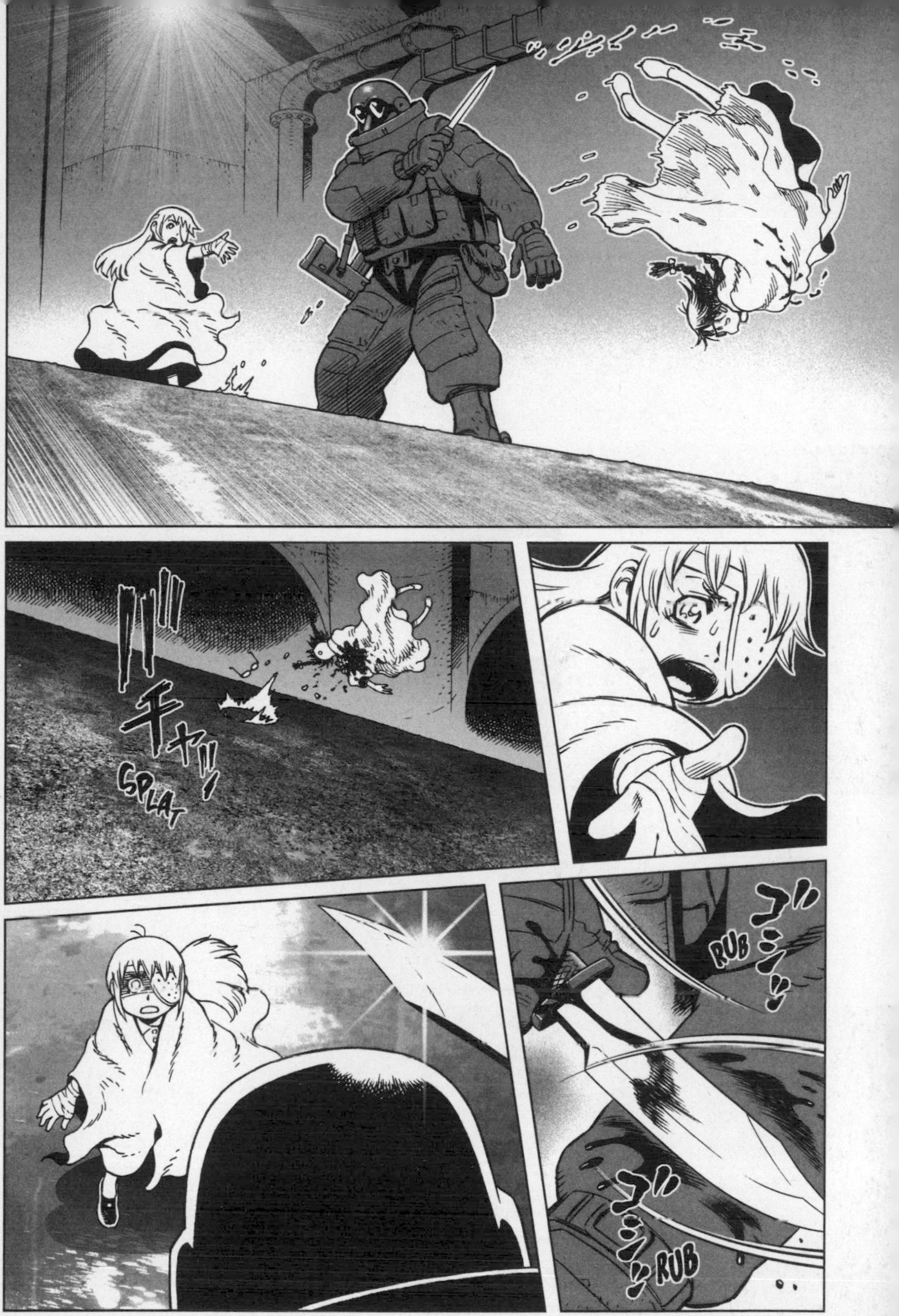
チャ!!
SPLAT
ゴシ!!
RUB
ゴシ!!
RUB

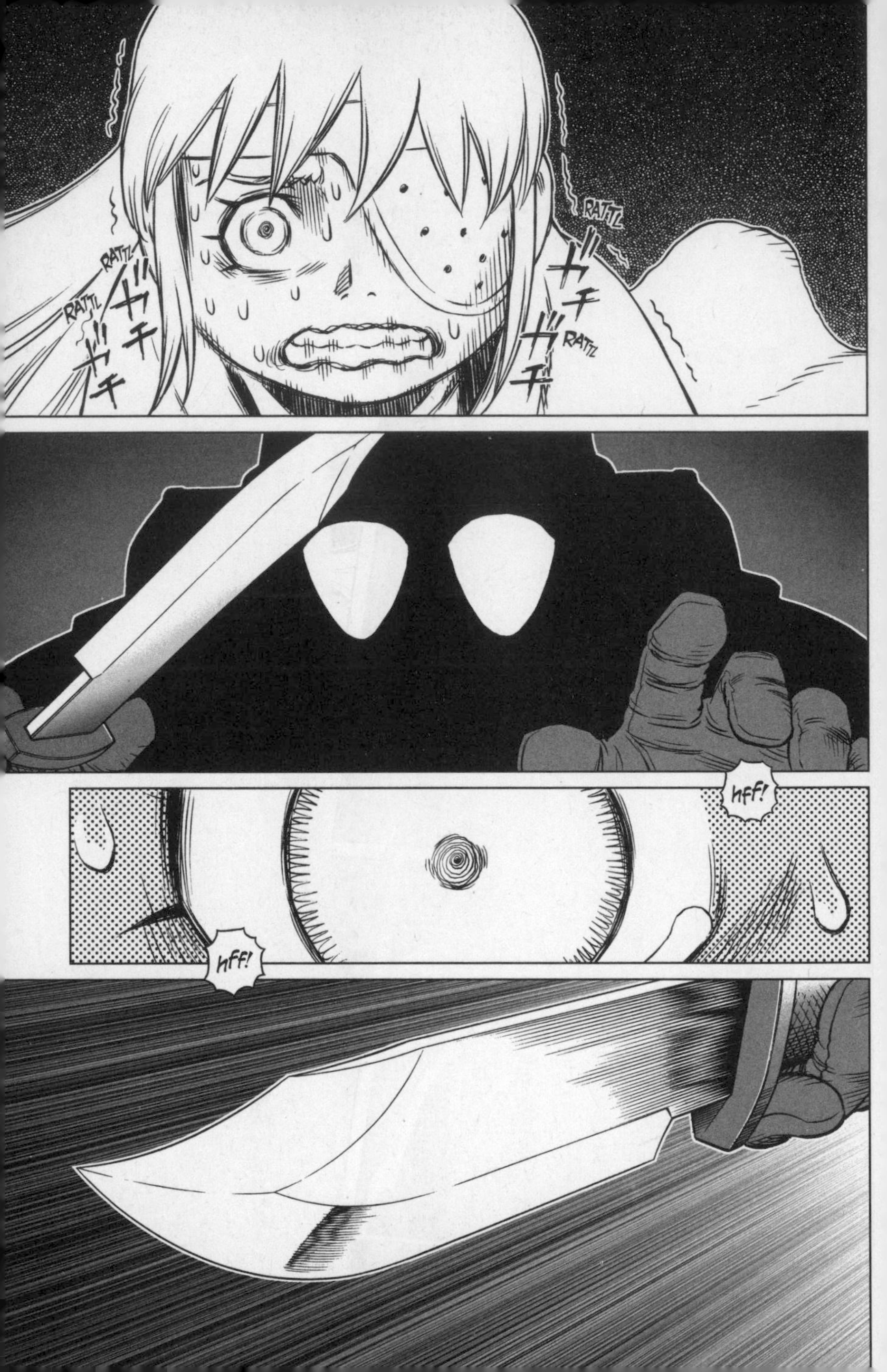
RATTL
ガチガチ
RATTL
RATTL
RATTL
ガチガチ
hff!
hff!

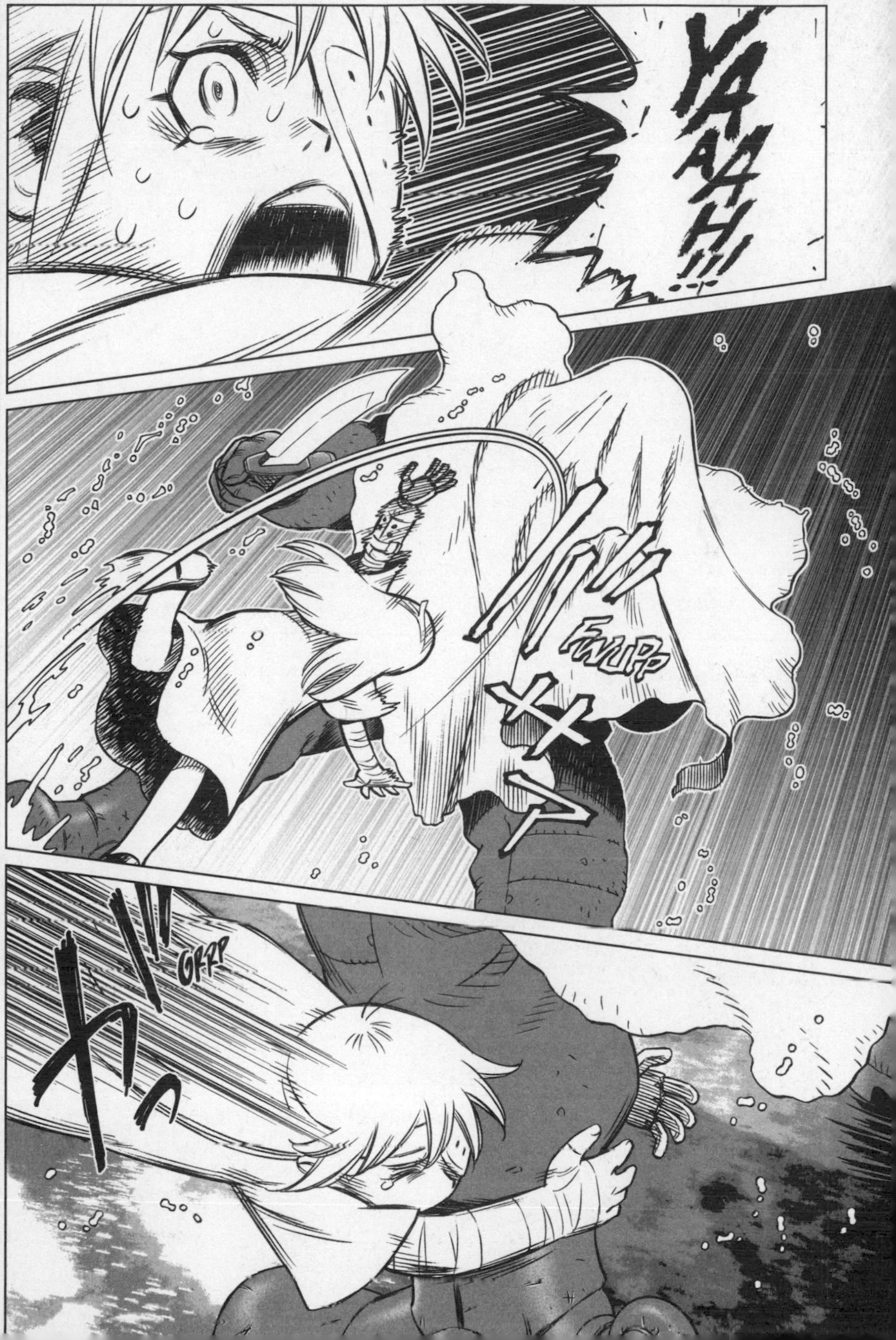
YAAAH!!!
FWUPP
GRRP

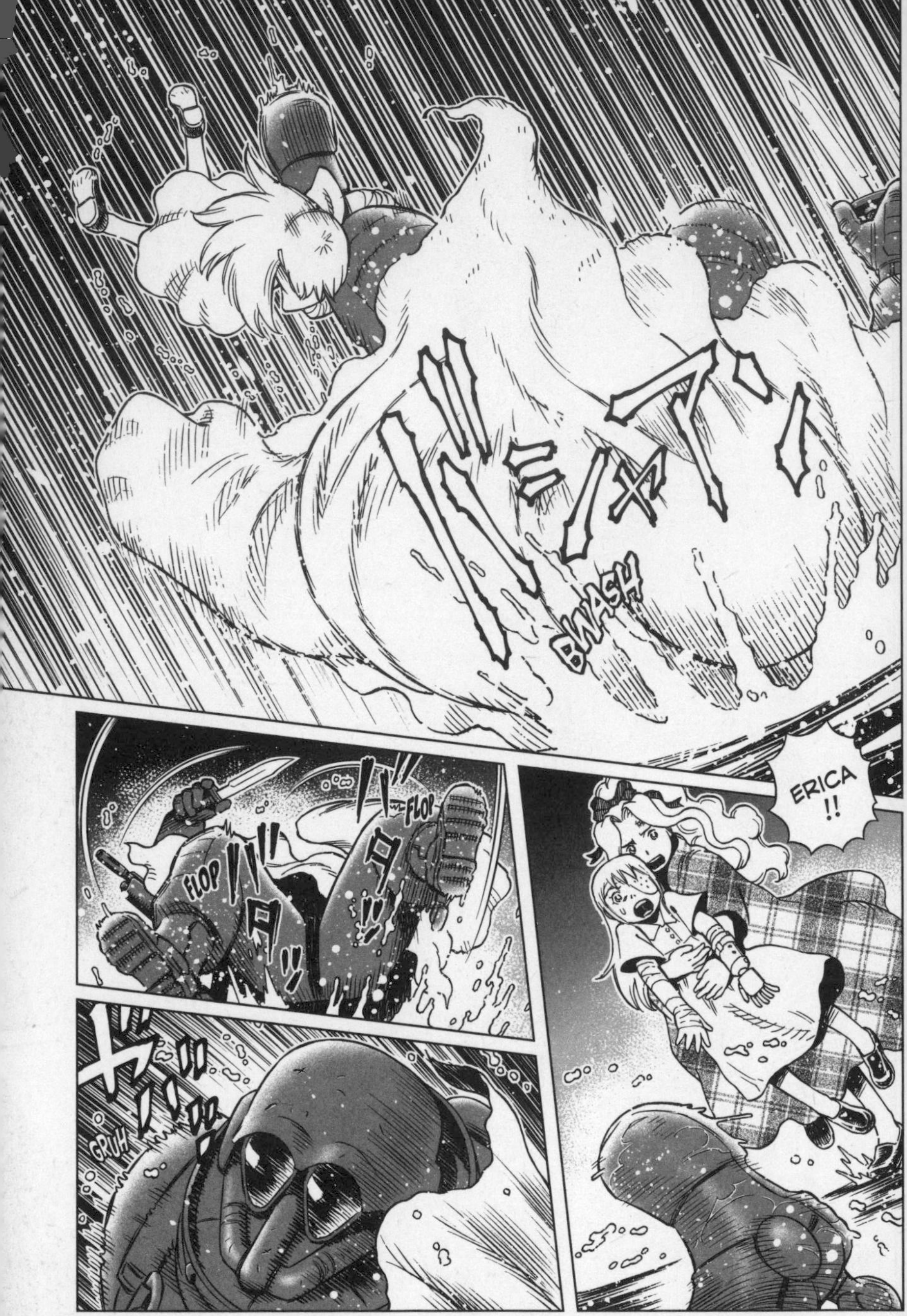
BWASH
ERICA !!
FLOP
FLOP
GRUH

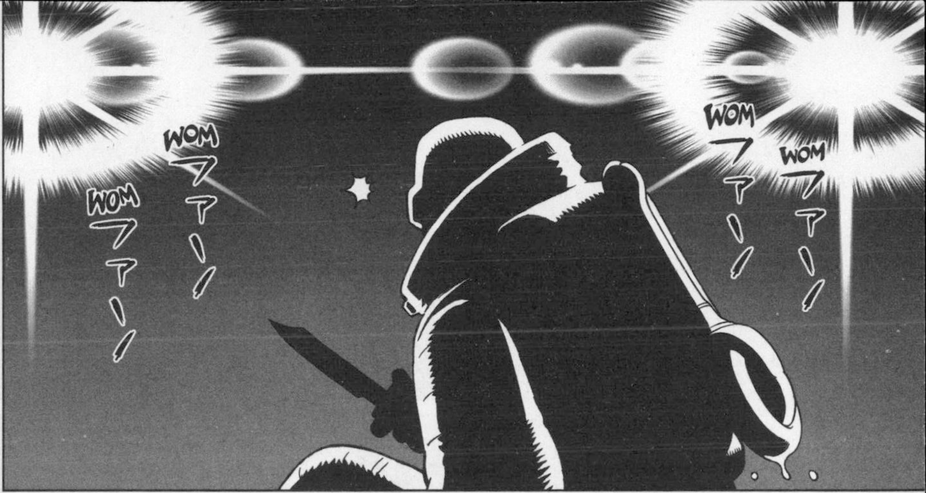
WOM
ファーン
WOM
ファーン
WOM
ファーン
WOM
ファーン
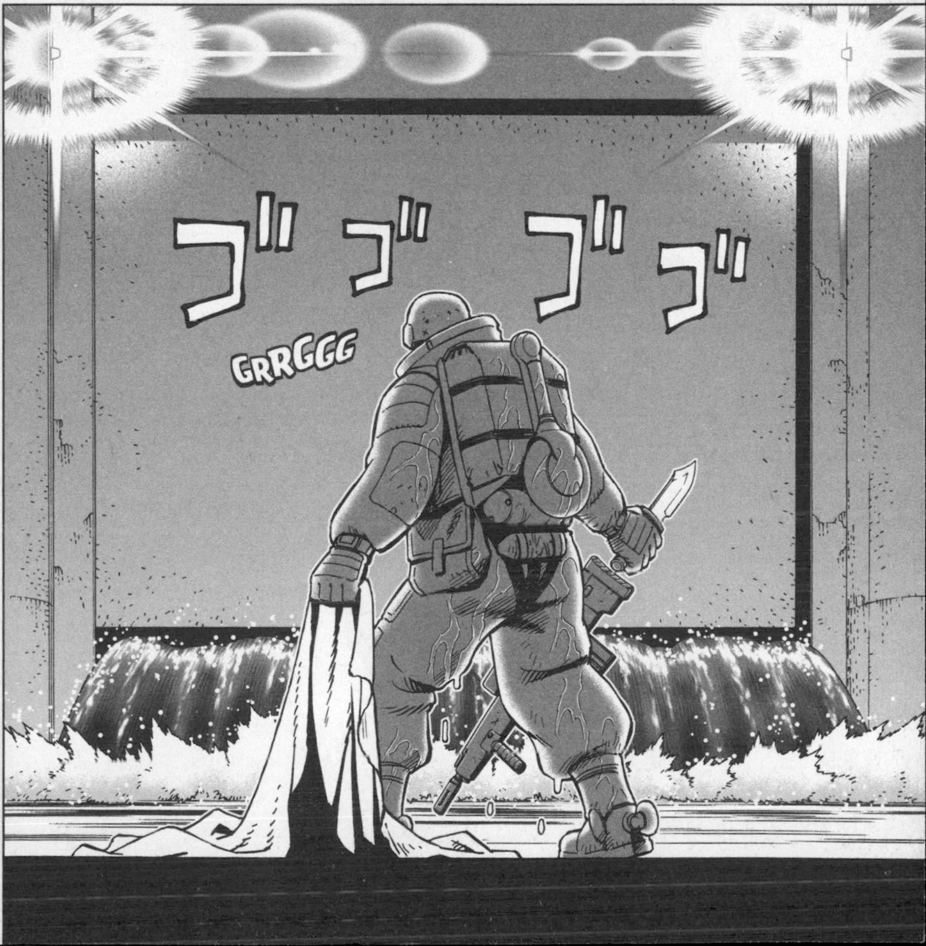
ゴゴゴゴ
GRRGGG

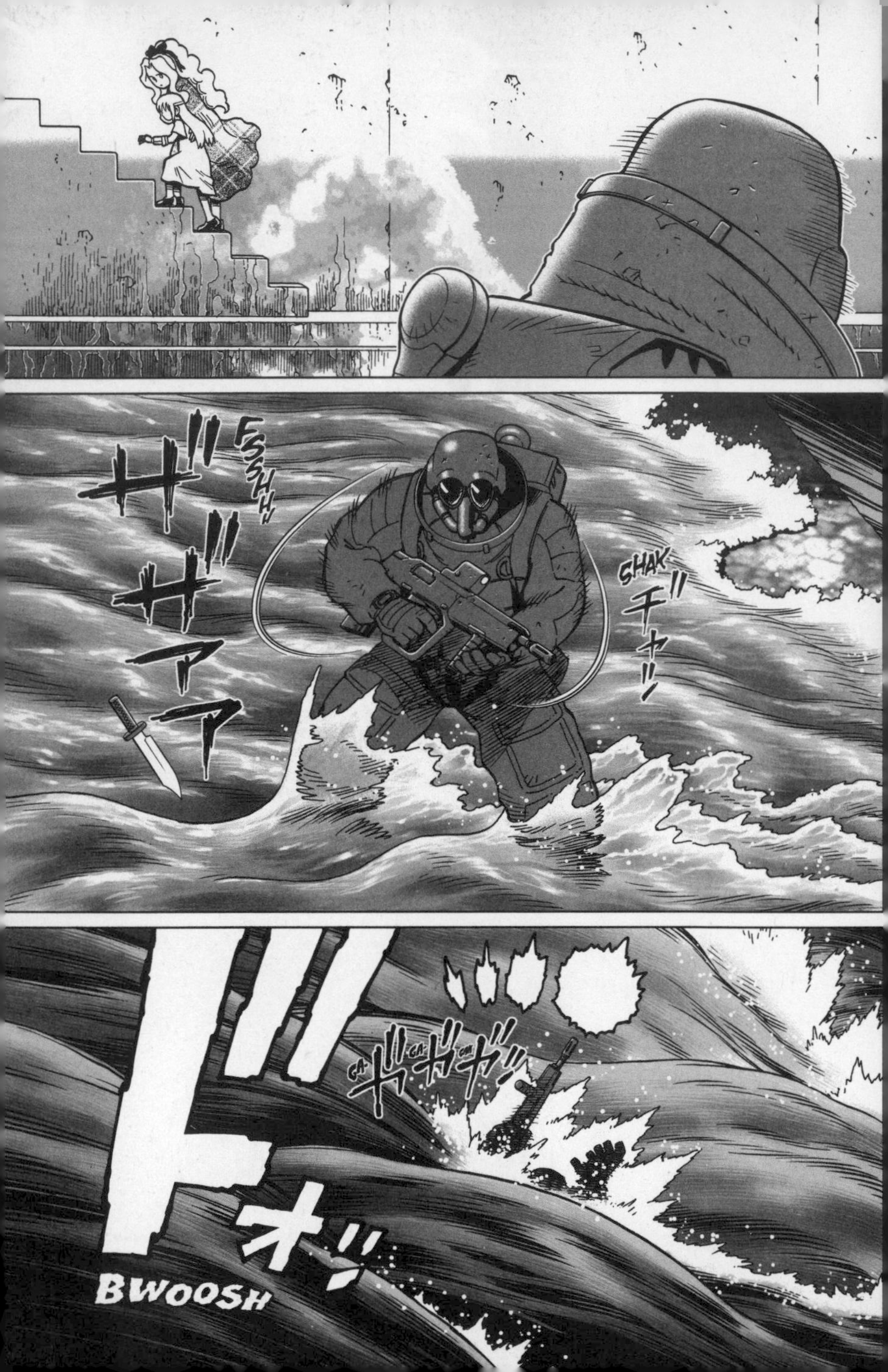
SHAK
チャ!!
FSSHH
ザザザァァ
GA- GA- GA
ガガガ!!
ドォッ
BWOOSH

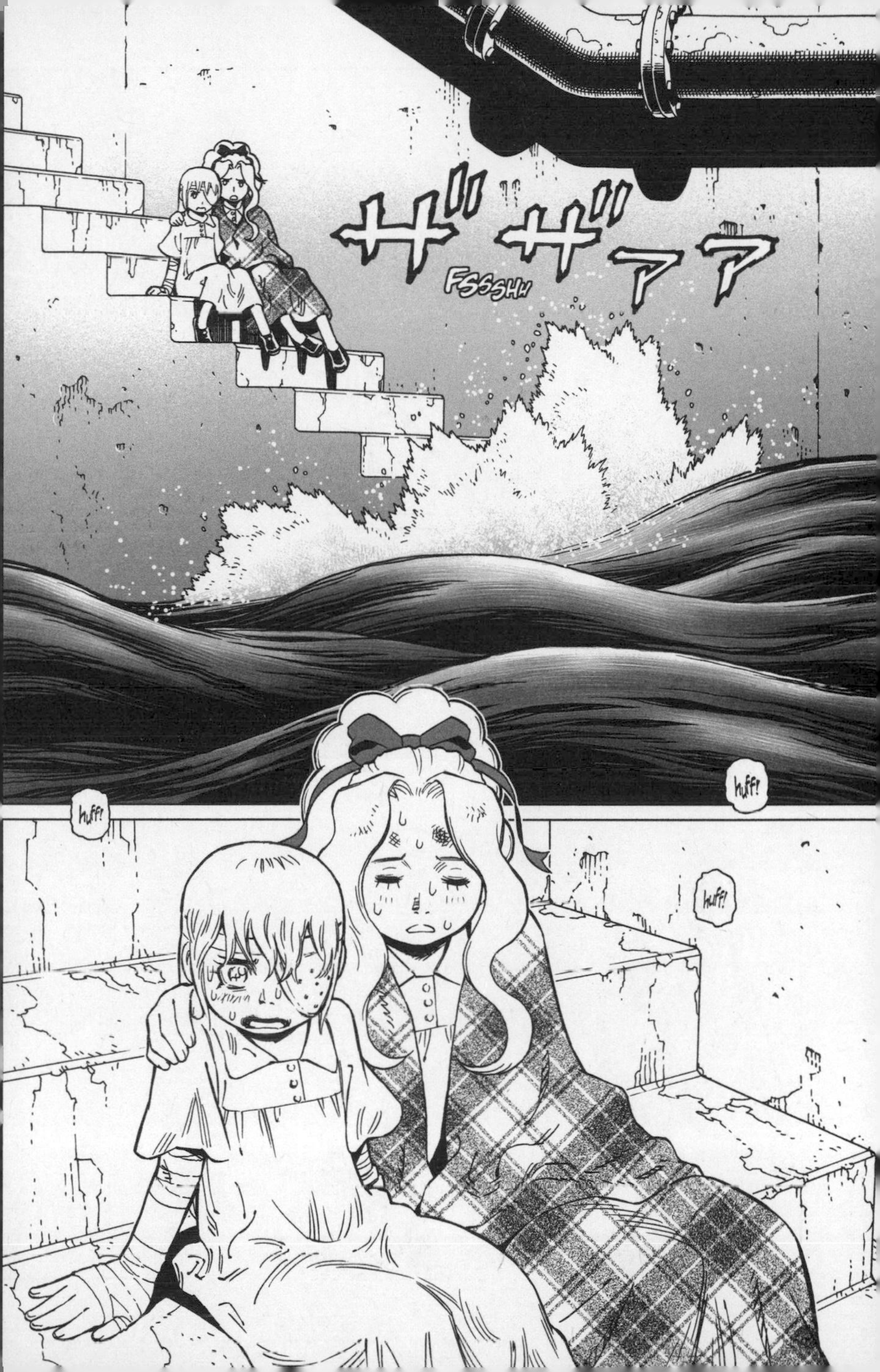
ザザァア
FSSSHH
huff!
huff!
huff!

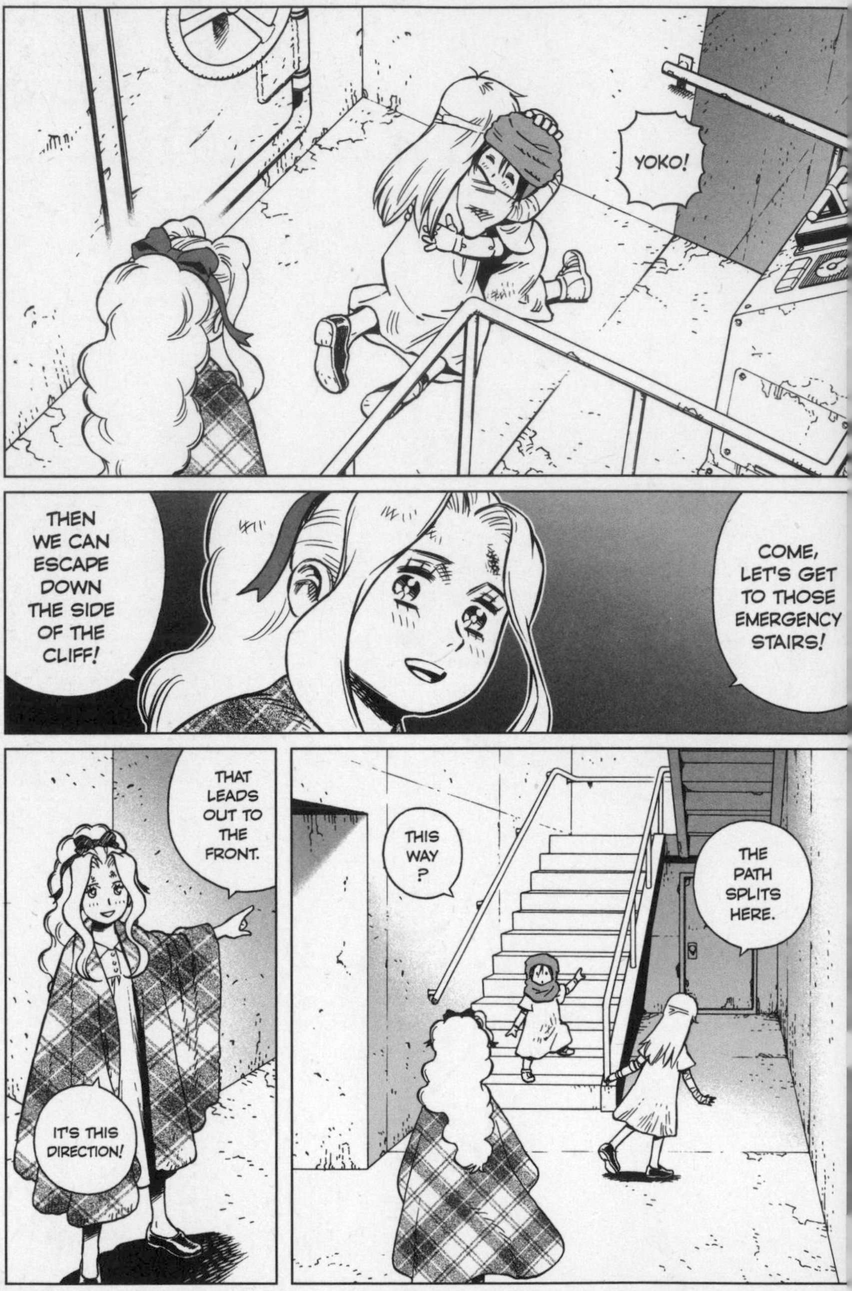
YOKO!
COME, LET'S GET TO THOSE EMERGENCY STAIRS!
THEN WE CAN ESCAPE DOWN THE SIDE OF THE CLIFF!
THE PATH SPLITS HERE.
THIS WAY ?
THAT LEADS OUT TO THE FRONT.
IT'S THIS DIRECTION!

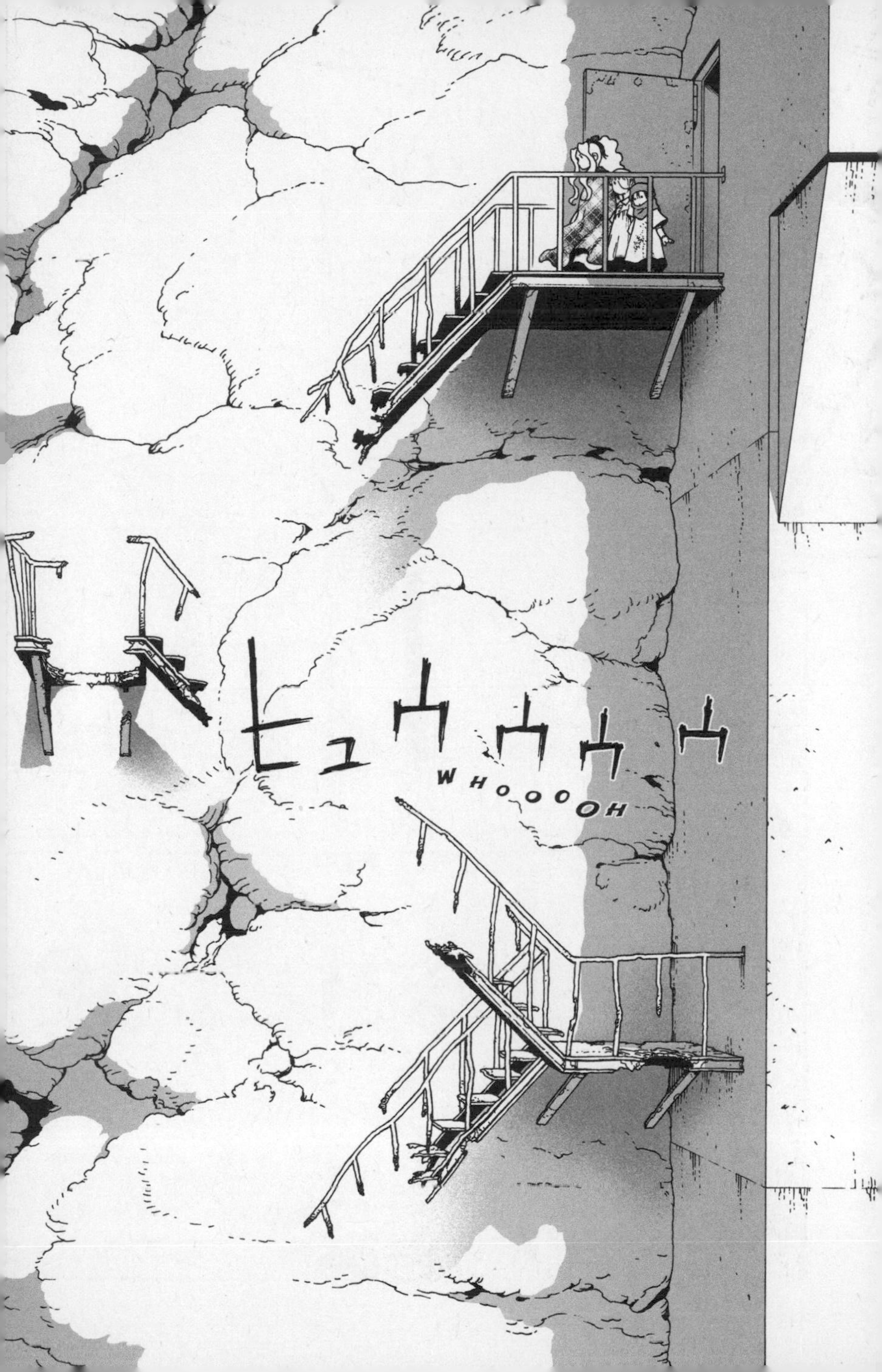
ヒュウウウウ
WHOOOOOH

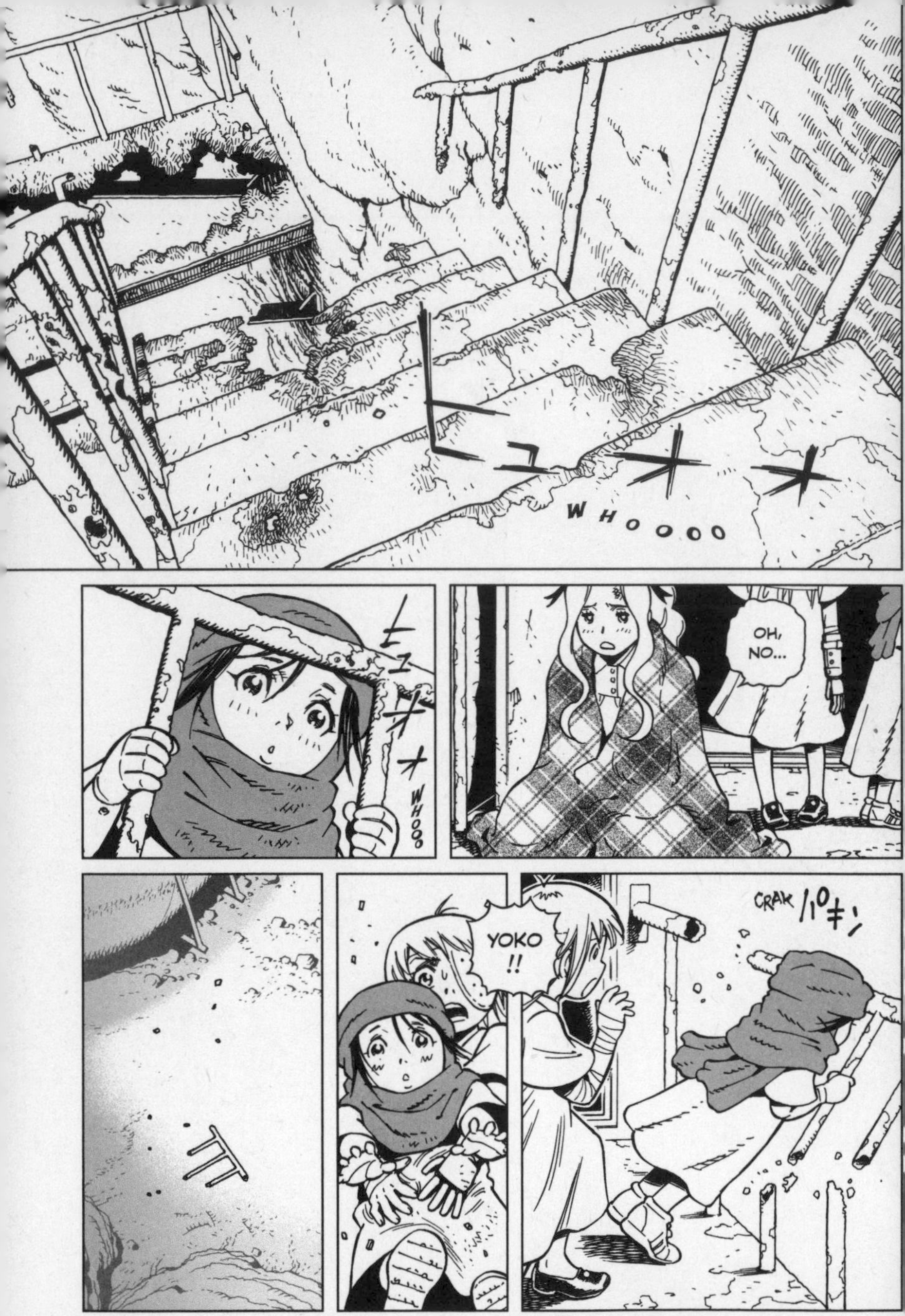
ヒュオオオ
WHOOOOO
OH, NO...
ヒュオオ
WHOOO
CRAK
パキン
YOKO !!

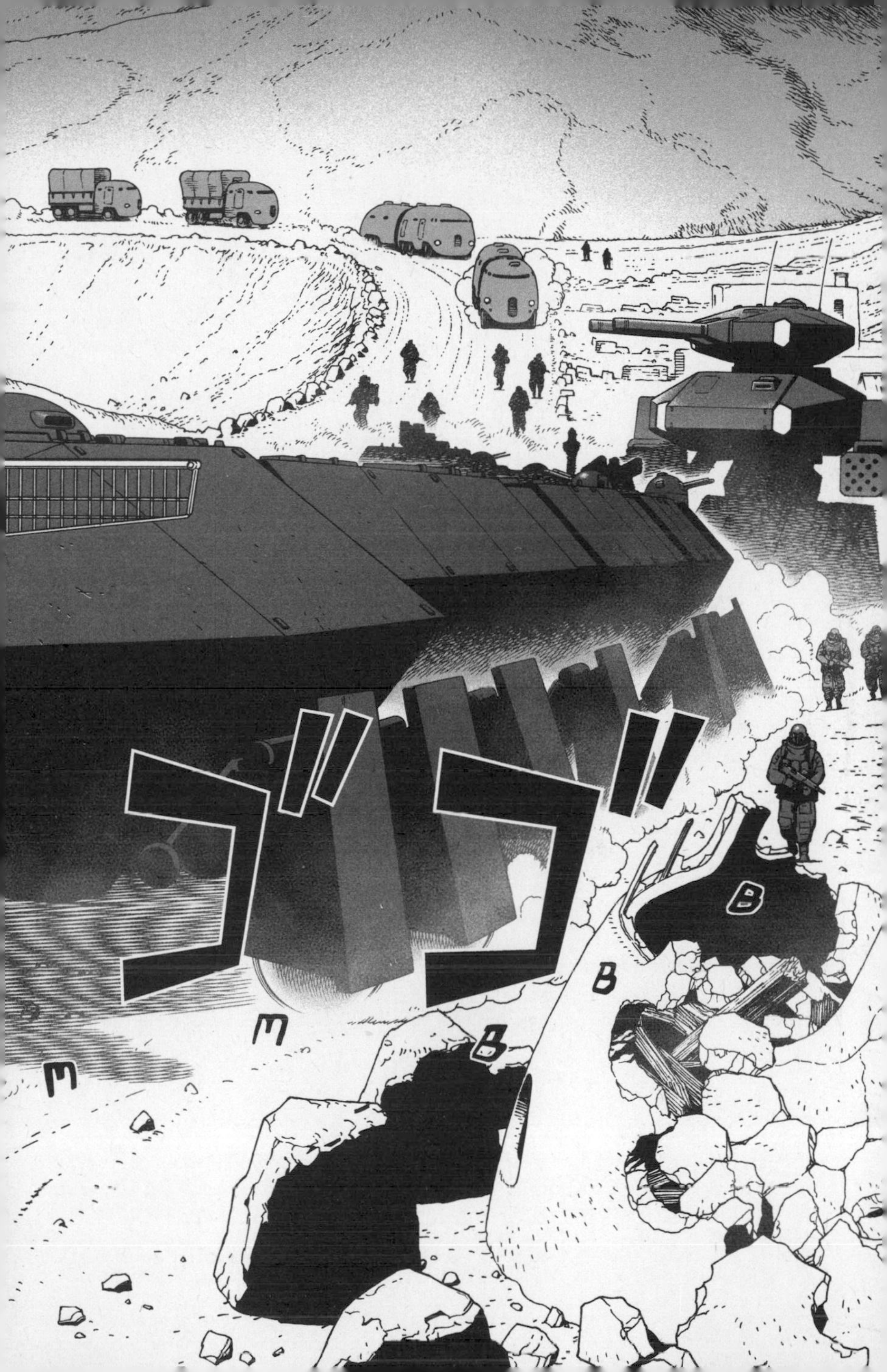
ゴゴ

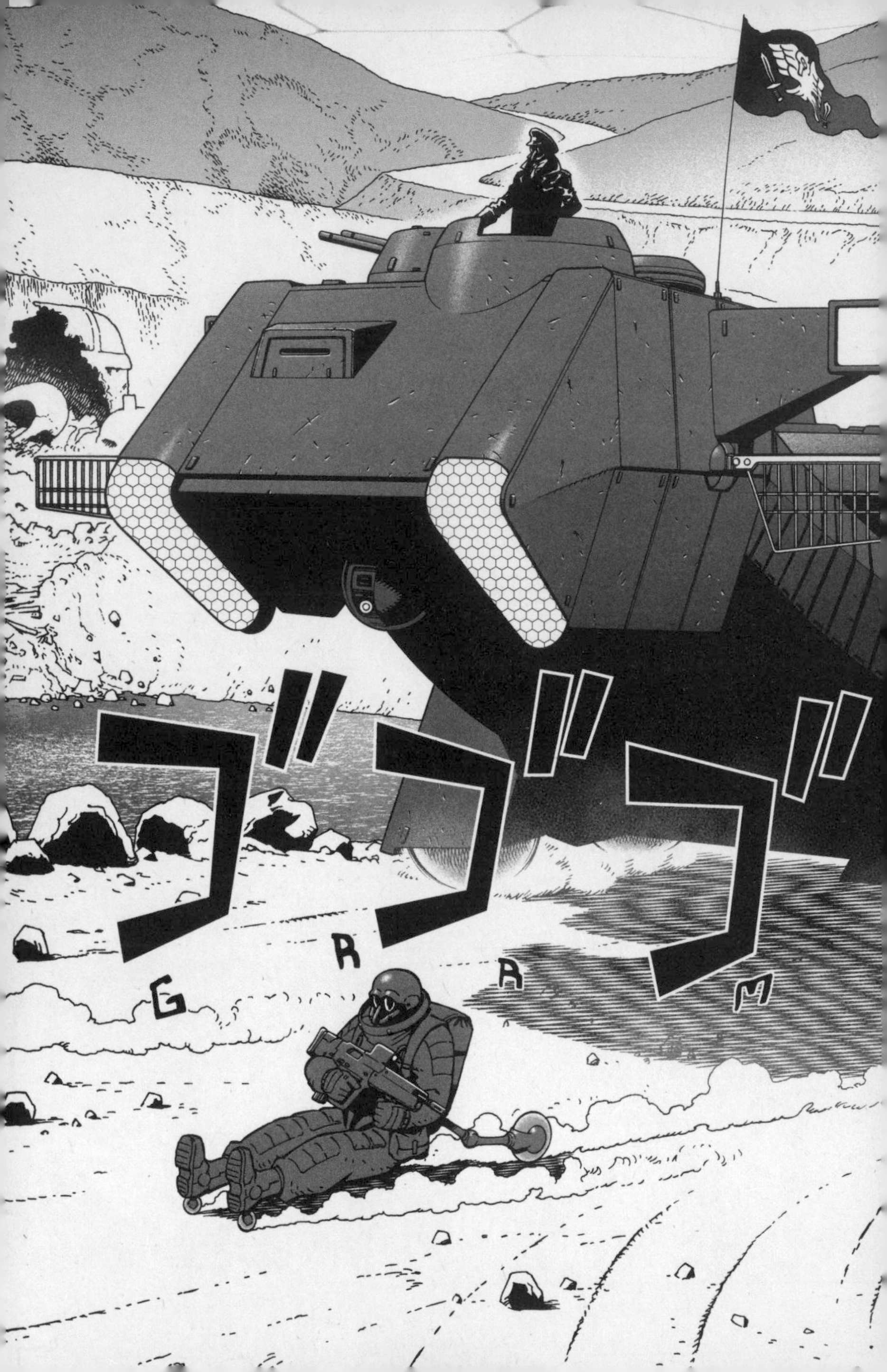
ゴゴゴ
G R A M

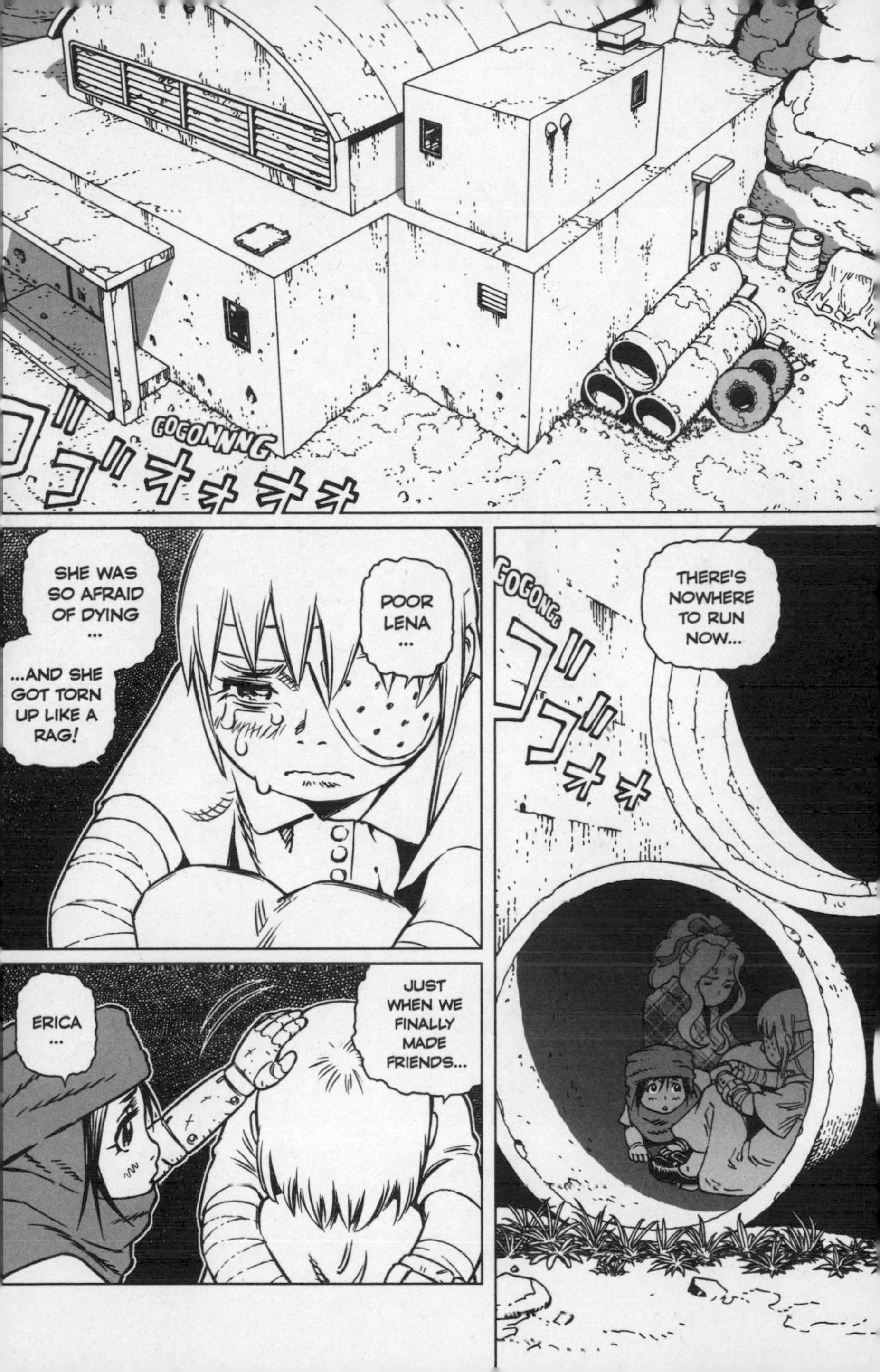
GOGONNNG
GOGONGG
THERE'S NOWHERE TO RUN NOW...
POOR LENA ...
SHE WAS SO AFRAID OF DYING ...
...AND SHE GOT TORN UP LIKE A RAG!
JUST WHEN WE FINALLY MADE FRIENDS...
ERICA ...

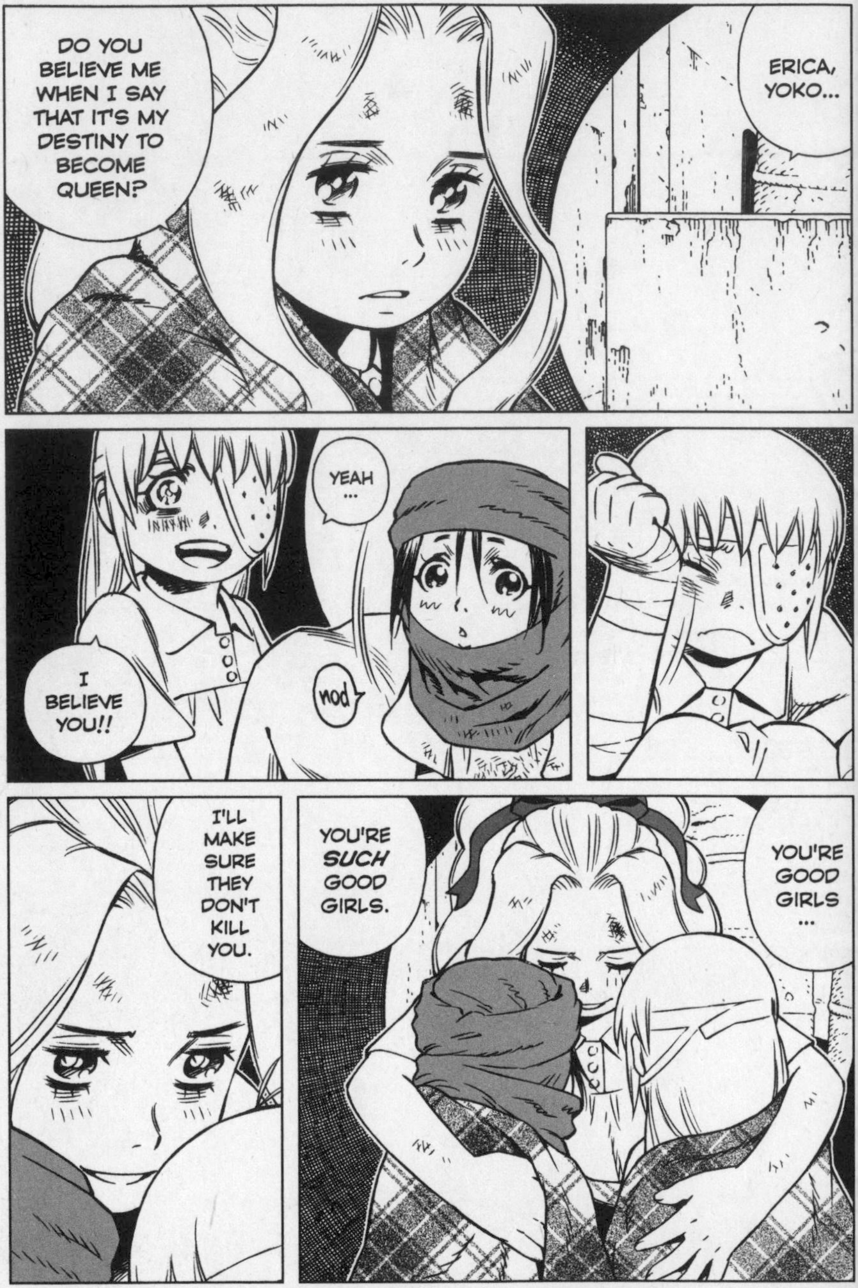
ERICA, YOKO...
DO YOU BELIEVE ME WHEN I SAY THAT IT'S MY DESTINY TO BECOME QUEEN?
YEAH ...
nod
I BELIEVE YOU!!
YOU'RE GOOD GIRLS ...
YOU'RE *SUCH* GOOD GIRLS.
I'LL MAKE SURE THEY DON'T KILL YOU.

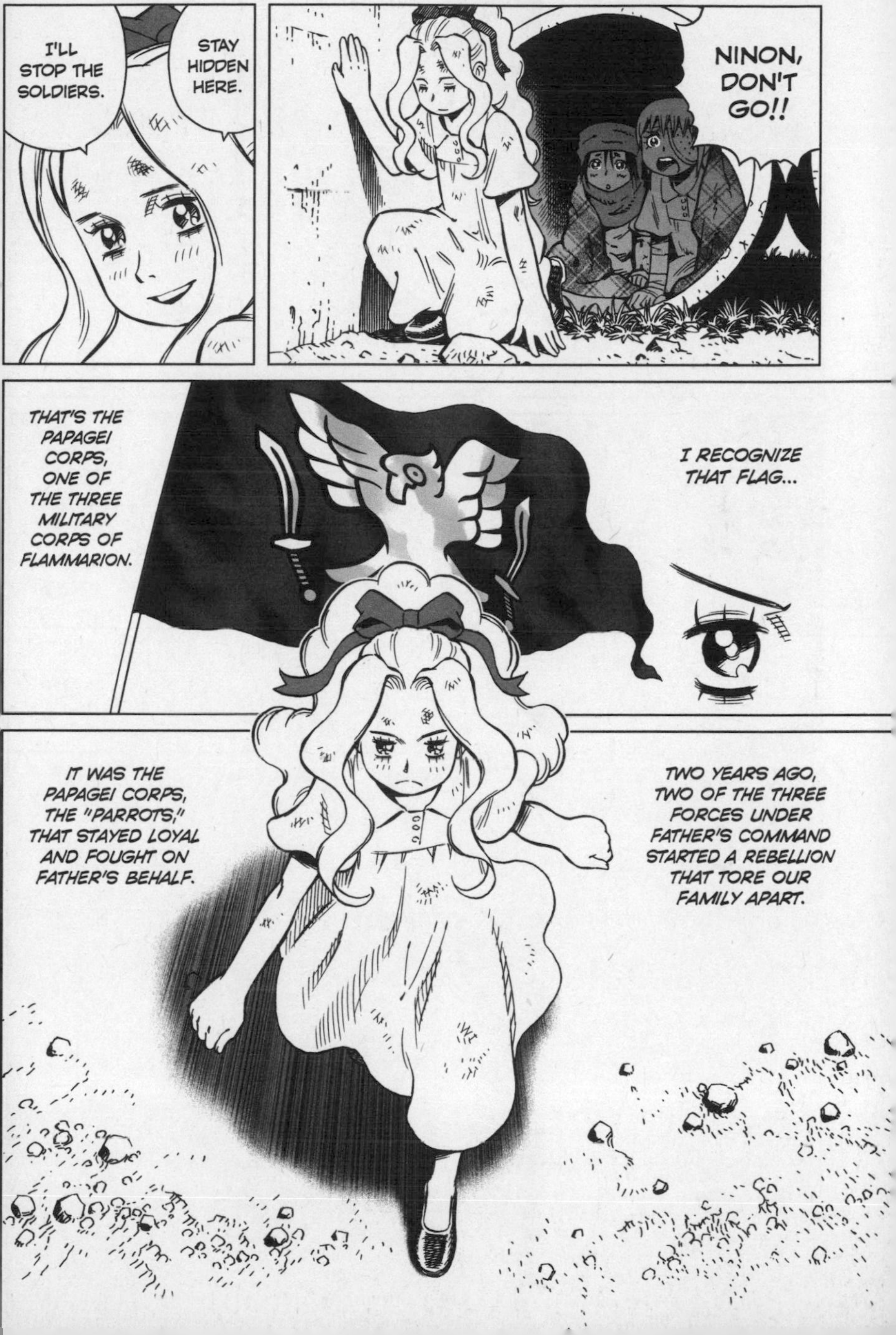
NINON, DON'T GO!!
STAY HIDDEN HERE.
I'LL STOP THE SOLDIERS.
I RECOGNIZE THAT FLAG...
THAT'S THE PAPAGEI CORPS, ONE OF THE THREE MILITARY CORPS OF FLAMMARION.
TWO YEARS AGO, TWO OF THE THREE FORCES UNDER FATHER'S COMMAND STARTED A REBELLION THAT TORE OUR FAMILY APART.
IT WAS THE PAPAGEI CORPS, THE "PARROTS," THAT STAYED LOYAL AND FOUGHT ON FATHER'S BEHALF.

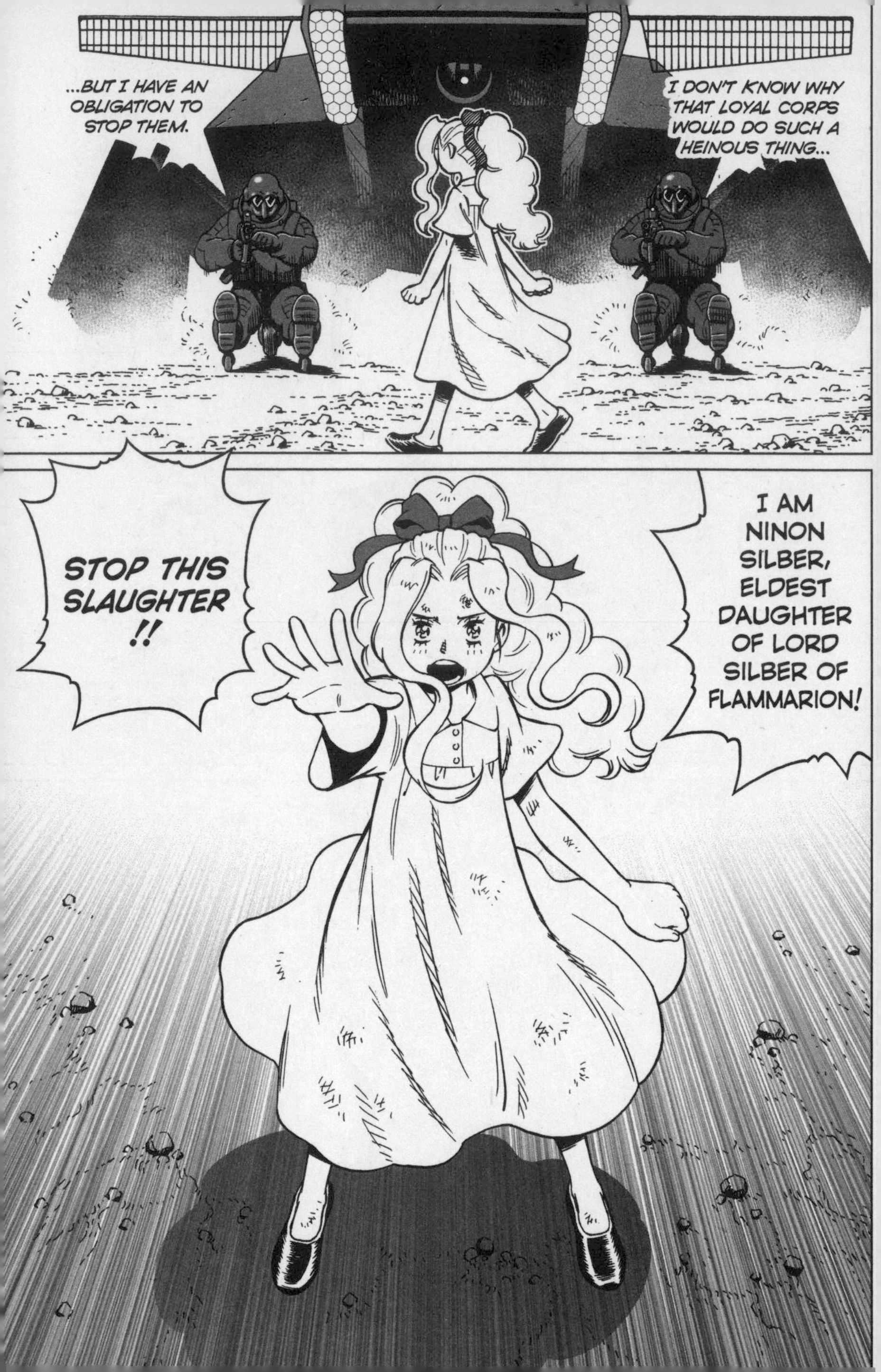
I DON'T KNOW WHY THAT LOYAL CORPS WOULD DO SUCH A HEINOUS THING...
...BUT I HAVE AN OBLIGATION TO STOP THEM.
I AM NINON SILBER, ELDEST DAUGHTER OF LORD SILBER OF FLAMMARION!
STOP THIS SLAUGHTER !!

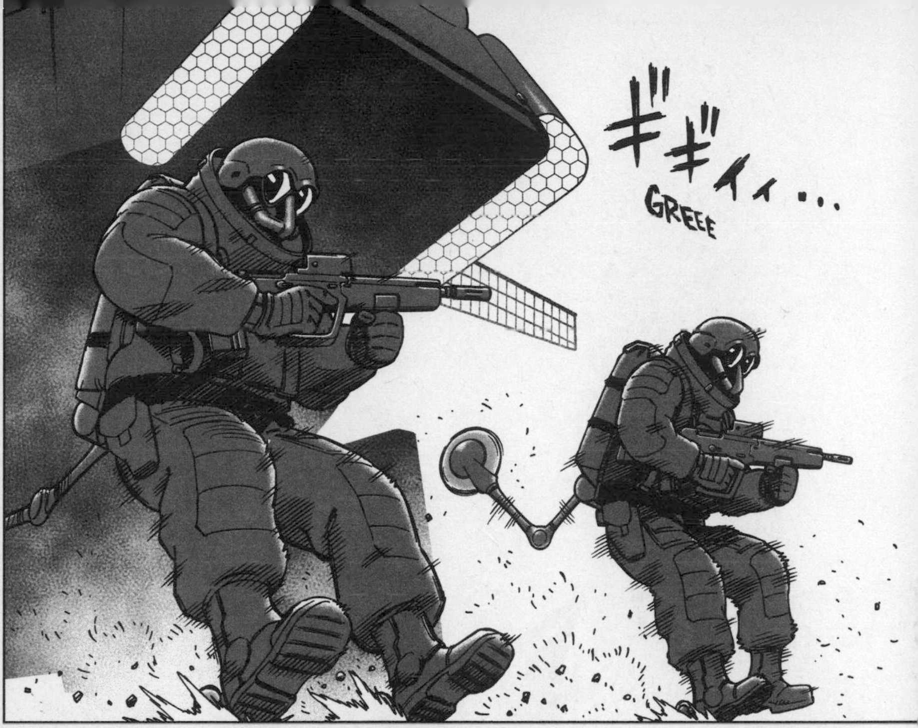
ギギィィ…
GREEE

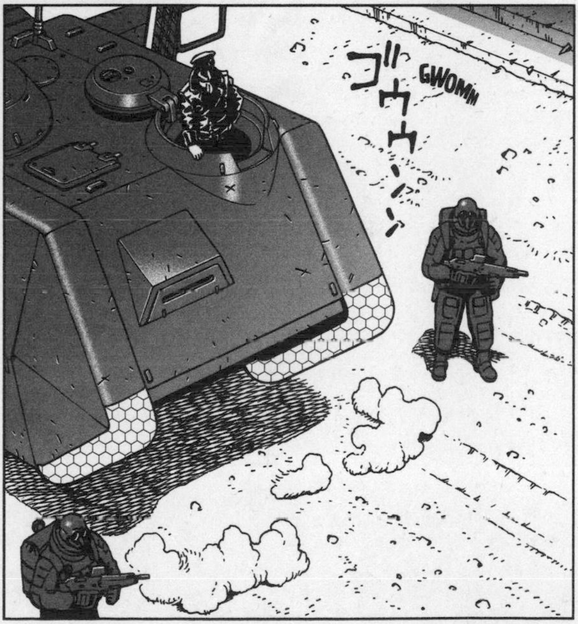
ゴウウーン
GWOMM

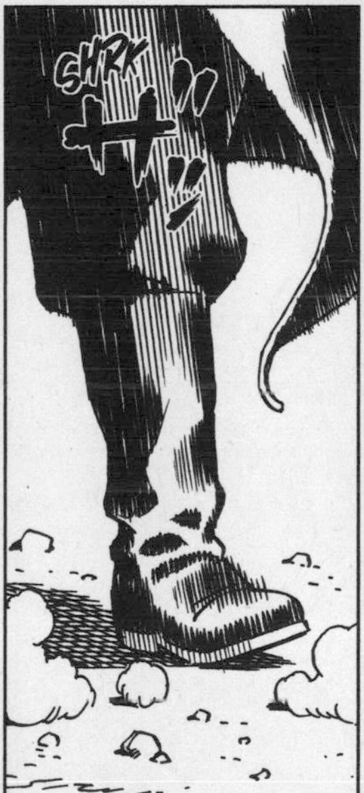
ザッ
SHRK

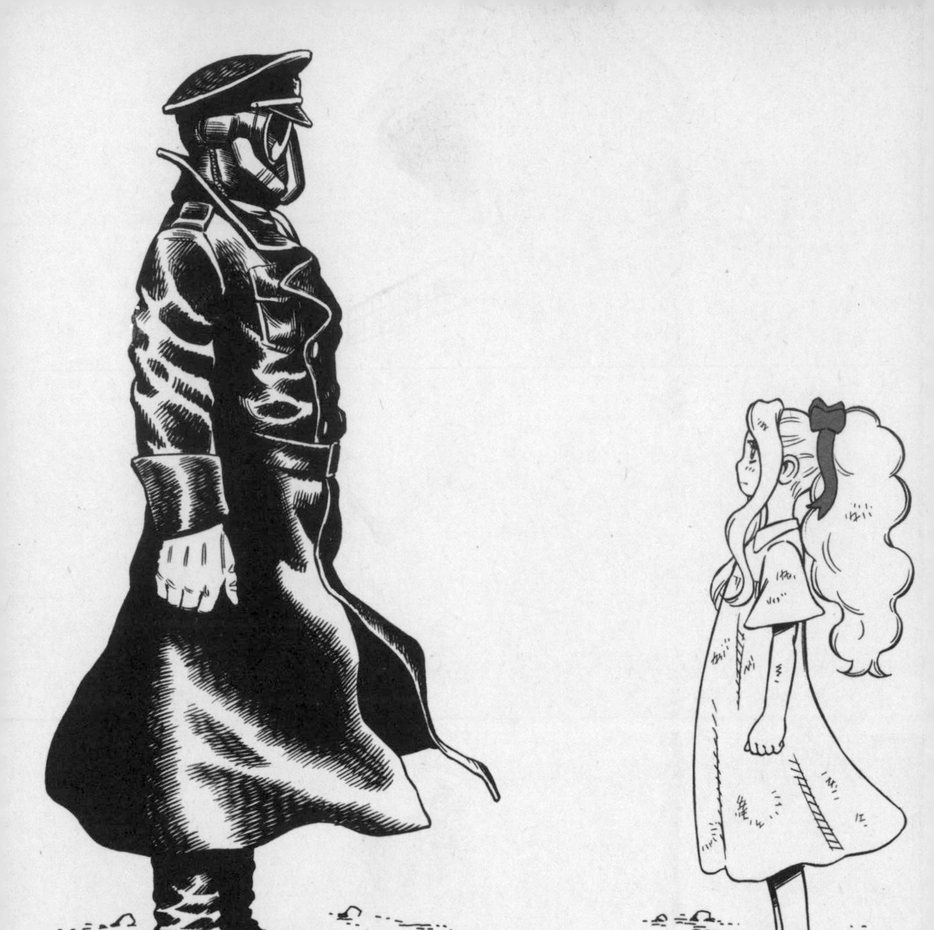

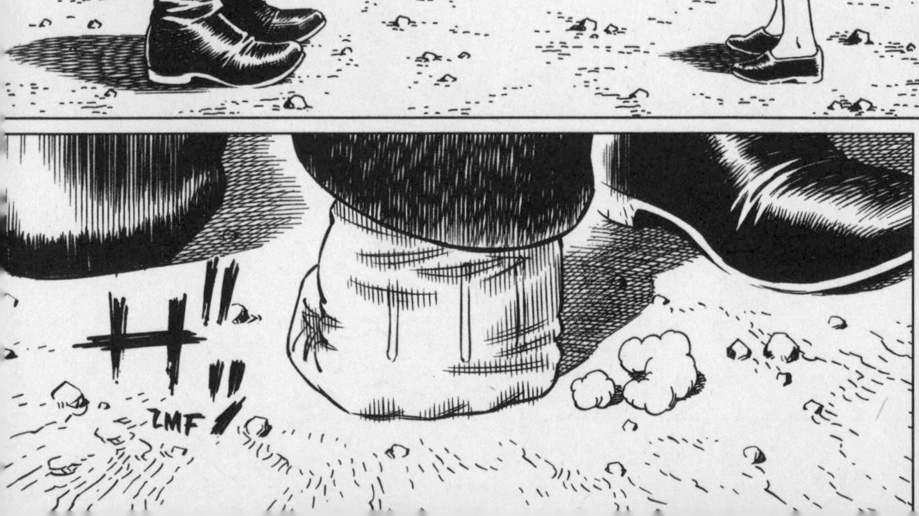
ZMF

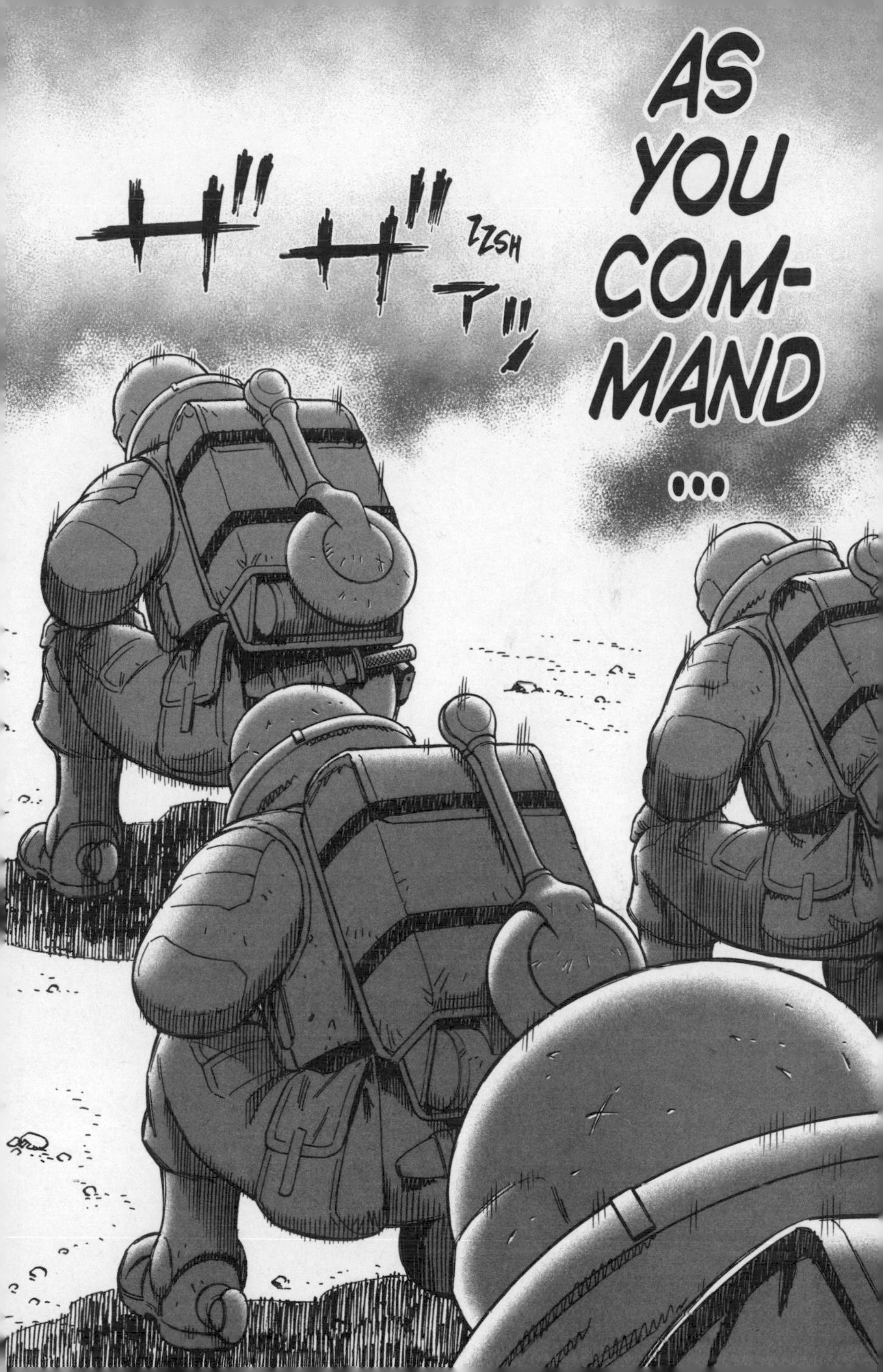
AS YOU COM-MAND...
ZZSH

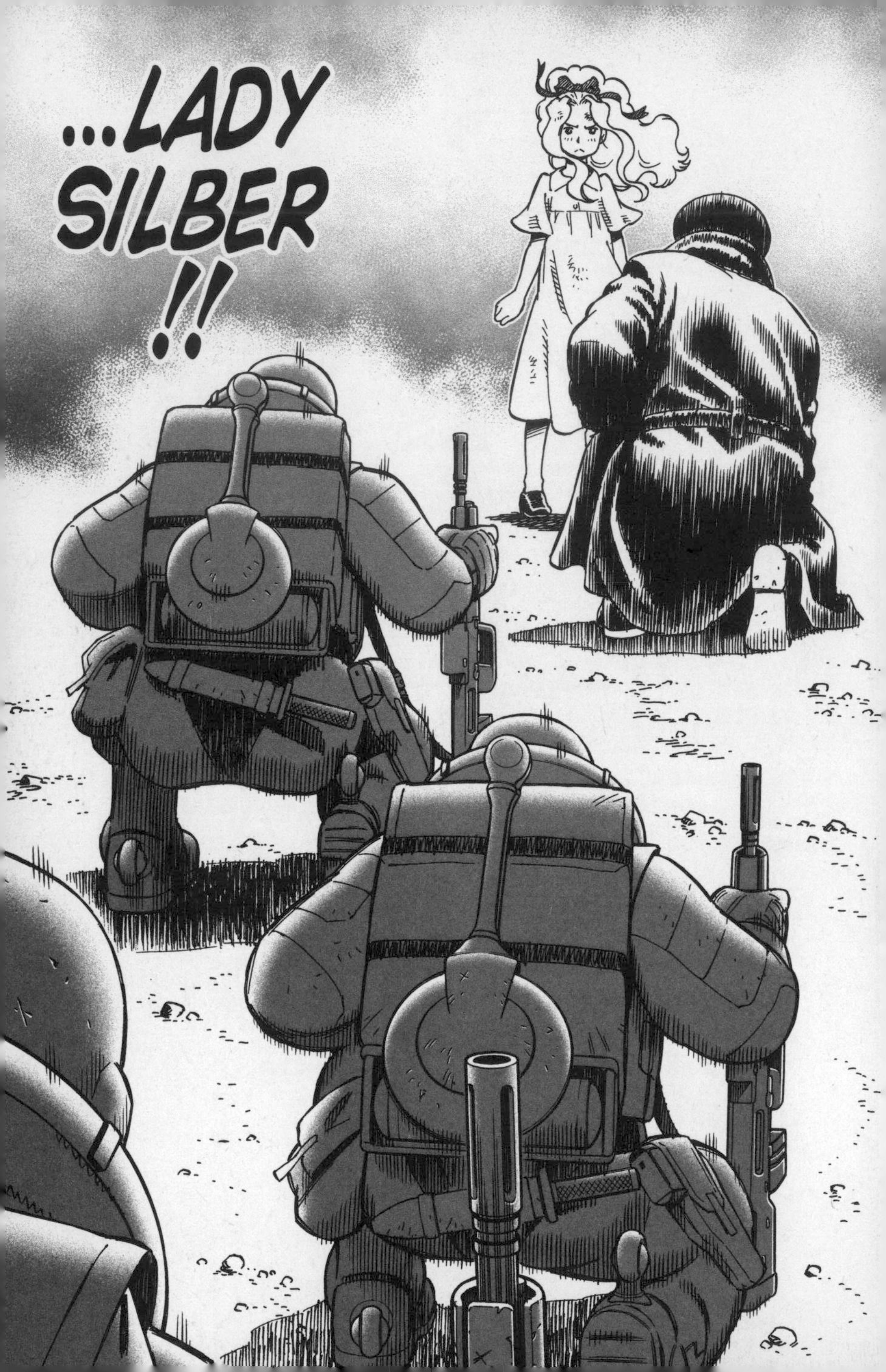
...LADY SILBER!!

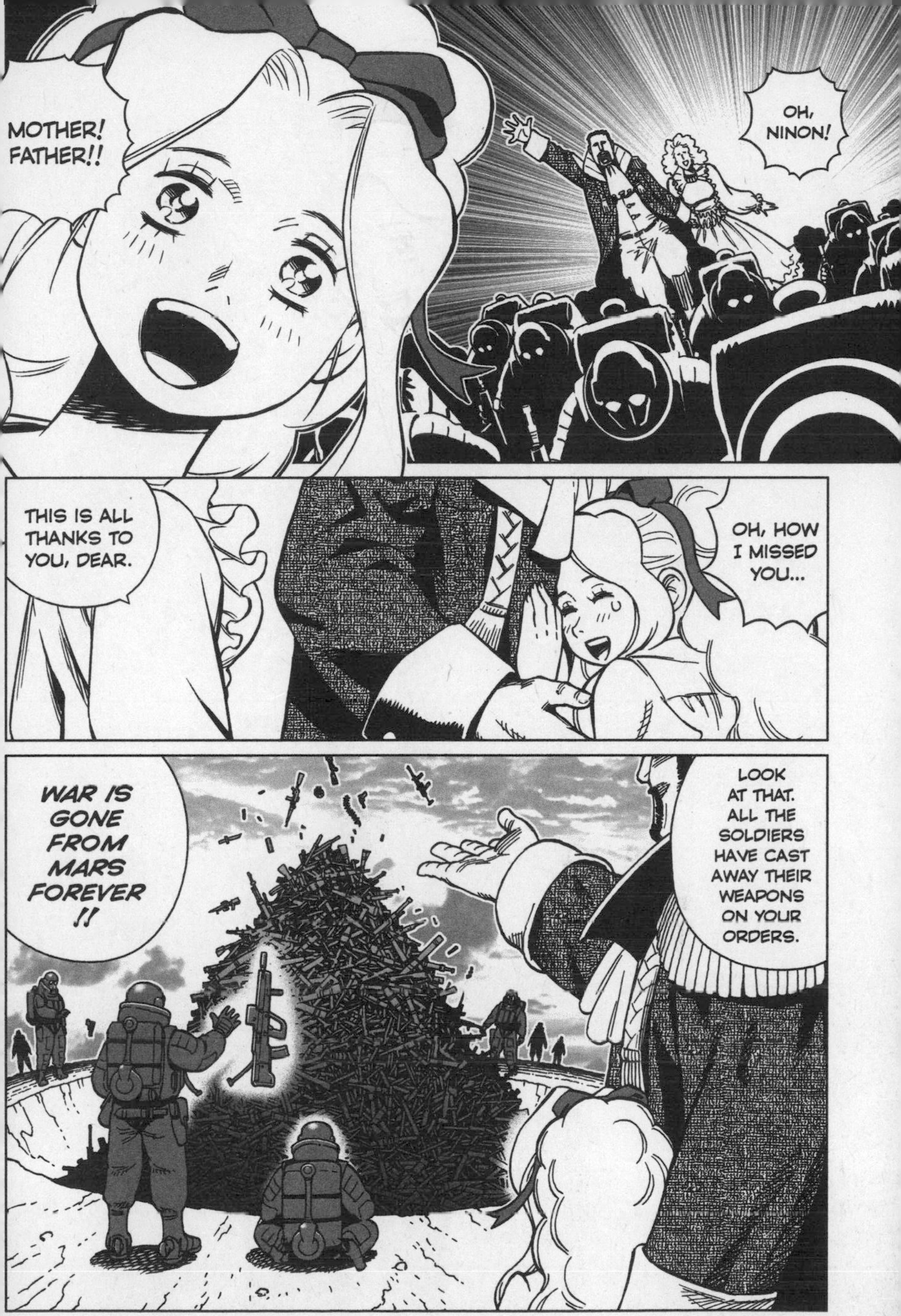

OH, NINON!
MOTHER! FATHER!!
OH, HOW I MISSED YOU...
THIS IS ALL THANKS TO YOU, DEAR.
LOOK AT THAT. ALL THE SOLDIERS HAVE CAST AWAY THEIR WEAPONS ON YOUR ORDERS.
WAR IS GONE FROM MARS FOREVER !!

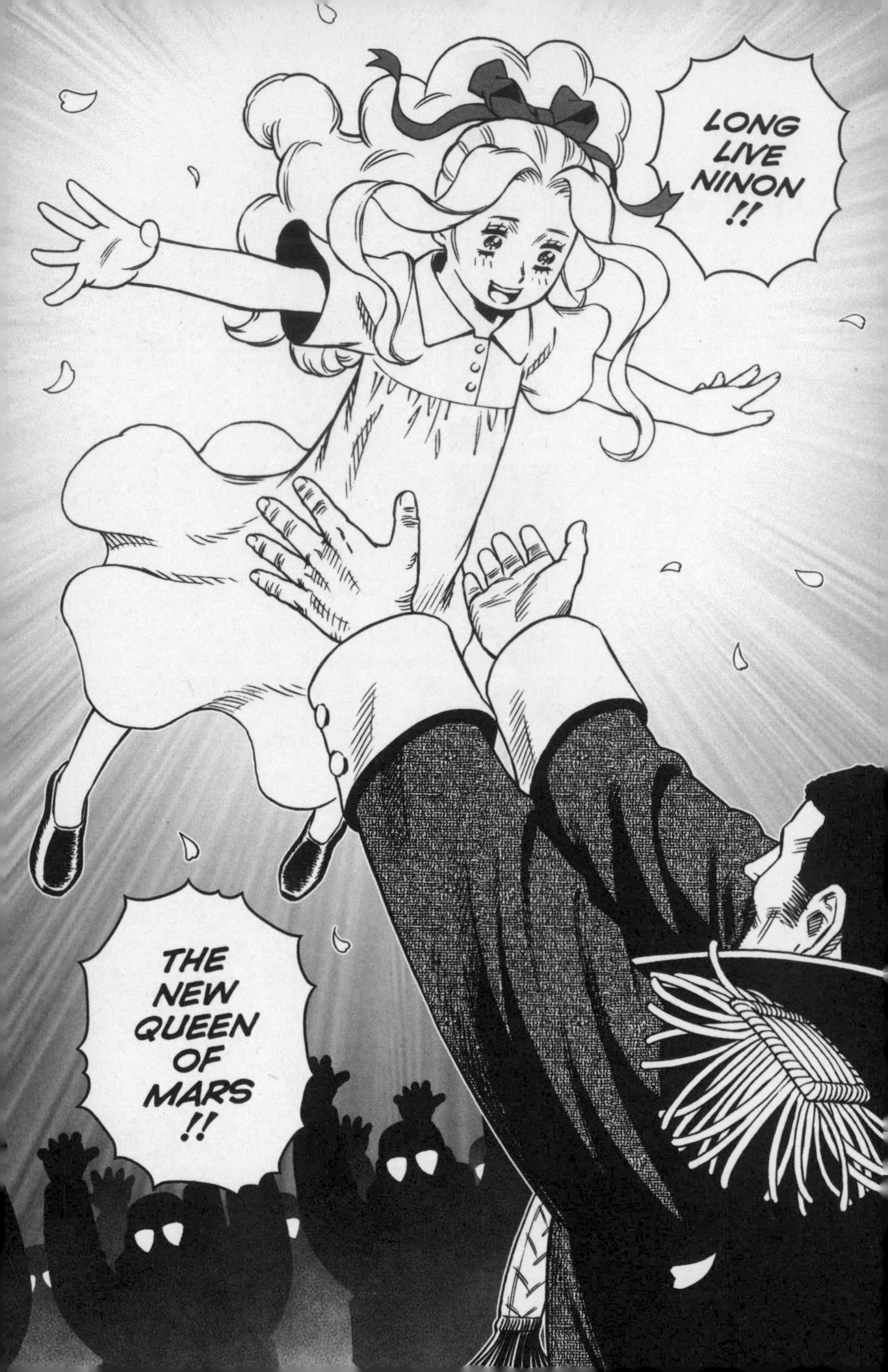
LONG LIVE NINON !!
THE NEW QUEEN OF MARS !!

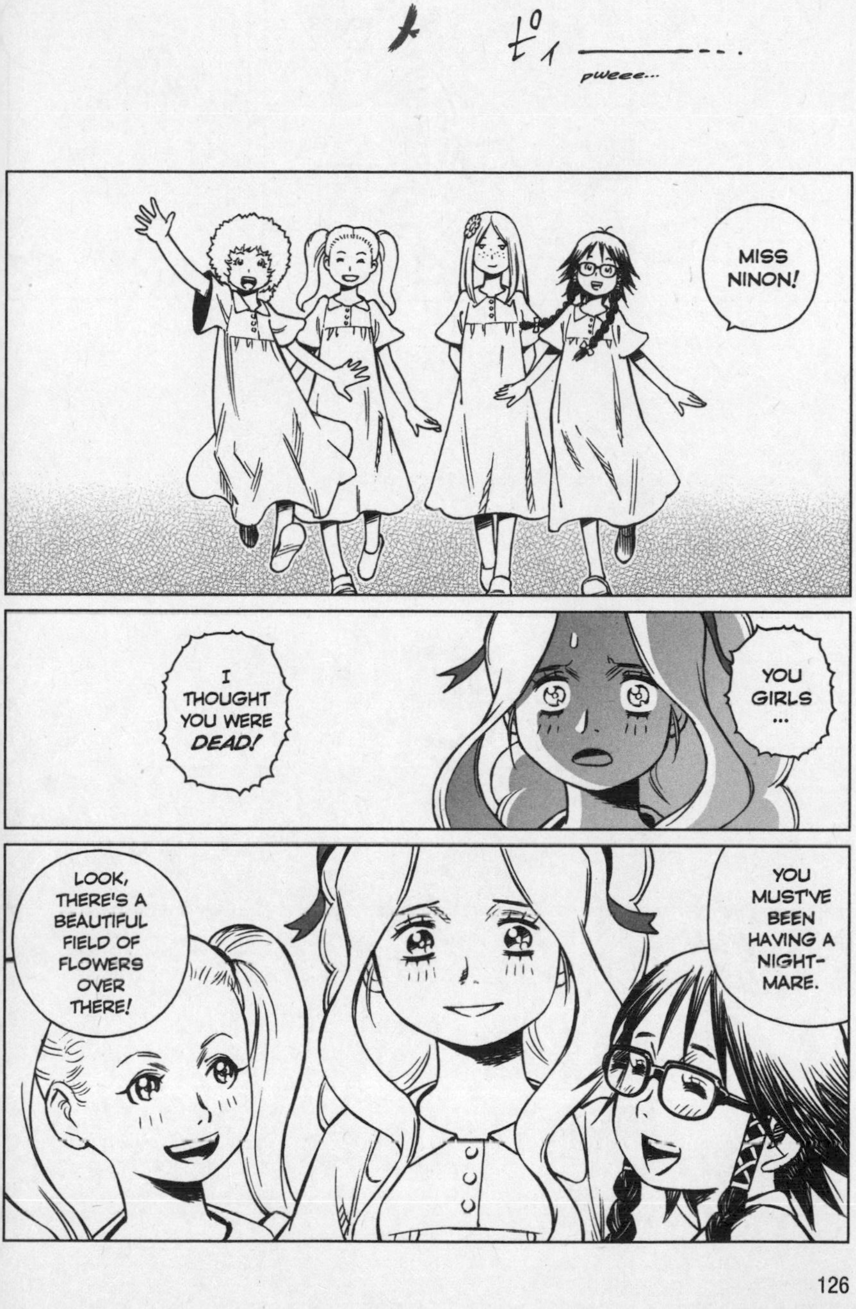
ピィ———…
pweee...
MISS NINON!
YOU GIRLS ...
I THOUGHT YOU WERE DEAD!
YOU MUST'VE BEEN HAVING A NIGHT-MARE.
LOOK, THERE'S A BEAUTIFUL FIELD OF FLOWERS OVER THERE!

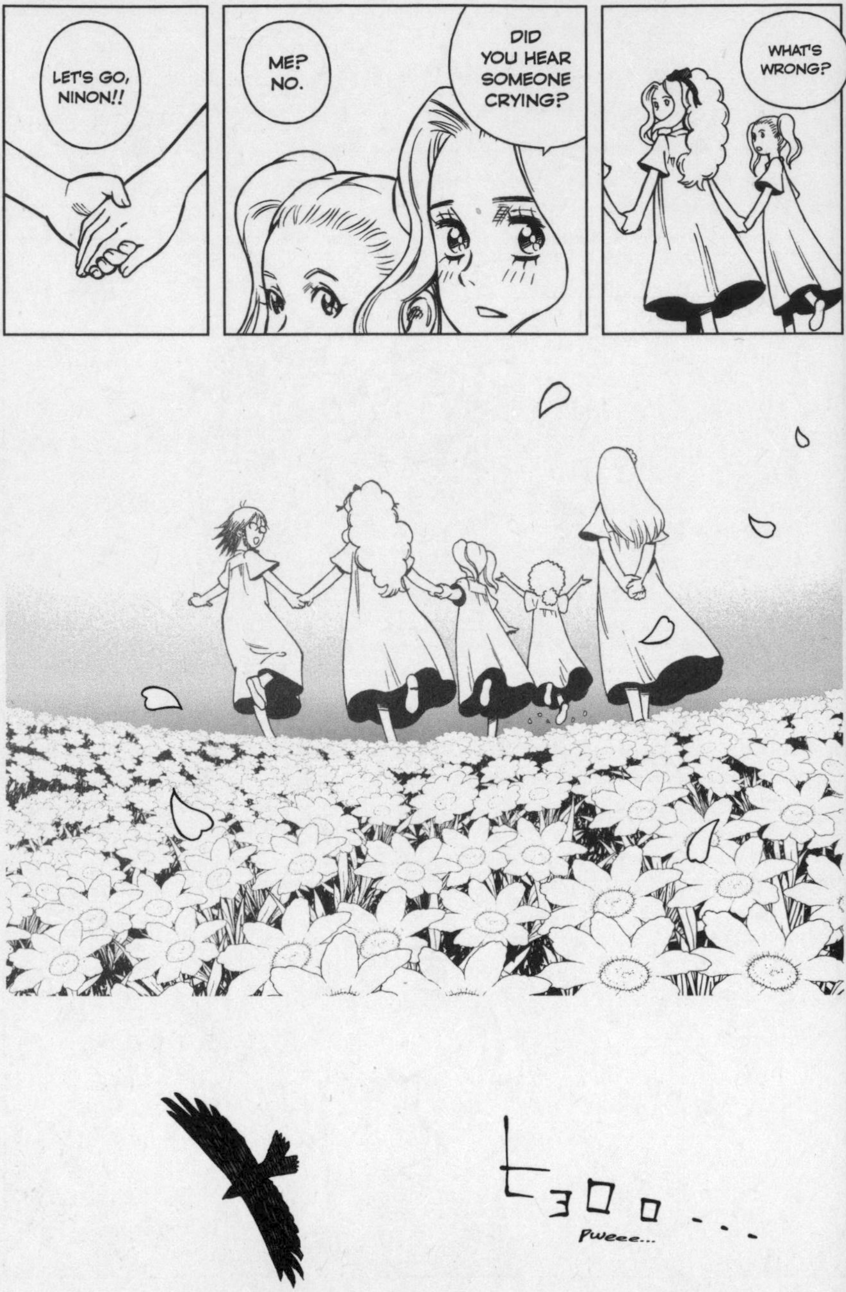
WHAT'S WRONG?
DID YOU HEAR SOMEONE CRYING?
ME? NO.
LET'S GO, NINON!!
Pweee...

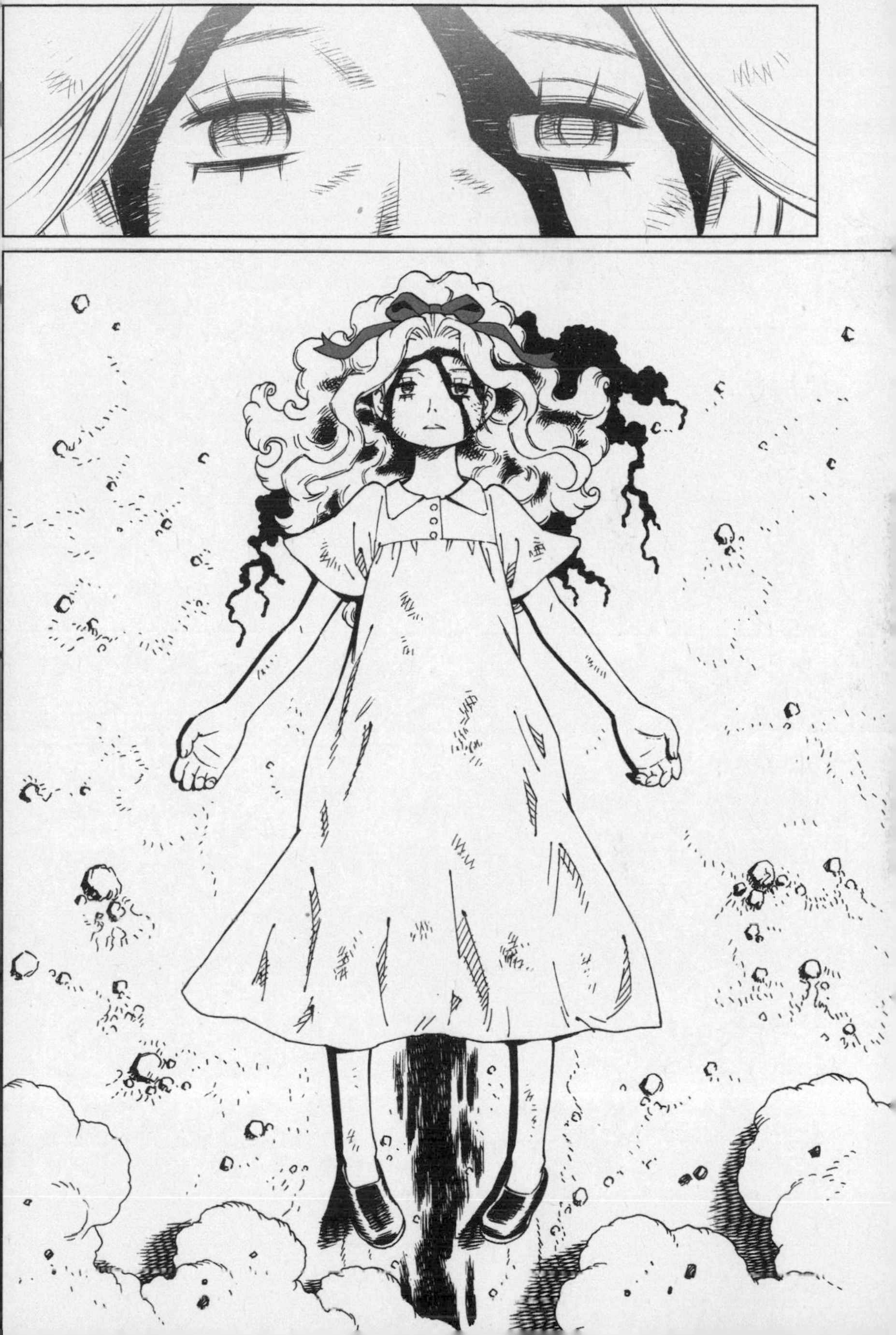

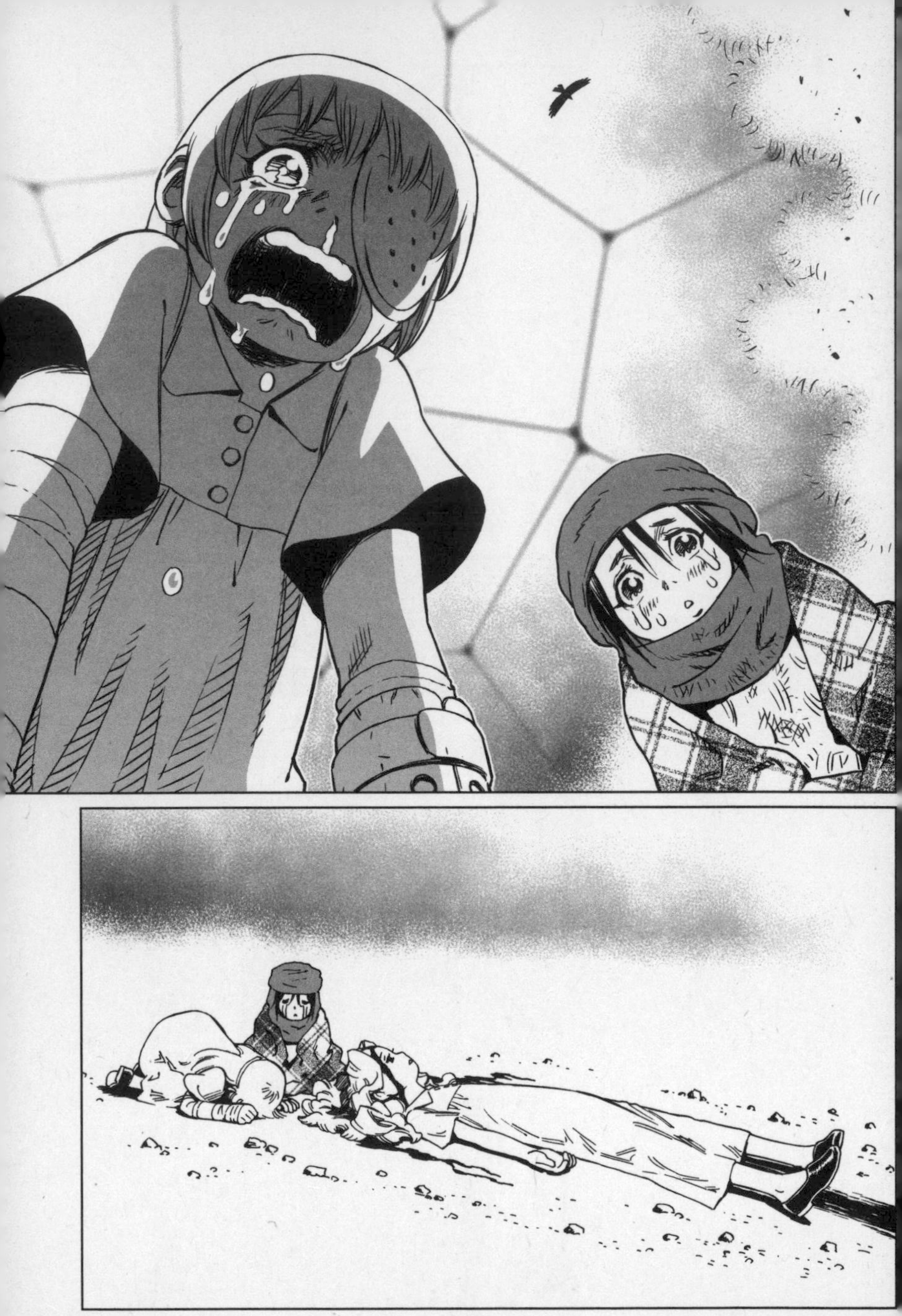

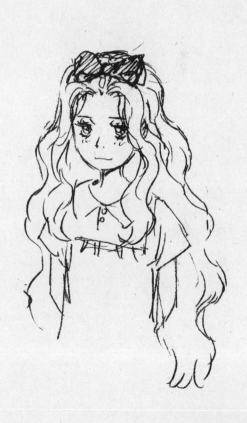

LOG:005

THE TRAIL OF REFUGEES

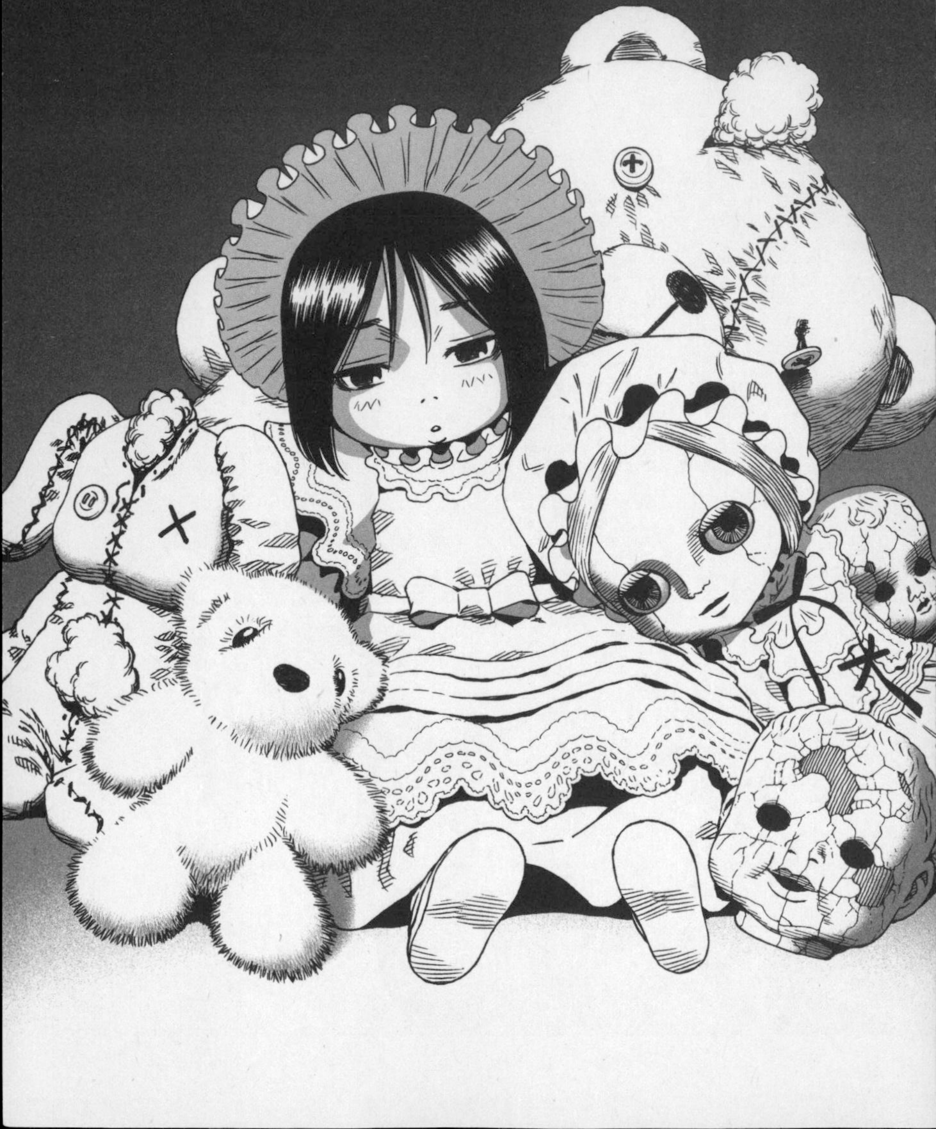

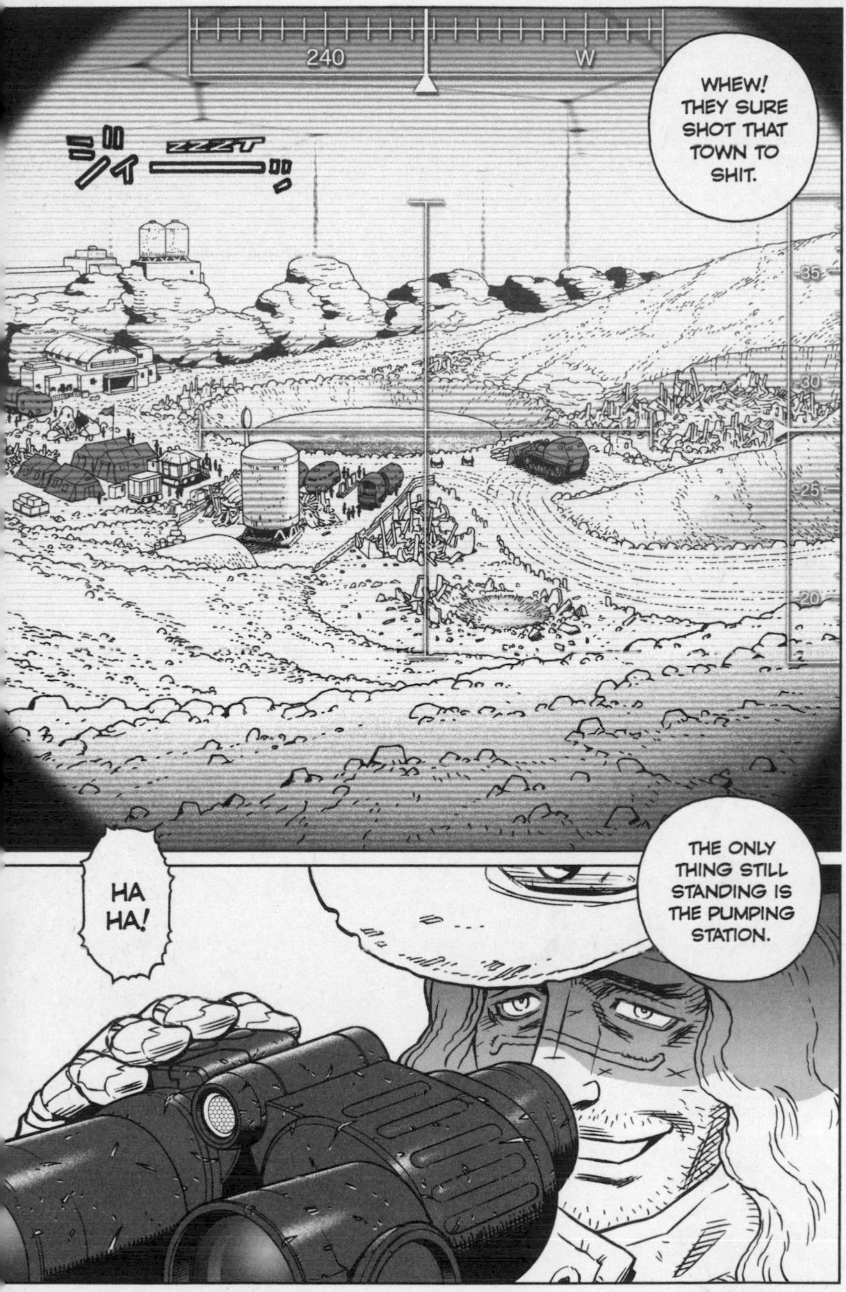
240
W
WHEW! THEY SURE SHOT THAT TOWN TO SHIT.
ZZZT
35
30
25
20
THE ONLY THING STILL STANDING IS THE PUMPING STATION.
HA HA!

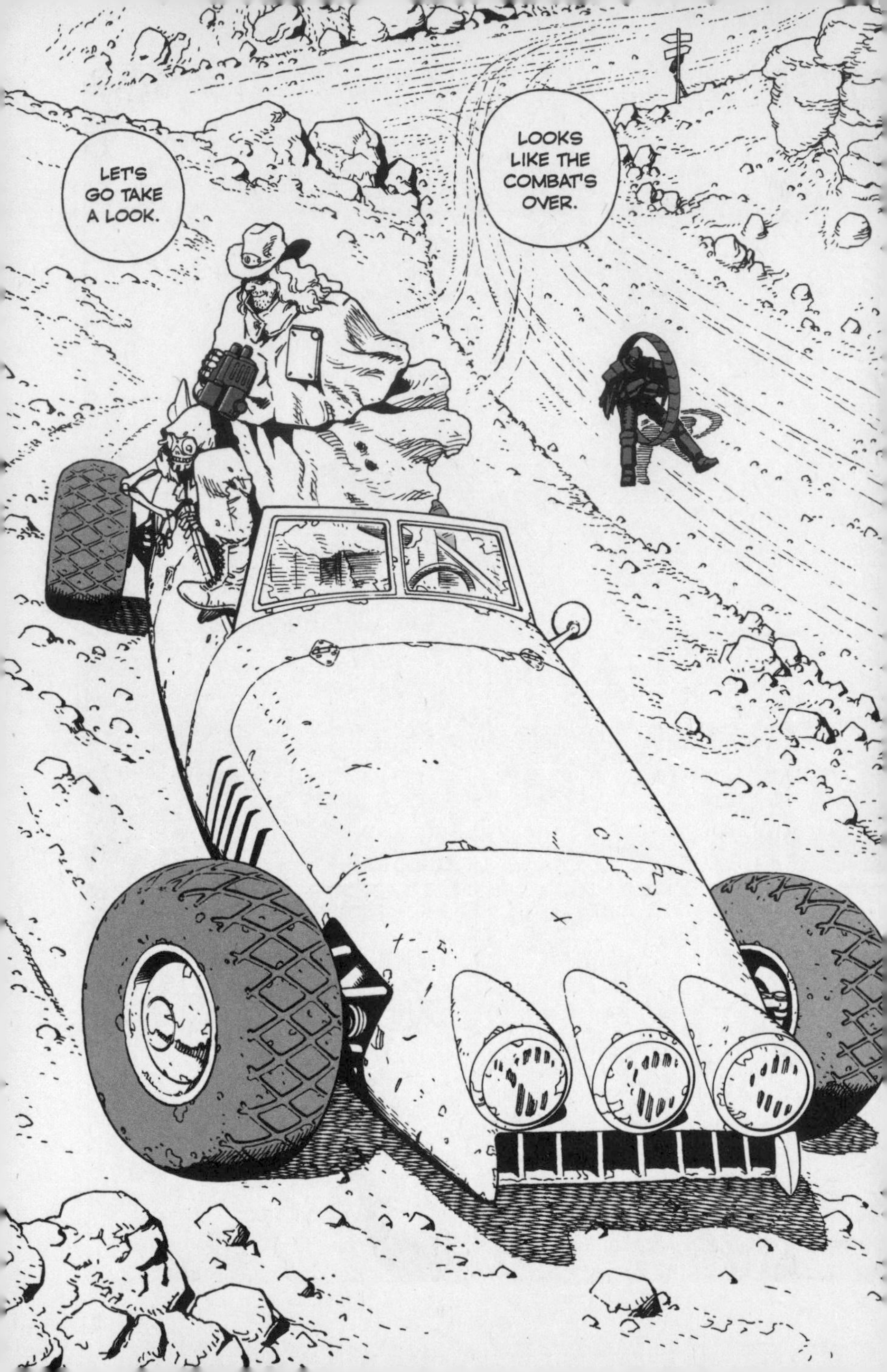
LOOKS LIKE THE COMBAT'S OVER.
LET'S GO TAKE A LOOK.

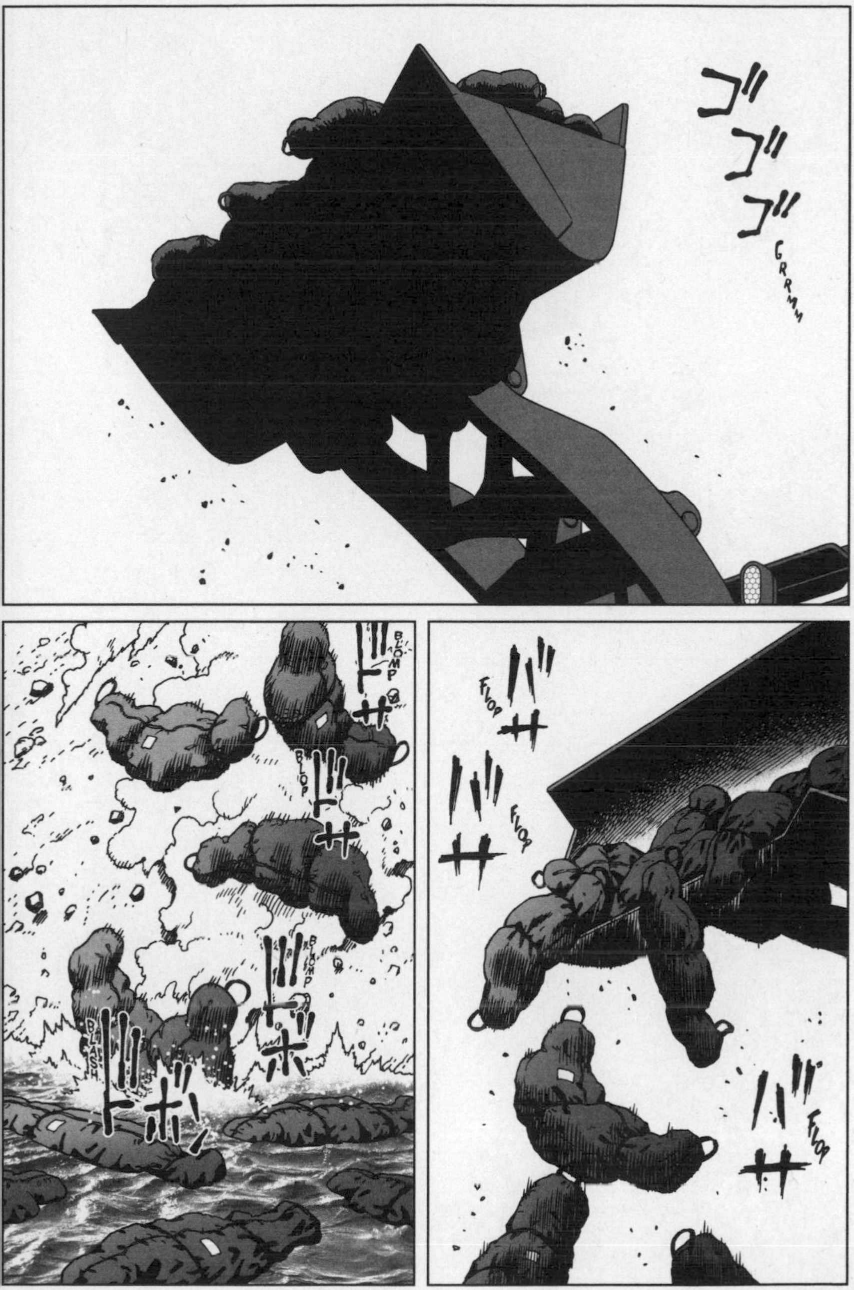
ゴゴゴ
GRRMM
バサ
FLOP
バサ
FLOP
バサ
FLOP
ドサ
BLOMP
ドサ
BLOP
ドボ
BLOMP
ドボン
BLASH

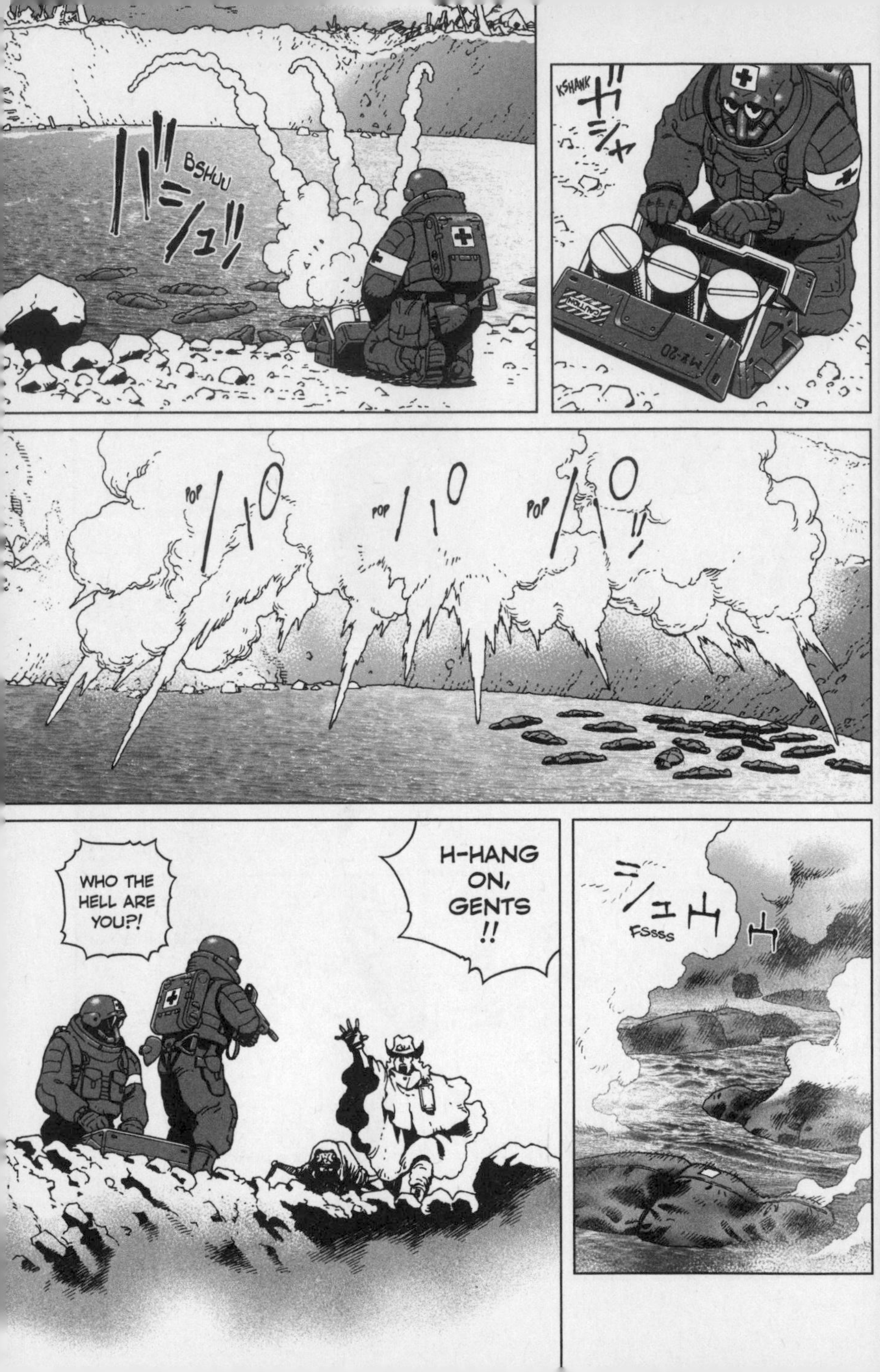
KSHANK
ガシャ
BSHUU
バシュ!!
POP
POP
POP
FSSSS
H-HANG ON, GENTS!!
WHO THE HELL ARE YOU?!

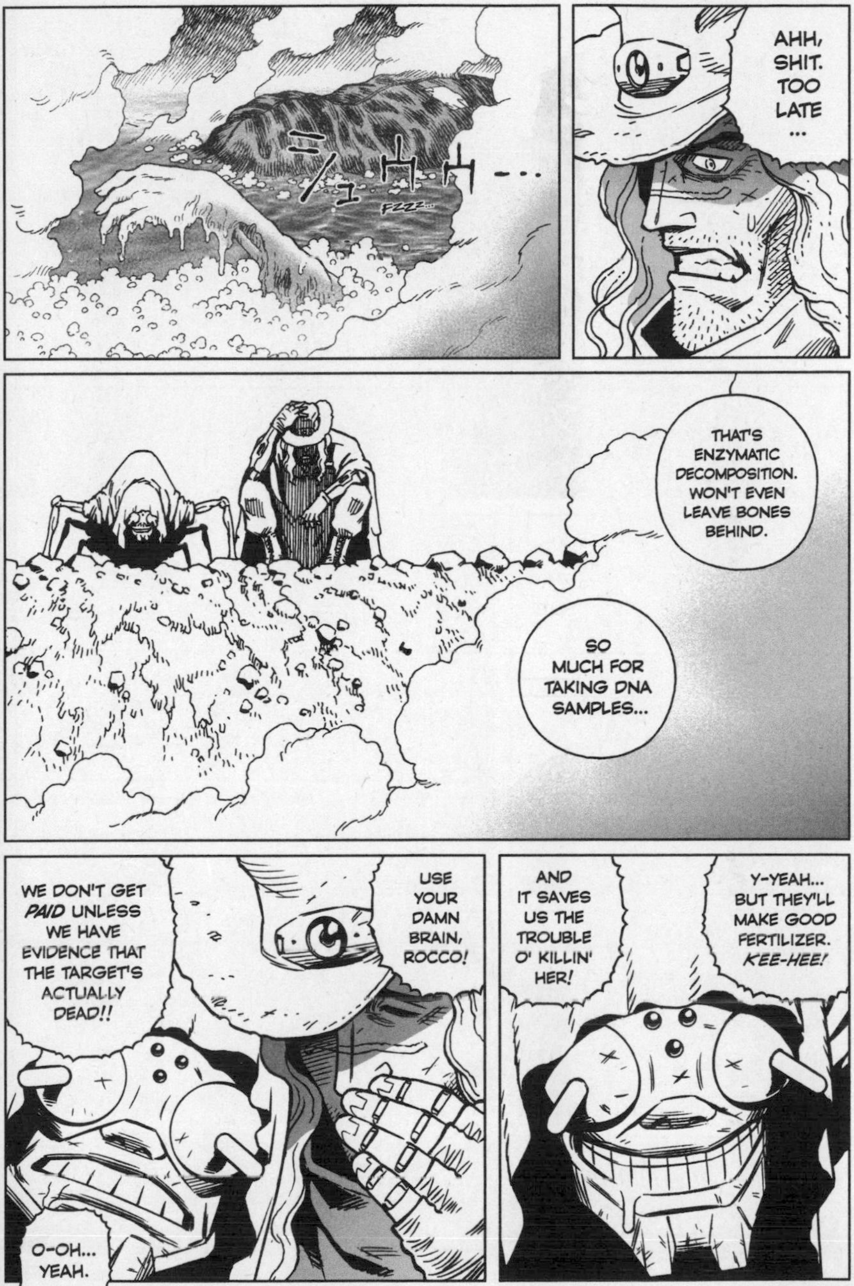
AHH, SHIT. TOO LATE ...
FZZZ...
THAT'S ENZYMATIC DECOMPOSITION. WON'T EVEN LEAVE BONES BEHIND.
SO MUCH FOR TAKING DNA SAMPLES...
Y-YEAH... BUT THEY'LL MAKE GOOD FERTILIZER. *KEE-HEE!*
AND IT SAVES US THE TROUBLE O' KILLIN' HER!
USE YOUR DAMN BRAIN, ROCCO!
WE DON'T GET *PAID* UNLESS WE HAVE EVIDENCE THAT THE TARGET'S ACTUALLY DEAD!!
O-OH... YEAH.

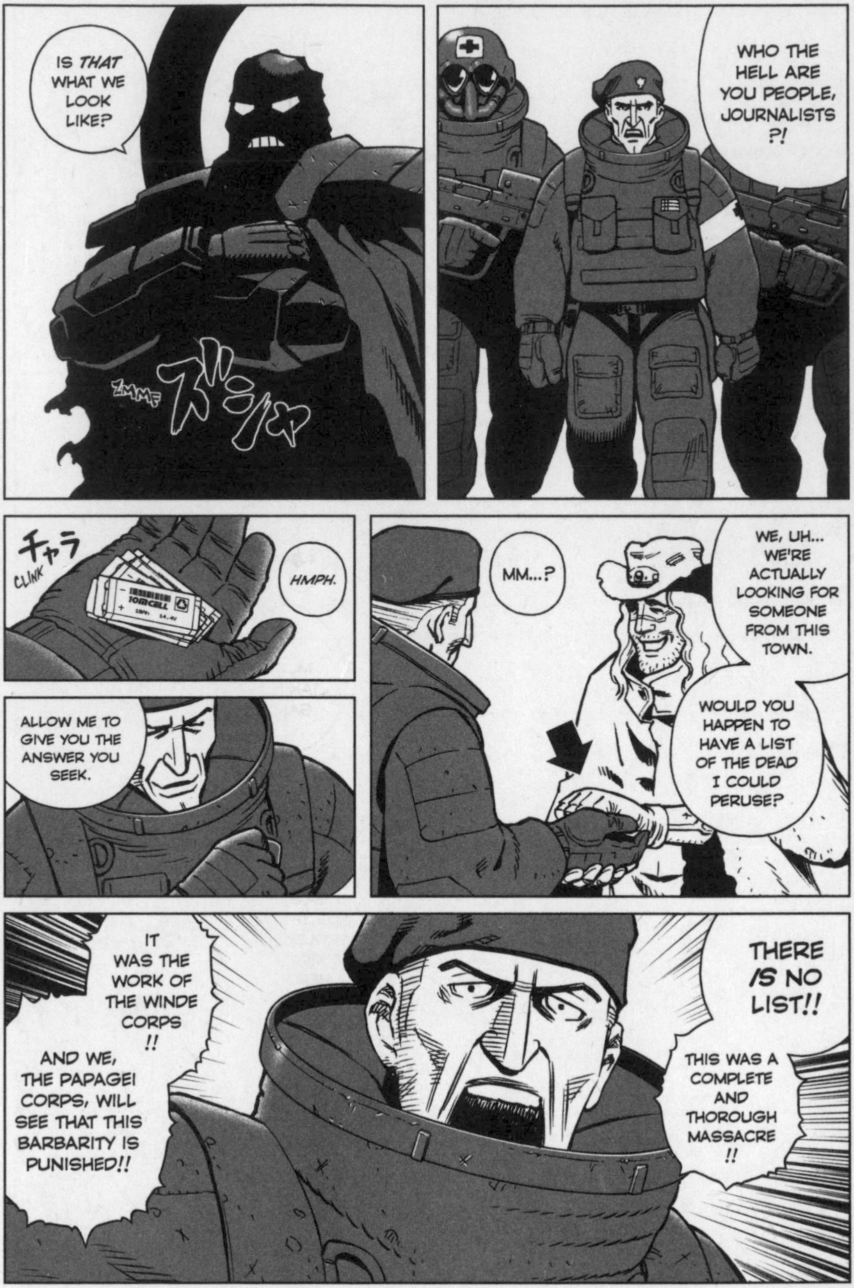
WHO THE HELL ARE YOU PEOPLE, JOURNALISTS ?!
IS *THAT* WHAT WE LOOK LIKE?
ZMMF
ズシャ
MM...?
WE, UH... WE'RE ACTUALLY LOOKING FOR SOMEONE FROM THIS TOWN.
WOULD YOU HAPPEN TO HAVE A LIST OF THE DEAD I COULD PERUSE?
チャラ
CLINK
HMPH.
ALLOW ME TO GIVE YOU THE ANSWER YOU SEEK.
THERE *IS* NO LIST!!
THIS WAS A COMPLETE AND THOROUGH MASSACRE !!
IT WAS THE WORK OF THE WINDE CORPS !!
AND WE, THE PAPAGEI CORPS, WILL SEE THAT THIS BARBARITY IS PUNISHED!!

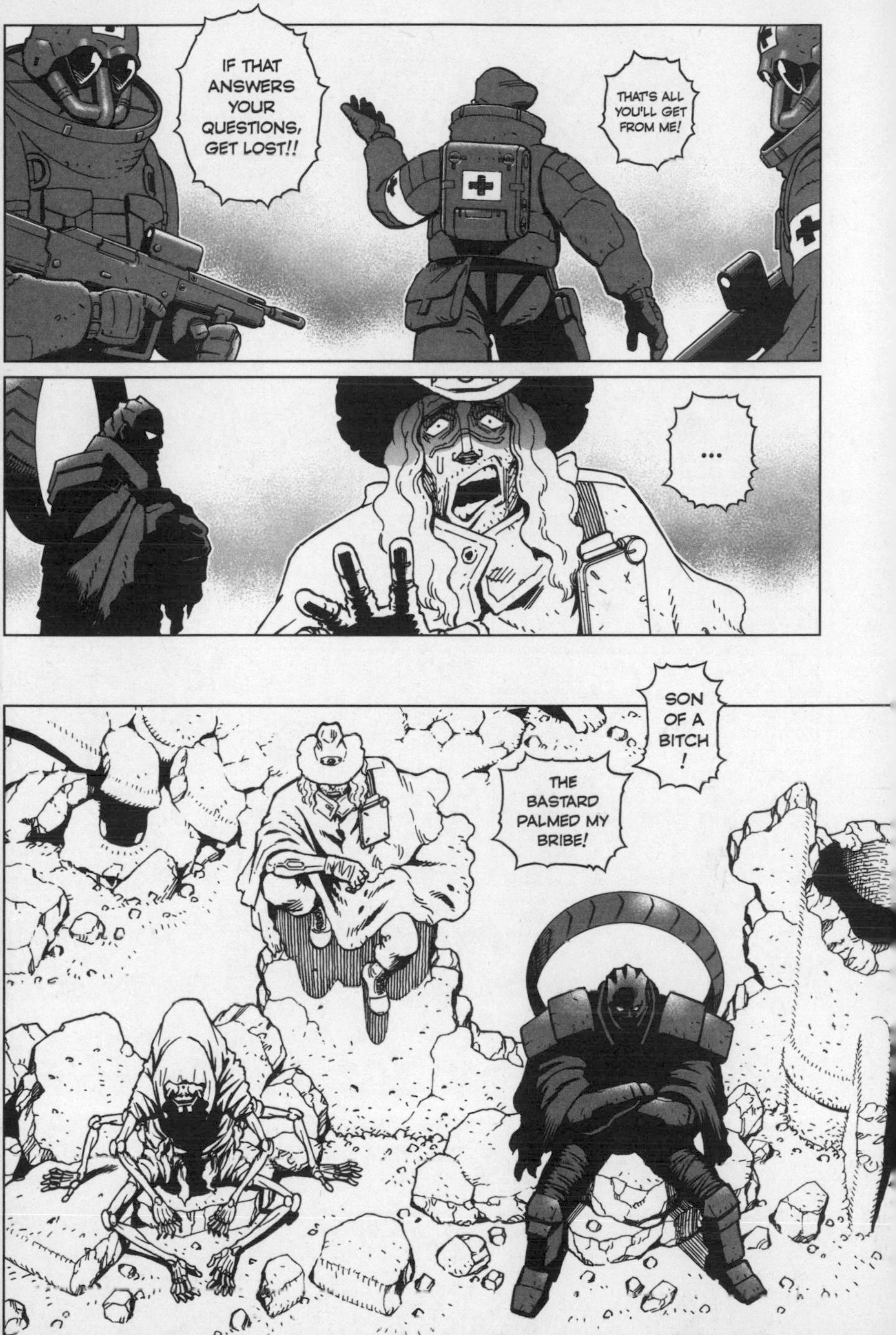
THAT'S ALL YOU'LL GET FROM ME!
IF THAT ANSWERS YOUR QUESTIONS, GET LOST!!
...
SON OF A BITCH!
THE BASTARD PALMED MY BRIBE!

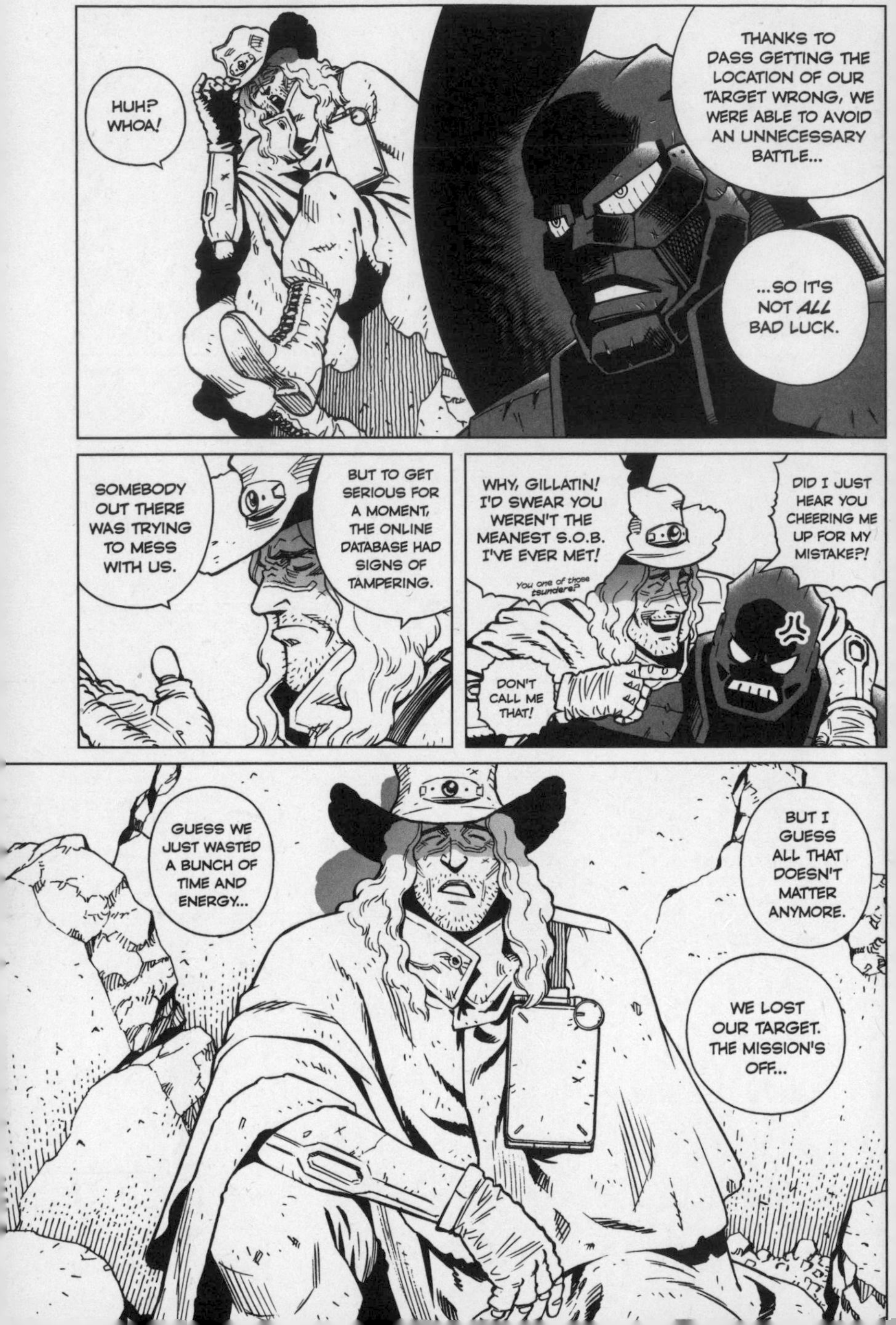
THANKS TO DASS GETTING THE LOCATION OF OUR TARGET WRONG, WE WERE ABLE TO AVOID AN UNNECESSARY BATTLE...
...SO IT'S NOT *ALL* BAD LUCK.
HUH? WHOA!
DID I JUST HEAR YOU CHEERING ME UP FOR MY MISTAKE?!
WHY, GILLATIN! I'D SWEAR YOU WEREN'T THE MEANEST S.O.B. I'VE EVER MET!
You one of those *tsundere*?
DON'T CALL ME THAT!
BUT TO GET SERIOUS FOR A MOMENT, THE ONLINE DATABASE HAD SIGNS OF TAMPERING.
SOMEBODY OUT THERE WAS TRYING TO MESS WITH US.
BUT I GUESS ALL THAT DOESN'T MATTER ANYMORE.
WE LOST OUR TARGET. THE MISSION'S OFF...
GUESS WE JUST WASTED A BUNCH OF TIME AND ENERGY...

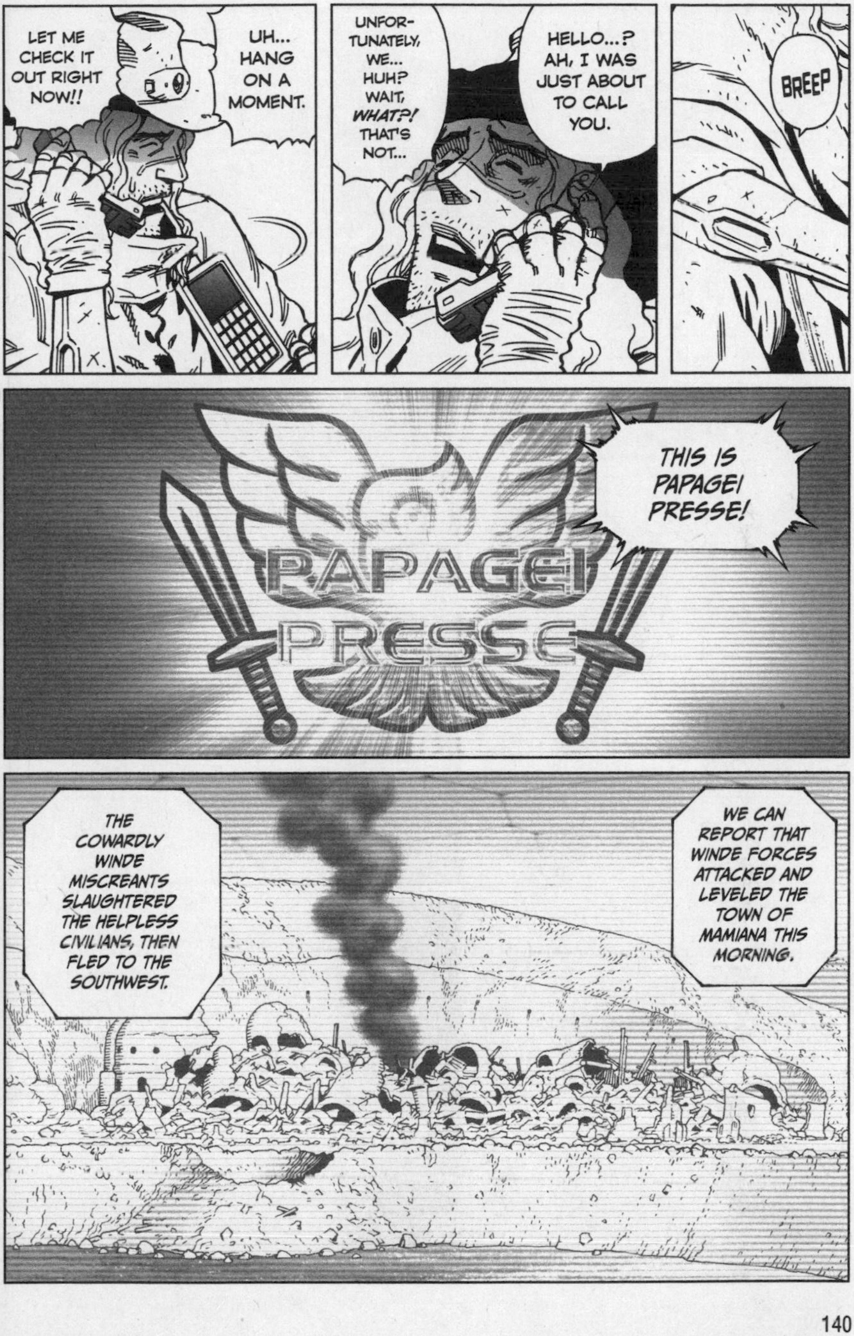
BREEP
HELLO...? AH, I WAS JUST ABOUT TO CALL YOU.
UNFOR-TUNATELY, WE... HUH? WAIT, *WHAT?!* THAT'S NOT...
UH... HANG ON A MOMENT.
LET ME CHECK IT OUT RIGHT NOW!!
THIS IS PAPAGEI PRESSE!
PAPAGEI PRESSE
WE CAN REPORT THAT WINDE FORCES ATTACKED AND LEVELED THE TOWN OF MAMIANA THIS MORNING.
THE COWARDLY WINDE MISCREANTS SLAUGHTERED THE HELPLESS CIVILIANS, THEN FLED TO THE SOUTHWEST.

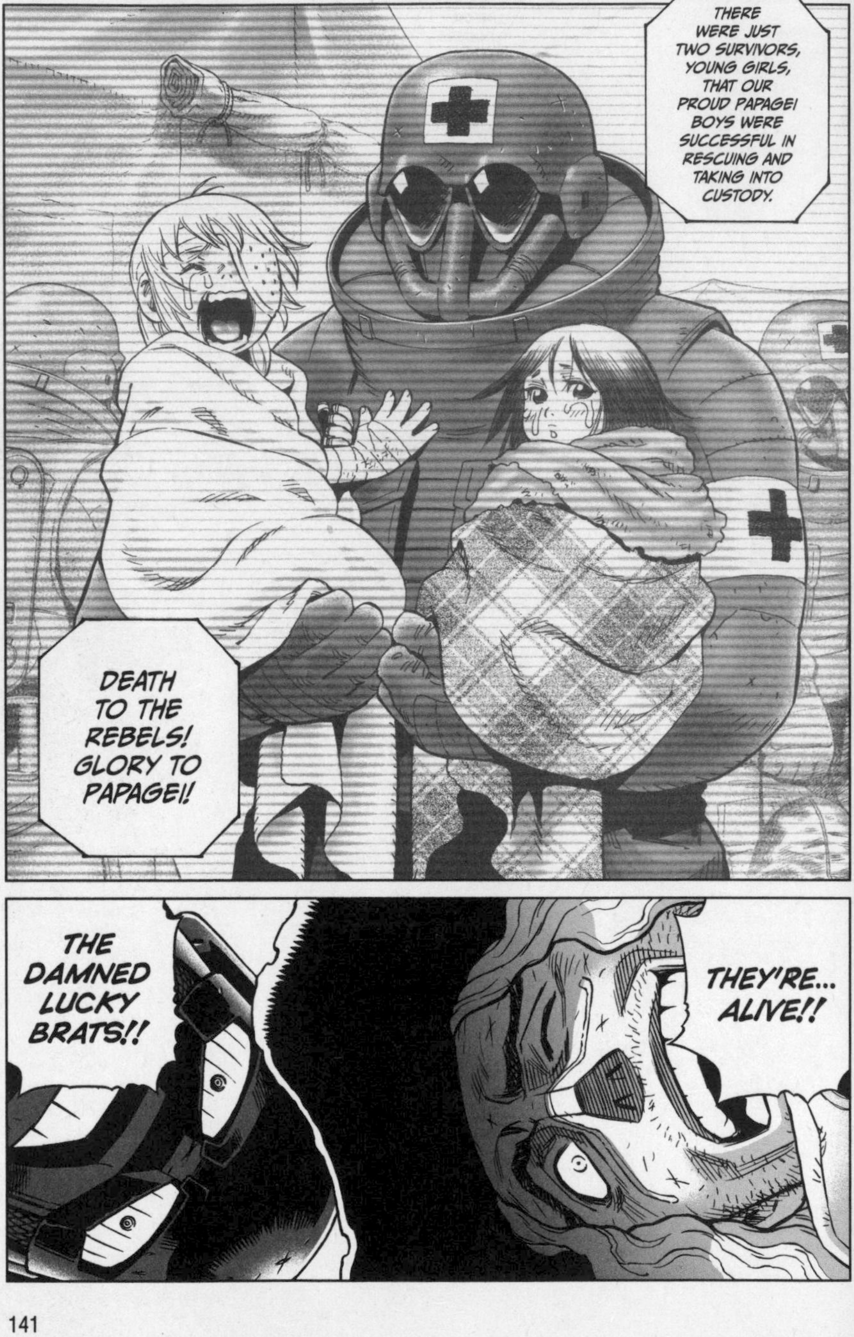
THERE WERE JUST TWO SURVIVORS, YOUNG GIRLS, THAT OUR PROUD PAPAGEI BOYS WERE SUCCESSFUL IN RESCUING AND TAKING INTO CUSTODY.
DEATH TO THE REBELS! GLORY TO PAPAGEI!
THEY'RE... ALIVE!!
THE DAMNED LUCKY BRATS!!

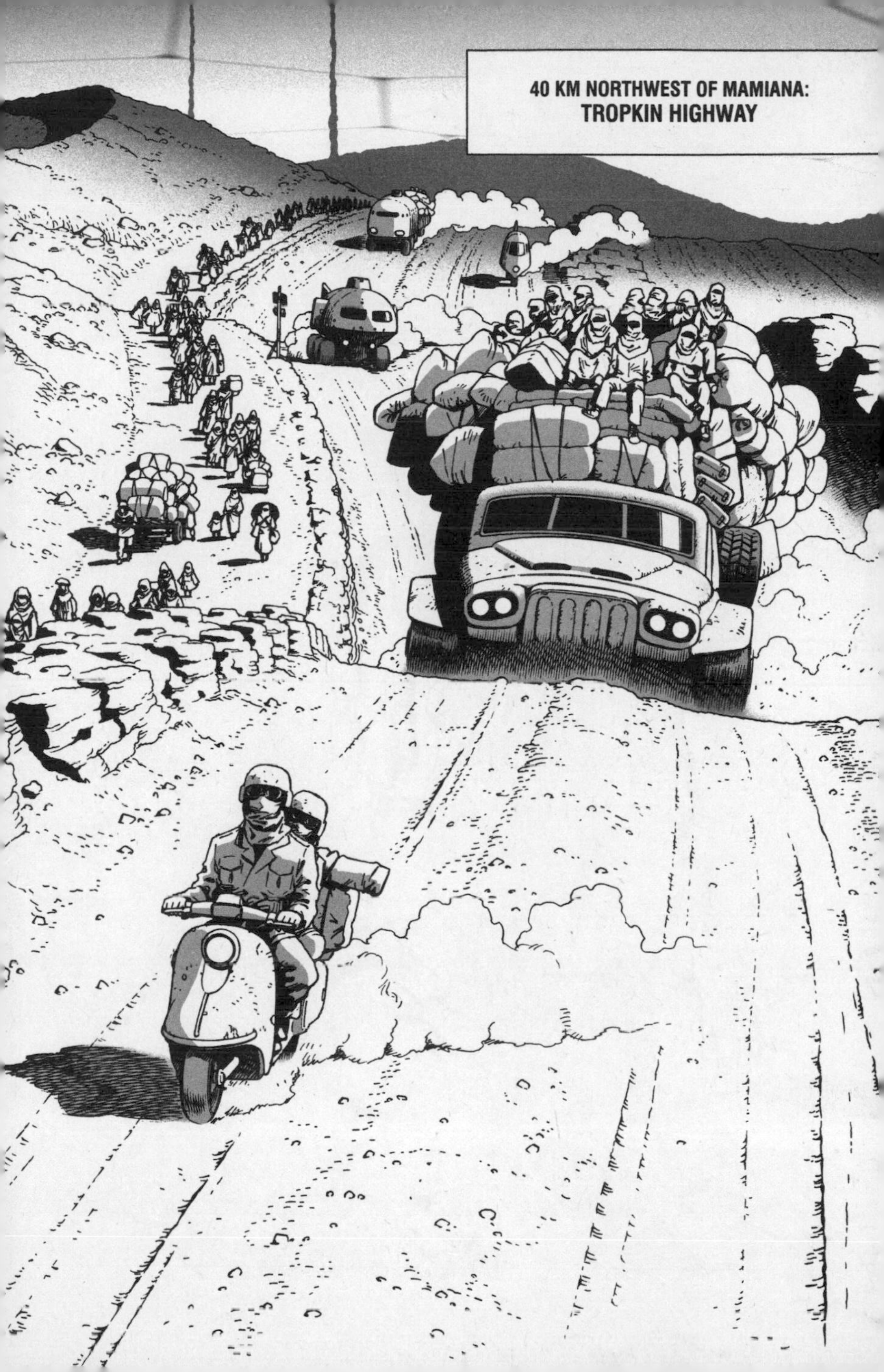
40 KM NORTHWEST OF MAMIANA:
TROPKIN HIGHWAY

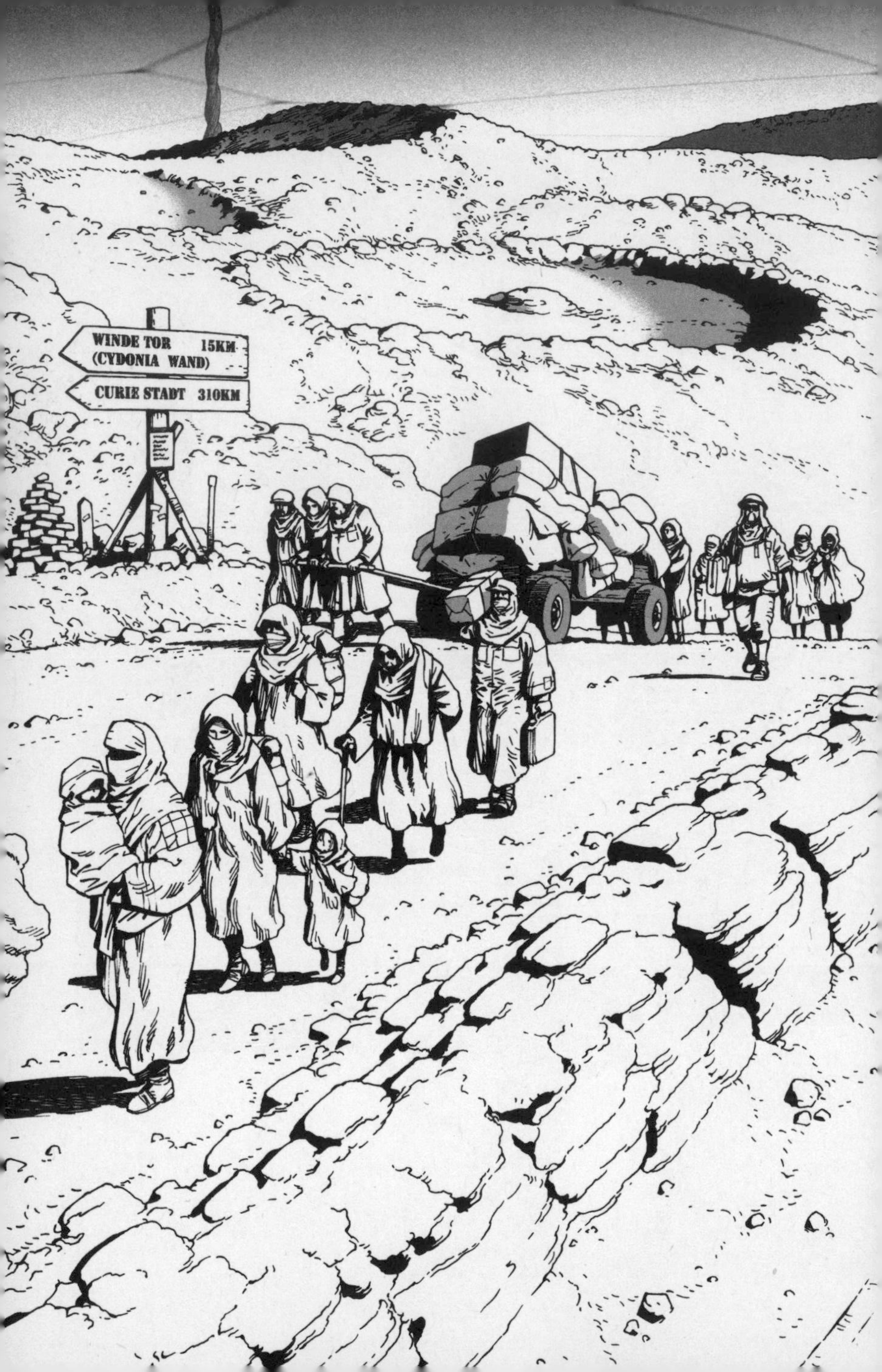
WINDE TOR 15KM
(CYDONIA WAND)
CURIE STADT 310KM

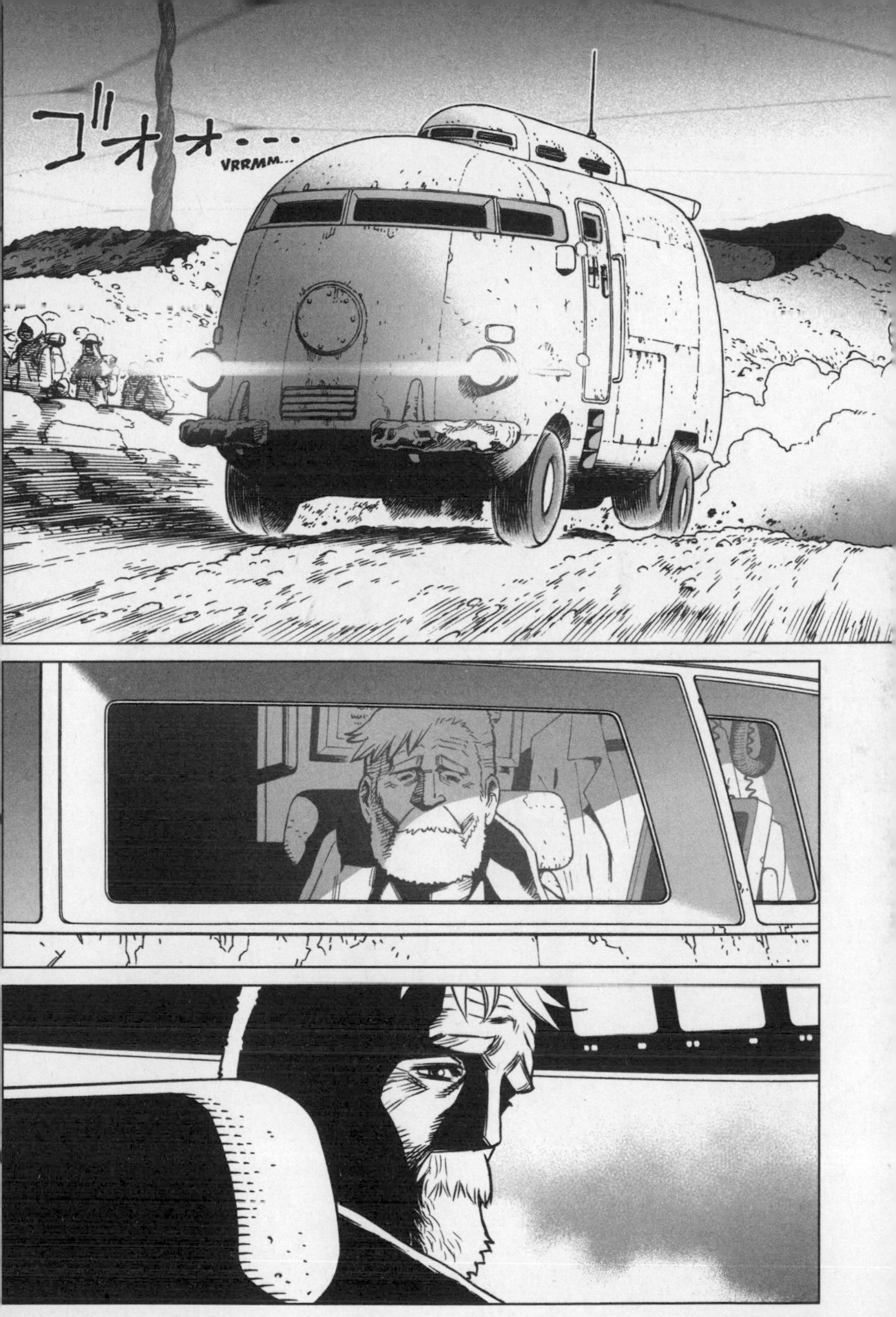
ゴオオ・・・
VRRMM...

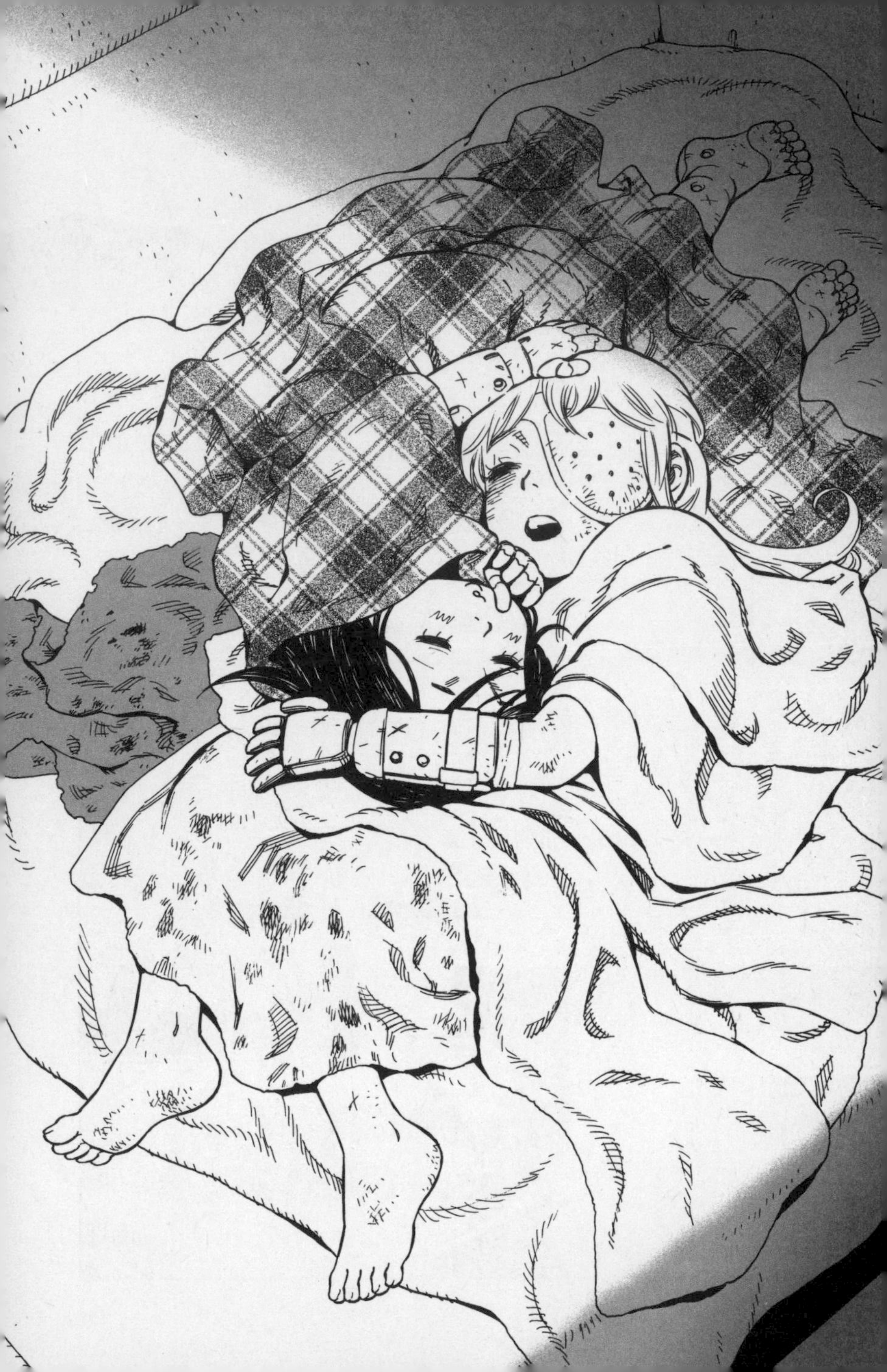

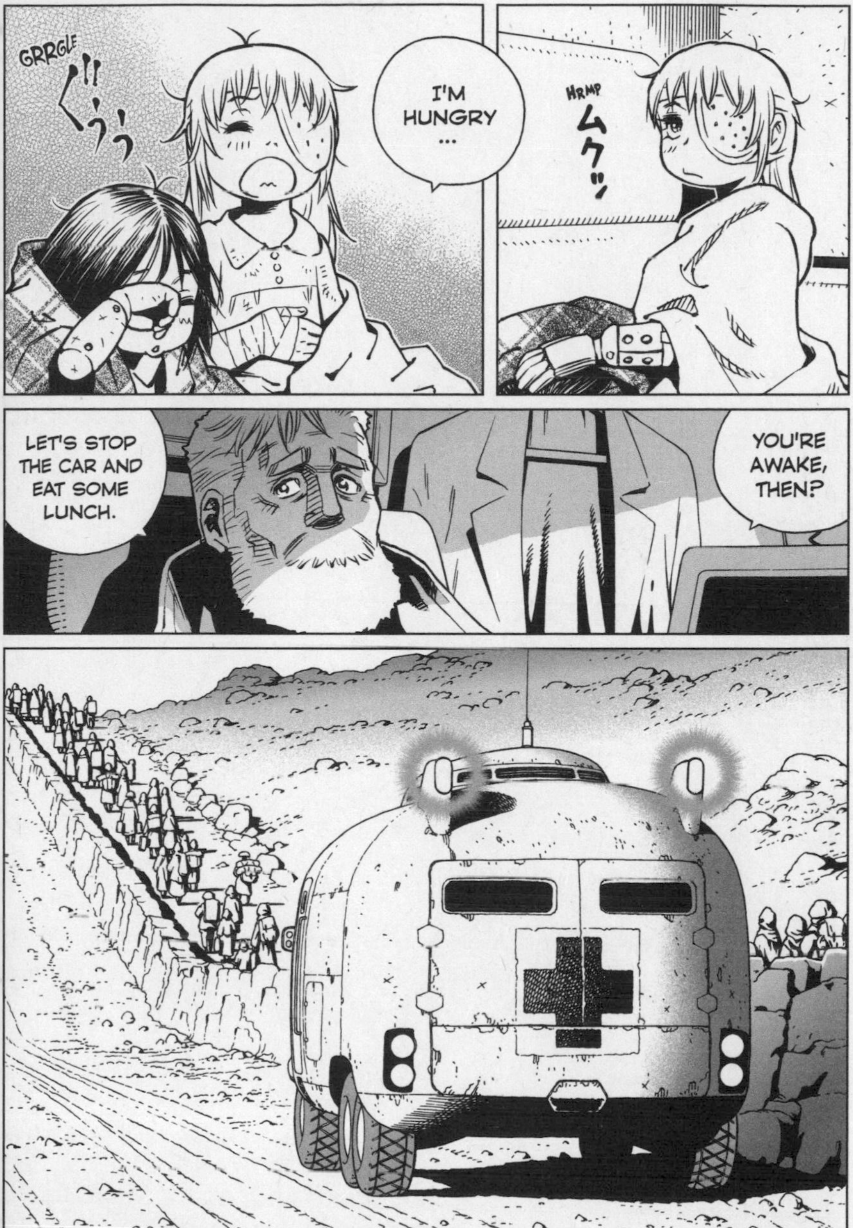
HRMP
ムクッ
I'M HUNGRY ...
GRRGLE
!!
くうぅ
YOU'RE AWAKE, THEN?
LET'S STOP THE CAR AND EAT SOME LUNCH.

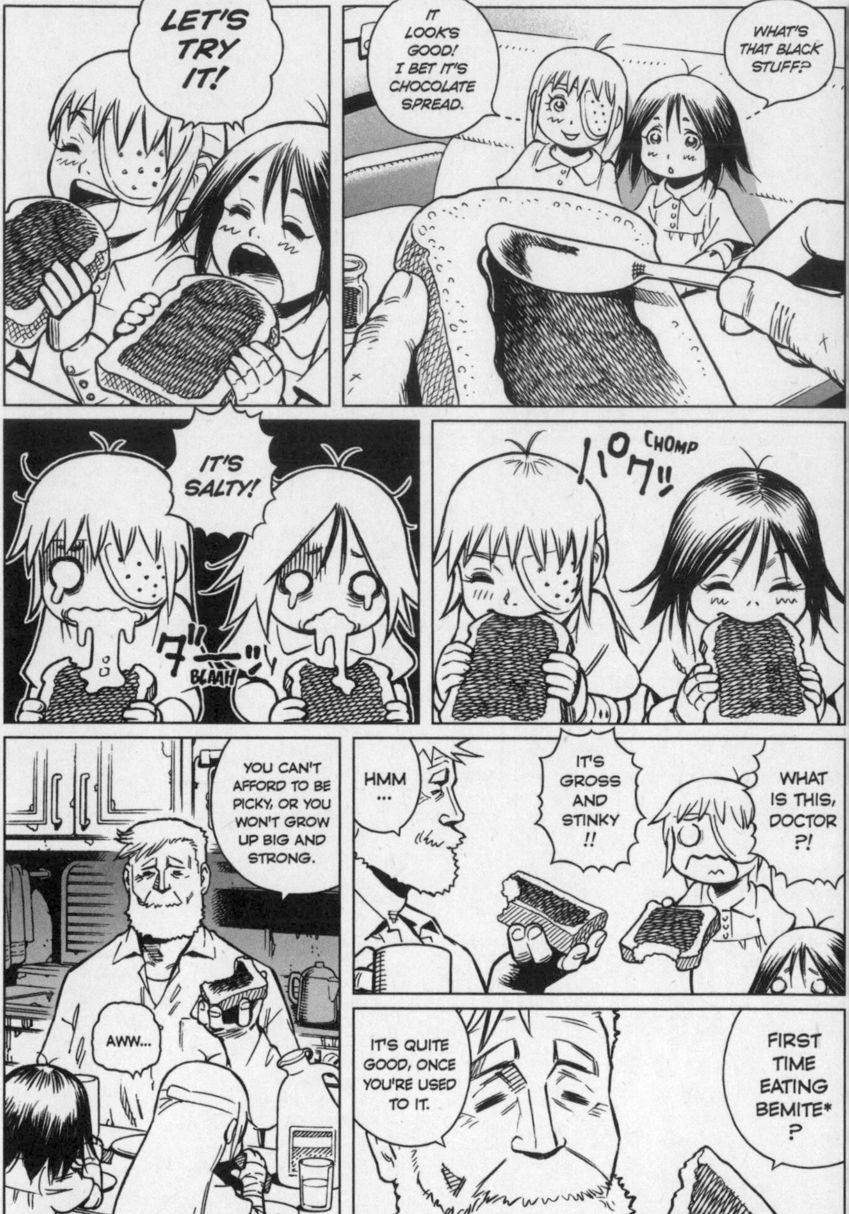
WHAT'S THAT BLACK STUFF?
IT LOOKS GOOD! I BET IT'S CHOCOLATE SPREAD.
LET'S TRY IT!
パク!!
CHOMP
IT'S SALTY!
ブーッ
BLAAH
WHAT IS THIS, DOCTOR ?!
IT'S GROSS AND STINKY !!
HMM ...
FIRST TIME EATING BEMITE* ?
IT'S QUITE GOOD, ONCE YOU'RE USED TO IT.
YOU CAN'T AFFORD TO BE PICKY, OR YOU WON'T GROW UP BIG AND STRONG.
AWW...

***Bemite:** An edible paste made from yeast created in the beer-brewing process. It's quite salty and has a strong odor. In England, Australia, and New Zealand it is sold under the brand names Marmite and Vegemite.

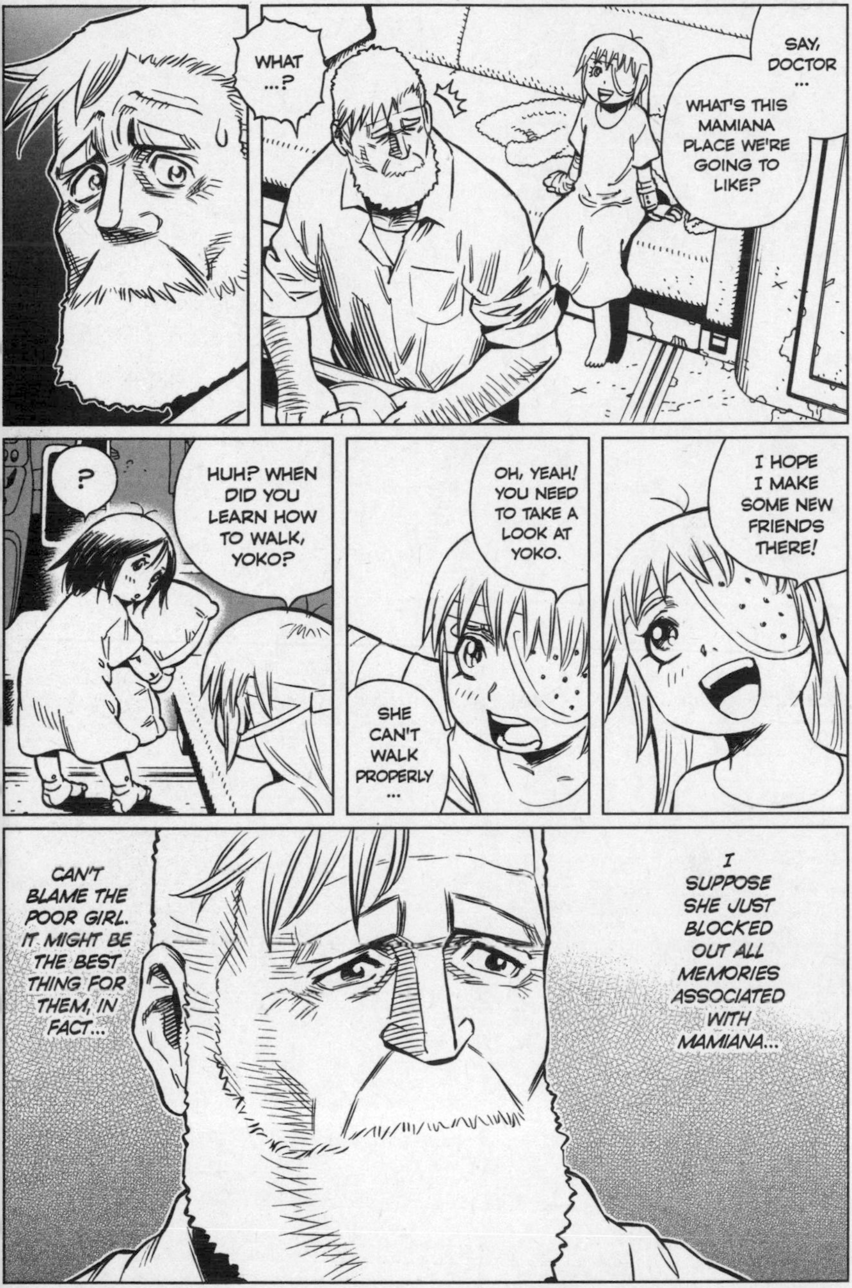
SAY, DOCTOR ...
WHAT'S THIS MAMIANA PLACE WE'RE GOING TO LIKE?
WHAT ...?
I HOPE I MAKE SOME NEW FRIENDS THERE!
OH, YEAH! YOU NEED TO TAKE A LOOK AT YOKO.
SHE CAN'T WALK PROPERLY ...
HUH? WHEN DID YOU LEARN HOW TO WALK, YOKO?
?
I SUPPOSE SHE JUST BLOCKED OUT ALL MEMORIES ASSOCIATED WITH MAMIANA...
CAN'T BLAME THE POOR GIRL. IT MIGHT BE THE BEST THING FOR THEM, IN FACT...

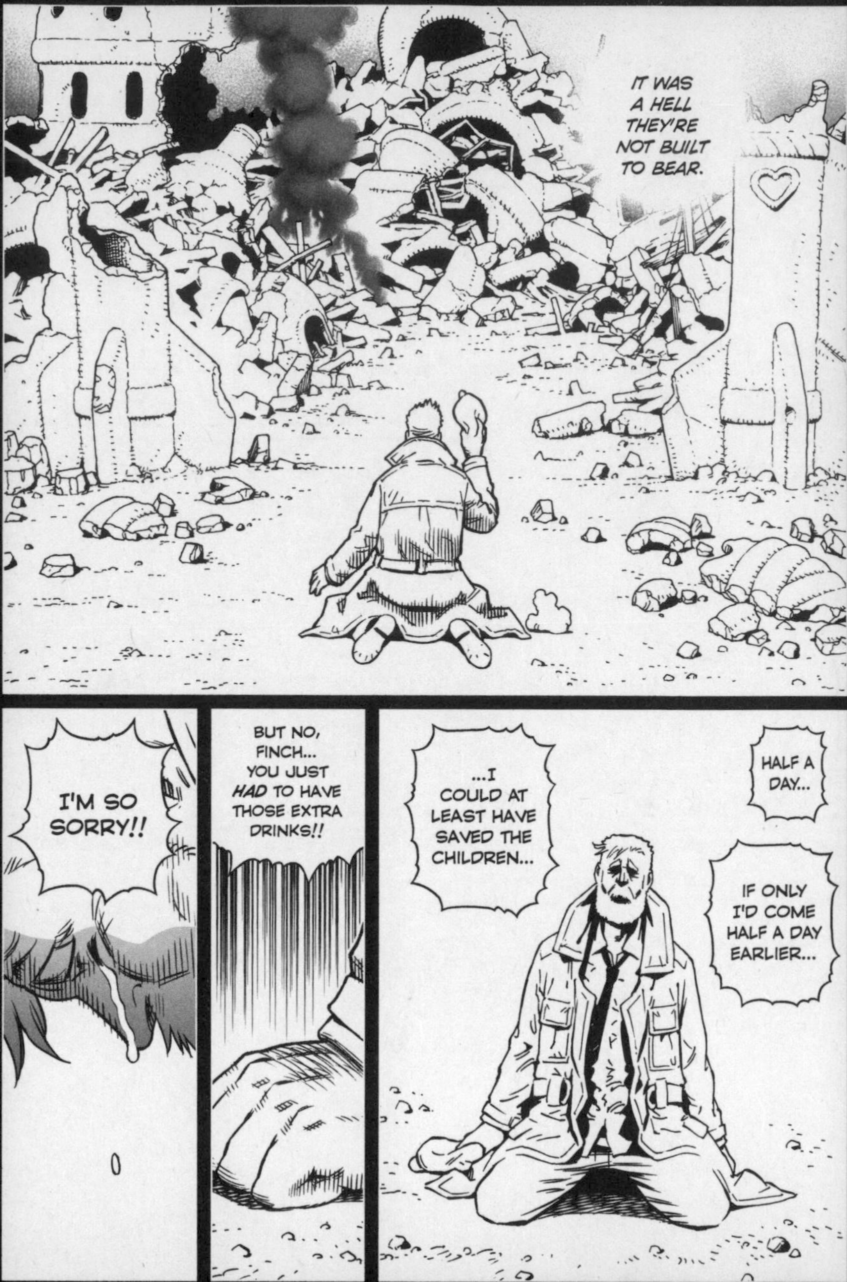
IT WAS A HELL THEY'RE NOT BUILT TO BEAR.
HALF A DAY...
IF ONLY I'D COME HALF A DAY EARLIER...
...I COULD AT LEAST HAVE SAVED THE CHILDREN...
BUT NO, FINCH... YOU JUST *HAD* TO HAVE THOSE EXTRA DRINKS!!
I'M SO SORRY!!

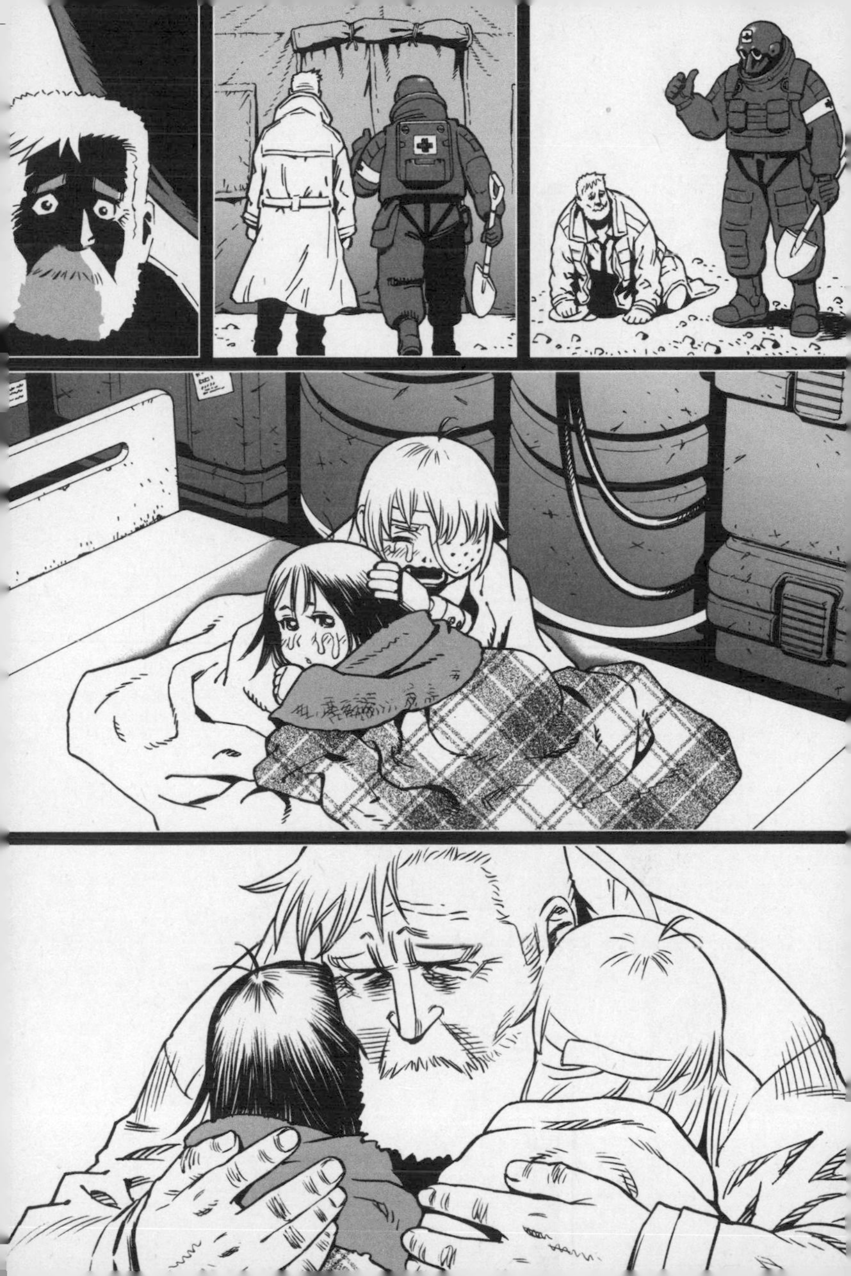

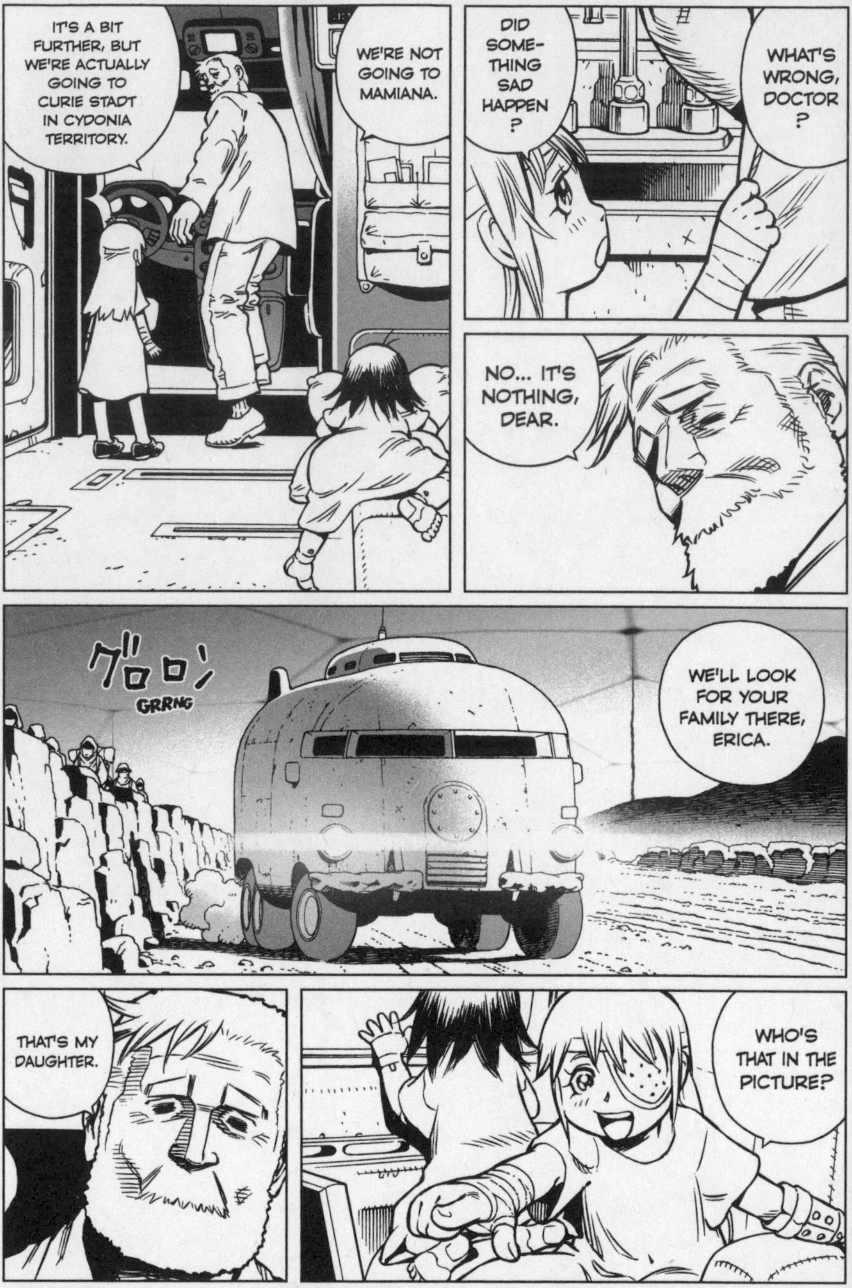
WHAT'S WRONG, DOCTOR?
DID SOMETHING SAD HAPPEN?
NO... IT'S NOTHING, DEAR.
WE'RE NOT GOING TO MAMIANA.
IT'S A BIT FURTHER, BUT WE'RE ACTUALLY GOING TO CURIE STADT IN CYDONIA TERRITORY.
グロロン
GRRNG
WE'LL LOOK FOR YOUR FAMILY THERE, ERICA.
WHO'S THAT IN THE PICTURE?
THAT'S MY DAUGHTER.

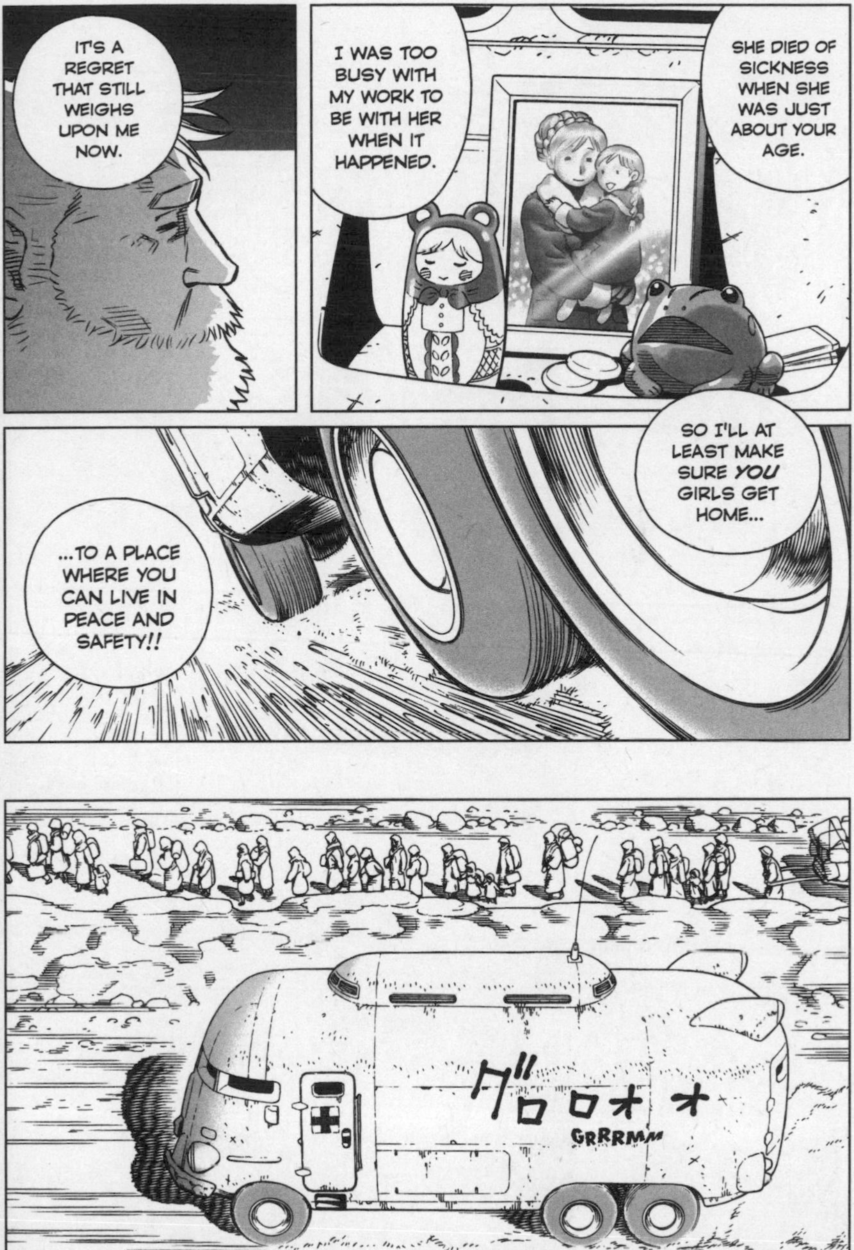
SHE DIED OF SICKNESS WHEN SHE WAS JUST ABOUT YOUR AGE.
I WAS TOO BUSY WITH MY WORK TO BE WITH HER WHEN IT HAPPENED.
IT'S A REGRET THAT STILL WEIGHS UPON ME NOW.
SO I'LL AT LEAST MAKE SURE *YOU* GIRLS GET HOME...
...TO A PLACE WHERE YOU CAN LIVE IN PEACE AND SAFETY!!
グロロオオ
GRRRMM

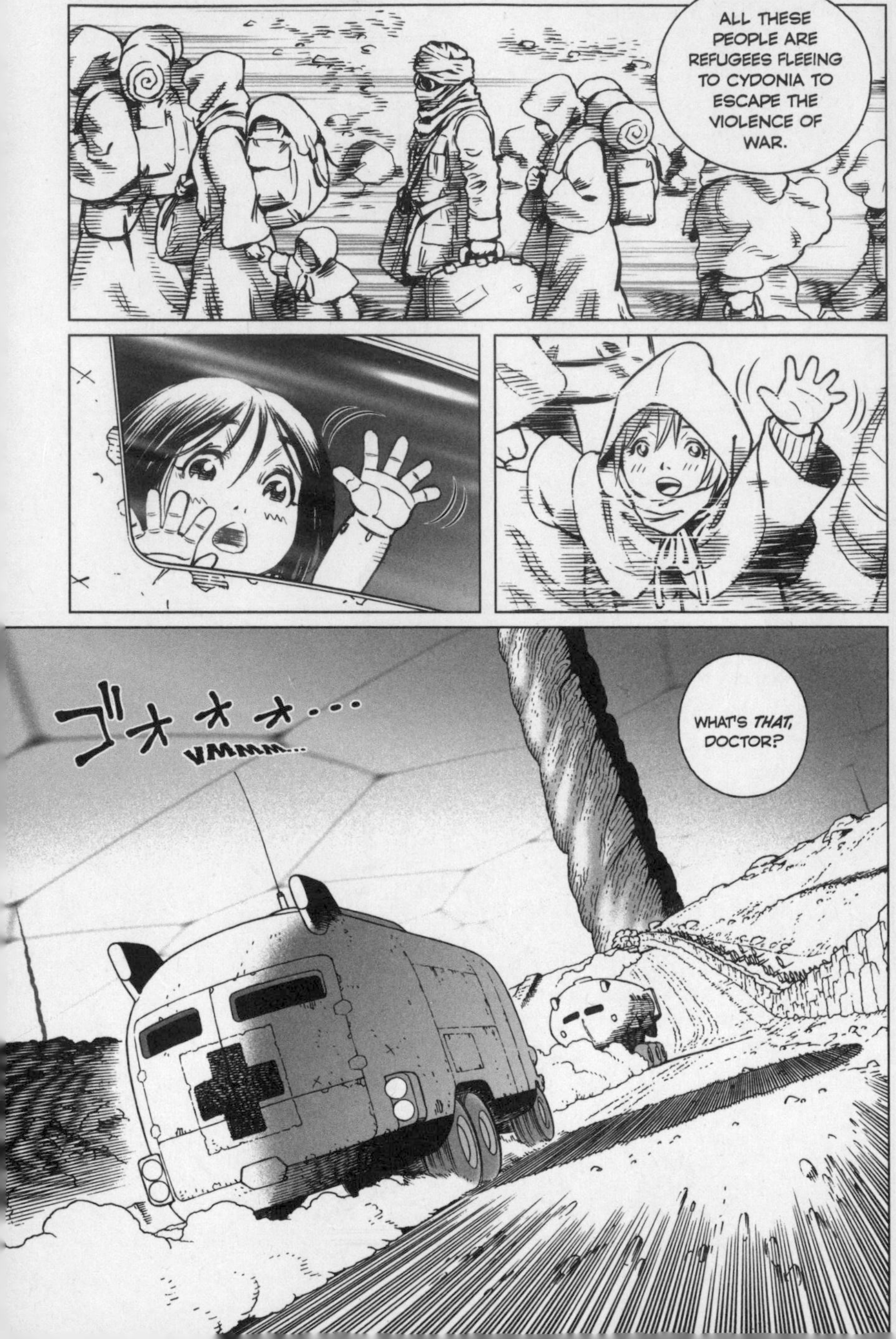
ALL THESE PEOPLE ARE REFUGEES FLEEING TO CYDONIA TO ESCAPE THE VIOLENCE OF WAR.
WHAT'S *THAT,* DOCTOR?
ゴオオオ…
VMMM...

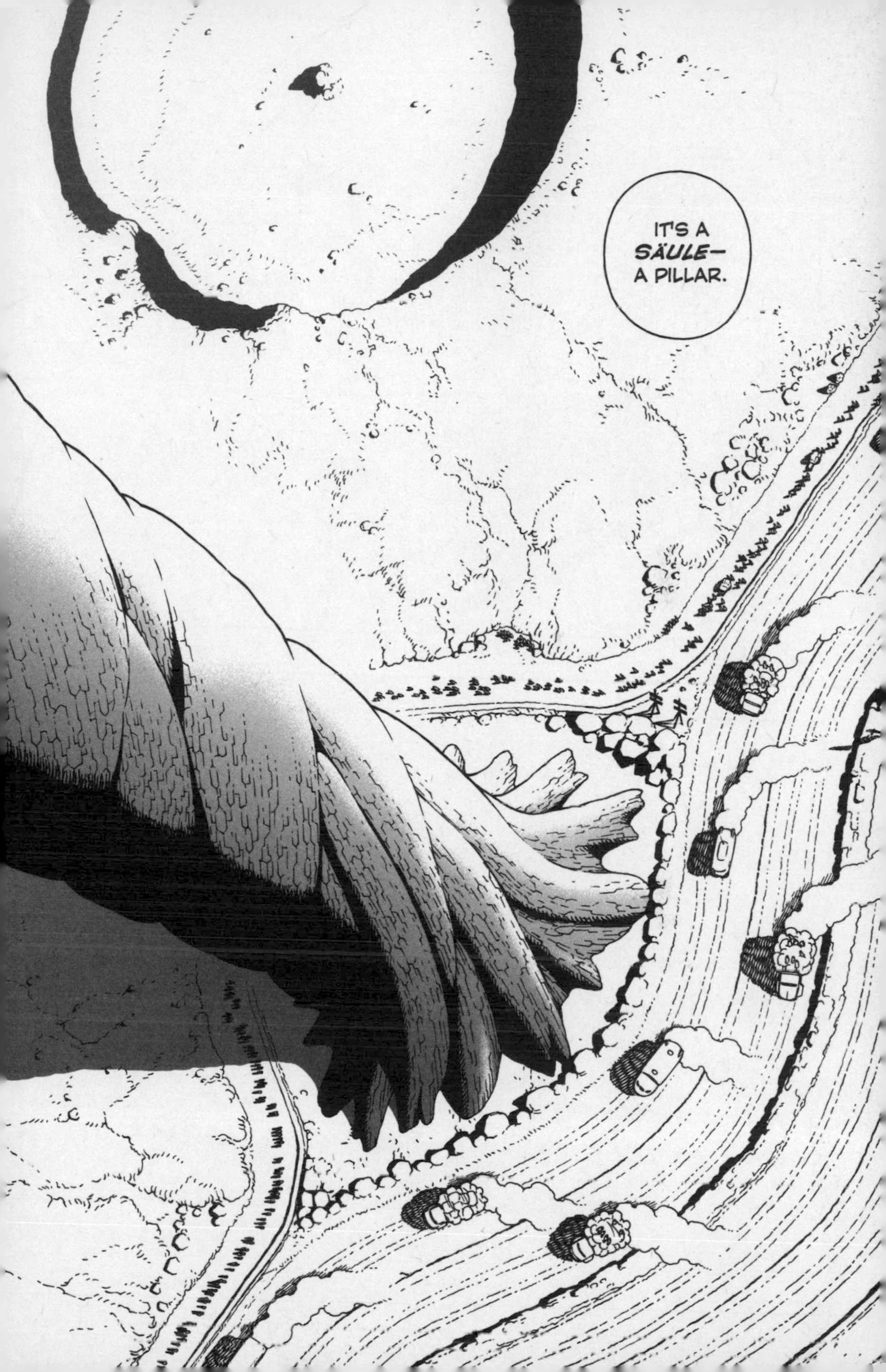
IT'S A *SÄULE*—
A PILLAR.

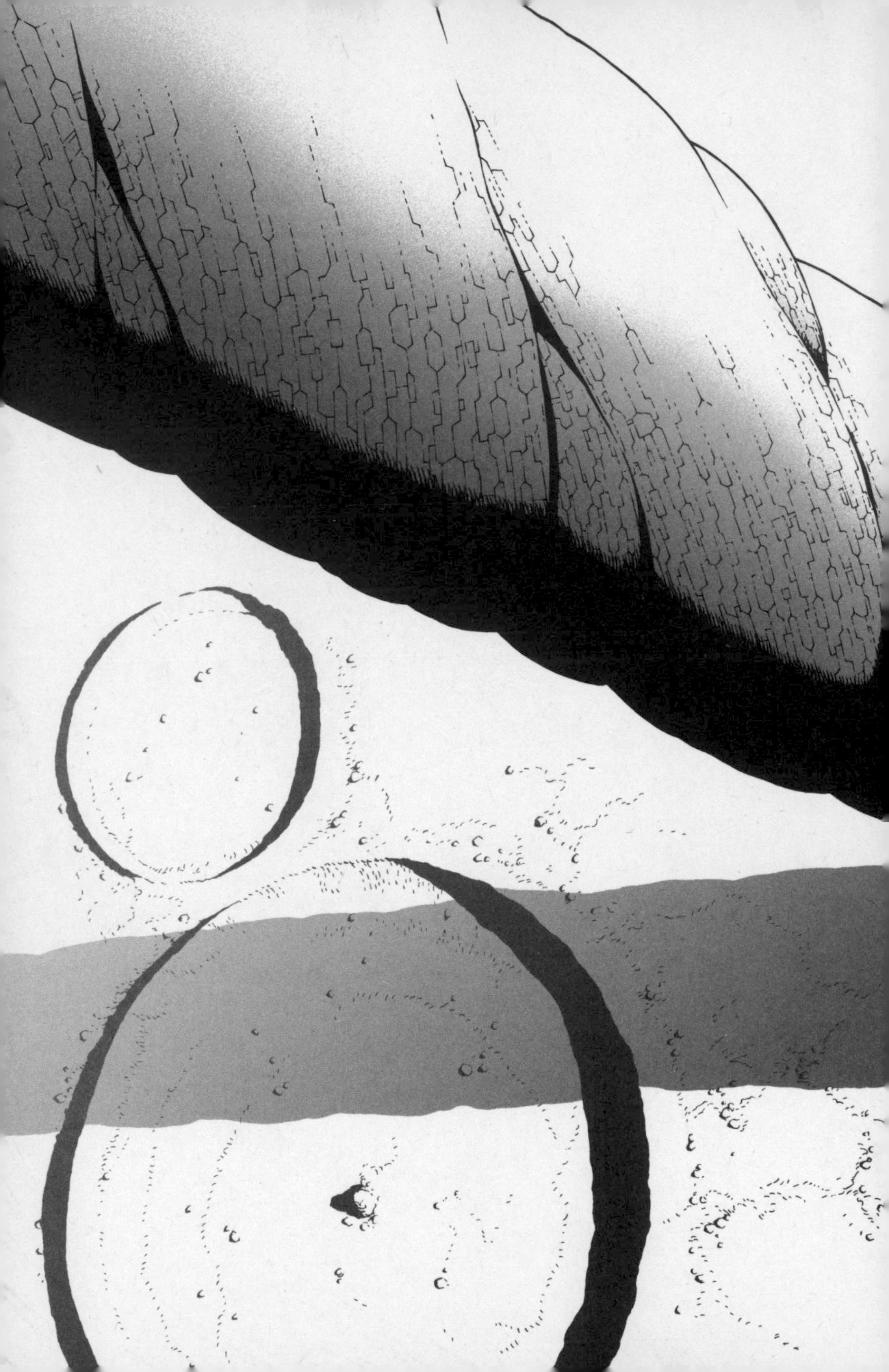

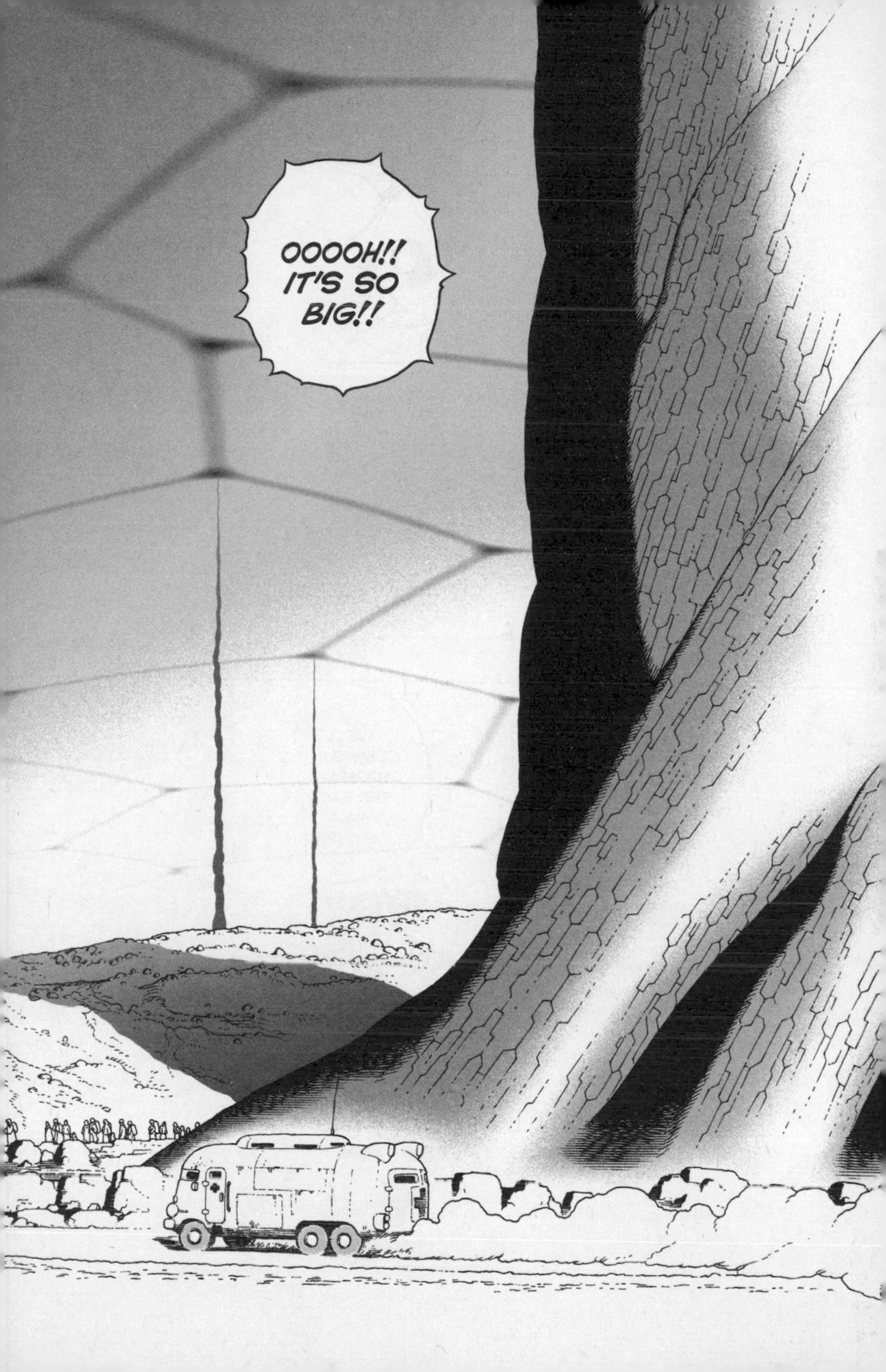
OOOOH!! IT'S SO BIG!!

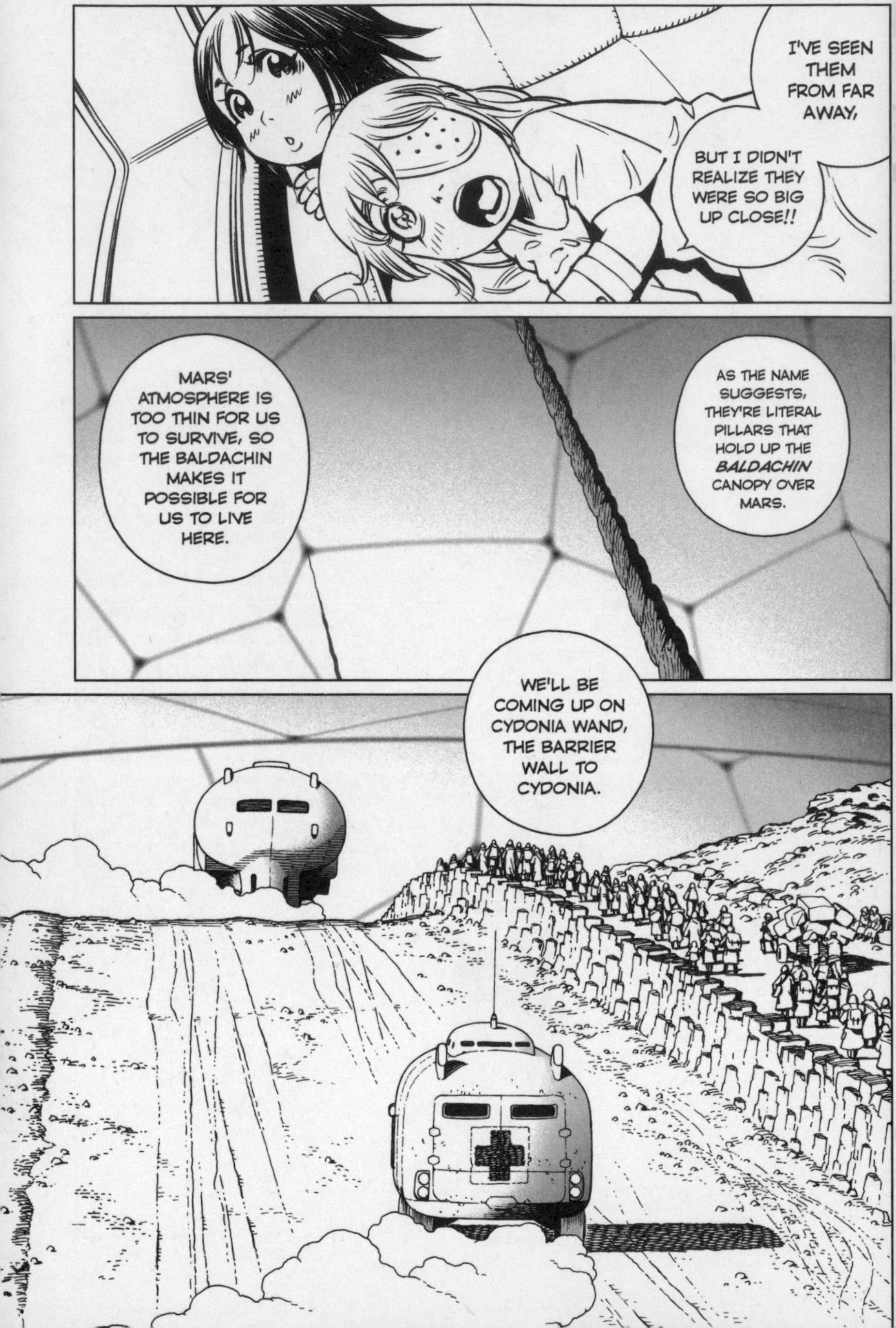
I'VE SEEN THEM FROM FAR AWAY,
BUT I DIDN'T REALIZE THEY WERE SO BIG UP CLOSE!!
AS THE NAME SUGGESTS, THEY'RE LITERAL PILLARS THAT HOLD UP THE *BALDACHIN* CANOPY OVER MARS.
MARS' ATMOSPHERE IS TOO THIN FOR US TO SURVIVE, SO THE BALDACHIN MAKES IT POSSIBLE FOR US TO LIVE HERE.
WE'LL BE COMING UP ON CYDONIA WAND, THE BARRIER WALL TO CYDONIA.

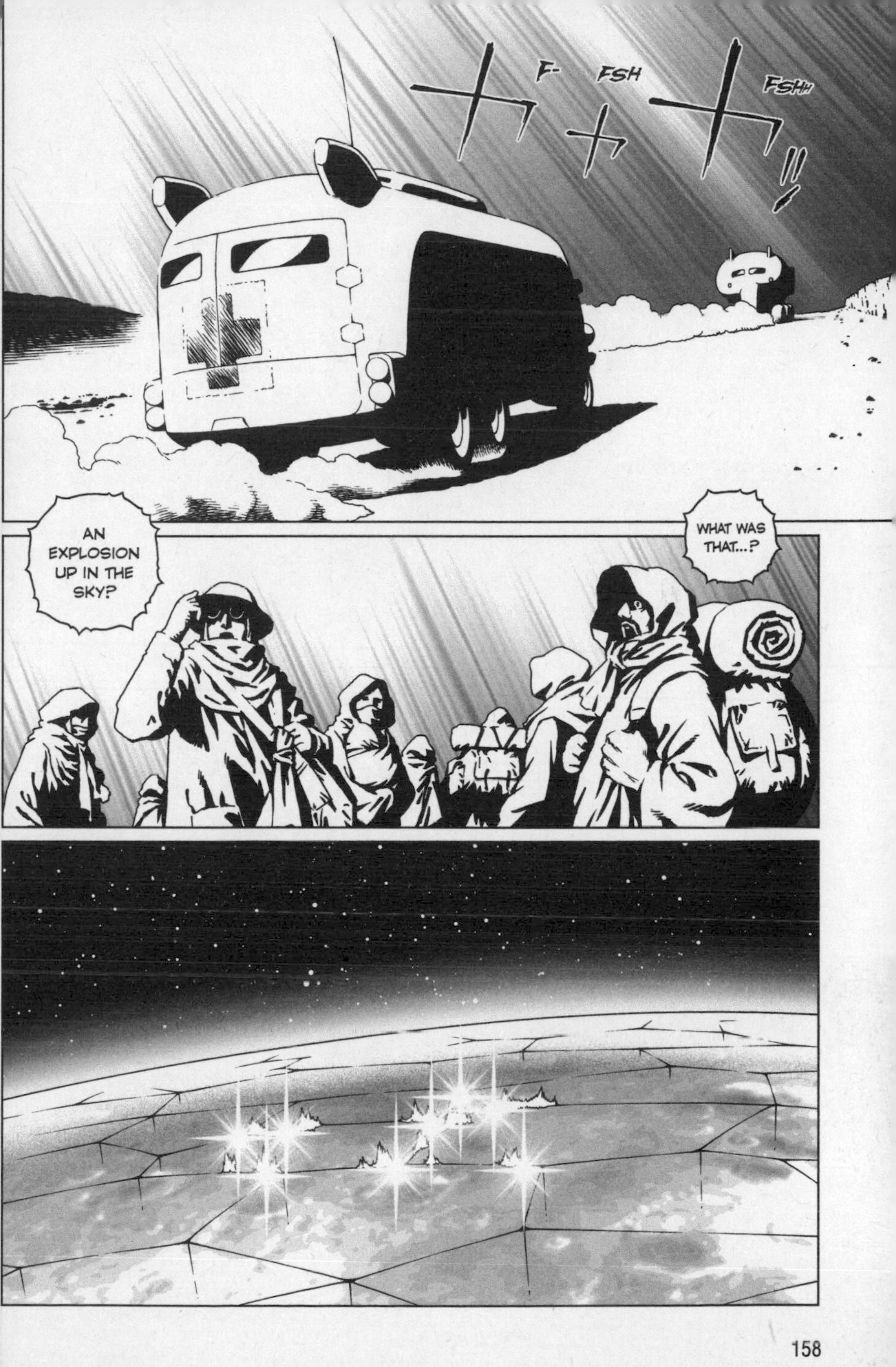
F- FSH FSHH
WHAT WAS THAT...?
AN EXPLOSION UP IN THE SKY?

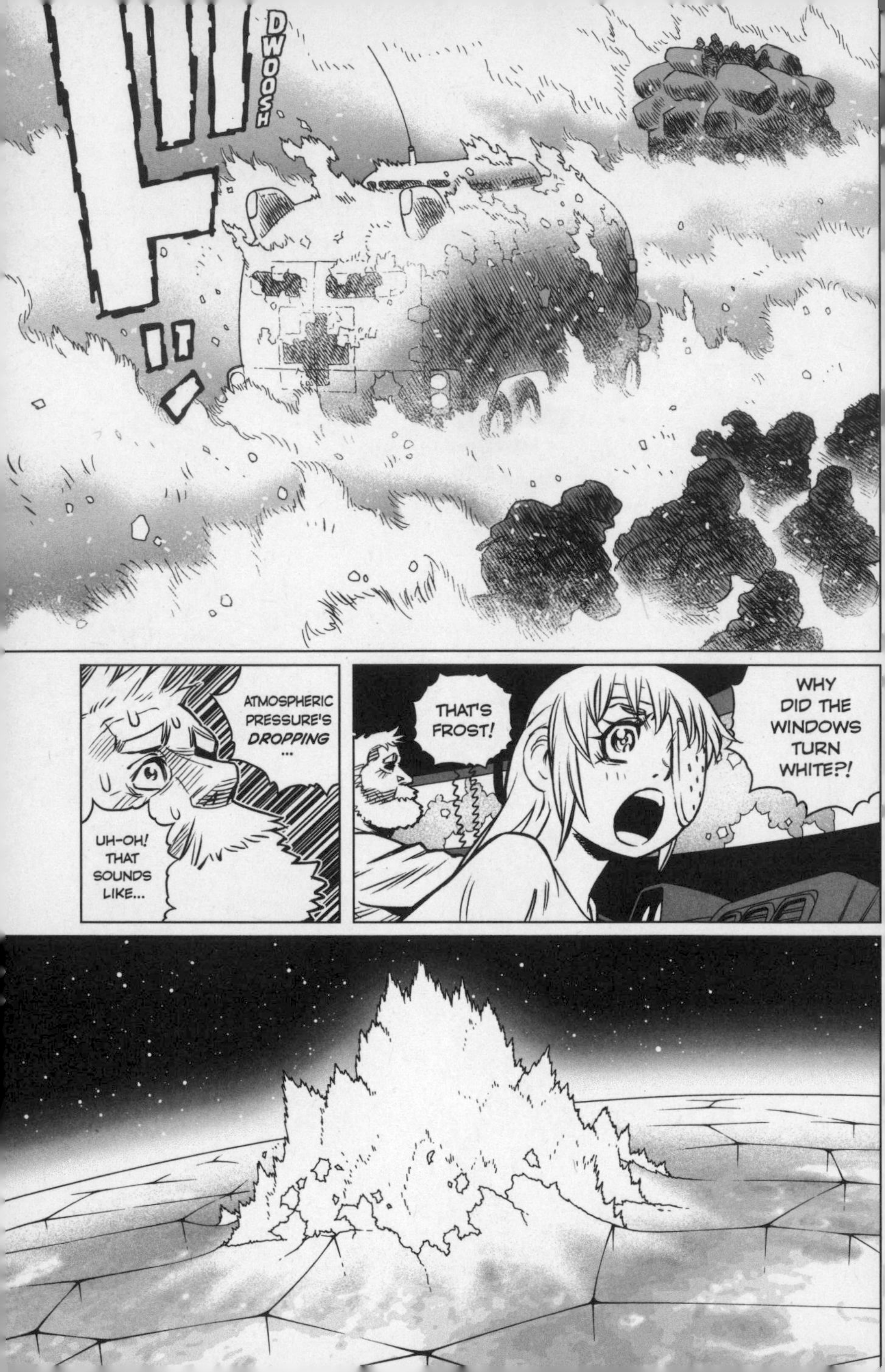
DWOOSH
WHY DID THE WINDOWS TURN WHITE?!
THAT'S FROST!
ATMOSPHERIC PRESSURE'S DROPPING ...
UH-OH! THAT SOUNDS LIKE...

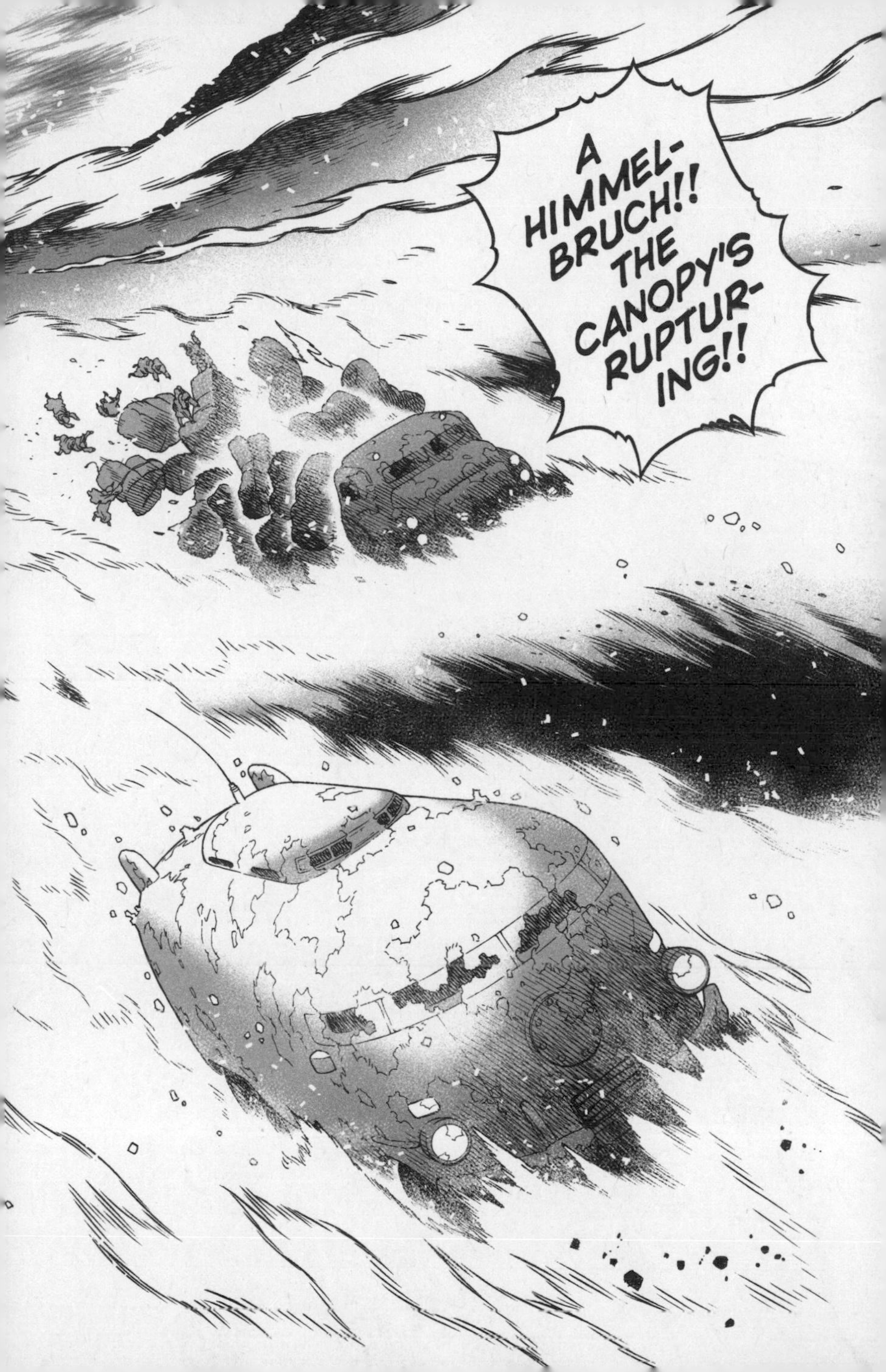
A HIMMEL-BRUCH!! THE CANOPY'S RUPTUR-ING!!

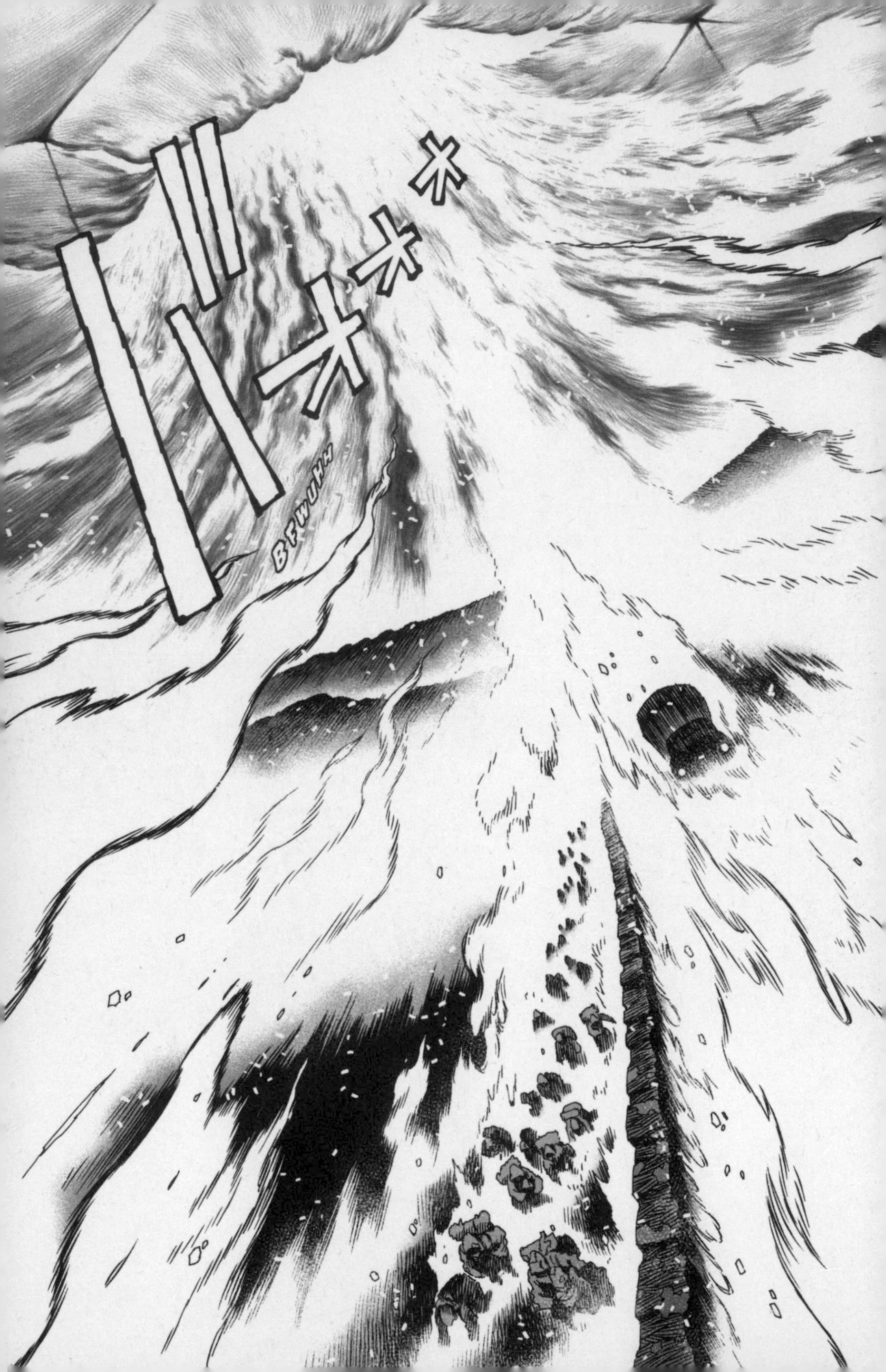
BFWUHH

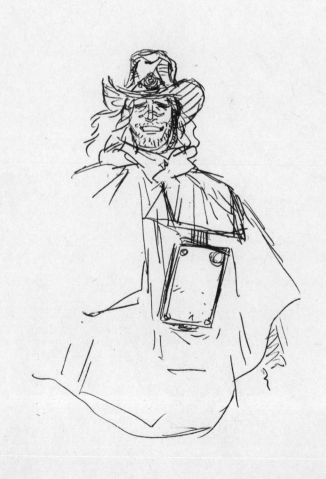

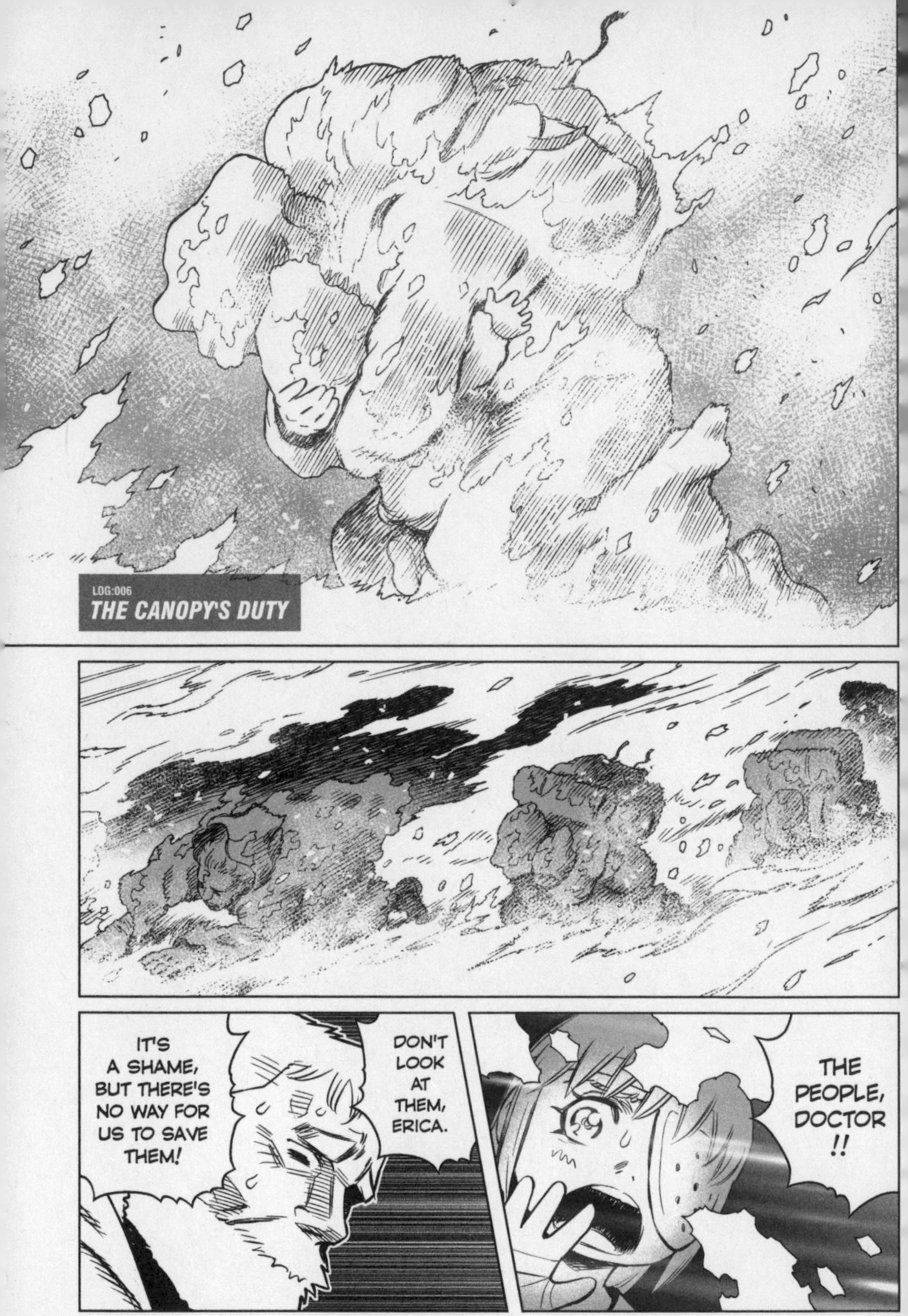
LOG:006
THE CANOPY'S DUTY
THE PEOPLE, DOCTOR!!
DON'T LOOK AT THEM, ERICA.
IT'S A SHAME, BUT THERE'S NO WAY FOR US TO SAVE THEM!

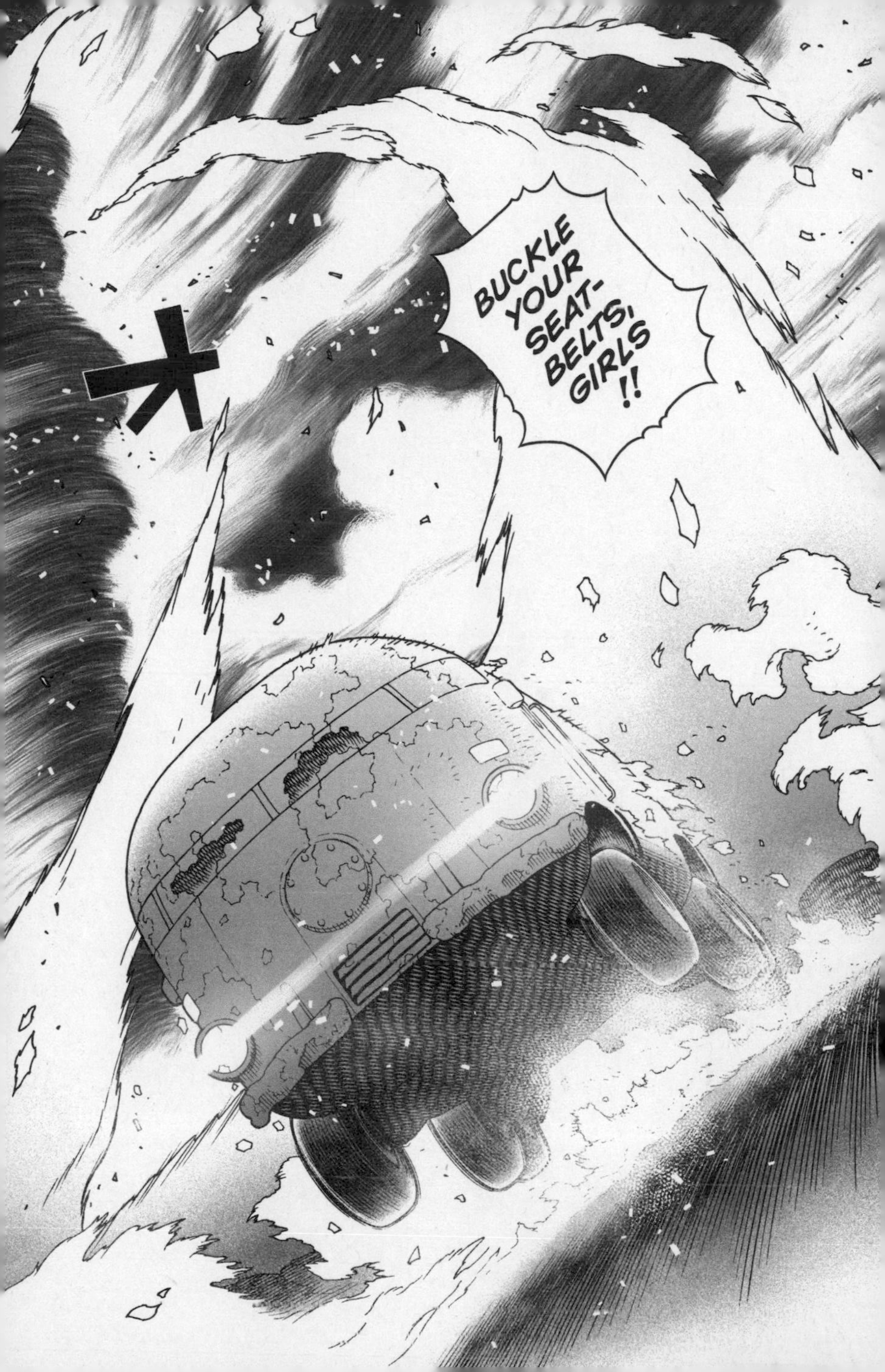
BUCKLE YOUR SEAT-BELTS, GIRLS!!

LOG:006

THE CANOPY'S DUTY

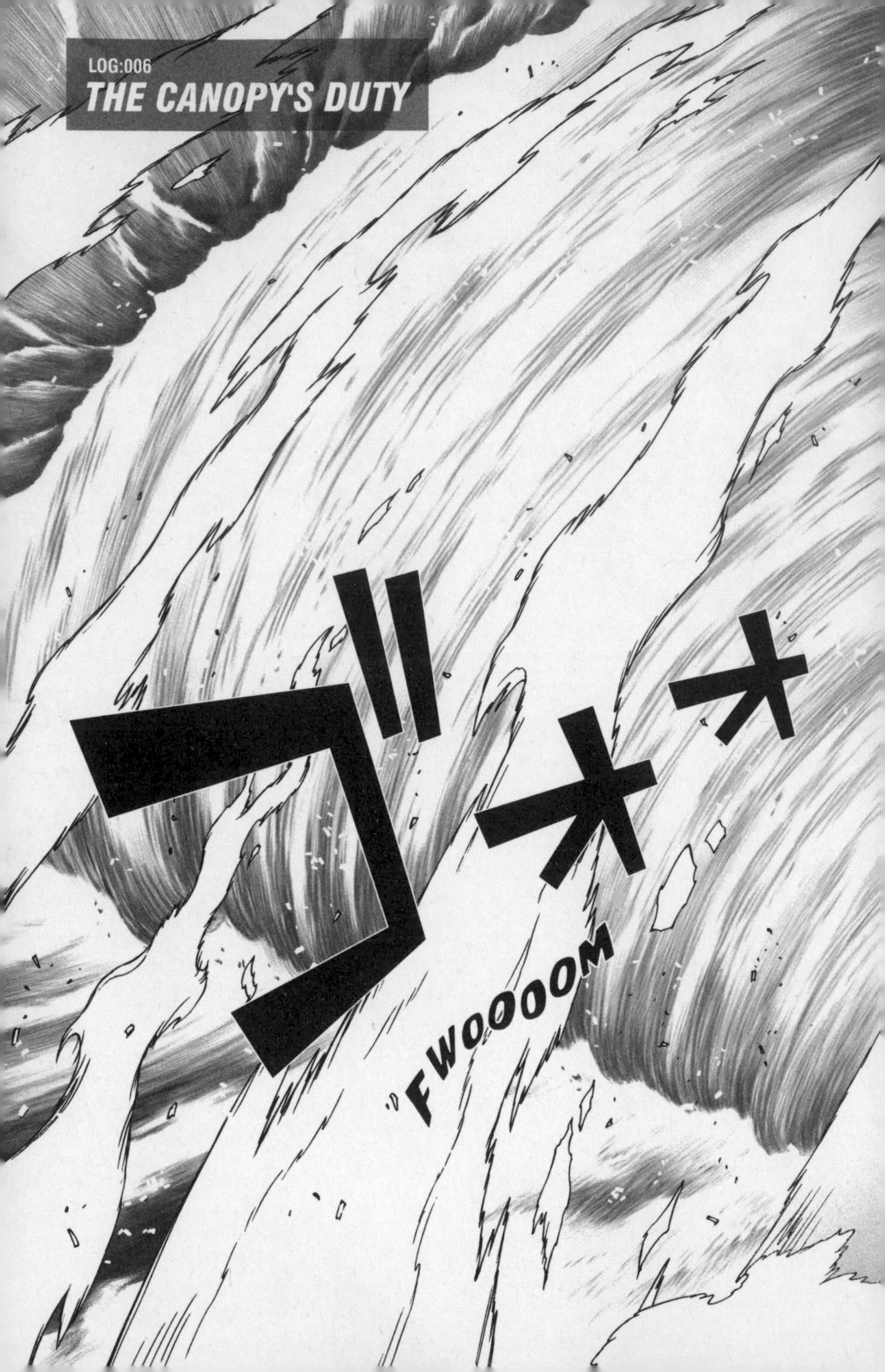
ゴォォ
FWOOOOM

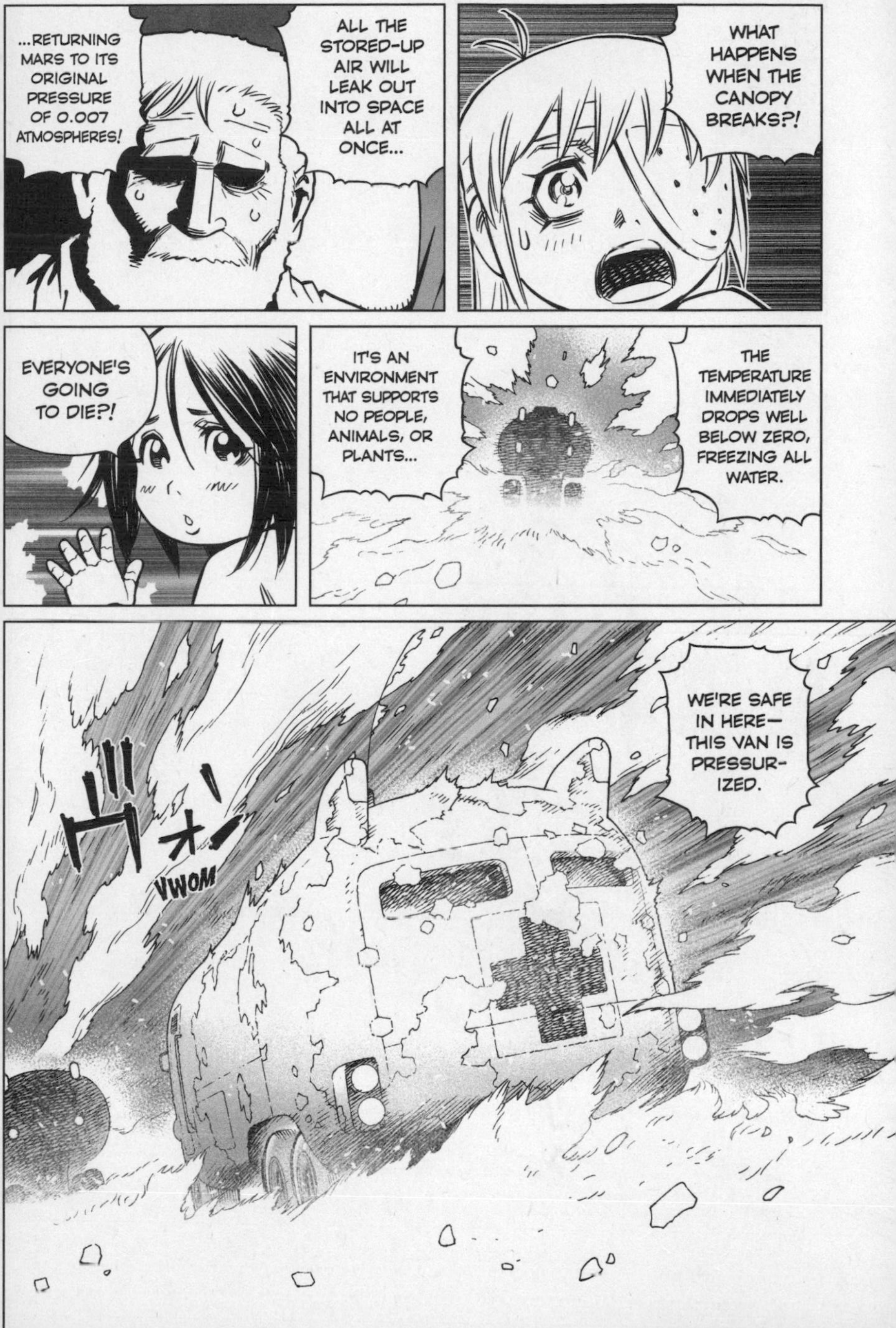
WHAT HAPPENS WHEN THE CANOPY BREAKS?!
ALL THE STORED-UP AIR WILL LEAK OUT INTO SPACE ALL AT ONCE...
...RETURNING MARS TO ITS ORIGINAL PRESSURE OF 0.007 ATMOSPHERES!
THE TEMPERATURE IMMEDIATELY DROPS WELL BELOW ZERO, FREEZING ALL WATER.
IT'S AN ENVIRONMENT THAT SUPPORTS NO PEOPLE, ANIMALS, OR PLANTS...
EVERYONE'S GOING TO DIE?!
WE'RE SAFE IN HERE— THIS VAN IS PRESSURIZED.
VWOM

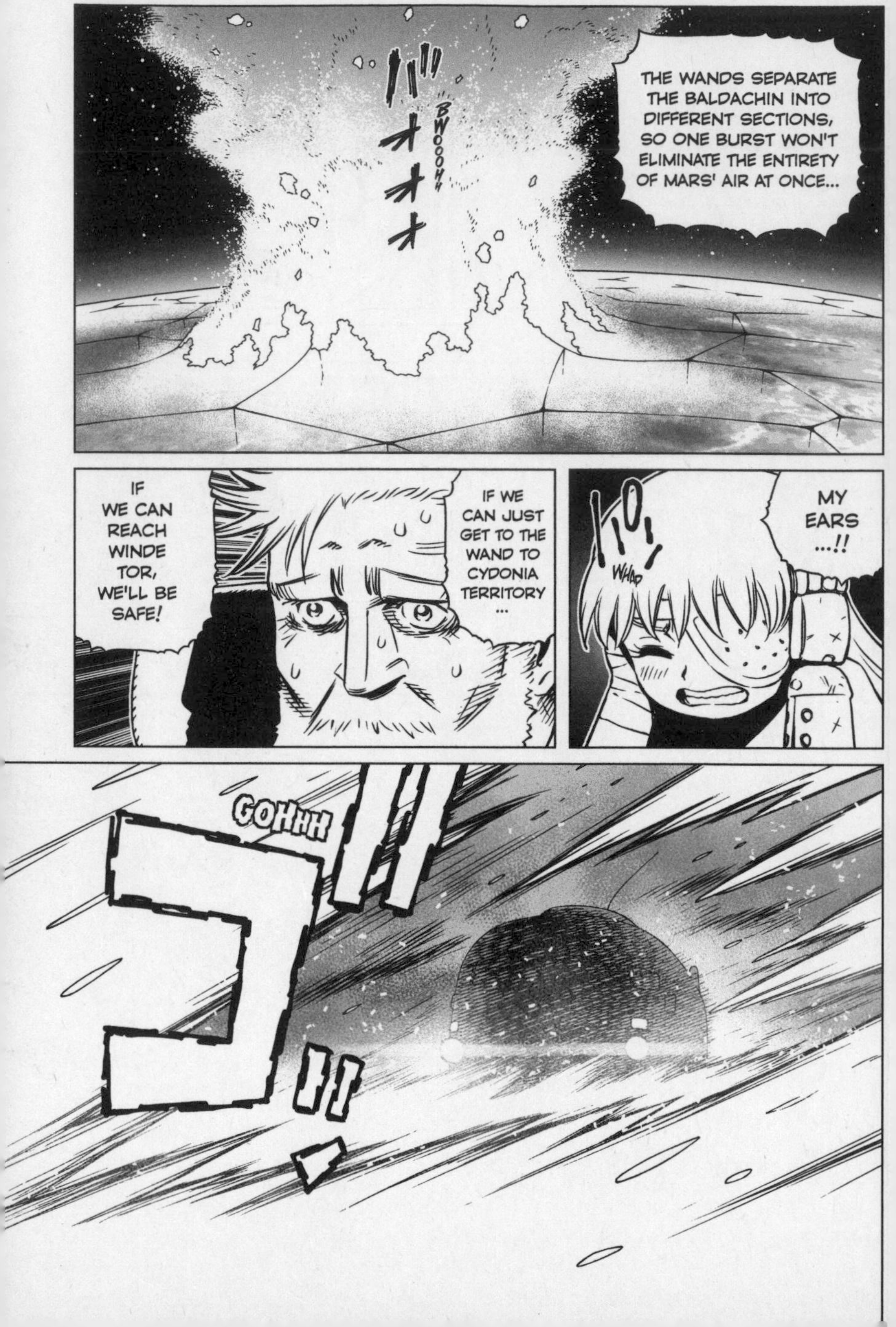
BWOOOHHH
THE WANDS SEPARATE THE BALDACHIN INTO DIFFERENT SECTIONS, SO ONE BURST WON'T ELIMINATE THE ENTIRETY OF MARS' AIR AT ONCE...
MY EARS ...!!
WHAP
IF WE CAN JUST GET TO THE WAND TO CYDONIA TERRITORY ...
IF WE CAN REACH WINDE TOR, WE'LL BE SAFE!
GOHHH

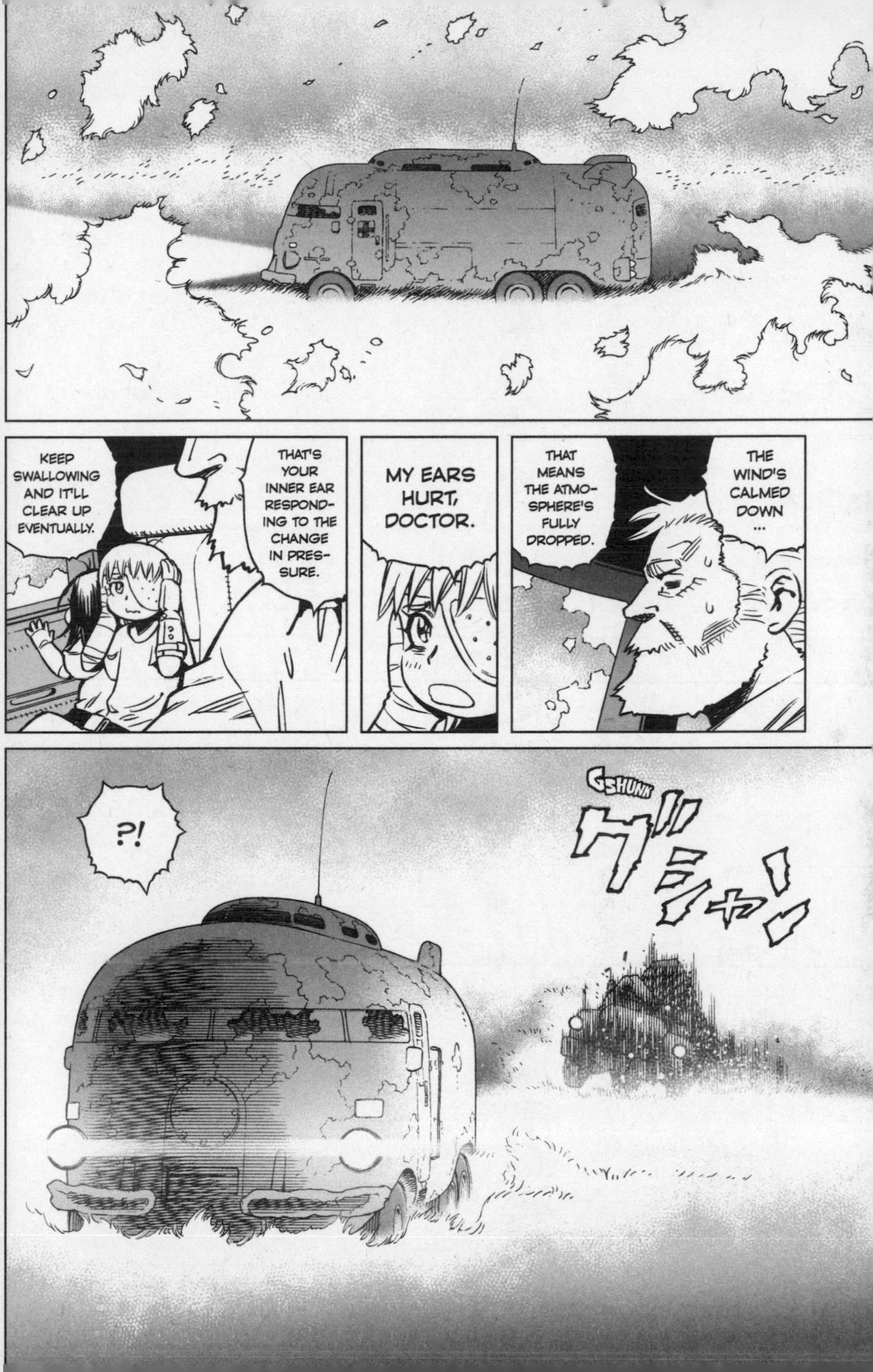
THE WIND'S CALMED DOWN ...
THAT MEANS THE ATMOSPHERE'S FULLY DROPPED.
MY EARS HURT, DOCTOR.
THAT'S YOUR INNER EAR RESPONDING TO THE CHANGE IN PRESSURE.
KEEP SWALLOWING AND IT'LL CLEAR UP EVENTUALLY.
GSHUNK
グシャン
?!

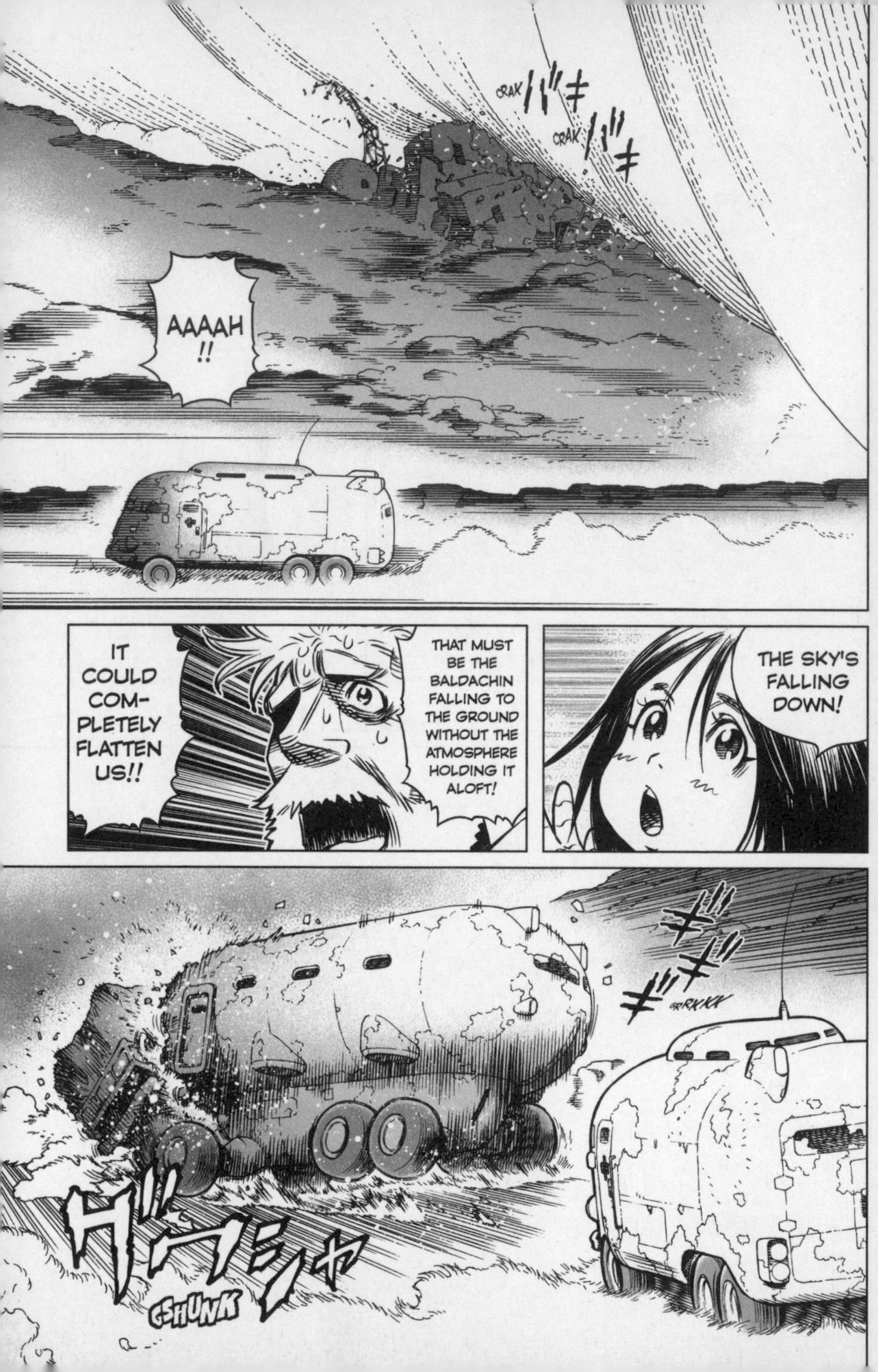

CRAK
CRAK
AAAAH!!
THE SKY'S FALLING DOWN!
THAT MUST BE THE BALDACHIN FALLING TO THE GROUND WITHOUT THE ATMOSPHERE HOLDING IT ALOFT!
IT COULD COMPLETELY FLATTEN US!!
GRRKKK
GSHUNK

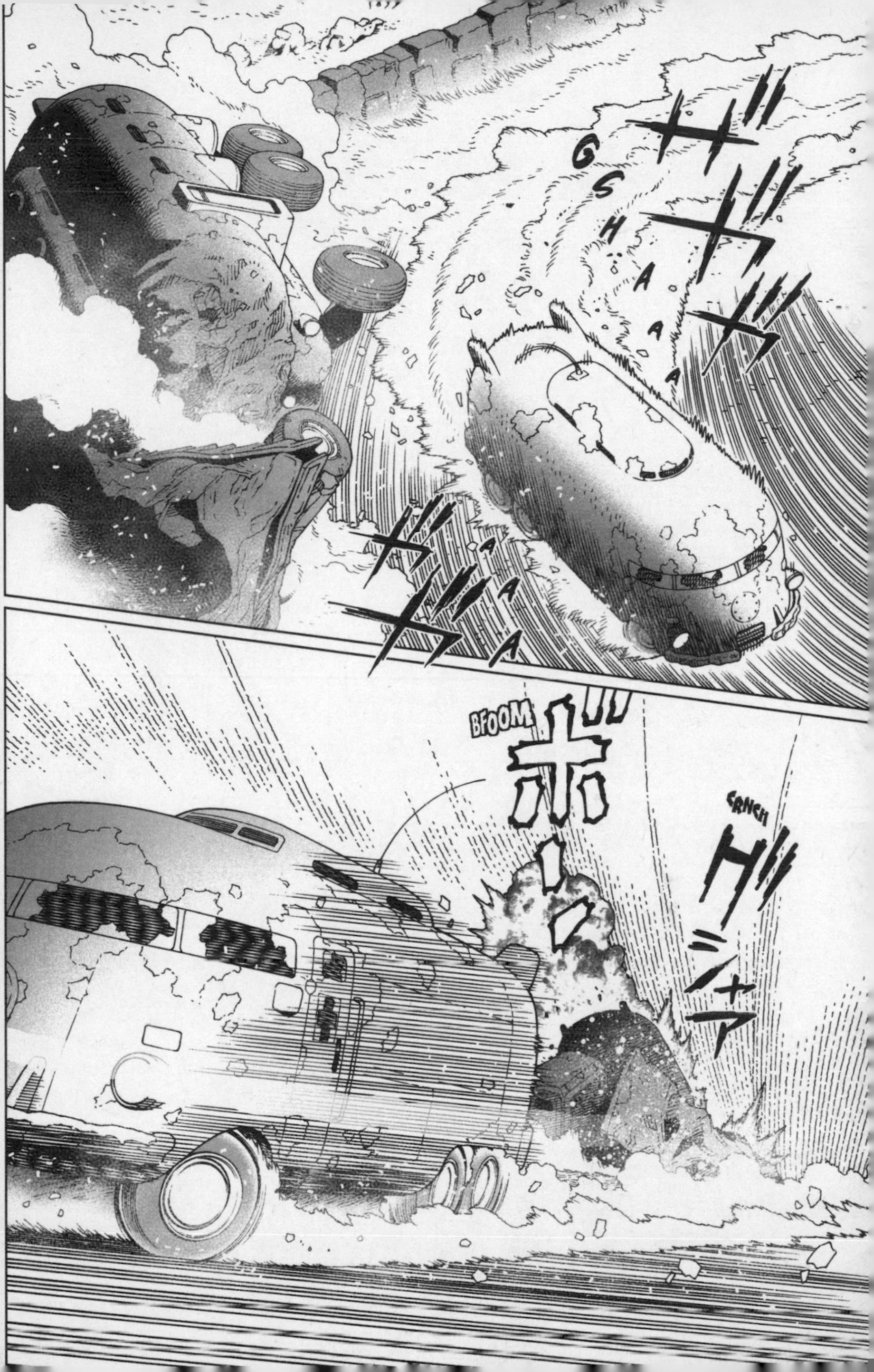
GSHAAAA
AAAA
BFOOM
CRNCH

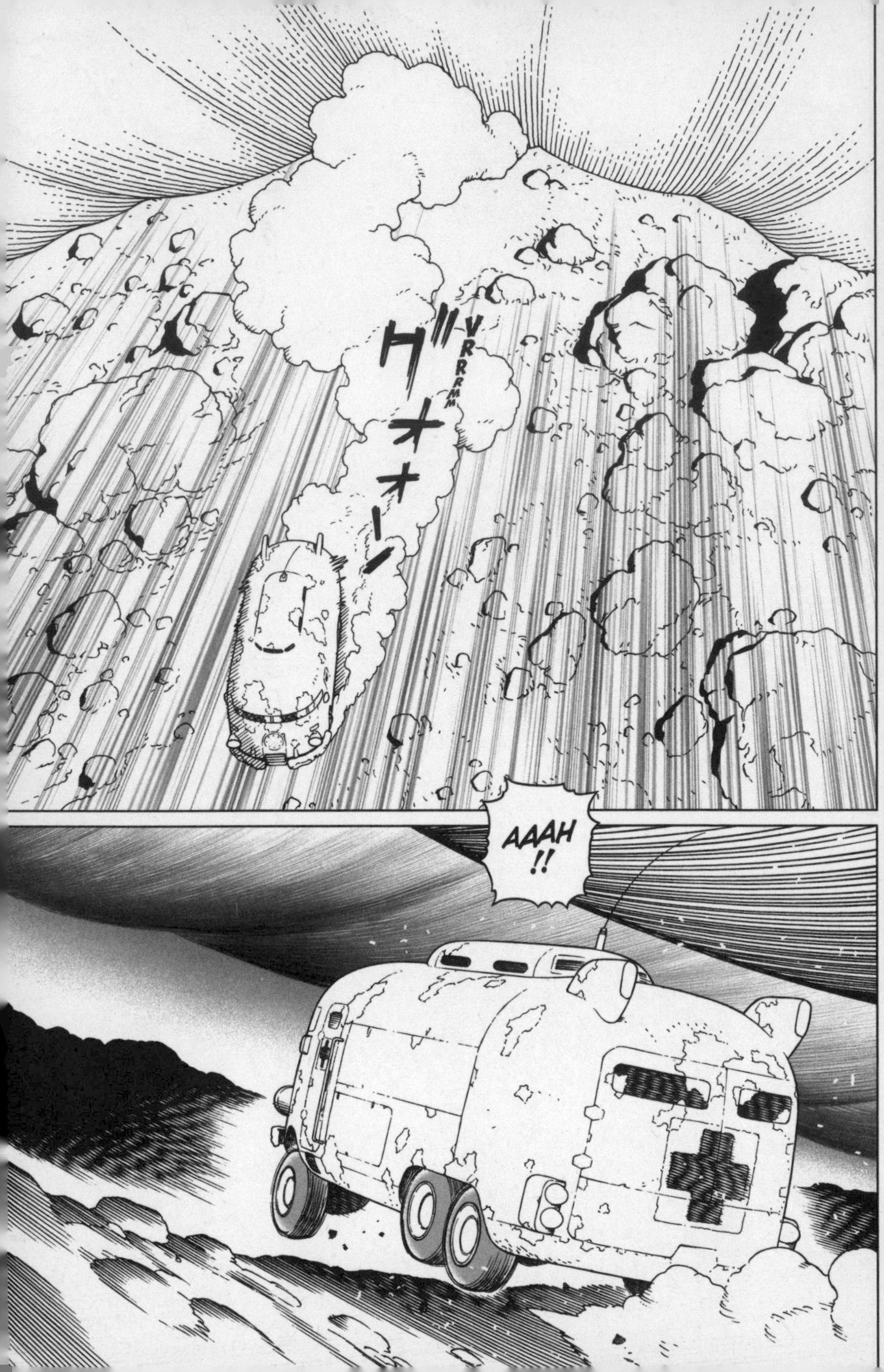
ゴオオーン
VRRRMM
AAAH!!

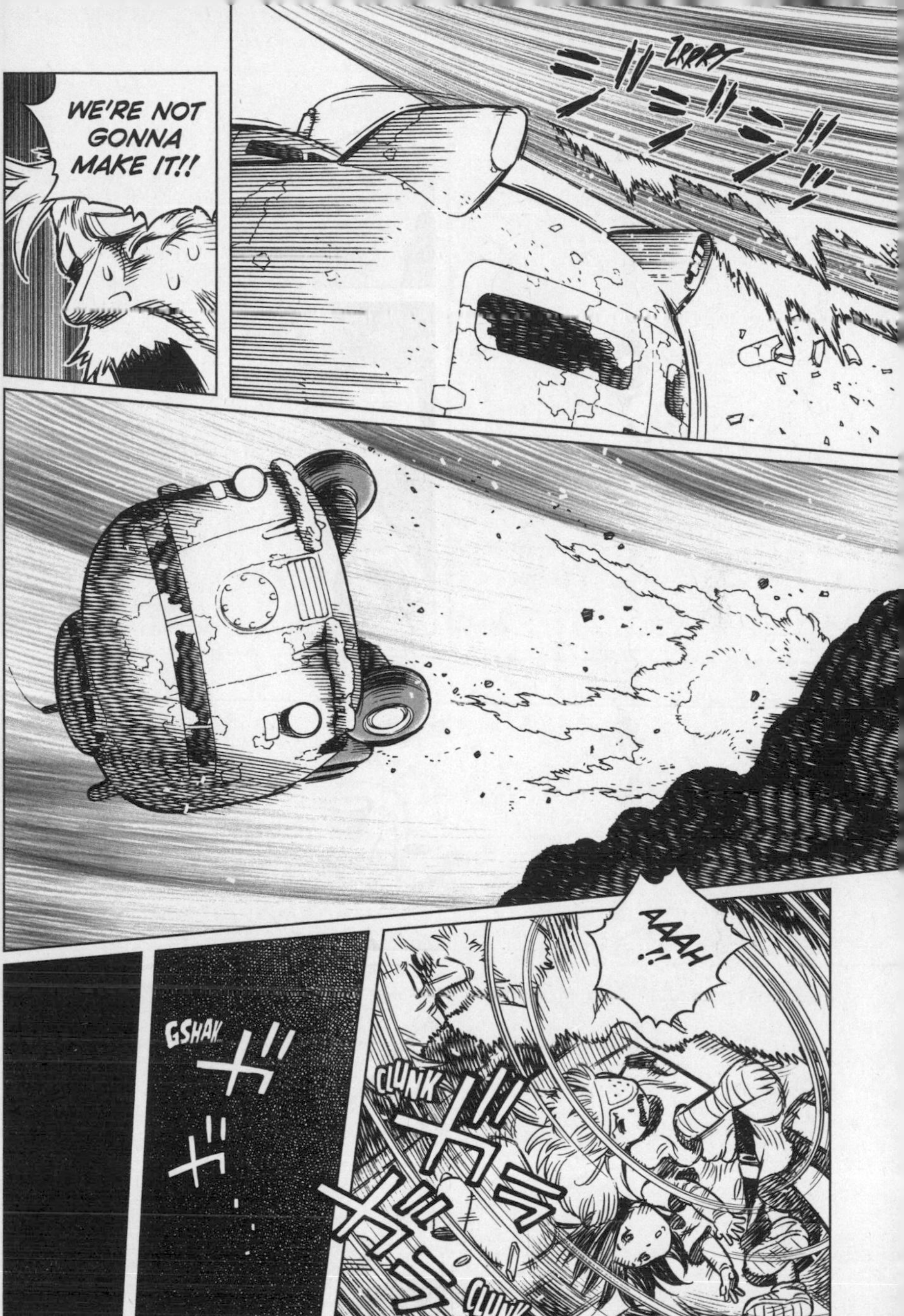
ZRRRT
WE'RE NOT GONNA MAKE IT!!
AAAH!!
CLUNK
CLUNK
GSHAK...

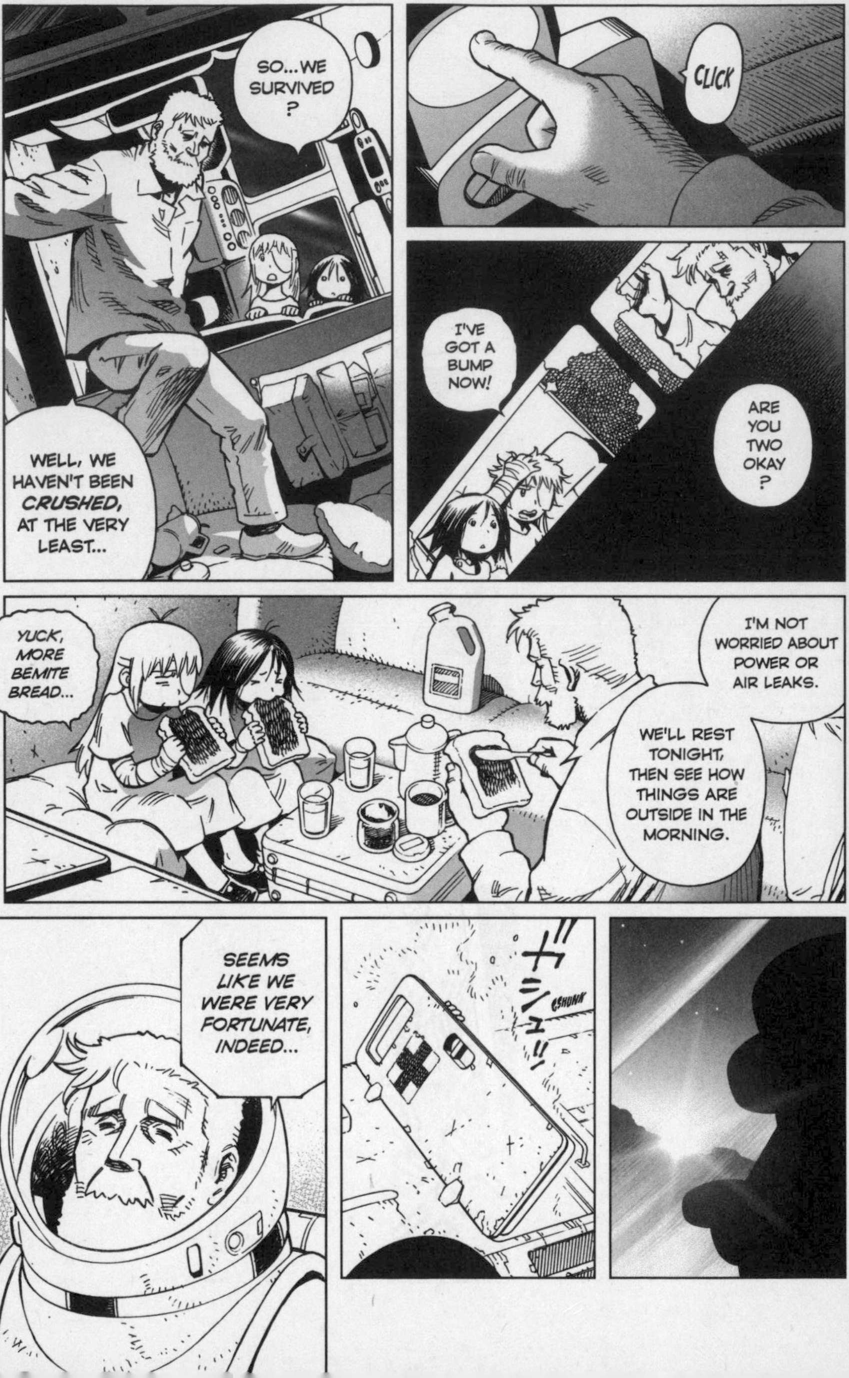
CLICK
ARE YOU TWO OKAY?
I'VE GOT A BUMP NOW!
SO...WE SURVIVED?
WELL, WE HAVEN'T BEEN CRUSHED, AT THE VERY LEAST...
I'M NOT WORRIED ABOUT POWER OR AIR LEAKS.
WE'LL REST TONIGHT, THEN SEE HOW THINGS ARE OUTSIDE IN THE MORNING.
YUCK, MORE BEMITE BREAD...
ガシュ!!
GSHUNK
SEEMS LIKE WE WERE VERY FORTUNATE, INDEED...

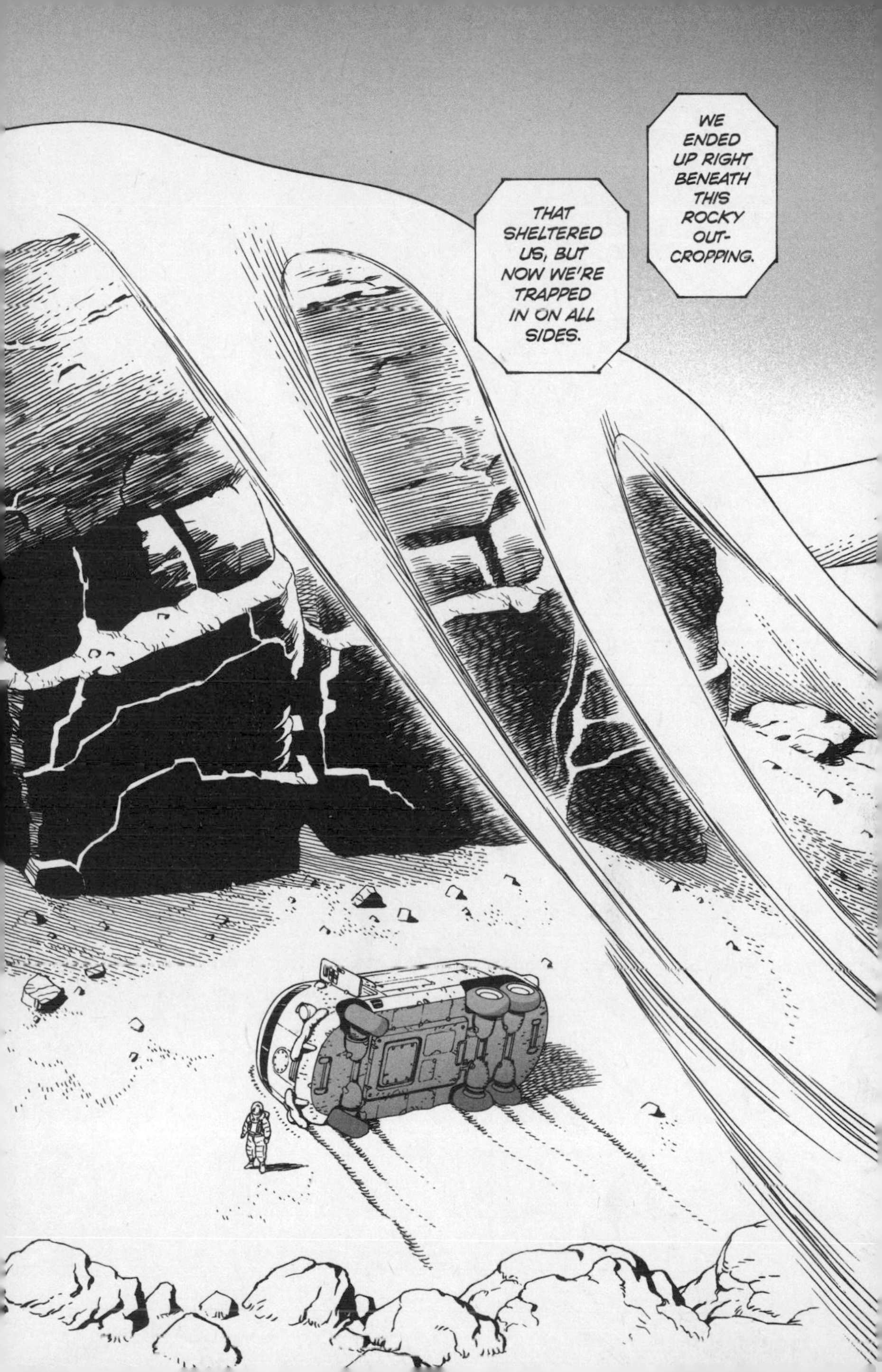
WE ENDED UP RIGHT BENEATH THIS ROCKY OUT-CROPPING.
THAT SHELTERED US, BUT NOW WE'RE TRAPPED IN ON ALL SIDES.

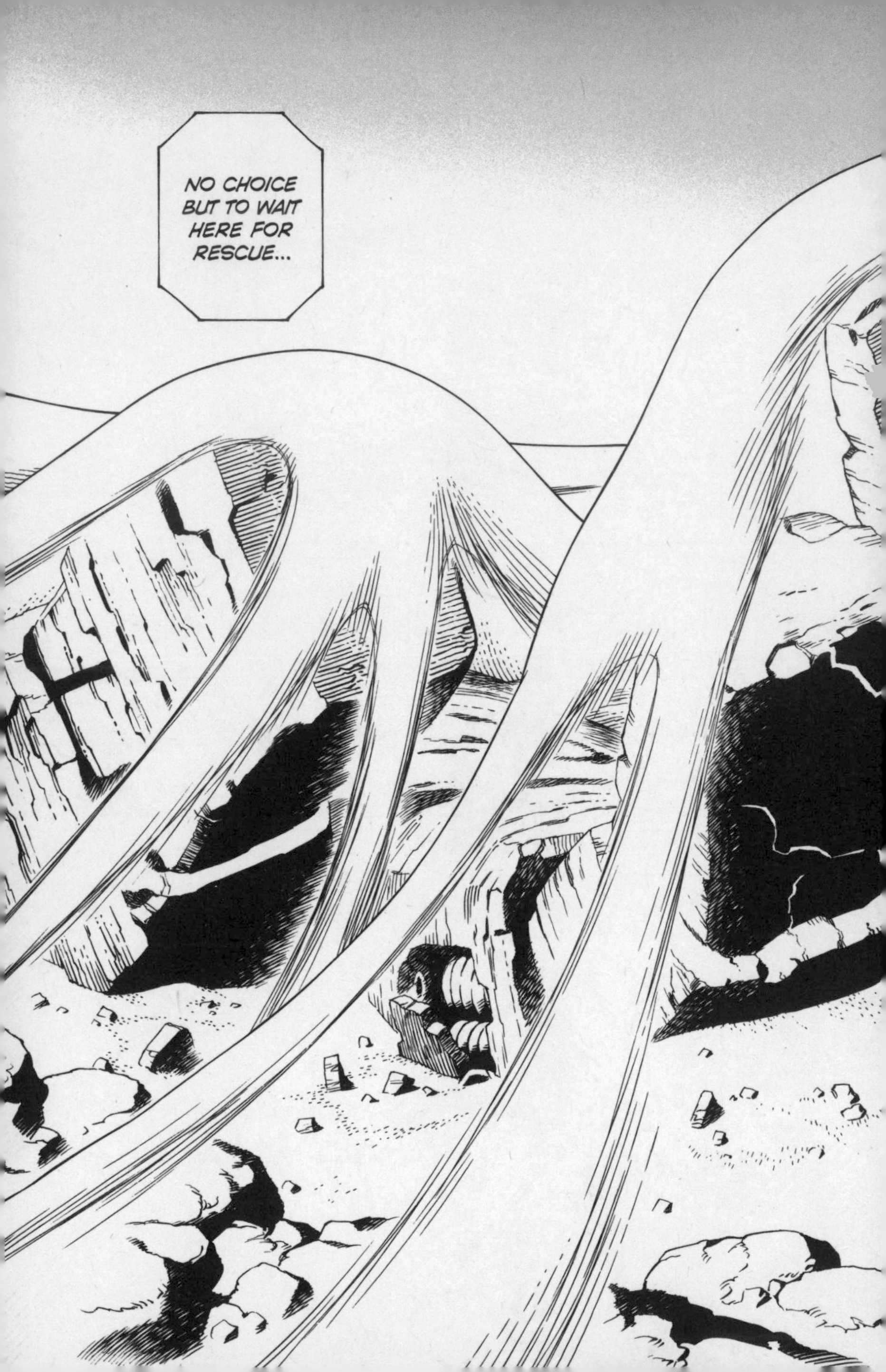
NO CHOICE BUT TO WAIT HERE FOR RESCUE...

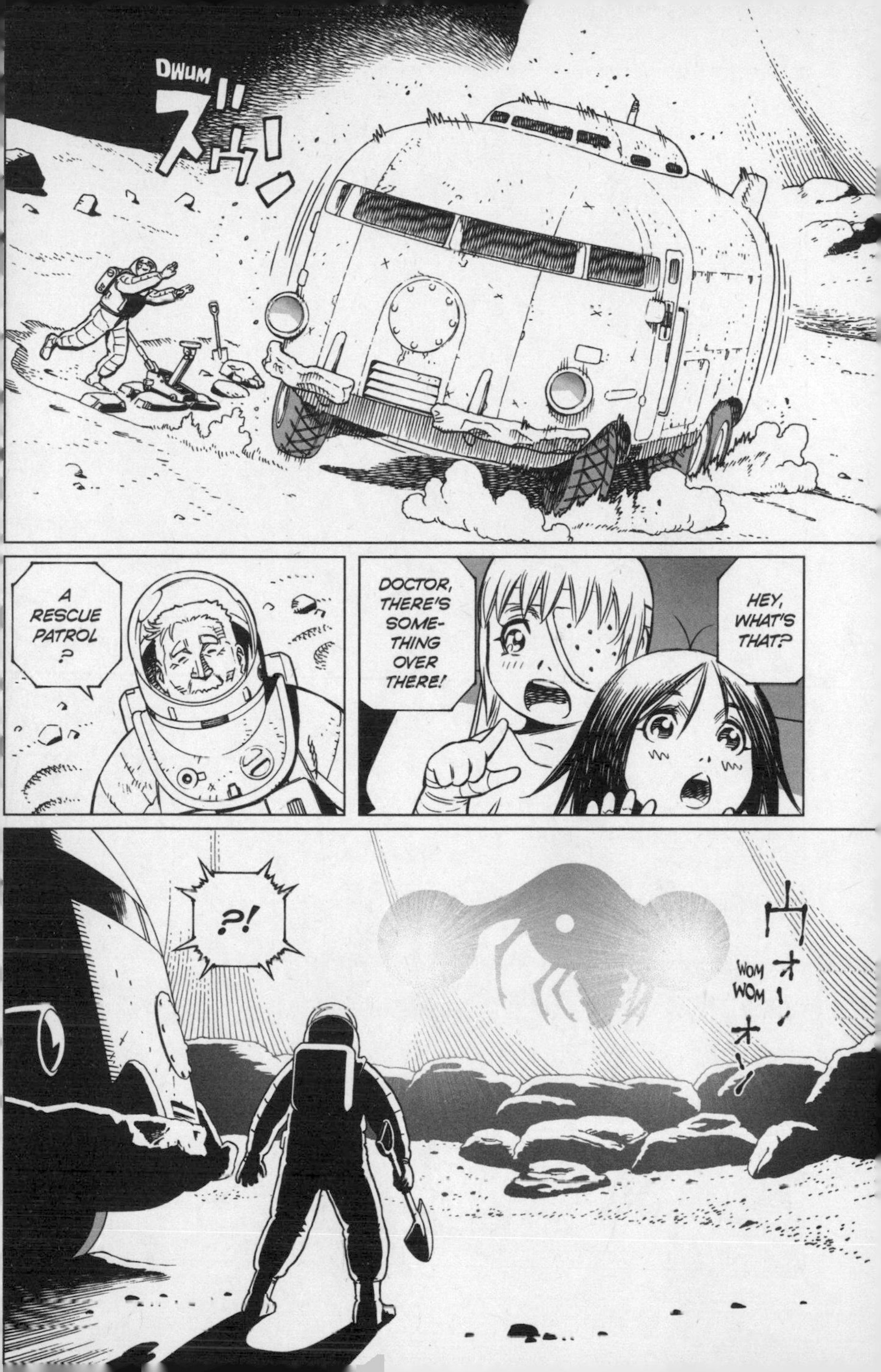
DWUM
HEY, WHAT'S THAT?
DOCTOR, THERE'S SOME-THING OVER THERE!
A RESCUE PATROL?
?!
WOM WOM

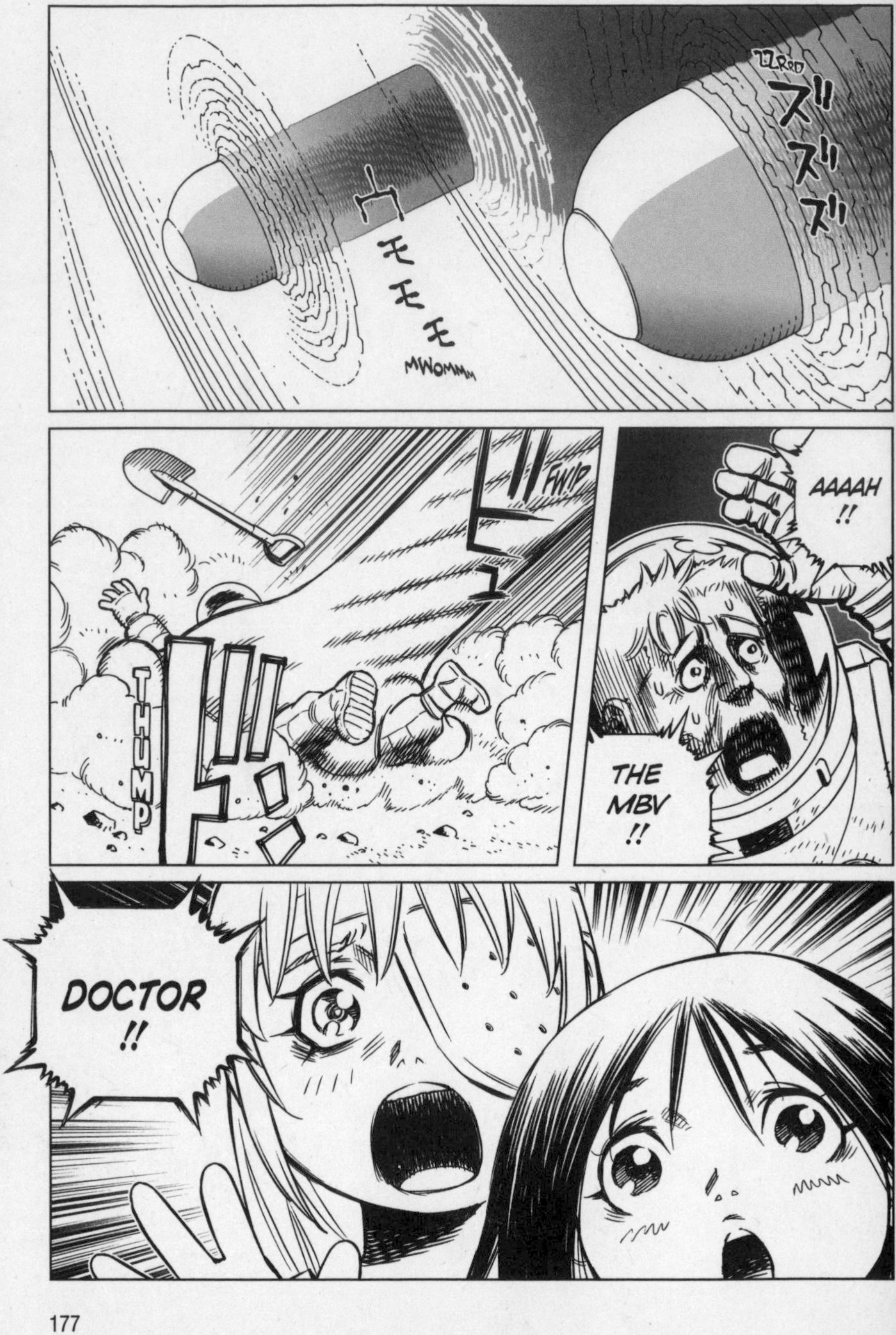
ZZRRD
ズズズズ
ムモモモ
MWOMMM
AAAAH!!
THE MBV!!
FWIP
THUMP
DOCTOR!!

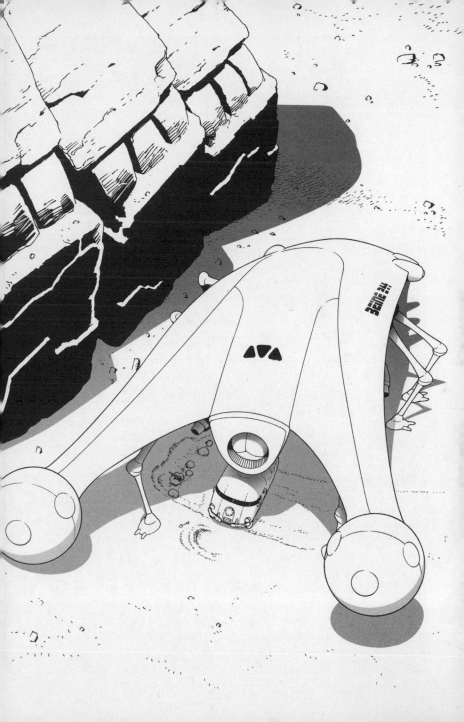

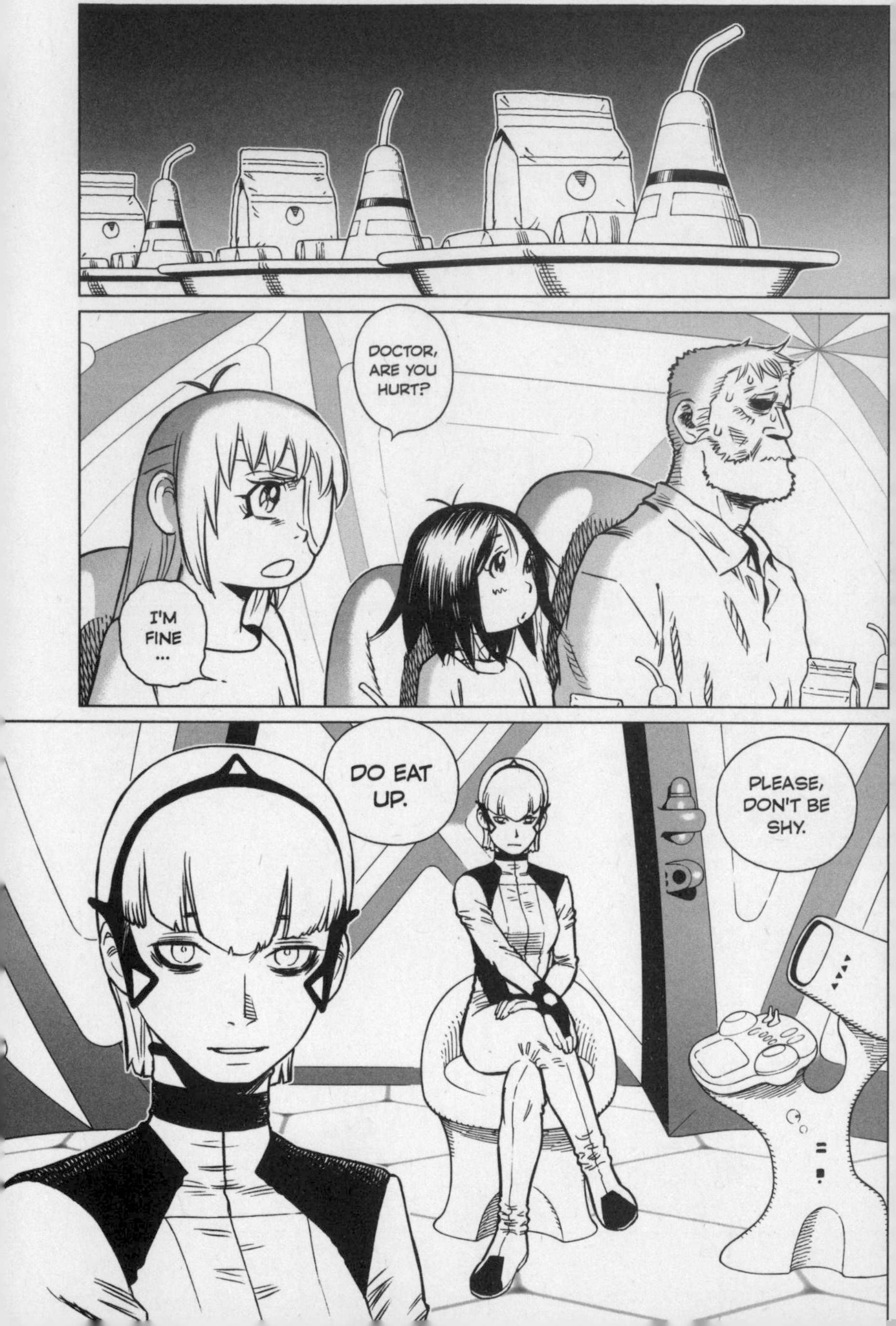
DOCTOR, ARE YOU HURT?
I'M FINE ...
PLEASE, DON'T BE SHY.
DO EAT UP.

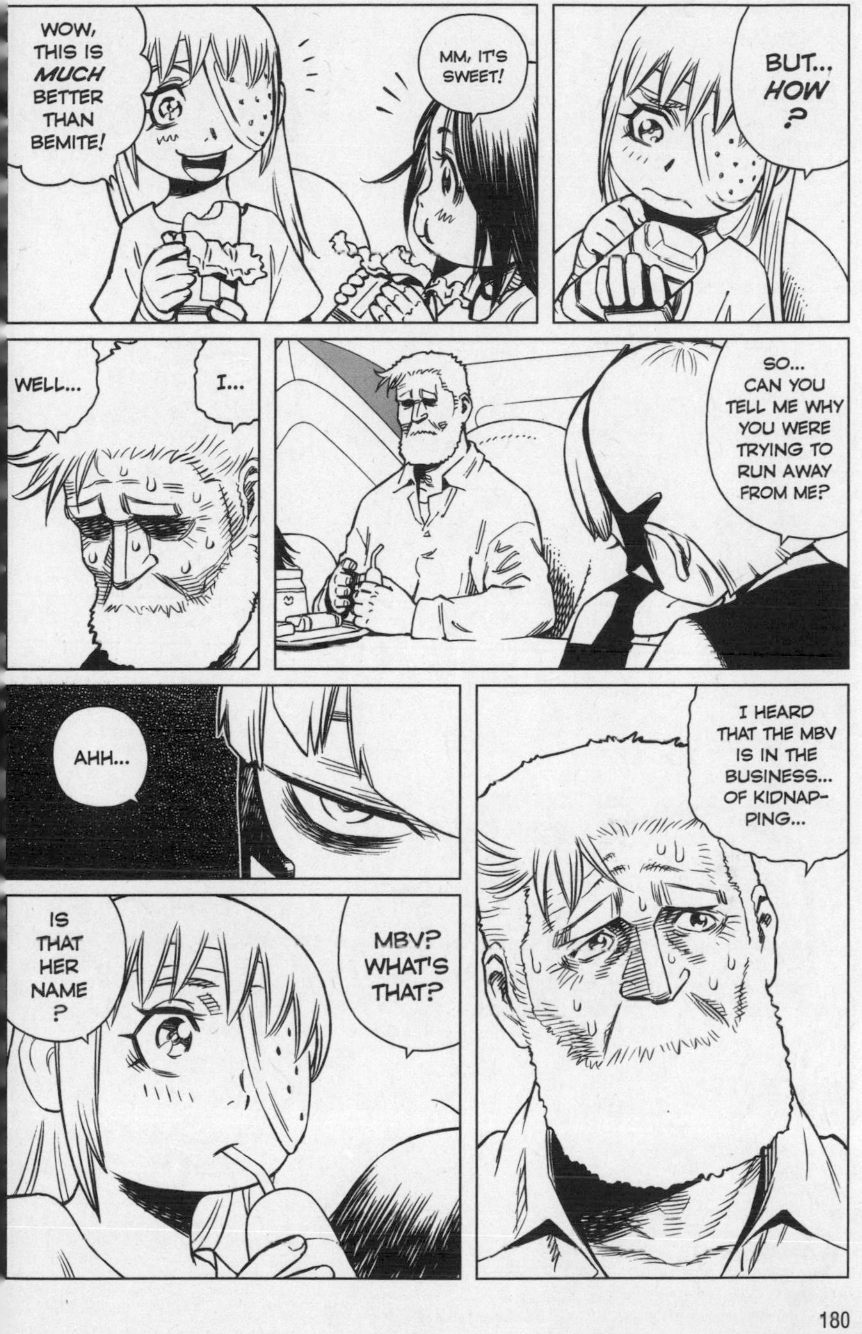
BUT... *HOW* ?
MM, IT'S SWEET!
WOW, THIS IS *MUCH* BETTER THAN BEMITE!
SO... CAN YOU TELL ME WHY YOU WERE TRYING TO RUN AWAY FROM ME?
I...
WELL...
I HEARD THAT THE MBV IS IN THE BUSINESS... OF KIDNAP-PING...
AHH...
MBV? WHAT'S THAT?
IS THAT HER NAME ?

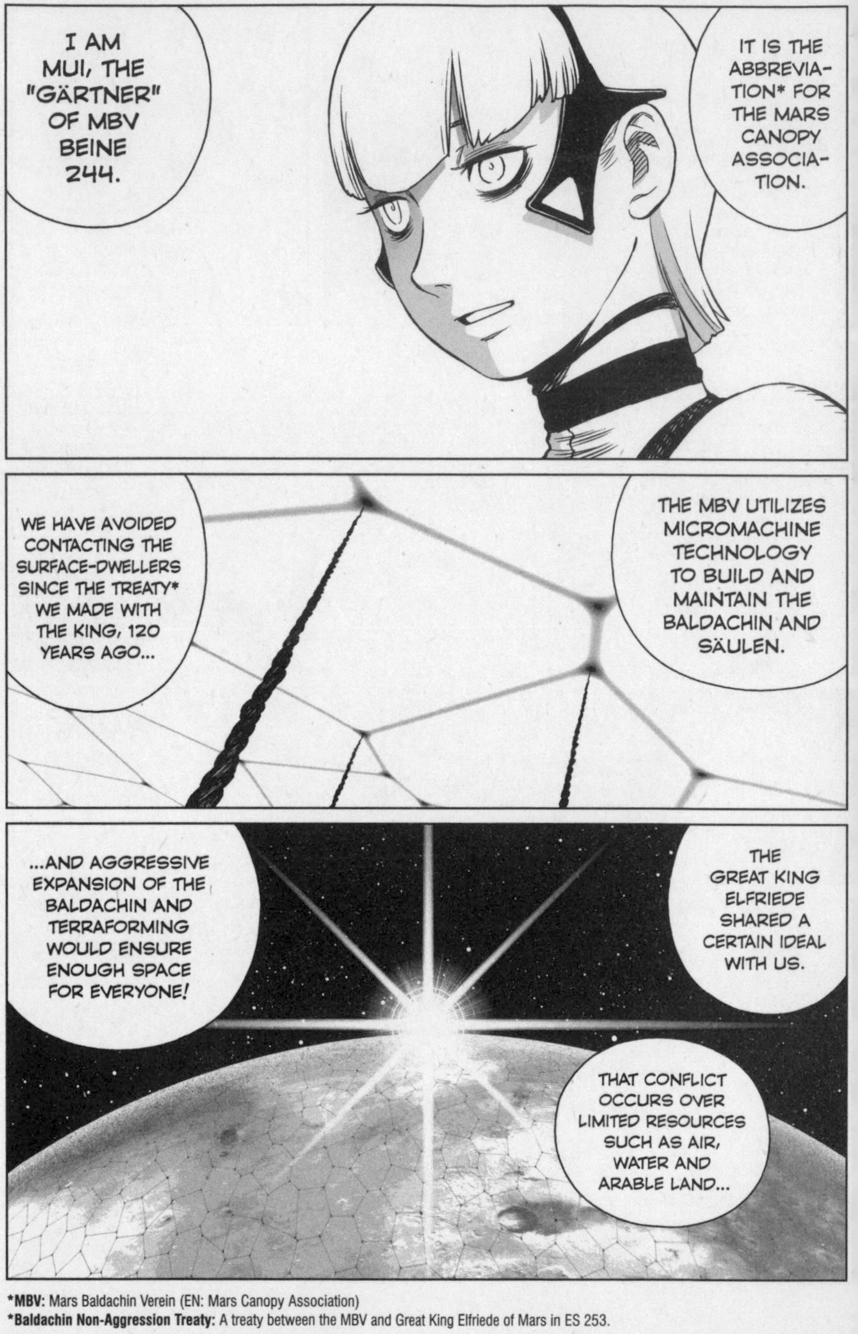
IT IS THE ABBREVIATION* FOR THE MARS CANOPY ASSOCIATION.
I AM MUI, THE "GÄRTNER" OF MBV BEINE 244.
THE MBV UTILIZES MICROMACHINE TECHNOLOGY TO BUILD AND MAINTAIN THE BALDACHIN AND SÄULEN.
WE HAVE AVOIDED CONTACTING THE SURFACE-DWELLERS SINCE THE TREATY* WE MADE WITH THE KING, 120 YEARS AGO...
THE GREAT KING ELFRIEDE SHARED A CERTAIN IDEAL WITH US.
...AND AGGRESSIVE EXPANSION OF THE BALDACHIN AND TERRAFORMING WOULD ENSURE ENOUGH SPACE FOR EVERYONE!
THAT CONFLICT OCCURS OVER LIMITED RESOURCES SUCH AS AIR, WATER AND ARABLE LAND...

***MBV:** Mars Baldachin Verein (EN: Mars Canopy Association)
***Baldachin Non-Aggression Treaty:** A treaty between the MBV and Great King Elfriede of Mars in ES 253.

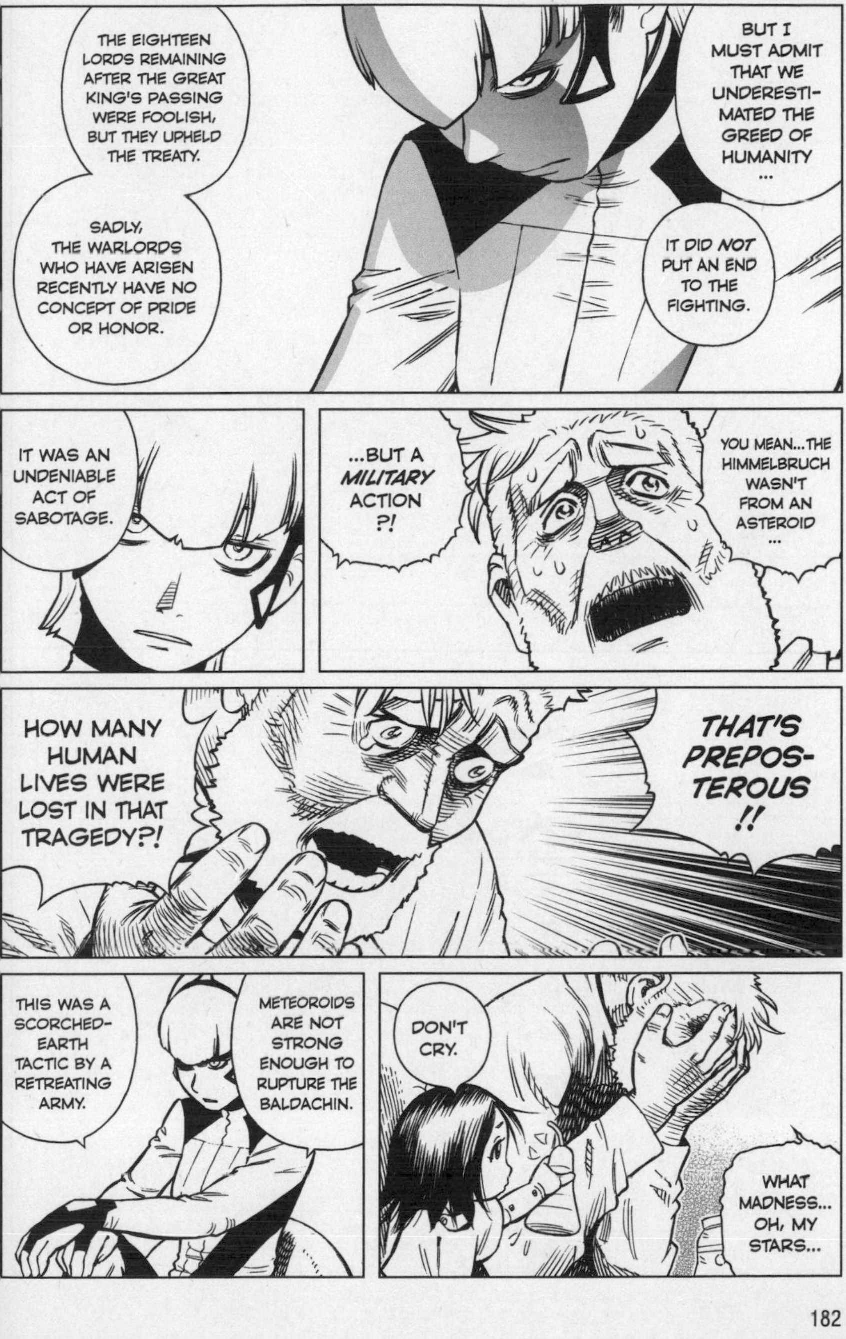
BUT I MUST ADMIT THAT WE UNDERESTIMATED THE GREED OF HUMANITY...
IT DID *NOT* PUT AN END TO THE FIGHTING.
THE EIGHTEEN LORDS REMAINING AFTER THE GREAT KING'S PASSING WERE FOOLISH, BUT THEY UPHELD THE TREATY.
SADLY, THE WARLORDS WHO HAVE ARISEN RECENTLY HAVE NO CONCEPT OF PRIDE OR HONOR.
YOU MEAN...THE HIMMELBRUCH WASN'T FROM AN ASTEROID...
...BUT A *MILITARY* ACTION?!
IT WAS AN UNDENIABLE ACT OF SABOTAGE.
THAT'S PREPOSTEROUS!!
HOW MANY HUMAN LIVES WERE LOST IN THAT TRAGEDY?!
WHAT MADNESS... OH, MY STARS...
DON'T CRY.
METEOROIDS ARE NOT STRONG ENOUGH TO RUPTURE THE BALDACHIN.
THIS WAS A SCORCHED-EARTH TACTIC BY A RETREATING ARMY.

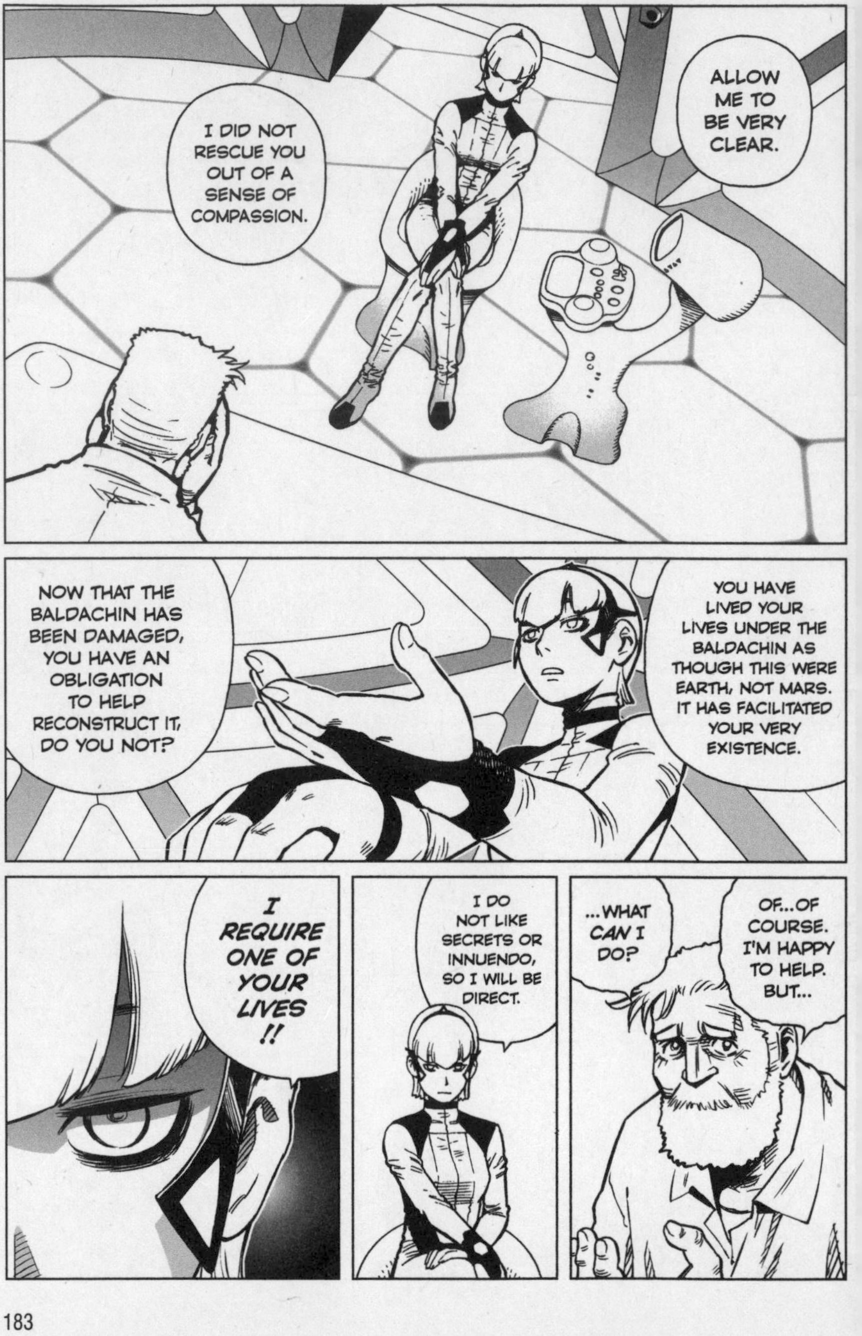
ALLOW ME TO BE VERY CLEAR.
I DID NOT RESCUE YOU OUT OF A SENSE OF COMPASSION.
YOU HAVE LIVED YOUR LIVES UNDER THE BALDACHIN AS THOUGH THIS WERE EARTH, NOT MARS. IT HAS FACILITATED YOUR VERY EXISTENCE.
NOW THAT THE BALDACHIN HAS BEEN DAMAGED, YOU HAVE AN OBLIGATION TO HELP RECONSTRUCT IT, DO YOU NOT?
OF...OF COURSE. I'M HAPPY TO HELP. BUT...
...WHAT *CAN* I DO?
I DO NOT LIKE SECRETS OR INNUENDO, SO I WILL BE DIRECT.
I REQUIRE ONE OF YOUR LIVES !!

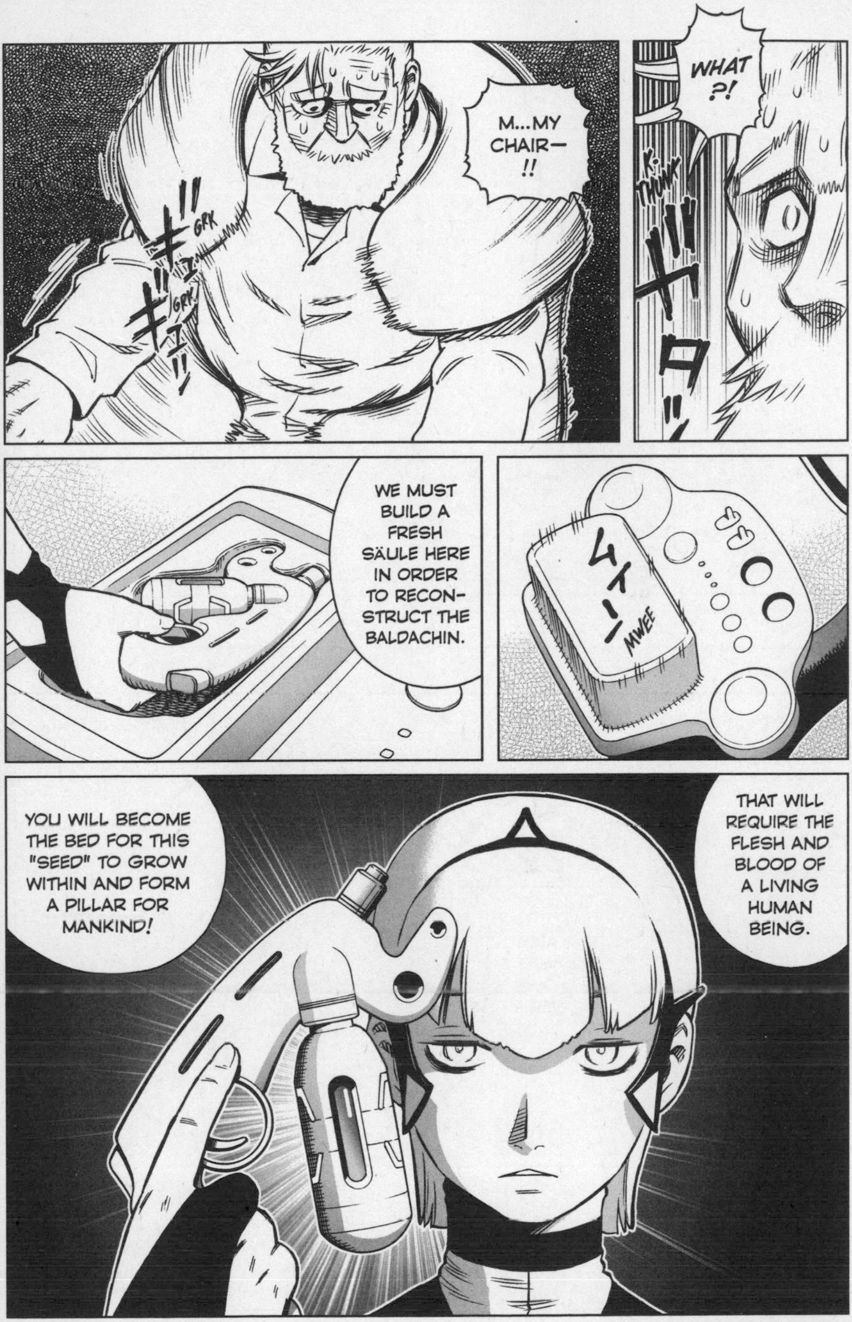
WHAT?!
K-THUNK
M...MY CHAIR—!!
GRK
GRK
MWEE
WE MUST BUILD A FRESH SÄULE HERE IN ORDER TO RECONSTRUCT THE BALDACHIN.
THAT WILL REQUIRE THE FLESH AND BLOOD OF A LIVING HUMAN BEING.
YOU WILL BECOME THE BED FOR THIS "SEED" TO GROW WITHIN AND FORM A PILLAR FOR MANKIND!

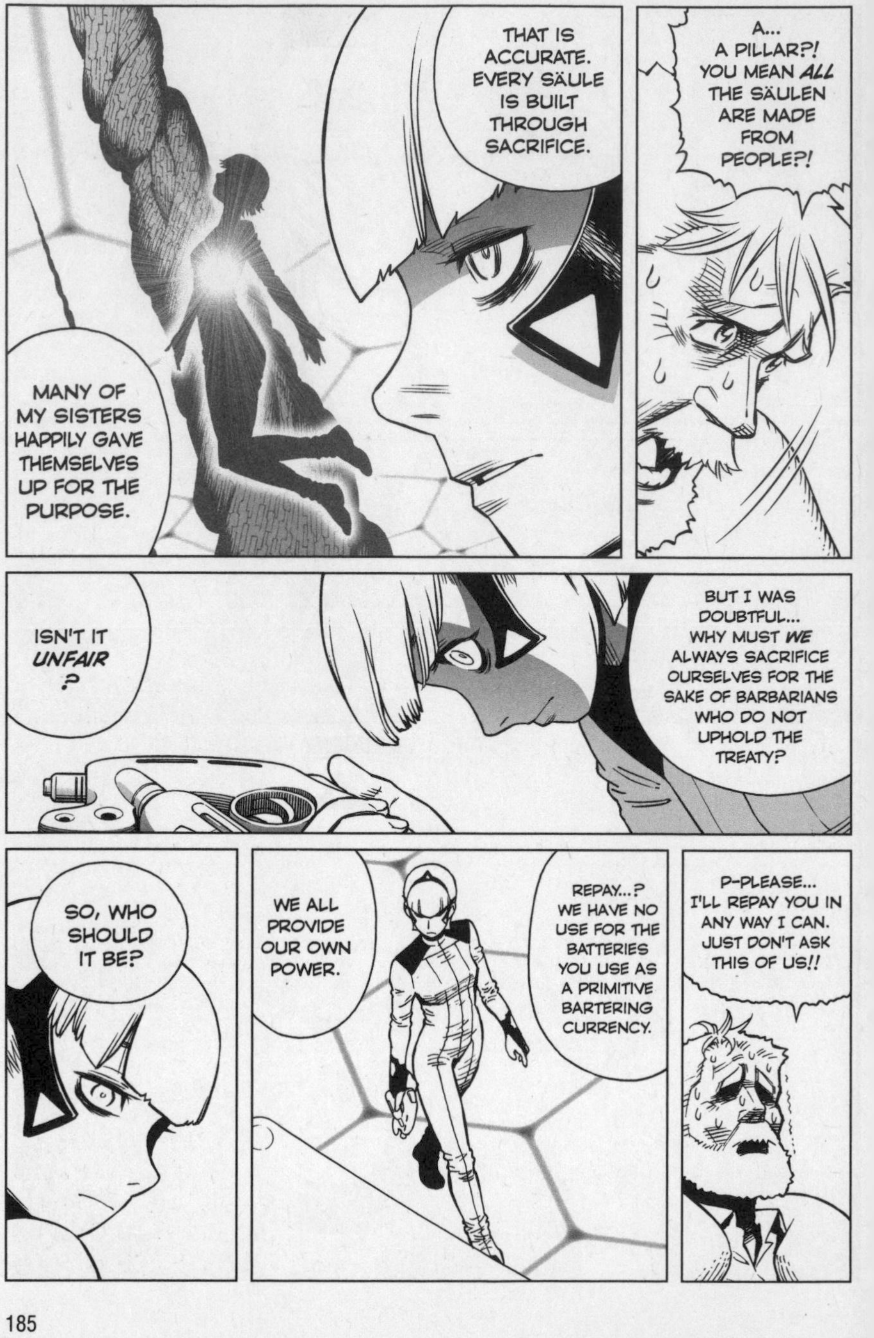
A... A PILLAR?! YOU MEAN ALL THE SÄULEN ARE MADE FROM PEOPLE?!
THAT IS ACCURATE. EVERY SÄULE IS BUILT THROUGH SACRIFICE.
MANY OF MY SISTERS HAPPILY GAVE THEMSELVES UP FOR THE PURPOSE.
BUT I WAS DOUBTFUL... WHY MUST WE ALWAYS SACRIFICE OURSELVES FOR THE SAKE OF BARBARIANS WHO DO NOT UPHOLD THE TREATY?
ISN'T IT UNFAIR?
P-PLEASE... I'LL REPAY YOU IN ANY WAY I CAN. JUST DON'T ASK THIS OF US!!
REPAY...? WE HAVE NO USE FOR THE BATTERIES YOU USE AS A PRIMITIVE BARTERING CURRENCY.
WE ALL PROVIDE OUR OWN POWER.
SO, WHO SHOULD IT BE?

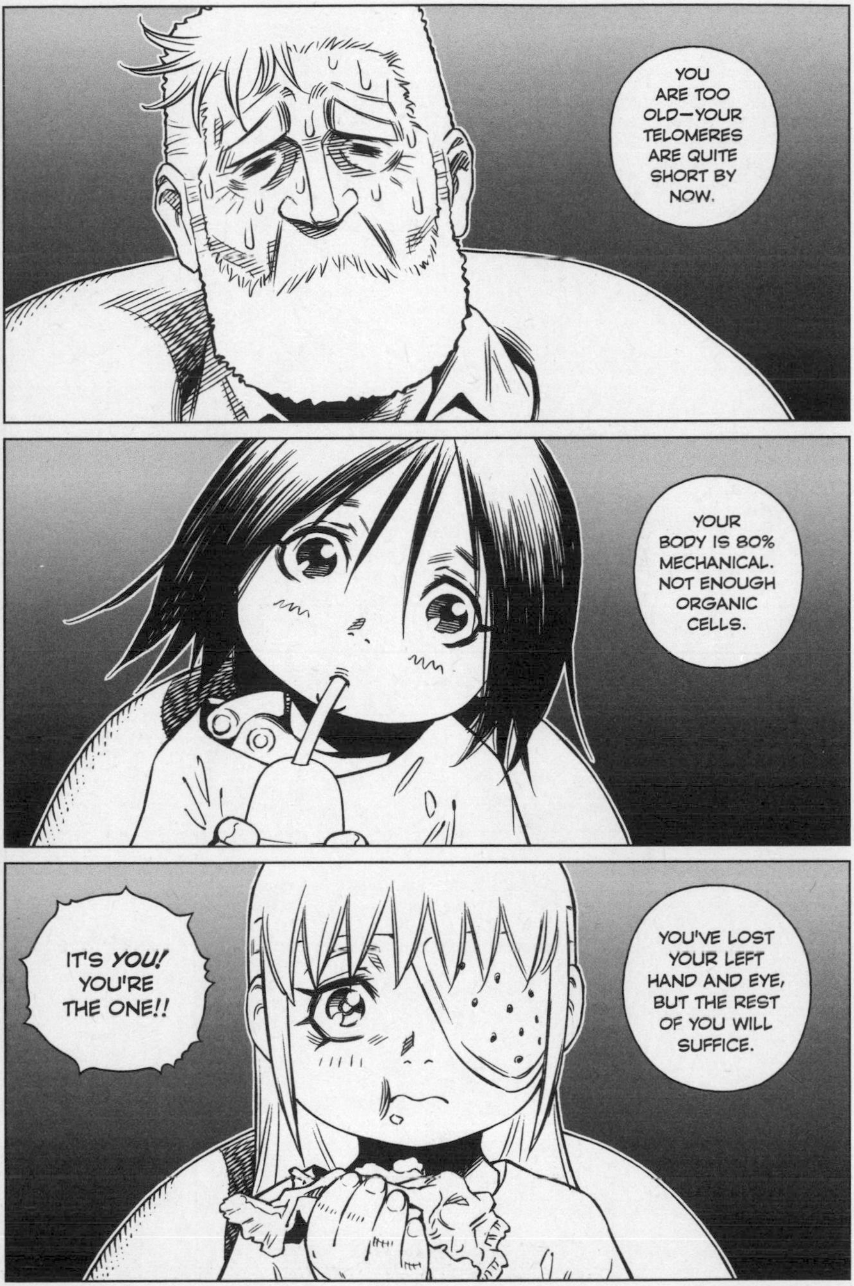
YOU ARE TOO OLD—YOUR TELOMERES ARE QUITE SHORT BY NOW.
YOUR BODY IS 80% MECHANICAL. NOT ENOUGH ORGANIC CELLS.
YOU'VE LOST YOUR LEFT HAND AND EYE, BUT THE REST OF YOU WILL SUFFICE.
IT'S *YOU!* YOU'RE THE ONE!!

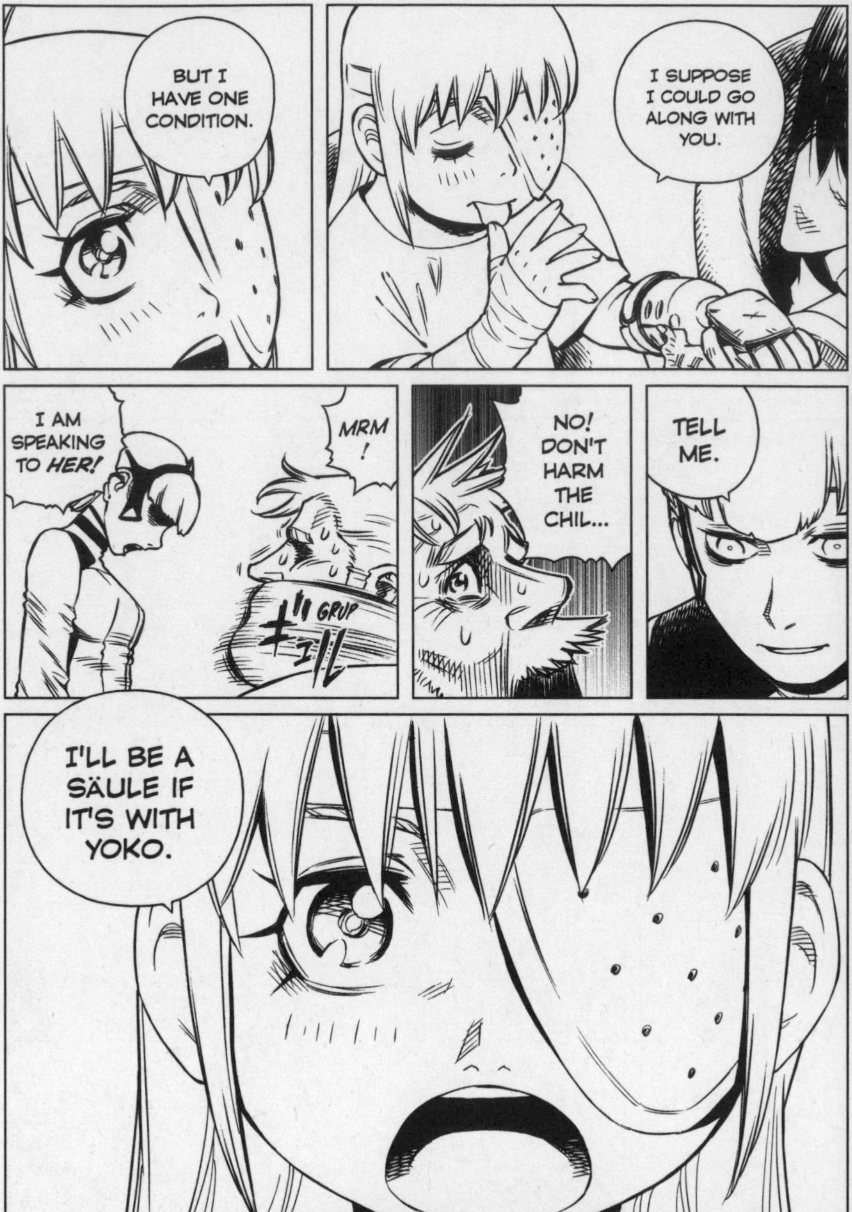
I SUPPOSE I COULD GO ALONG WITH YOU.
BUT I HAVE ONE CONDITION.
TELL ME.
NO! DON'T HARM THE CHIL...
MRM !
I AM SPEAKING TO *HER!*
GRUP
I'LL BE A SÄULE IF IT'S WITH YOKO.

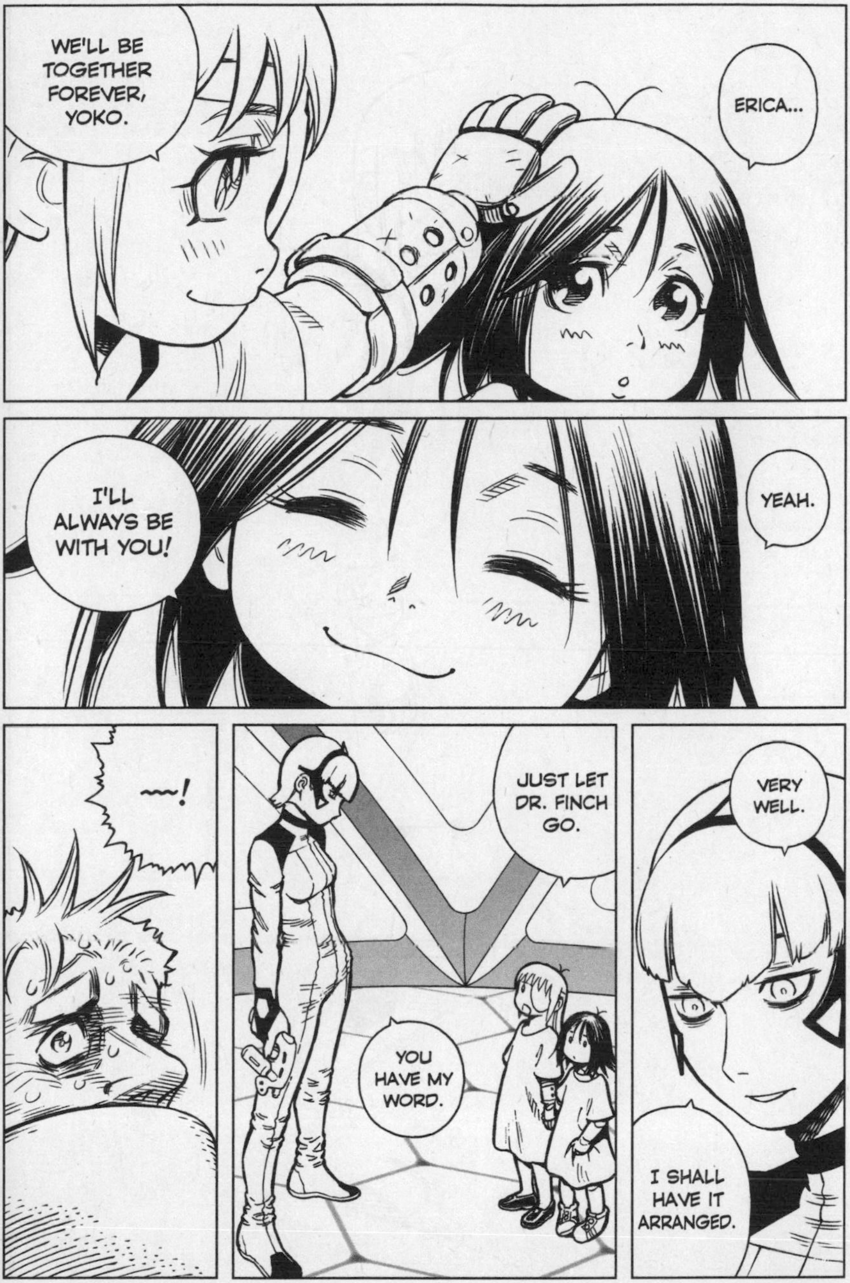
ERICA...
WE'LL BE TOGETHER FOREVER, YOKO.
YEAH.
I'LL ALWAYS BE WITH YOU!
VERY WELL.
I SHALL HAVE IT ARRANGED.
JUST LET DR. FINCH GO.
YOU HAVE MY WORD.
~~!

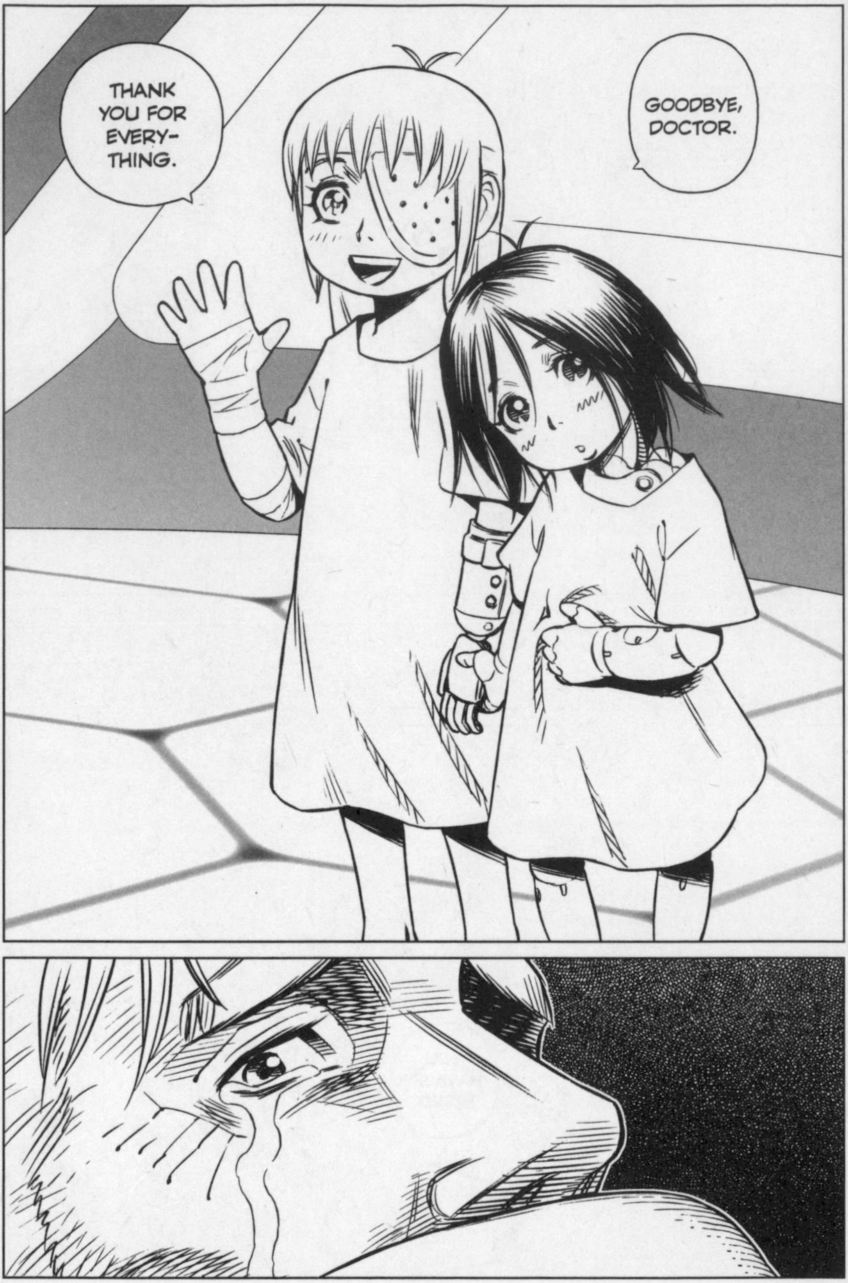
GOODBYE, DOCTOR.
THANK YOU FOR EVERY-THING.

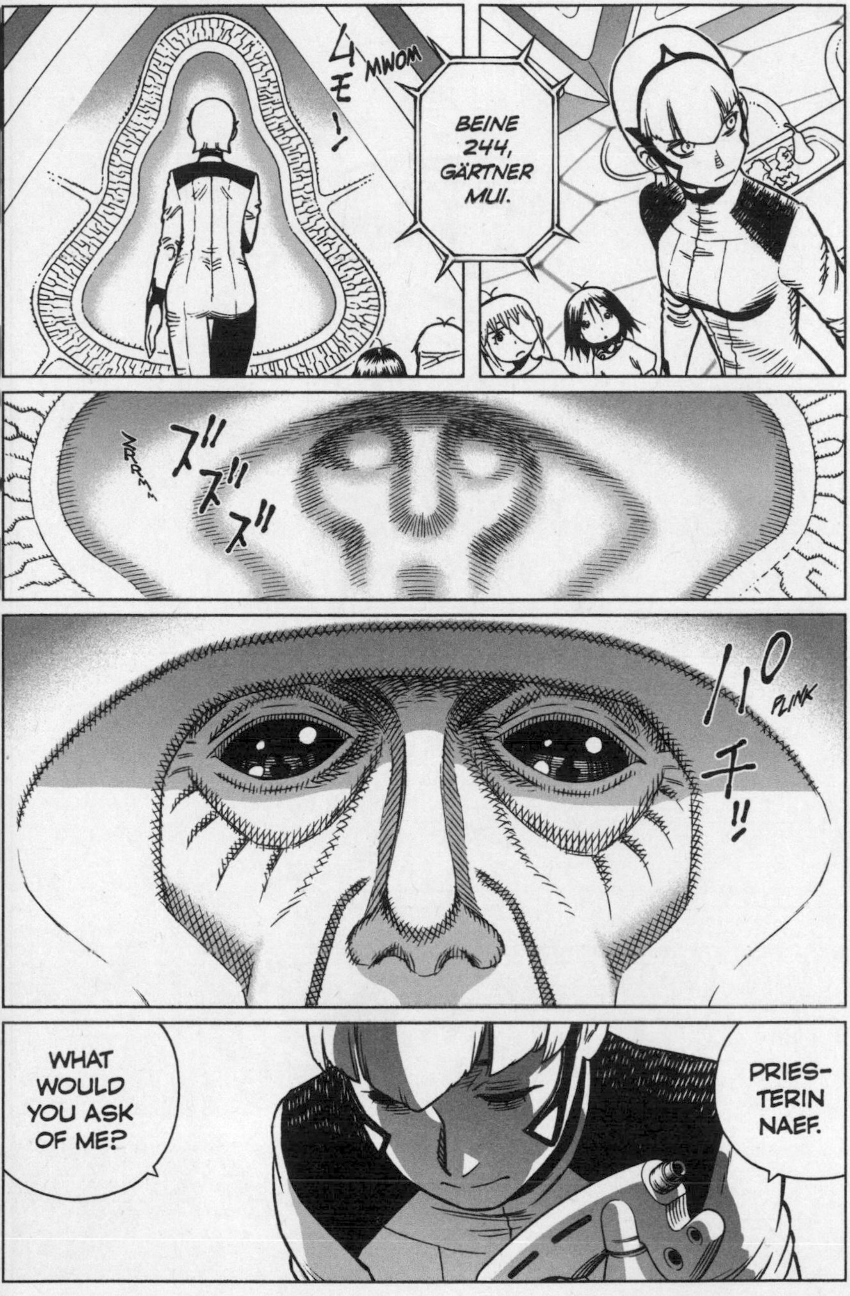

BEINE 244, GÄRTNER MUI.
MWOM
ZRRMM
PLINK
PRIES-TERIN NAEF.
WHAT WOULD YOU ASK OF ME?

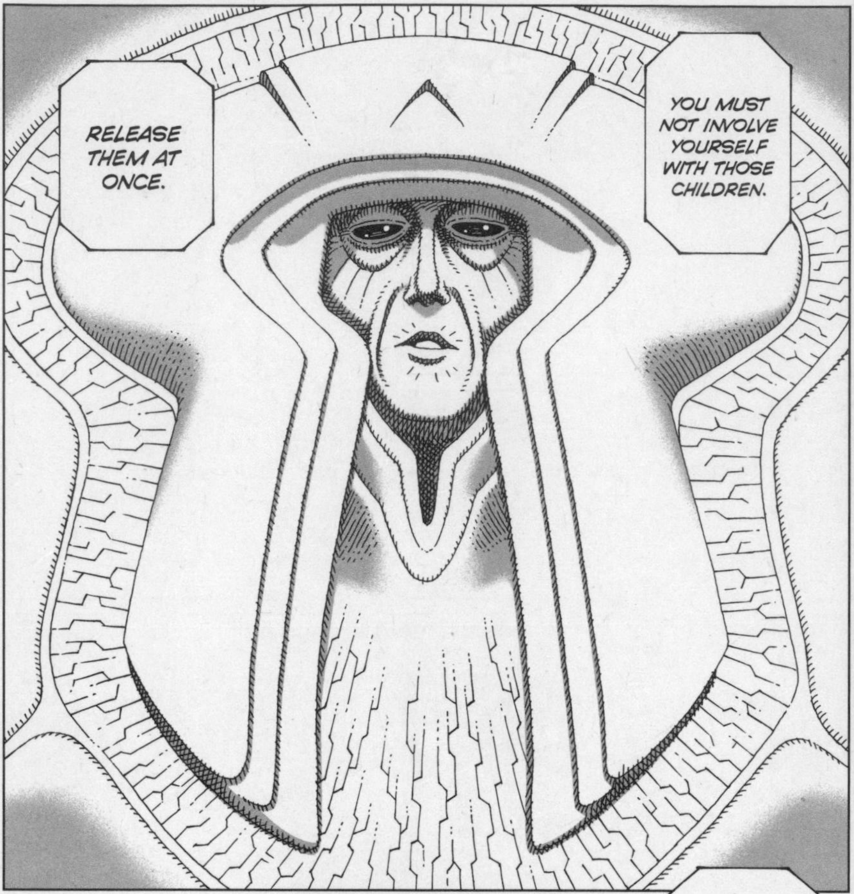
YOU MUST NOT INVOLVE YOURSELF WITH THOSE CHILDREN.
RELEASE THEM AT ONCE.
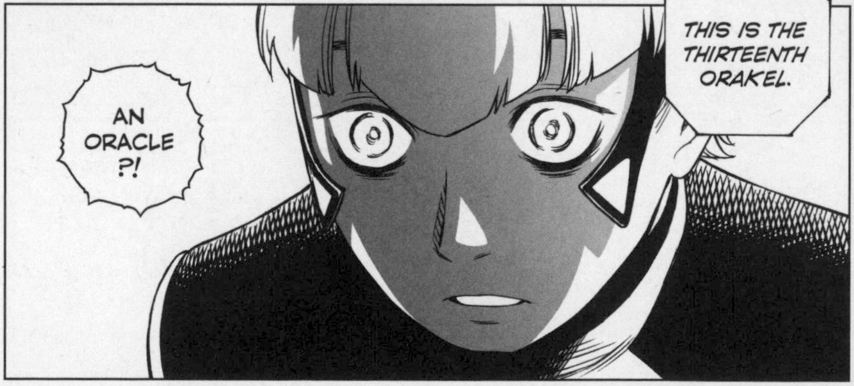
THIS IS THE THIRTEENTH ORAKEL.
AN ORACLE ?!

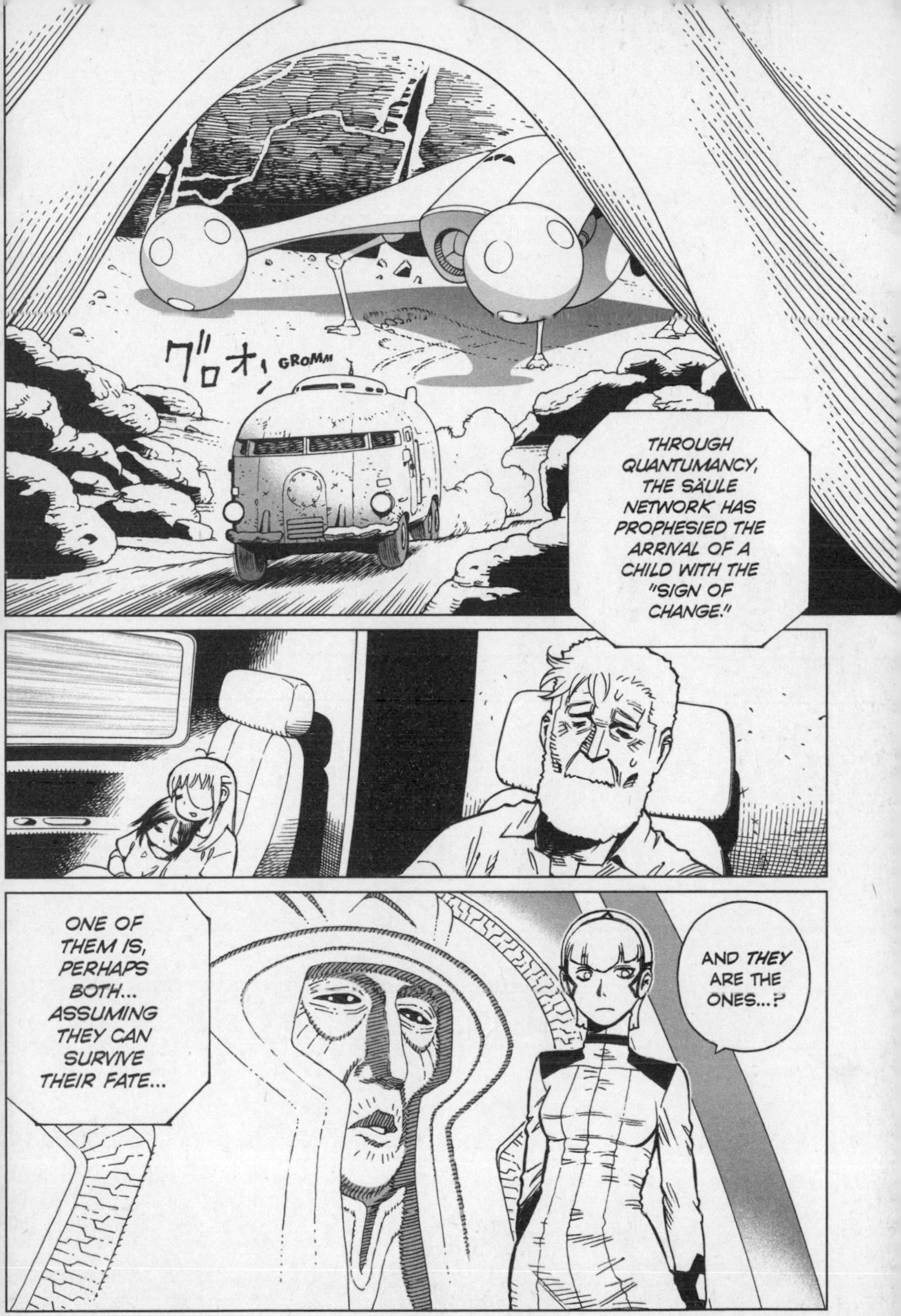

グロオ, GROMM
THROUGH QUANTUMANCY, THE SÄULE NETWORK HAS PROPHESIED THE ARRIVAL OF A CHILD WITH THE "SIGN OF CHANGE."
AND *THEY* ARE THE ONES...?
ONE OF THEM IS, PERHAPS BOTH... ASSUMING THEY CAN SURVIVE THEIR FATE...

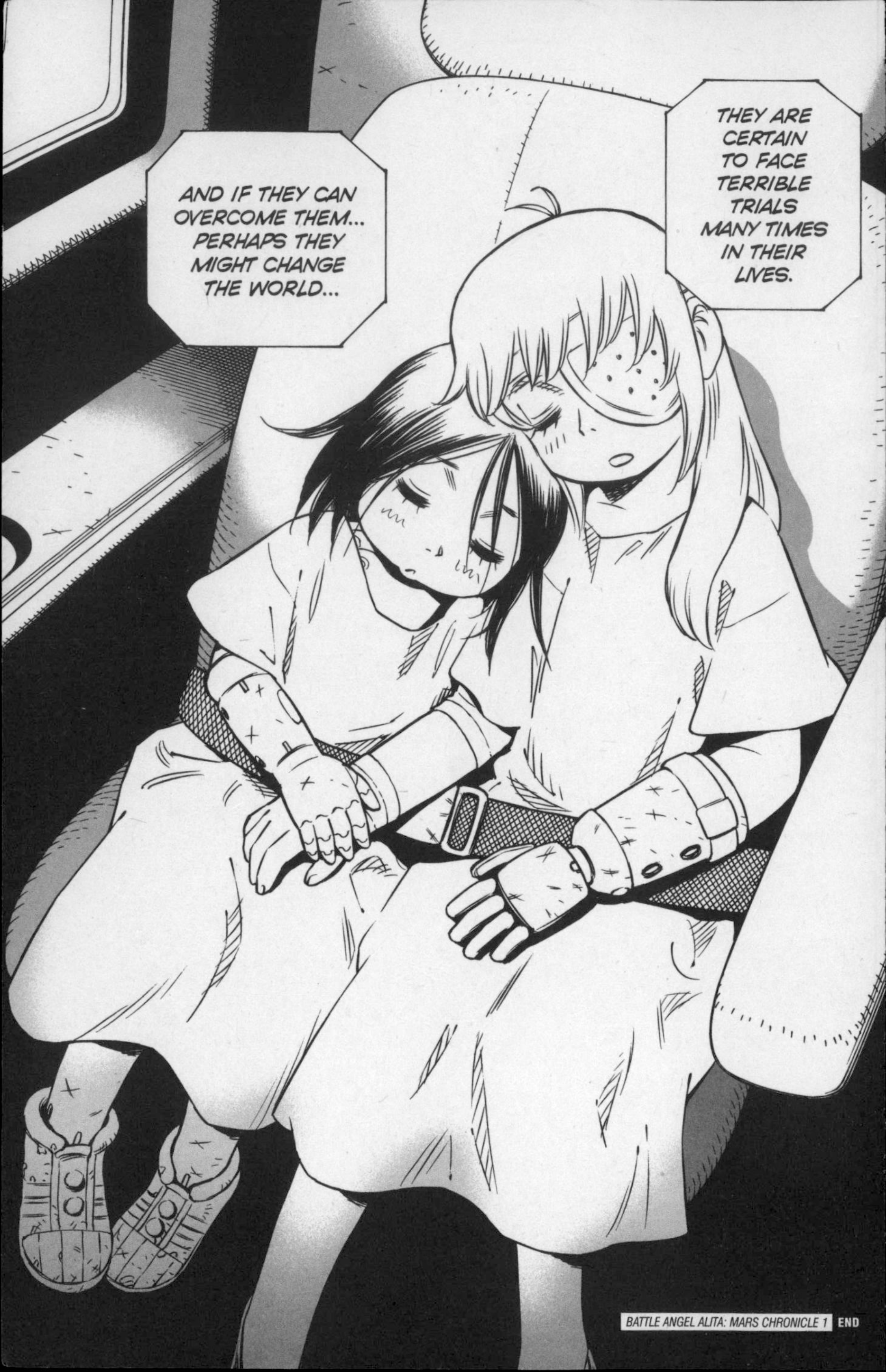
THEY ARE CERTAIN TO FACE TERRIBLE TRIALS MANY TIMES IN THEIR LIVES.
AND IF THEY CAN OVERCOME THEM... PERHAPS THEY MIGHT CHANGE THE WORLD...

BATTLE ANGEL ALITA: MARS CHRONICLE 1 END

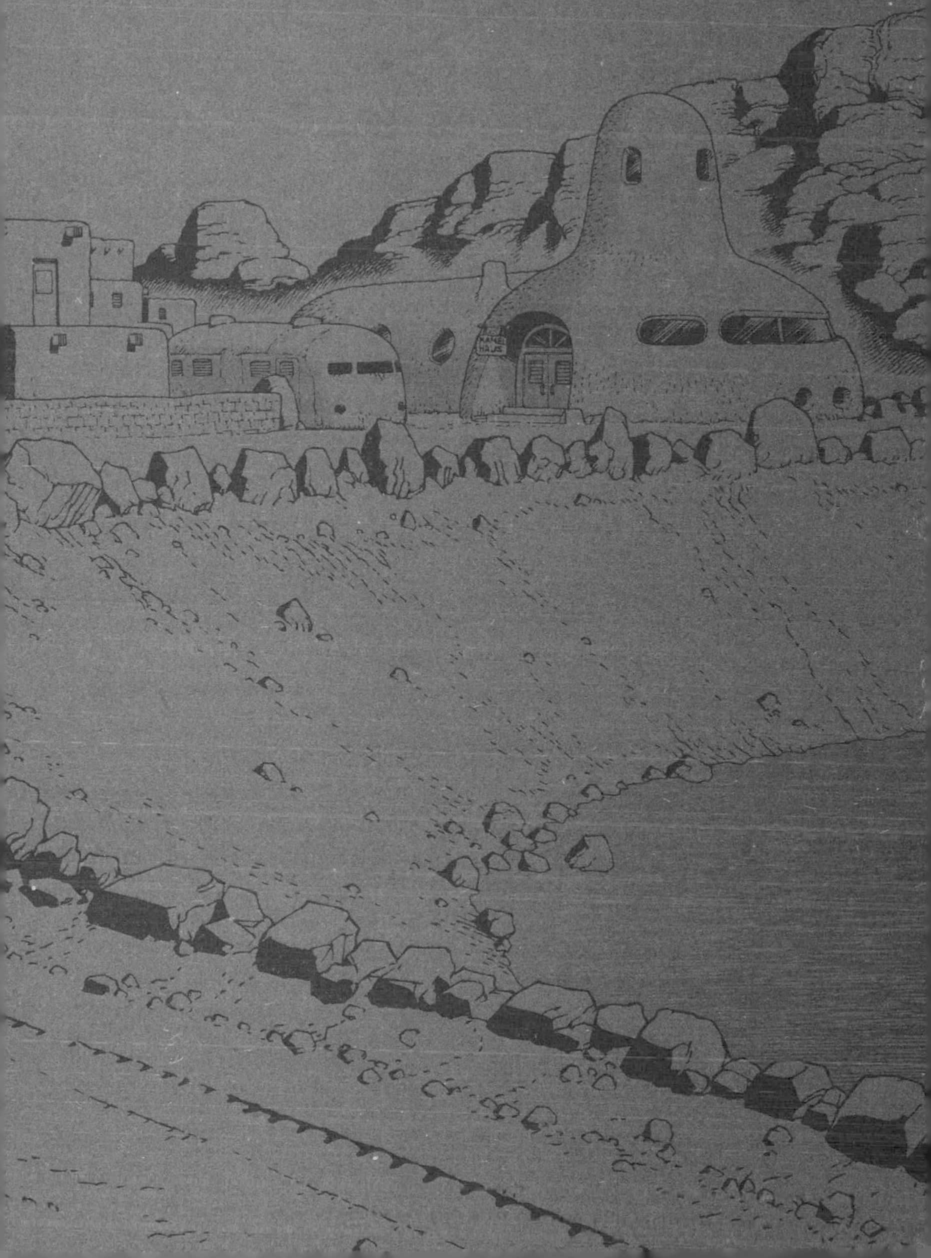
KAME HAUS

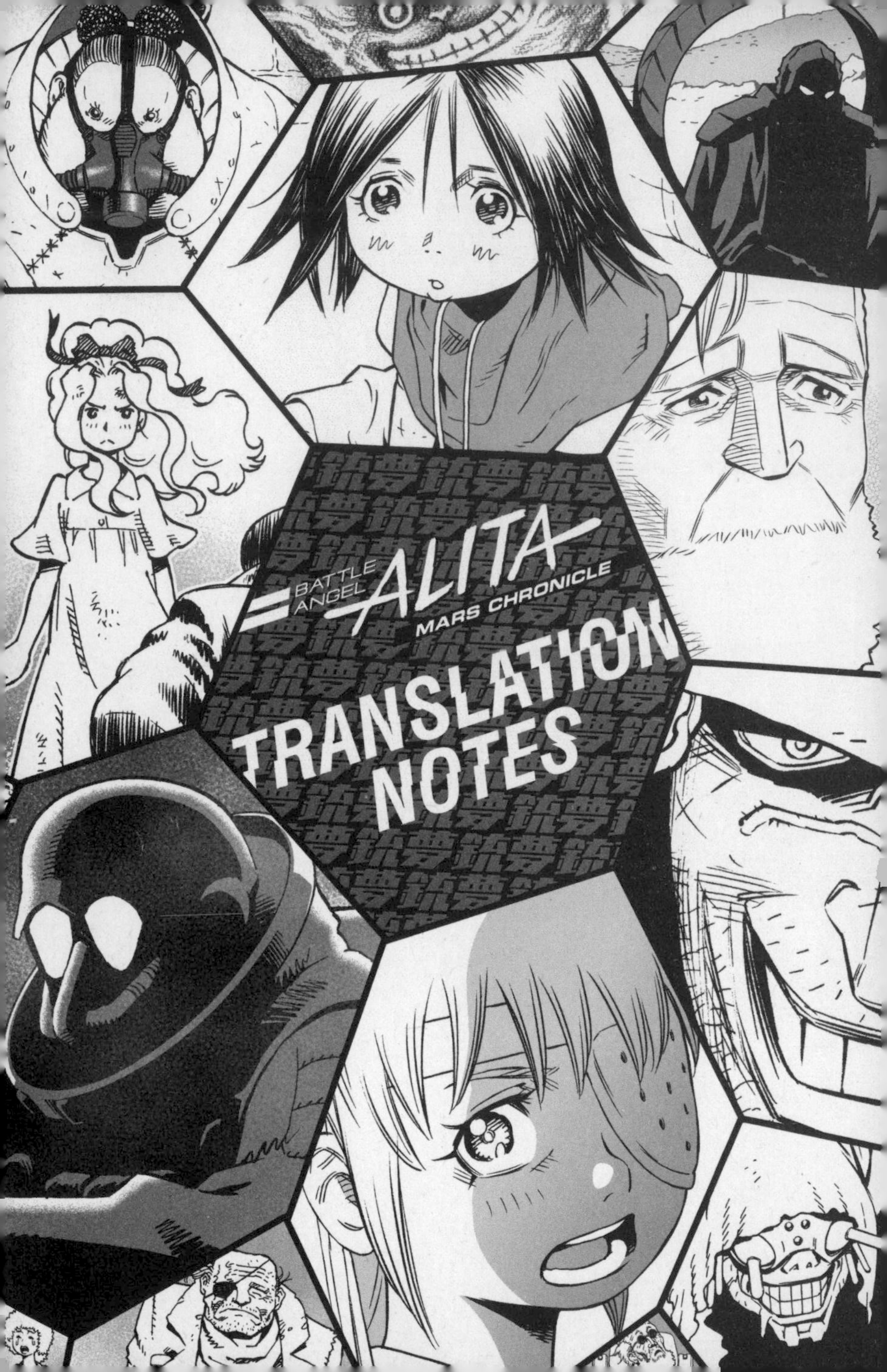
BATTLE ANGEL ALITA
MARS CHRONICLE
TRANSLATION NOTES

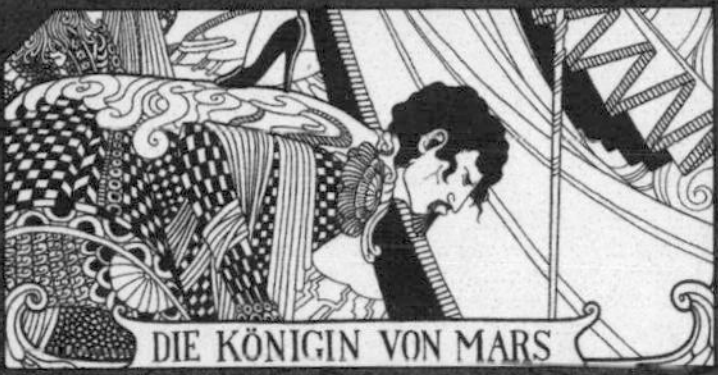
DIE KÖNIGIN VON MARS

DIE KÖNIGIN VON MARS

pg. 17

"The Queen of Mars" in German.

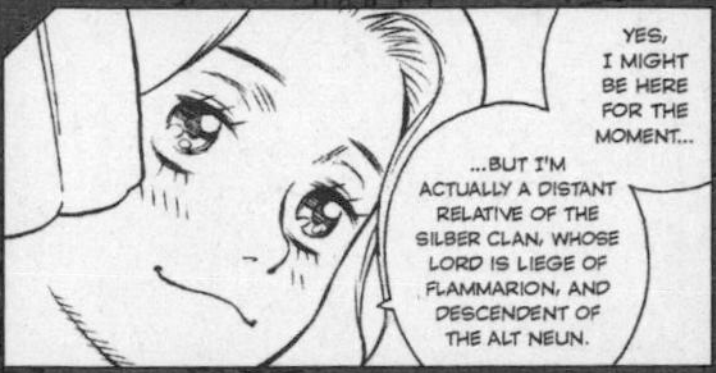
YES, I MIGHT BE HERE FOR THE MOMENT...
...BUT I'M ACTUALLY A DISTANT RELATIVE OF THE SILBER CLAN, WHOSE LORD IS LIEGE OF FLAMMARION, AND DESCENDENT OF THE ALT NEUN.

ALT NEUN

pg. 11

German for "Old Nine." The *kanji* used define this term as meaning "the nine great founders."

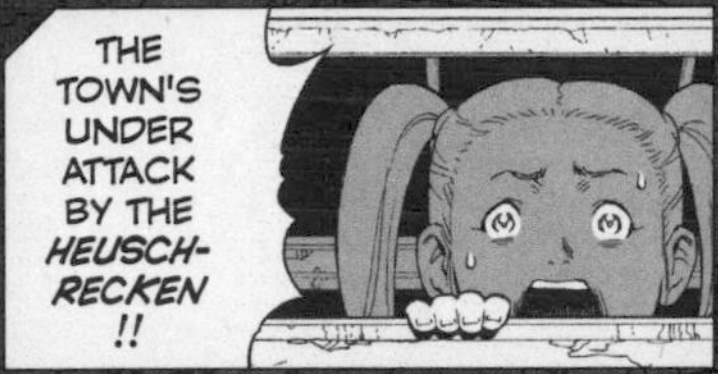
THE TOWN'S UNDER ATTACK BY THE *HEUSCH-RECKEN* !!

HEUSCHRECKEN

pg. 55

German for "grasshoppers."

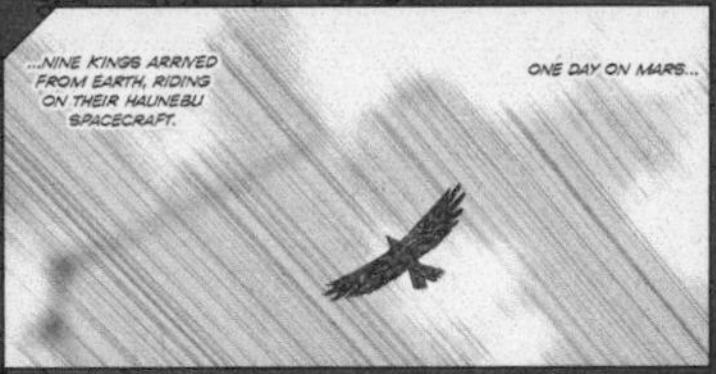
ONE DAY ON MARS...
...NINE KINGS ARRIVED FROM EARTH, RIDING ON THEIR HAUNEBU SPACECRAFT.

HAUNEBU

pg. 47

One of the alleged codenames for rumored Nazi German experiments in building UFOs before and during World War II, either on their own or with alien assistance.

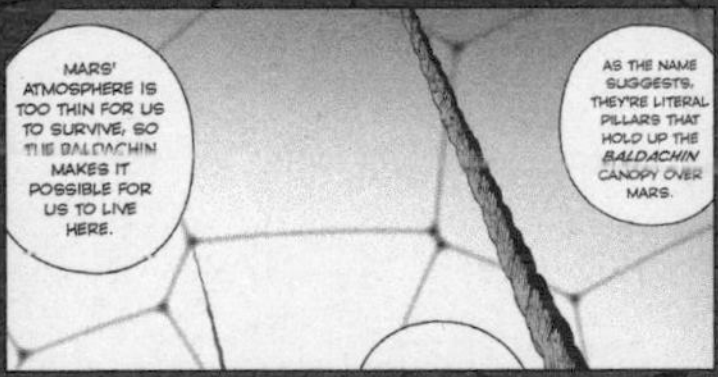
AS THE NAME SUGGESTS, THEY'RE LITERAL PILLARS THAT HOLD UP THE *BALDACHIN* CANOPY OVER MARS.
MARS' ATMOSPHERE IS TOO THIN FOR US TO SURVIVE, SO THE BALDACHIN MAKES IT POSSIBLE FOR US TO LIVE HERE.

BALDACHIN

pg. 157

In its original usage, this word refers to a special canopy that is placed over a throne, altar, or some other symbol of great authority. This feature was particularly prominent during the Middle Ages and Renaissance in Europe.

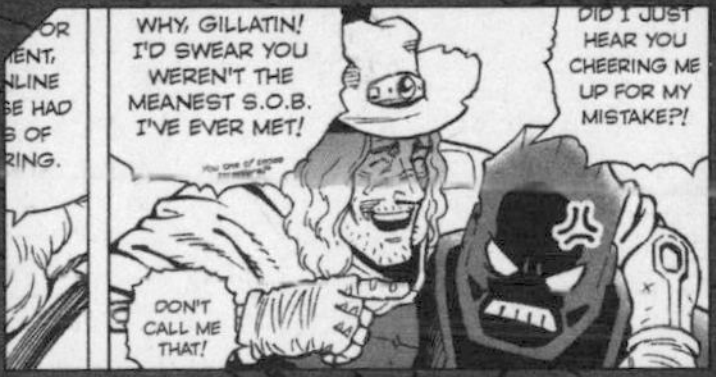
DID I JUST HEAR YOU CHEERING ME UP FOR MY MISTAKE?!
WHY, GILLATIN! I'D SWEAR YOU WEREN'T THE MEANEST S.O.B. I'VE EVER MET!
DON'T CALL ME THAT!

TSUNDERE

pg. 139

A common anime archetype of a character who is outwardly hostile but eventually reveals a sweet and affectionate core when their guard is down. Typically refers to female characters, not menacing cyborgs like Gillatin.

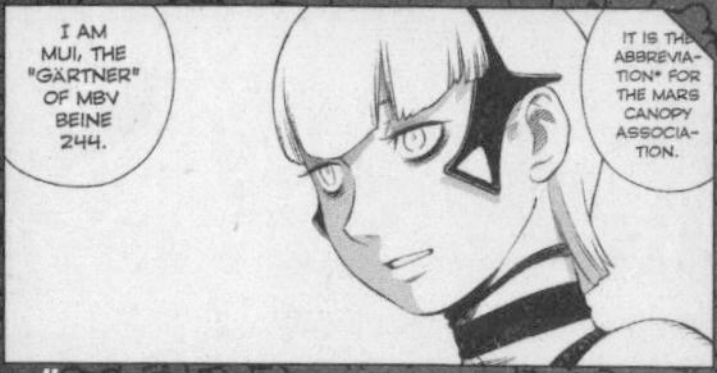
I AM MUI, THE "GÄRTNER" OF MBV BEINE 244.
IT IS THE ABBREVIATION* FOR THE MARS CANOPY ASSOCIATION.

GÄRTNER

pg. 181

The German word for "gardener." This perhaps ties in to the "seed" and "plant" motif of the Säule pillars.

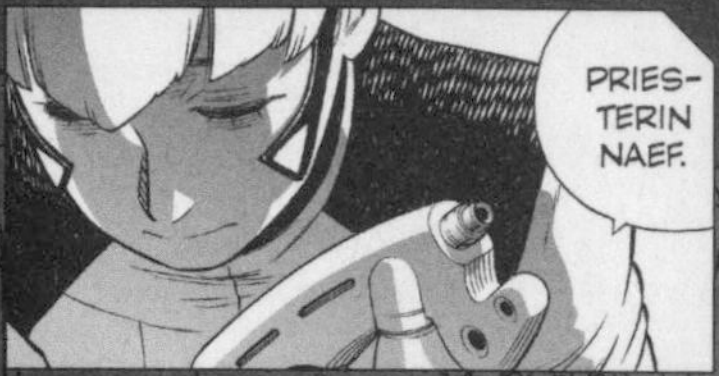
PRIES-TERIN NAEF.

PRIESTERIN

pg. 190

The German term for "high priestess."

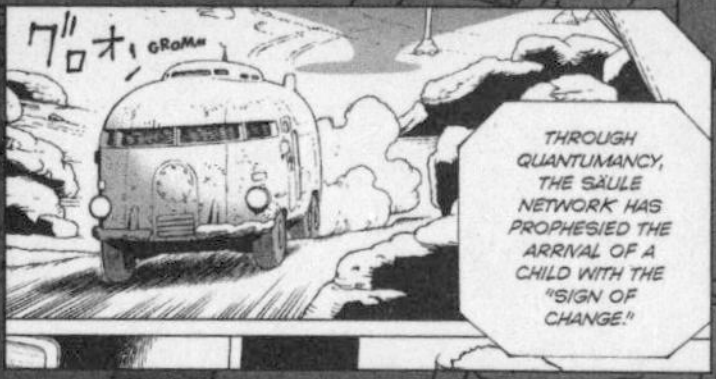
THROUGH QUANTUMANCY, THE SÄULE NETWORK HAS PROPHESIED THE ARRIVAL OF A CHILD WITH THE "SIGN OF CHANGE."
グロオ
GROMM

QUANTUMANCY

pg. 192

Although it isn't explained with an author's footnote, the *kanji* used with the English term quantumancy define it as "quantum divination" or fortune-telling.

DELUXE EDITION

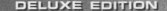

BATTLE ANGEL ALITA

After more than a decade out of print, the original cyberpunk action classic returns in glorious 400-page hardcover deluxe editions, featuring an all-new translation, color pages, and new cover designs!

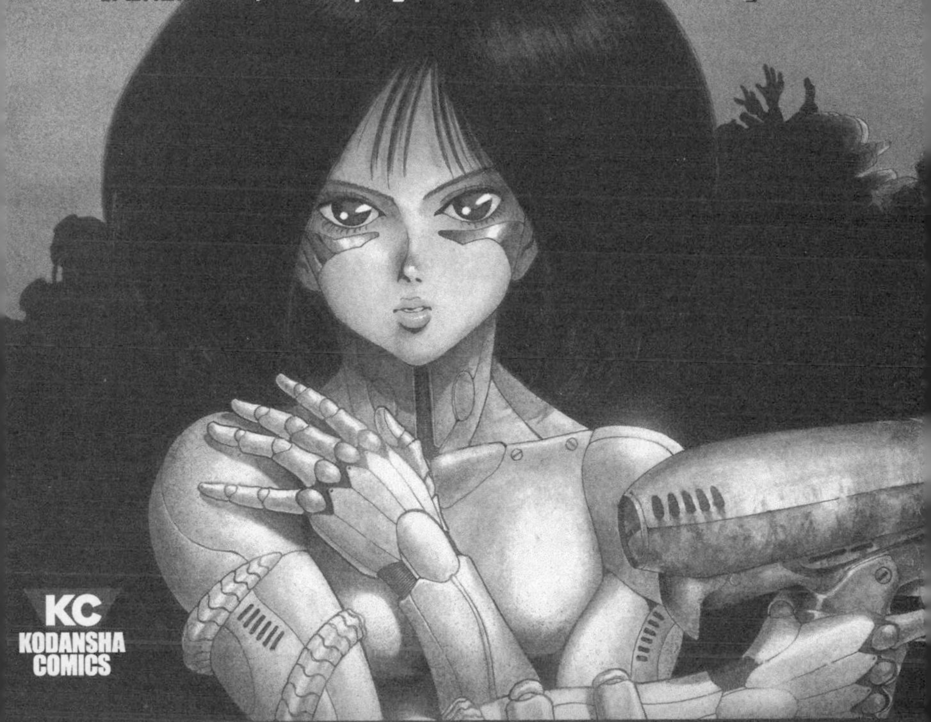
KC
KODANSHA COMICS

Far beneath the shimmering space-city of Zalem lie the trash-heaps of The Scrapyard... Here, cyber-doctor and bounty hunter Daisuke Ido finds the head and torso of an amnesiac cyborg girl. He names her Alita and vows to fill her life with beauty, but in a moment of desperation, a fragment of Alita's mysterious past awakens in her. She discovers that she possesses uncanny prowess in the legendary martial art known as panzerkunst. With her newfound skills, Alita decides to become a hunter-warrior - tracking down and taking out those who prey on the weak. But can she hold onto her humanity in the dark and gritty world of The Scrapyard?

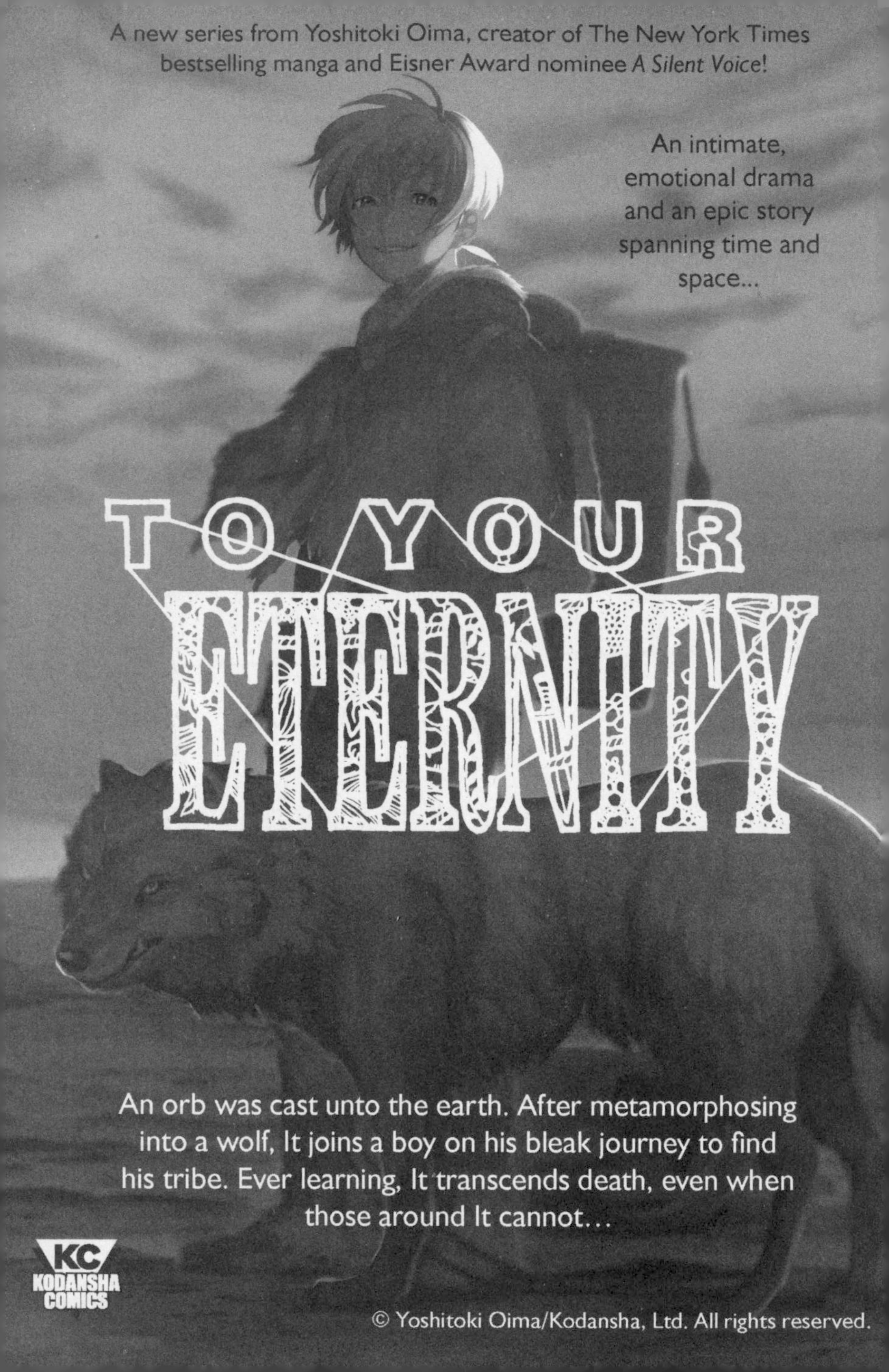
A new series from Yoshitoki Oima, creator of The New York Times bestselling manga and Eisner Award nominee *A Silent Voice*!
An intimate, emotional drama and an epic story spanning time and space...
TO YOUR ETERNITY
An orb was cast unto the earth. After metamorphosing into a wolf, It joins a boy on his bleak journey to find his tribe. Ever learning, It transcends death, even when those around It cannot...
KC KODANSHA COMICS
© Yoshitoki Oima/Kodansha, Ltd. All rights reserved.

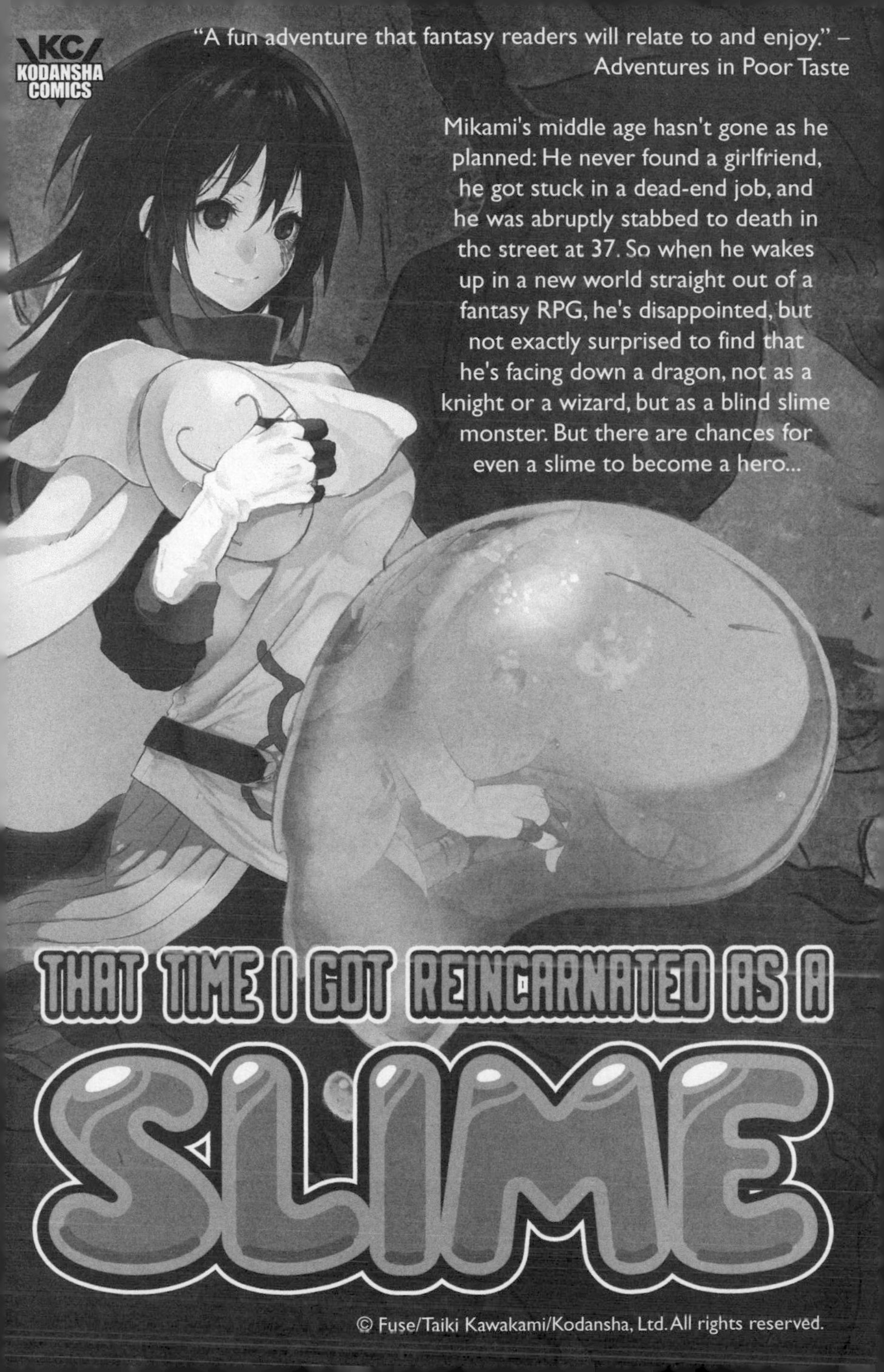
KC KODANSHA COMICS
"A fun adventure that fantasy readers will relate to and enjoy." –
Adventures in Poor Taste
Mikami's middle age hasn't gone as he planned: He never found a girlfriend, he got stuck in a dead-end job, and he was abruptly stabbed to death in the street at 37. So when he wakes up in a new world straight out of a fantasy RPG, he's disappointed, but not exactly surprised to find that he's facing down a dragon, not as a knight or a wizard, but as a blind slime monster. But there are chances for even a slime to become a hero...
THAT TIME I GOT REINCARNATED AS A
SLIME
© Fuse/Taiki Kawakami/Kodansha, Ltd. All rights reserved.

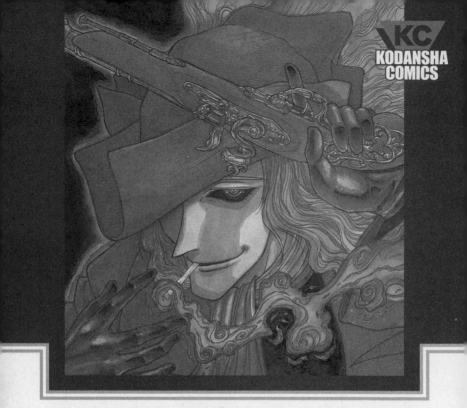

The Black Museum
The Ghost and the Lady

By Kazuhiro Fujita

Deep in Scotland Yard in London sits an evidence room dedicated to the greatest mysteries of British history. In this "Black Museum" sits a misshapen hunk of lead—two bullets fused together—the key to a wartime encounter between Florence Nightingale, the mother of modern nursing, and a supernatural Man in Grey. This story is unknown to most scholars of history, but a special guest of the museum will tell the tale of *The Ghost and the Lady*...

Praise for Kazuhiro Fujita's *Ushio and Tora*

"A charming revival that combines a classic look with modern depth and pacing... **Essential viewing both for curmudgeons and new fans alike.**" — Anime News Network

"**GREAT!** The first episode of *Ushio and Tora* captures the essence of '90s anime." — IGN

Japan's most powerful spirit medium delves into the ghost world's greatest mysteries!

Story by Kyo Shirodaira, famed author of mystery fiction and creator of *Spiral*, *Blast of Tempest*, and *The Record of a Fallen Vampire*.

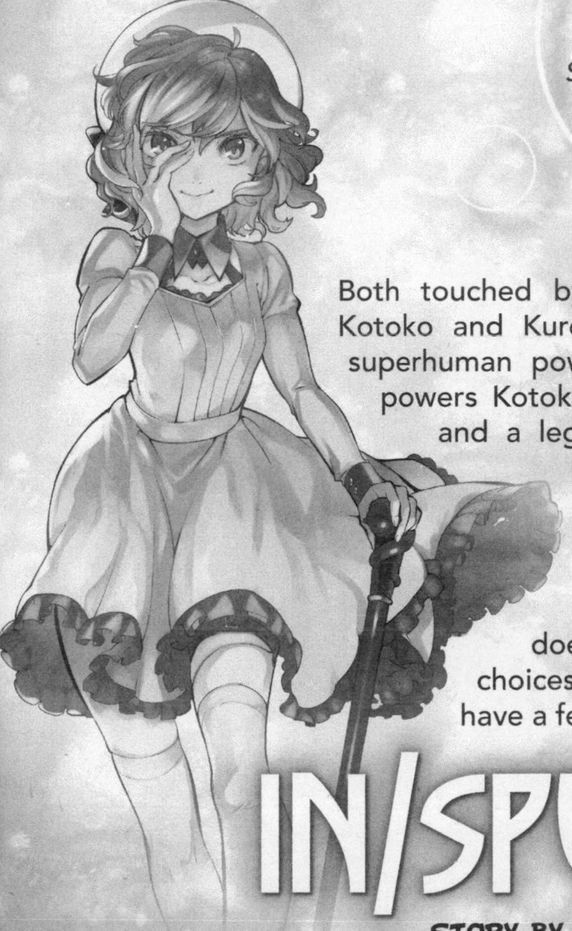

Both touched by spirits called yôkai, Kotoko and Kurô have gained unique superhuman powers. But to gain her powers Kotoko has given up an eye and a leg, and Kurô's personal life is in shambles. So when Kotoko suggests they team up to deal with renegades from the spirit world, Kurô doesn't have many other choices, but Kotoko might just have a few ulterior motives...

IN/SPECTRE

STORY BY KYO SHIRODAIRA
ART BY CHASHIBA KATASE

KC
KODANSHA COMICS

New action series from Hiroyuki Takei, creator of the classic shonen franchise Shaman King!

In medieval Japan, a bell hanging on the collar is a sign that a cat has a master. Norachiyo's bell hangs from his katana sheath, but he is nonetheless a stray — a ronin. This one-eyed cat samurai travels across a dishonest world, cutting through pretense and deception with his blade.

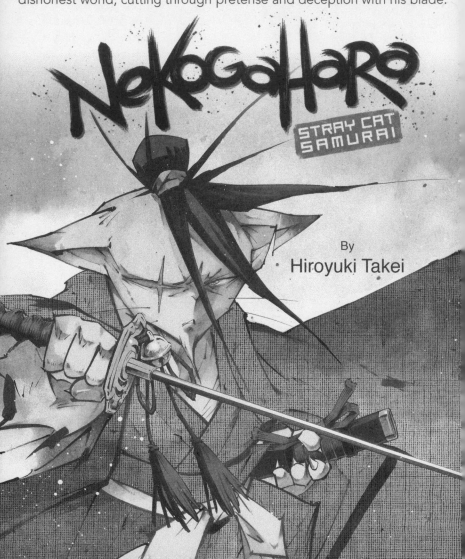

Nekogahara

STRAY CAT SAMURAI

By

Hiroyuki Takei

HAPPINESS

—ハピネス—

By Shuzo Oshimi

From the creator of *The Flowers of Evil*

Nothing interesting is happening in Makoto Ozaki's first year of high school. HIs life is a series of quiet humiliations: low-grade bullies, unreliable friends, and the constant frustration of his adolescent lust. But one night, a pale, thin girl knocks him to the ground in an alley and offers him a choice.

Now everything is different. Daylight is searingly bright. Food tastes awful. And worse than anything is the terrible, consuming thirst...

Praise for Shuzo Oshimi's *The Flowers of Evil*

"A shockingly readable story that vividly—one might even say queasily—evokes the fear and confusion of discovering one's own sexuality. Recommended." —The Manga Critic

"A page-turning tale of sordid middle school blackmail." —Otaku USA Magazine

"A stunning new horror manga." —Third Eye Comics

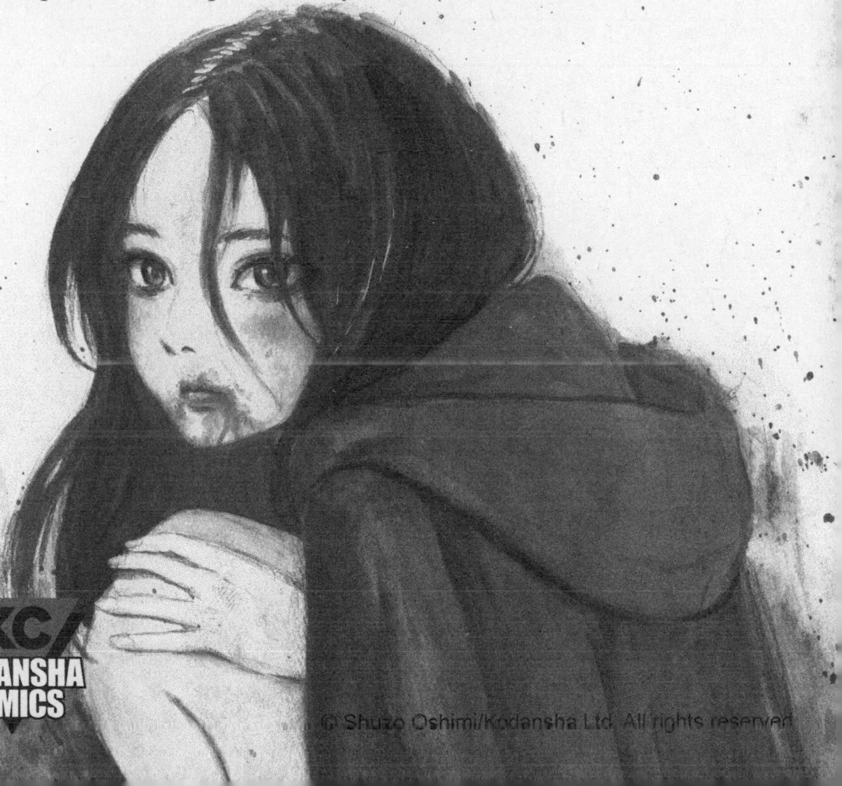

KODANSHA COMICS

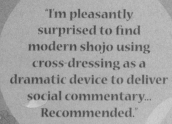

"I'm pleasantly
surprised to find
modern shojo using
cross-dressing as a
dramatic device to deliver
social commentary...
Recommended."

-Otaku USA
Magazine

The prince in his dark days

By **Hico Yamanaka**

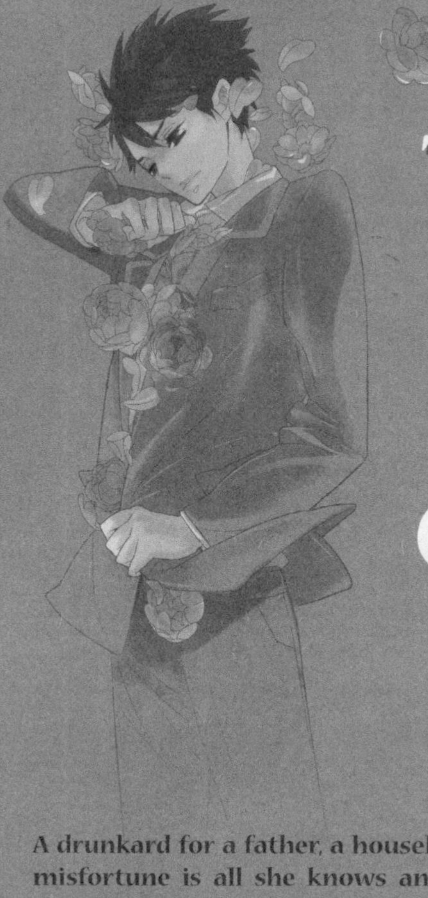

A drunkard for a father, a household of poverty... For 17-year-old Atsuko, misfortune is all she knows and believes in. Until one day, a chance encounter with Itaru–the wealthy heir of a huge corporation–changes everything. The two look identical, uncannily so. When Itaru curiously goes missing, Atsuko is roped into being his stand-in. There, in his shoes, Atsuko must parade like a prince in a palace. She encounters many new experiences, but at what cost...?

Having lost his wife, high school teacher Kōhei Inuzuka is doing his best to raise his young daughter Tsumugi as a single father. He's pretty bad at cooking and doesn't have a huge appetite to begin with, but chance brings his little family together with one of his students, the lonely Kotori. The three of them are anything but comfortable in the kitchen, but the healing power of home cooking might just work on their grieving hearts.

"This season's number-one feel-good anime!" —Anime News Network

"A beautifully-drawn story about comfort food and family and grief. Recommended." —Otaku USA Magazine

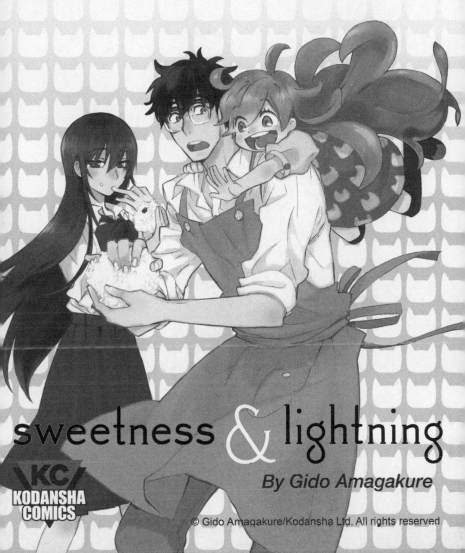

sweetness & lightning

By Gido Amagakure

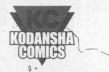

INUYASHIKI

A superhero like none you've ever seen, from the creator of "Gantz"!

ICHIRO INUYASHIKI IS DOWN ON HIS LUCK. HE LOOKS MUCH OLDER THAN HIS 58 YEARS, HIS CHILDREN DESPISE HIM, AND HIS WIFE THINKS HE'S A USELESS COWARD. SO WHEN HE'S DIAGNOSED WITH STOMACH CANCER AND GIVEN THREE MONTHS TO LIVE, IT SEEMS THE ONLY ONE WHO'LL MISS HIM IS HIS DOG.

THEN A BLINDING LIGHT FILLS THE SKY, AND THE OLD MAN IS KILLED... ONLY TO WAKE UP LATER IN A BODY HE ALMOST RECOGNIZES AS HIS OWN. CAN IT BE THAT ICHIRO INUYASHIKI IS NO LONGER HUMAN?

COMES IN EXTRA-LARGE EDITIONS WITH COLOR PAGES!

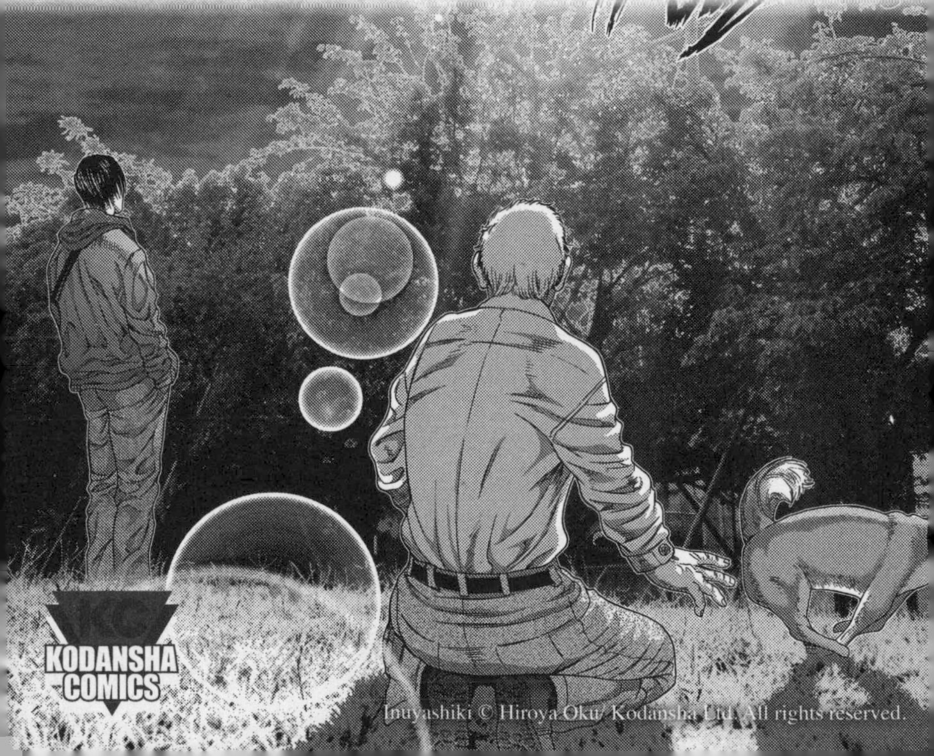
KODANSHA COMICS

D0198846

Battle Angel Alita: Mars Chronicle volume 1 is a work of fiction. Names, characters, places, and incidents are the products of the author's imagination or are used fictitiously. Any resemblance to actual events, locales, or persons, living or dead, is entirely coincidental.

A Kodansha Comics Trade Paperback Original.

Battle Angel Alita: Mars Chronicle volume 1 copyright © 2015 Yukito Kishiro
English translation copyright © 2018 Yukito Kishiro

All rights reserved.

Published in the United States by Kodansha Comics, an imprint of Kodansha USA Publishing, LLC, New York.

Publication rights for this English edition arranged through Kodansha Ltd., Tokyo.

First published in Japan in 2015 by Kodansha Ltd., Tokyo, as *Gunnm: Mars Chronicle 1*.

ISBN 978-1-63236-615-3

Printed in the United States of America.

www.kodanshacomics.com

9 8 7 6 5 4 3 2

Translator: Stephen Paul
Lettering: Evan Hayden
Editing: Ajani Oloye
Kodansha Comics edition cover design: Phil Balsman